Addressing Pupils' Behaviour: Responses at District, School and Individual Levels

The companion volumes in this series are:

Inclusion and Behaviour Management in Schools: Issues and Challenges, edited by Janice Wearmouth, Ted Glynn, Robin C. Richmond and Mere Berryman

Understanding Pupil Behaviour in Schools: A Diversity of Approaches, edited by Janice Wearmouth, Robin C. Richmond, Ted Glynn and Mere Berryman

These three volumes constitute part of a course jointly developed by the Open University in the UK and the University of Waikato in New Zealand. The Open University course is E804 *Managing Behaviour in Schools*. The University of Waikato course comprises three modules: HDCO534 - Theorising Behaviour in Schools; HDCO535 - Behaviour Assessment and Intervention in Schools; HDCO536 - School Behaviour Policies.

The Open University Course E804 - *Managing Behaviour in Schools*

The course is offered within the Open University Master's Programme in Education. The Master's Programme provides great flexibility. Students study at their own pace and in their own time anywhere in the European Union. They receive specially prepared study materials, supported by face-to-face tutorials where they can work with other students.

The MA is modular. Students may select modules from the programme which fit their personal and professional interests and goals. Specialist lines of study are also available and include special and inclusive education, management, applied linguistics and lifelong learning. The attainment of an MA entitles students to apply for entry to the Open University Doctorate in Education Programme.

How to apply

If you would like to find out more information about available courses, please write, requesting the *Professional Development in Education* prospectus, to the Call Centre, PO Box 200, The Open University, Walton Hall, Milton Keynes, MK7 6ZW, UK (tel: 0 (0 44) 1908 653231). Details can also be viewed on our web page http://www.open.ac.uk

The University of Waikato *Postgraduate Diploma in Managing Behaviour in Schools PGDip (MBS)*

This postgraduate diploma is offered within the University of Waikato Master of Education programme, and utilises the same specially prepared study materials, supported by face-to-face classes and tutorials offered flexibly through summer school sessions and intermittent Saturday sessions. Each module is offered as a Master's level course, and can be credited towards a Master's degree in Education. The PGDipMBS requires one additional course in research methodology (on-line options available). Holders of the Postgraduate Diploma are able to complete a one-year Master's Degree in Education by thesis or course work, across a wide range of areas, such as inclusive education, Maori and bilingual education, educational policy and educational leadership.

How to apply

If you would like to find out more about the PGDipMBS and other available courses, please contact the Administrator, Graduate Studies in Education, School of Education, University of Waikato, Private Bag 3105, Hamilton, New Zealand (tel: 64-7-838-4500 or fax 64-7-838-4555). Details can also be accessed via e-mail: educ_grad@waikato.ac.nz or viewed on our website: http://www.waikato.ac.nz/education/grad

Addressing Pupil's Behaviour: Responses at District, School and Individual Levels

Janice Wearmouth, Robin C. Richmond and Ted Glynn

David Fulton Publishers
London

in association with
The Open University and
the University of Waikato

The
University
of Waikato
Te Whare Wānanga
o Waikato

The Open
University

David Fulton Publishers Ltd
The Chiswick Centre, 414 Chiswick High Road, London W4 5TF

www.fultonpublishers.co.uk

First published in Great Britain in 2004 by David Fulton Publishers
David Fulton Publishers is a division of Granada Learning, Part of ITV plc.

10 9 8 7 6 5 4 3 2 1

Note: The right of the individual contributors to be identified as the authors of their work has been asserted by them in accordance with the Copyright, Designs and Patents Act 1988.

British Library Cataloguing in Publication Data
A catalogue record for this book is available from the British Library.

ISBN 1 84312 231 6

Typeset by RefineCatch Limited, Bungay, Suffolk
Printed in Great Britain

Contents

Acknowledgements

We would like to thank all those who have contributed chapters to this reader or have approved their reprinting from other publications. Grateful acknowledgement is made to the following sources for permission to reproduce material in this book. Chapters not listed have been newly written. All chapters have been edited.

Chapter 2: Hopkins, B. (2002) 'Restorative justice in schools', *Support for Learning*, 17(3), 144–9.

Chapter 4: Head, G., Kane, J. and Cogan, N. (2003) 'Behaviour support in secondary schools', *Emotional and Behavioural Difficulties*, 8(1), 33–42. Reproduced by permission of Sage Publications, Thousand Oaks, London and Delhi (www.sagepub.co.uk).

Chapter 6: Blair, M. (2001) 'The education of black children: why do some schools do better than others?' In R. Majors (ed.) *Educating Our Black Children: New Directions and Radical Approaches*. London: Falmer.

Chapter 7: MacFarlane, A. (1997) 'The Hiraiko Rationale teaching students with emotional and behavioural difficulties: a bicultural approach', *Waikato Journal of Education*, 3, 153–68.

Chapter 8: Neville-Tisdall, M. and Milne, A. (2002) '"One size fits few": the case study of a school that has defied the constraints of a European system for Polynesian students'. Paper presented at the Teacher Education Forum of Aotearoa/New Zealand (TEFANZ) Conference, Wellington, NZ, August.

Chapter 9: Creese, A., Norwich, B. and Daniels, H. (2000) 'Evaluating teacher support teams in secondary schools: supporting teachers for SEN and other needs', *Research Papers in Education*, 15(3), 307–24. Reproduced with permission of Taylor & Francis Ltd (www.tandf.co.uk/journals).

Chapter 10: Tew, M. (1998) 'Circle time: a much-neglected resource in secondary schools', *Pastoral Care*, September, 18–27.

Chapter 11: Demko, L. (1996) 'Bullying at school: the no-blame approach', *Health Education*, 1, 26–30.

Chapter 14: Rogers, W.A. (2002) 'The language of behaviour management'. In W.A. Rogers (ed.) *Classroom Behaviour: A Practical Guide to Effective Teaching, Behaviour Management and Colleague Support*. London: Paul Chapman, pp 55–74. Reproduced with permission of Sage Publications, Thousand Oaks, London and Delhi (www.sagepub.co.uk).

Chapter 15: Watkins, C. and Wagner, P. (2000) 'Improving classroom behaviour'. In C. Watkins and P. Wagner (eds) *Improving School Behaviour*. London: Paul Chapman, pp 51–90.

Chapter 17: Williams, H. and Birmingham City Council (1998) 'A three-level approach to intervention for individual behaviour difficulties'. In *Behaviour in Schools: Framework for Intervention*. Birmingham City Council Education Department, pp 21–40.

Chapter 20: Shearman, S. (2003) 'What is the reality of inclusion for children with emotional and behavioural difficulties in the primary classroom?', *Emotional and Behavioural Difficulties*, 8(1), 53–76. Reproduced with permission of Sage Publications, Thousand Oaks, London and Delhi (www.sagepub.co.uk).

Chapter 21: Rigby, K. (2002) 'What is to be done about bullying?' *New Perspectives on Bullying*. London: Jessica Kingsley. Reproduced with permission of Jessica Kingsley Publishers. Copyright © Ken Rigby 2002.

Chapter 22: Cornwall, J. (2000) 'Might is right? A discussion of the ethics and practicalities of control and restraint in education', *Emotional and Behavioural Difficulties*, 5(4), 19–25. Reproduced with permission of Sage Publications, Thousand Oaks, London and Delhi (www.sagepub.co.uk).

Preface

Janice Wearmouth

The human mind develops in a social context. Young people's meaning-making is situated within that context (Bruner, 1996). Behaviour in schools which is disruptive, challenging or worrying to teachers and seems to relate to a particular student may be indicative of a range of contextual factors associated with the family, school, classroom, peer group or teacher, as well as the individual student (Watkins and Wagner, 2000). If interventions designed to improve student behaviour in schools are to be effective they need to be based on an understanding of these factors.

The book looks first at issues associated with students' behaviour in relation to community and family background and ways in which school responses might be conceptualised in partnership with members of the local community, including external agencies. It goes on to consider behaviour management at whole-school and classroom level as well as interventions to address individual behaviours regarded as problematic in some way.

In the Introduction, chapter 1 by Wearmouth, Richmond and Connors views student behaviour in schools as influenced by almost every aspect of the school's organisation and structure and by its relationship to the community it serves (DES/Elton, 1989) and, therefore, effective interventions as potentially needing to be based at any one of these levels.

Part 1, *District and community level*, opens with a chapter by Hopkins in which she outlines the potential in the context of the UK for building links between local communities and school in introducing restorative justice principles to address challenging or disruptive behaviour in schools. The emphasis on involving members of the local community as well as the community within the school is built on an assumption that all those within the community both within and outside the school wish to repair the harm or hurt that has been done and have the skills and power to do so. Chapter 3 by Berryman and Glynn follows the same line in describing a case study of an intervention in a New Zealand Māori context that was designed collaboratively between local community members and their neighbourhood school to prevent the suspension from school of students accused of substance abuse. Next, in chapter 4, Head, Kane and Cogan discuss an evaluation of the effectiveness of

behaviour support to schools in one local education authority (LEA) in
Scotland. The context in which the evaluation took place was the incentives to
LEAs from the Scottish Executive to develop more inclusive approaches to
young people whose behaviour is perceived as challenging or troublesome in
schools. The LEA in which the evaluation took place facilitated a range of
forms of behaviour support which were designed to suit the context of
individual schools.

   Part 2, *School level*, begins with chapter 5 by McCall in which he describes a
case study of behaviour change in a secondary school on the east coast of
England between the years 1998 and 2003. It continues with chapter 6 where
Blair examines the question of why some schools do better than others in
providing for the education of Black students in British schools. She uses the
example of one particularly successful school to draw the conclusion that what
is needed, above all, is the creation of a 'we' ethos which ensures that no
student or parent feels in any way marginalised. In chapter 7, Macfarlane
reports an approach to behaviour management in schools, the 'Hikairo
Rationale', which is assertive but also responsive to cultural and individual
differences. This chapter has been written with specific reference to Maori
cultural values, but in the respect shown for the dignity and value of all
students of all backgrounds its principles have a generic significance in the
context of behaviour management in all schools. In the following chapter
Neville-Tisdale and Milne illustrate how Clover Park Middle School in South
Auckland, New Zealand, has employed an innovative approach to developing
a culturally-sensitive curriculum in order to ensure that all students are
included in the school's community of learners (Lave and Wenger, 1991). In
chapter 9, Creese, Norwich and Daniels report on the development of teacher
support teams (TSTs) to assist teachers in responding positively to the demands
of planning and teaching the curriculum and managing learning support for an
increasingly diverse student body. It includes an evaluation of the working and
impact of TSTs in four secondary schools. Chapter 10 goes on to discuss
potential uses of 'Circle Time' (Mosley, 1988, 1996) to support moral and
social development among students of secondary school age. Demko then
outlines a case study of one school's attempts to introduce the 'No-blame
approach' (Maines and Robinson, 1991) to address issues of bullying in
one independent school. She illustrates how new initiatives need to be
introduced at whole-school level with support from senior management,
clear objectives, appropriate training for the staff and with an agreed strategy
for awareness-raising of relevant issues among both students and parents.
In chapter 12, Sproson examines the origins and current uses of learning
support units (LSUs) attached to mainstream schools in one LEA in England.
In the following chapter Cooper evaluates an intervention in the early years
through 'nurture groups'.

Part 3, *Classroom level*, begins with chapter 14 in which Rogers offers many examples of ways in which teachers might adopt a firm but respectful approach to behaviour management in classrooms through their use of assertive language. In chapter 15, Watkins and Wagner describe and discuss ways of understanding the complex nature of the school classroom and a variety of effective approaches to potentially difficult situations in which teachers might find themselves. Smith then goes on to consider issues surrounding confrontation in classrooms and ways in which this might be prevented and/or de-escalated, in chapter 16.

In Part 4, *Individual student level*, chapter 17 outlines a model of intervention for individual behaviour problems that was developed as part of Birmingham, England's, strategy 'Behaviour in schools: Framework for intervention'. Three levels of intervention are proposed: Level 1 which is marked by an audit of the behavioural environment, Level 2 by a plan to improve the behavioural environment together with the use of an Individual Behaviour Plan, and Level 3 by an emphasis on the IBP together with involvement from outside agencies. In chapter 18, Moore discusses the rationale underpinning functional assessment of student behaviour and discusses its potential use in schools. In the following chapter, Pitchford then describes the theory and practice of 'multi-element planning' for conceptualising the root causes of individual student behaviour that is seen as difficult to manage in schools predominantly from a behavioural standpoint. He goes on to discuss appropriate ways of addressing such behaviour that take into account individual students' learning and behavioural needs. In chapter 20, Shearman draws on psycho-analytic concepts to discuss the reality of the experience of inclusion in a mainstream primary school for three students whose behaviour is seen as the focus of teachers' concerns. In chapter 21, Rigby examines issues related to bullying in general terms and goes on to outline a range of strategies commonly adopted to address bullying behaviour in schools. In the final chapter, Cornwall addresses issues of controlling student behaviour through physical restraint and raises important questions of ethics.

References

Bruner, J. (1996) *The Culture of Education*, London: Harvard

Department of Education and Science (DES) (1989) *Discipline in Schools*. Report of the committee of enquiry chaired by Lord Elton (the Elton Report), London: Her Majesty's Stationery Office (HMSO)

Lave, J. and Wenger, E. (1991) *Situated Learning: legitimate peripheral participation*, Cambridge: Cambridge University Press

Maines, B. and Robinson, G. (1991) *Stamp out Bullying*, Bristol: Lame Duck
 Publishers
Mosley, J. (1988) 'Some Implications Arising from a Small-scale Study of a
 Circle-based Programme Initiated for the Tutorial Period', *Pastoral Care in
 Education* 6 (2), 10–16
Mosley, J. (1996) *Quality Circle Time*. Cambridge: LDA
Watkins, C. and Wagner, P. (2000) *Improving School Behaviour*, London: Paul
 Chapman

Chapter 1

Multi-level responses to behavioural issues in schools

Janice Wearmouth, Robin Richmond and Bushra Connors

Introduction

Student behaviour in schools does not occur in a vacuum (Watkins and Wagner, 2000). Students operate inside classrooms inside schools within neighbourhoods and also within their own families and communities, and each influences student outcomes (Bronfenbrenner, 1979). Society at large imposes significant demands on individual students. These demands vary from one community to another. Students growing up in the UK, for example, face a number of demands which are specific to the UK context and others which are shared by other societies. 'Formalised education, commencing at the age of five years, imposes a whole range of requirements including the need for compliance, focused concentration and the willingness to listen and reflect' (BPS, 1996, p 13). The hurdles facing students in the UK education system 'reflect, in part, modern society's emphasis on competition and achievement' (ibid, p 13). It is inevitable that students who experience difficulties in meeting these demands must face 'a range of social, educational and psychological consequences' which will be 'compounded by personal unhappiness' (BPS, 1996, p 13).

It is undoubtedly true that 'difficult' neighbourhoods tend to produce more 'difficult' students than neighbourhoods in more affluent circumstances (Watkins and Wagner, 2000). Gewirtz et al (1995), for example, note the increase in inequality along lines of social class especially where, as currently in many countries, education is viewed as a 'commodity' and the market system ensures the flow of resources from children with greatest need to those with the least. However, research outcomes do not support the application of a simple cause

and effect model. Economic impoverishment in the neighbourhood does
not necessarily lead to disruptive behaviour in schools. Even in areas of
disadvantage, the structure and organisation of schools, including the way
they relate to their local communities, as well as classroom management and
intervention at the level of the individual student can make a difference to
student behaviour (Rutter et al, 1979; OFSTED, 2003).

In this chapter we look first at issues associated with students' behaviour in
relation to community and family background and ways in which school
responses might be conceptualised. We go on to consider behaviour with
regard to whole-school and classroom practices and individual attributes, and
discuss approaches at these levels also.

Student behaviour, community and family background

The development of the human mind depends on its evolution within a
society. The 'reality' of individual experience is represented through a shared
symbolism through which that community's way of life is organised and
understood. Young people's meaning-making is therefore situated in a cultural
context (Bruner, 1996). Culture is often linked with membership of ethnic
groups or communities. Working with a group of Māori Year 9 and 10 students
in mainstream New Zealand schools, Bishop, Berryman, Richardson & Tiakiwai
(2001) found, for example, that if teachers were to effectively engage them
with classroom activities and education in general, teachers needed to provide
a responsive context in which Māori students believed they could safely
bring their 'Selves' into the classroom. The alternative was for students to leave
their Māori identity at the school gate and behave according to the constraints
set by the majority culture or to resist teachers and have their behaviour
misinterpreted as challenging. Bishop et al (2001) concluded that culture
should not be something that is put aside while the 'real' educational issues
are addressed. Failing to support the development of students' understanding
and ability to act in a cultural context risks marginalising and alienating young
people and rendering them incompetent, with the consequent threat to the
stability of society as a whole.

Collaboration between schools and local support agencies

The role envisaged by central government in the UK for schools in preventing
social exclusion and in reintegrating those already socially excluded into
mainstream society involves collaboration with external agencies: social, health
and community education services, housing agencies and local community

groups. The kind of collaboration expected is exemplified in England by the Circular 10/99 *Social Inclusion: Pupil Support* which was published as part of the government's 'social inclusion' agenda and recognised wider influences on student behaviour than simply personal attributes. This document identifies certain groups of students as being at particular risk of exclusion from education:

- those with special educational needs;
- children in the care of local authorities;
- minority ethnic children;
- Travellers;
- young carers;
- those from families under stress;
- pregnant schoolgirls and teenage mothers.

(DfEE, 1999, ch 3, p 1, downloaded from
http://www.dfes.gov.uk/publications/guidanceonthelaw/10–99/risk.htm)

Teachers are exhorted to identify students who do not respond to actions in school to address disaffection and to design a Pastoral Support Programme (PSP) in liaison with external support services. A PSP

> needs to be agreed with parents, who should be regularly informed about their child's progress. To set up a PSP, the school should invite the parents and an LEA representative to discuss the causes of concern and what is reasonably required of the pupil to put right the situation, both academically and socially. The LEA should agree with the school what monitoring and help it will offer. LEAs may either offer support free to the school, or, if that is its policy, supplement the school's budget to enable it to buy the extra support outlined in the PSP. The LEA may, alternatively, offer support to a different school to receive and educate the child (see below).

The involvement of 'other agencies' in designing and implementing PSPs can be seen as an acknowledgement of the influence of external factors on student behaviour:

> Social Services Departments may be able to resolve home problems...
> Housing Departments can help to resolve accommodation difficulties or uncertainties that may be contributing to problems at school...
> Voluntary organisations and the Youth Service, both statutory and voluntary, can help to support young people both in and out of school...
> Careers Services can help young people make informed decisions about their future and encourage them not to drop out of learning at 16...
> Ethnic minority community groups can help schools with mentoring programmes, and provide them with advice and guidance on framing PSPs.

(DfEE, 1999, ch 3, pp 1–2)

This collaboration is not straightforward however. A great deal is known about the problems and pitfalls of schools' work with other agencies. These include territorial battles over budgets, different professional ideologies and structural barriers in terms of line management and reporting (Dyson and Robson, 1999; Lloyd, 1997; Kendrick, 1995; Armstrong and Galloway, 1994). In a study of the nature, extent and effectiveness of links between schools and local agencies and communities in Scotland, Tett el al (2001) concluded that 'most schools did not have strong links with their communities (ibid, p 7). Control of schools was dominated by professional community groups and customer groups were less common in schools' leading to a speculation that 'most schools defined their communities primarily in terms of their student constituency rather than their locales' (ibid, p 7). To maximise the chances of the school playing a leading role in community development it should ensure that it remains connected to its historical, social and cultural contexts, such that the school 'belongs' to the community in which it is located.

Collaboration between schools and community

Braithwaite (1997) claims that many responses to young people with problems fail because they treat young people as isolated individuals and do not operate in the context of the community of people who know and care about an individual. Usually a caring, loving family is able to encourage its children to value and nurture learning and develop social responsibility. For some young people the immediate family does not or cannot always provide this. However, the wider community circle of people who know, care about and are respected by a young person could do this.

In some schools and local education authorities particular programmes have been devised to address issues of problematic behaviour which are based in general terms on the principles of 'restorative justice'. Individual freedom and equal participation are combined with a communitarian preference for defining moral expectations and reparation at the level of the local community. Restorative justice can employ traditional community conflict resolution processes and culturally appropriate mechanisms to address and resolve tension and make justice visible and more productive (Anderson et al, 1996). Such initiatives shift the focus on to whole communities and away from the victim or the perpetrator in order to harness the necessary resources to address the problems that have resulted in unacceptable, unsociable behaviours (Schweigert, 1999). By incorporating restorative justice principles in their behaviour management strategies, schools are not just assisting individual students or families, but are also helping to restore the integrity of their communities. Powerful mechanisms of situated learning (Lave and Wenger, 1991) are brought into play in a process that empowers community members to experience reciprocal accountability, respect and support.

A model proposed by Braithwaite, which draws from the experience of restorative justice within the criminal justice system to reduce criminal offending, advocates setting up 'family group circles'. Victims and offenders meet with people from the community whom the offender respects and trusts, and who care about the offender, to discuss what needs to be done to help the victim and the offender to right the wrongs and restore their lives. In educational settings, informal social support with education, relationships and employment from people trusted by the young person could be provided by 'youth development circles' where all members of the circles would be chosen by the young person concerned. The circles would remain in place for the whole period of compulsory schooling.

In practical terms, to set up such an initiative in school, family and community partnerships, Epstein et al (1997) propose five steps:

Step 1   Create an action team: at least three teachers, three parents and an administrator

Step 2   Obtain funds and other support: LEA funds, local businesses, school discretionary funds, separate fund-raising?

Step 3   Identify starting points: collect information about the school's current practices of partnerships – strengths, needed changes, expectations, sense of community, links to students' achievement

Step 4   Develop a three-year outline plan, and a one-year detailed starting plan

Step 5   Continue planning and working: annual presentation and discussion of progress and future developments.

Whole-school issues

Fundamental to understanding and addressing behavioural concerns in schools is an understanding that a sense of belonging and acceptance in a social group which shows care and respect for its members is a basic human need. A number of reports and studies refer to the influence of the beliefs of the leaders and managers of a school in sustaining appropriate values, attitude and beliefs (DES, 1989; DfE, 1994a and b; OFSTED, 2001; Richards, 1999; Visser, Cole and Daniels, 2002 for example). Visser, Cole and Daniels (2002) comment on the importance of the values, attitudes and beliefs of a school as a whole in which staff cared about students recognising and valuing diversity and the influence of what they describe as a 'critical mass' of staff which is not necessarily a majority of staff but influential staff who are key players in the school.

In an investigation into the characteristics of schools identified as successful in addressing the learning needs of minority ethnic students, in particular those of black students of African-Caribbean heritage, Blair (2001) puts strong emphasis on a school climate and ethos in which the views of black students along with all students are listened to and respected. The essential factor is teachers who respect diversity and are open to learning and understanding the issues that affect the students, including their political and social concerns. Students' needs and concerns as adolescents are recognised alongside needs arising from ethnic and racial identities. In the successful school the views of black students on poor behaviour and poor relations within school were sought and respected, as were those of all students. The commitment of teachers was essential to success and required their participation in frank discussions about the basic philosophy and culture of school, staff development on equality of opportunity and consultations with students to decide what they want from school. Blair's suggestions are conceived from the outset in an inclusive 'whole school' response. For her, school change to respond to a wider variety of needs is the issue. Black children need to know that they are not only wanted but welcome in school through respect for their culture and through awareness that the political issues that beset them as black people will be understood. The hopes of black parents for their children to benefit from education and school are the same as any other parents. Blair described the commitment of successful schools to work with black parents and the strong relationships forged between the school and the black community with consultation on policies and school governance.

A 'whole school' approach involves all those who have to operate or are affected by a policy and is likely to be most effective in creating and maintaining the necessary ethos and associated practice. Watkins and Wagner (2000) describe how staff can work cooperatively in improvement teams to create a behaviour policy and with the support of peers to develop practice. As a consequence school ethos can become more caring and supportive and the use of sanctions reduced. The notion of students, parents, staff, management and governors having a stake in the school through dialogue, participation and supportive relationships is recognised by Richards (1999). Radford (2000) claims that such a situation has given results in the form of a sense of ownership and empowerment through the willingness to work and act in cooperation and alongside others.

Behaviour improvement policies aimed at change at the individual, the classroom and the school levels are more likely to be effective than simple punishment and/or personal humiliation and take into account the cultural contexts of behaviour. For example, when resolving behavioural issues Māori will often refer to the concept of 'mana' or to ensuring that everyone's mana remains safe and intact. 'Mana tangata' is the authority one gains, according to one's ability to develop and maintain skills. Sometimes these skills are acquired through self-motivation and determination and sometimes skills are handed down from others.

'Circle Time (Mosley and Tew, 1999) is another example of an initiative associated with students' behaviour that is designed to permeate the structure and organisation of the whole school. Mosley (undated) notes seven key elements in the model:

1. Improving the Morale of Staff
   … If staff in a school are to respond in a positive and warm manner to children, they need to have the ability to support each other as members of a team. The first focus of the Quality Circle Time training is on the emotional health of adults … This puts listening at the centre of the school timetable. The aim is to work on maintaining emotional safety, and to promote specific relationship skills.
2. Three Listening Systems
   Quality Circle Time sets up three systems within which children can speak with themselves and each other. These are:
   Circle Time … the games and exercises used are designed to foster a sense of the class as a community, and to establish a safe boundary within which other activities can take place.
   Bubble Time and Talk are one-to-one listening systems, respectively for primary schools and for secondary schools.
   Think Books are offered as a daily non-verbal communication system.
3. Golden Rules … All members of a school are involved in the discussion and establishment of Golden Rules. Once agreed, they are displayed in every area of the school.
4. Incentives … Stickers and certificates are given to those who observe the rules. They are given by the whole school community – including lunchtime supervisors, caretakers and children – so that people can all congratulate each other…
5. Golden Time/Privilege Time … A regular half-hour slot of free time is given over to educational activities chosen by the children.
6. Lunchtime Policy … Good practice means creating possibilities for all kids to join in a range of different activities. It also means providing quiet places for them to go … Lunchtime supervisors are given the same rights as teachers, and are encouraged to use the same incentive and sanction system, whilst also being invited to regular Circle Time meetings with children and with members of staff…
7. Children Beyond … There are some children who … need the security of three other approaches, that incorporate behavioural, therapeutic and peer support. For them, teachers are introduced to a range of 'guaranteed success' programmes.

(Mosley, undated, pp 7–9)

The process of creating school behaviour policies and the way decisions are taken about policy content are crucial to the effectiveness of practice. Radford (2000) reports an initiative by a London Borough Education Authority to help schools with the creation of behaviour policies, which is aimed at involving all who are members of the school community. She used a model which provides a framework for reflection at each stage of the process of policy formulation. During Phase A of policy development staff discussed:

Aims and priority values
Rationale of policy
Key values in practice

(Radford, 2000, p 87)

Phase B comprised:

> Staff self-review
> Action plans
> Systems and training needs
> INSET

(Radford, ibid)

The final stage of the process, Phase C, involved:

> Monitoring
> Evaluation

(Radford, ibid)

She identifies the skills senior staff need if the process is to be successful:

- create an environment in which there are non-judgemental opportunities to reflect on one's beliefs, values, attitudes and feelings about behaviour;
- draw staff into active involvement, using their ideas as part of the process;
- invite staff to take responsibility for decisions taken;
- provide opportunities to formulate ideas that will influence future planning, including changes to practical arrangements;
- inspire confidence such that staff will be prepared to reflect on their own practice.

(Radford, 2000, p 88)

A sanctions-driven discipline policy at the level of the individual student can promote a type of behaviour that schools find acceptable. However, students can have different experiences of the use of those sanctions (Wright, Weekes and McGlaughlin, 2000). If students perceive sanctions or policies as unfair and are unable to get staff to listen to them, then conflict occurs in which students will contest the nature of power and control in the school. Radford (2000) states that:

> Whilst it may be possible to maintain order in classrooms by the fear of graduated responses to misdemeanours, there is a need to address the more fundamental issue of how to motivate youngsters to behave in a fashion conducive to creating a supportive social community, within the school, and beyond.

(Radford, 2000, p 86)

Watkins and Wagner (1995) conclude that effective approaches to addressing issues of school behaviour take into account the extent to which a school has practices and methods which can:

- identify behaviour patterns at the level of individual students, classrooms and the whole school and also
- facilitate the process of problem-solving through exploration of the problem situation, reaching new understandings through reflection on findings and re-framing the problem so that action can be taken.

Collecting evidence about behaviour at school level might include, for example, occasional informal surveys, reviews of school behaviour at staff meetings to identify locations and situations where difficult behaviour does, and does not, occur. At classroom level, information on behaviour patterns might be collected, for example through tracking individual students and observing class activities through the eyes of students as closely as possible and/or through reciprocal classroom observation by peers on the staff. It may well be important to structure the content of the classroom observation with an agreed list of areas to be observed.

School policies can be framed to support intervention in difficult patterns of behaviour. They may outline:

- ways for staff to review how the school organisation affects behaviour;
- ways of improving school facilities and environment to increase student involvement;
- developing statements of expectations in school and classroom;
- clarifying how the curriculum addresses behaviour and helps students learn;
- methods of reviewing classrooms and their management;
- systems for all staff learning/developing (including mid-day supervision team);
- improving the reward climate of the school.

(Watkins and Wagner, 1995, p 57)

Classroom management

In a summary report of research into some 8000 students' perceptions of classroom learning in 15,000 classes, Hobby and Smith (2002) argue that:

> pupils' motivation and desire to learn will significantly affect their academic progress (as well as promoting more rounded, social development).

(Hobby and Smith, 2002, p 8)

Teachers create learning environments, 'classroom climate', defined as:

> The collective perception of pupils of what it feels like, in intellectual, motivational and emotional terms, to be a pupil in any particular teacher's classroom; where those perceptions influence every pupil's motivation to learn and perform to the best of his or her ability.

(Hobby and Smith, 2002, p 9)

Teachers can directly influence classroom climate by their behaviour and skills. An instructional or teaching and learning approach aimed at creating a positive learning climate in classrooms is more effective than control and sanctions as a means of managing behaviour difficulties in classrooms (Carpenter and McKee-Higgins, 1996). Similarly, in a New Zealand Māori context, Macfarlane (1997) describes teaching approaches designed to encourage a positive learning climate through the provision of appropriate learning tasks, rewarding positive responses and developing positive interactions with students which stem from:

- the traditional Māori value of 'aroha', connoting, in the context of school discipline, 'co-operation, support, understanding, reciprocity and warmth' (Macfarlane, 1997, p 155),
- a sense of opening doorways by creating meaningful relationships, destroying unhelpful, negative myths associated with students' previous reputations and establishing clear, fair boundaries for behaviour,
- teachers' assertive communication which is 'part of an established order of Māori protocol' (Macfarlane, 1997, p 156) in speaking on the marae (traditional community meeting place),
- respect for all students and an awareness of the need to build students' self respect,
- an awareness of the reality of the situation of each of them,
- a secure and nurturing environment where students can taste success, feel valued as community members and be encouraged to take responsibility for the choices they make,
- shared ownership of the situation of the student by the student, the teacher and the whānau (extended family).

Teachers in schools can influence student and behaviour by assessing characteristics of the classroom learning environments in which students are placed, because these can be changed to support more effective learning (Ysseldyke and Christenson, 1987). Following an analysis of features in the learning environment that appeared to influence learning, Ysseldyke and Christenson designed 'The Instructional Environment Scale' (TIES) in order to support the systematic collection of data to analyse contextual barriers to pupils' learning. Ysseldyke and Christenson (1987, p 21–2) recommend that data should be gathered through classroom observation and interview with both student and teacher on twelve components of teaching: 'Instructional presentation', 'Classroom environment', 'Teacher expectations', 'Cognitive emphasis', 'Motivational strategies', 'Relevant practice', 'Academic engaged time', 'Informed feedback', 'Adaptive instruction', 'Progress evaluation', 'Instructional planning' and 'Student understanding'.

Individual attributes

As Watkins and Wagner (1995) note, 'difficult behaviour' of individual students may be indicative of issues in the immediate context as well as students' personal attributes. Compatible with this view is an approach adopted by Birmingham (England) City Council's strategy document *Behaviour in Schools: framework for intervention* (Birmingham City Council Education Department, 1998). In this approach, responses to difficult behaviour begin with an audit of the learning environment and considerations of alterations to it which are designed to make a positive impact on behaviour and learning. For a small minority of students whose behaviour continues to be a focus of teachers' concerns, it may be seen as appropriate to investigate learning and behavioural issues at the level of the individual. Where necessary, interventions continue with a greater focus on the individual student as well as the environment and may involve external agencies.

Effective solutions to problems associated with behavioural concerns in schools require 'effective problem definition' (Watkins and Wagner, 1995, p 6). As Watkins and Wagner (op cit) note, systematic collection of evidence about individual patterns of behaviour 'can identify and analyse the vicious and virtuous cycles in the pattern of behaviour, so that the means of creating further virtuous cycles may be found'. The following questions may offer a useful starting point for considering individual students' patterns of behaviour and the level at which this behaviour might be addressed:

> What specific behaviour is causing concern? In which particular contexts, and with whom, does the behaviour occur?
>> In which contexts does the behaviour not occur?
>> What leads up to the behaviour? Are there any triggers?
>> What are the consequences of the behaviour, that is, what is the payoff for the student?
>> What level of social and communication skills does the student possess?
>> What skills does the student lack?
>> What does the behaviour mean to the student?
>> How does the behaviour enhance the student's view of him/herself?
>> What views do other students and staff have of the individual student? Can these views be changed?
>> Whom does the individual student's behaviour most affect?
>> (adapted from Watkins and Wagner, 1995, p 6)

Within the area of student behaviour in schools there is a wide range of intervention strategies that might be adopted. It is very important, therefore, to have a clear view of which intervention might be appropriate to address which need, to understand its underpinning rationale and take account of any ethical issues this raises. One common intervention in response to problematic student behaviour in schools is that of behaviour modification programmes for individuals.

> *Behaviour modification* is an approach which takes as its starting point the Skinnerian notion that in any situation, or in response to any stimulus, the person has available a repertoire of possible responses, and emits the behaviour that is reinforced or rewarded. This principle is known as *operant conditioning* … Applied to individuals with behavioural problems, these ideas suggest that it is helpful to reward or reinforce desired or appropriate behaviour, and ignore inappropriate behaviour.
> …The effectiveness of behaviour modification and token economy programmes is highly dependent on the existence of a controlled social environment, in which the behaviour of the learner can be consistently reinforced in the intended direction … The technique can … be applied … in … situations like schools and families if key

participants such as teachers and parents are taught how to apply the technique. It is essential, however, that whoever is supplying the behaviour modification is skilled and motivated, so that the client is not exposed to contradictory reinforcement schedules.

(McLeod, 1998, p 66)

In any relationship where the role of a professional is to influence the behaviour of others, there is an important question of ethics. 'Underpinning ethical codes are a set of core moral principles: autonomy, non-maleficence, beneficence, justice and fidelity' (McLeod, 1998, p 289):

Furthermore, because behaviour modification relies on the fact that the person supplying the reinforcement has real power to give or withhold commodities which are highly valued by the client, there is the possibility of corruption and abuse...

Another way in which behaviour modification can be abusive in practice is by too much emphasis on the technique known as 'time out' ... problematic behaviour patterns, such as aggressive and violent behaviour, can be interrupted by placing the person in a room to 'cool off'. The intention is that violence is not rewarded by attention from staff or other residents, but that resumption of rationality is rewarded, by the person being allowed out of the room. In principle, this can be a valuable intervention strategy, which can help some people to change behaviour that can lead them into severe trouble. The danger is that staff may use time out in a punitive manner, to keep a resident quiet or to discharge their own anger at him or her. This technique may result in an abuse of the rights and civil liberties of the client.

(McLeod, 1998, p 67)

To these issues we might add cultural safety, that is, acceptance of students' values and preferences. One of the criticisms of behaviour management techniques in schools is that they tend to silence the cultural and community contexts, together with the traditional values, in which behaviour is defined and understood (Macfarlane, 1997; 2000a and b; Glynn and Bishop, 1995).

Conclusion

A school as a whole has to move from a simple focus on the student with behaviour difficulties to a focus on the incident. Behaviour improvement policies aimed at change at the individual, the classroom and the school levels are most likely to be effective. This position is a more positive basis for movement towards collaborative solutions, rather than simply to punishment and/or personal humiliation. It also takes into account the cultural contexts of behaviour. The Elton Report (DES, 1989) concludes that students' behaviour in schools is influenced by almost every aspect of the school's organisation and structure and by its relationship to the community it serves. By definition, therefore, addressing students' behaviour in schools:

may involve thinking about and intervening on almost every aspect of the way the school is run. This may include:

pupil behaviour (that is learning and social behaviour, individually and in groups)...

teacher behaviour (such as approaches to managing classrooms, styles of responding to difficulties, and so on); and

school behaviour (such as the style of the organisation and how it typically responds when difficulties or concerns are raised).

(Watkins and Wagner, 1995, p 55)

In conclusion, student behaviour in schools is influenced by a range of factors that operate at individual, institutional, family, community and societal levels. Effective interventions to address student behaviour need to be based on an understanding of these factors. Thus multi-level responses to behavioural issues in schools are far more realistic than responses that view these issues as the problems of isolated individuals operating in a vacuum.

References

Anderson, C., Gendler, G., Riestenberg, N., Anfang, C.C., Ellison, M. and Yates, B. (1996) *Restorative Measures: respecting everyone's ability to resolve problems*. St Paul, MN: Minnesota Department of Children, Families and Learning, Office of Community Services, 550 Cedar Street.

Armstrong, D. and Galloway, D. (1994) 'Special educational needs and problem behaviour: making policy in the classroom', in Riddell, S. and Brown, S. (eds) *Special Educational Needs Policy in the 90s*, London: Routledge.

Birmingham City Council Education Department (1998) *Behaviour in Schools: framework for intervention*, Birmingham: Birmingham City Council.

Bishop, R., Berryman, M., Glynn, T., McKinley, L., Devine, N. and Richardson, C. (2001) *The Experiences of Māori Children in the Year 9 and year 10 Classrooms: Part 1 the scoping exercise*. Report presented to the Research Division of the Ministry of Education, Wellington: Ministry of Education.

Bishop, R., Berryman, M., Richardson, C., and Tiakiwai, S. (2001) *Te Kotahitanga: Experiences of year 9 and 10 Māori students in mainstream classrooms*. Final Report prepared for the Ministry of Education, Wellington: Ministry of Education.

Blair, M. (2001) 'The education of Black children: why do some schools do better than others?' In R. Majors (ed.), *Educating our Black Children*, London: Routledge Falmer.

Braithwaite, J. (1997) *Restorative Justice: assessing an immodest theory and a pessimistic theory* (Australian Institute of Criminology, Australian National University).

British Psychological Society (1996) *Attention Deficit Hyperactivity Disorder (ADHD): a psychological response to an evolving concept*, Leicester: BPS.

Bronfenbrenner, U. (1979) *The Ecology of Human Development*. Cambridge, Mass: Harvard.

Bruner, J. (1996) *The Culture of Education*, London: Harvard.

Carpenter, S.L. and McKee-Higgins, E. (1996) 'Behaviour management in inclusive classrooms'. *Remedial and Special Education*, 17(4), 195.

Department for Education (DfE) (1994a) *Pupil Behaviour and Discipline* (Circular 8/94), London: DfE.

Department for Education (DfE) (1994b) *The Education of Children with Emotional and Behavioural Difficulties* (Circular 9/94), London: DfE.

Department for Education and Employment (DfEE) (1999) *Social Inclusion: pupil support* (Circular 10/99), London: DfEE.

Department of Education and Science (DES) (1989) *Discipline in Schools*. Report of the committee of enquiry chaired by Lord Elton (the Elton Report), London: Her Majesty's Stationery Office (HMSO).

Dyson, A. and Robson, E. (1999) *School Inclusion: the evidence. A review of the UK literature on school, family and community links*, Newcastle: University of Newcastle.

Epstein, J., Coates, L., Salinas, K., Sanders, M. and Simon, B. (1997) '*School Family and Community Partnerships: your handbook for action*, Thousand Oaks, CA: Corwin Press.

Gewirtz, S., Ball, S.J., and Bowe, R. (1995) *Markets, Choice and Equity in Education*, Buckingham: Open University Press.

Glynn, T. and Bishop, R. (1995) 'Cultural issues in educational research: a New Zealand perspective', *He Pūkengo Kōrero*, 1(1), 37–43.

Hobby, R. and Smith, F. (2002) *A National Development Agenda. What does it feel like to learn in our schools? Transforming learning*. London: The Hay Group.

Kendrick, A. (1995) 'The integration of child care services in Scotland', *Children and Youth Services Review*, 17, 5–16, 619–35.

Lave, J. and Wenger, E. (1991) *Situated Learning: legitimate peripheral participation*, Cambridge: Cambridge University Press.

Lloyd, G. (1997) 'Can the law support children's rights in school in Scotland and prevent the development of a climate of blame?', *Pastoral Care*, 15, 13–16.

Macfarlane, A. (1997) 'The Hikairo rationale: a bicultural approach to teaching students experiencing behaviour difficulties', *Waikato Journal of Education*, 3, 153–168.

Macfarlane, A. (2000a) 'Māori perspectives on development', in L. Bird and W. Drewery (eds) *Human Development in Aotearoa: a journey through life*, 42–45, Auckland: McGraw-Hill Book Company.

Macfarlane, A. (2000b) 'The value of Māori ecologies in special education', in

D. Fraser, R. Moltzen and K. Ryba (eds) *Learners with Special Needs in Aotearoa New Zealand*, 2nd edn, Palmerston North, NZ: Dunmore Press.

McLeod, J. (1998) *An Introduction to Counselling*, 2nd edn, Buckingham: Open University Press.

Mosley, J. (undated) *Quality Circle Time: the heart of the curriculum,* Trowbridge: Jenny Mosley Consultancies.

Mosley, J. and Tew, M. (1999) *Quality Circle Time in the Secondary School – A Handbook of Good Practice*, London: David Fulton Publishers.

Office for Standards in Education (OFSTED) (2001) *Improving Attendance and Behaviour in Secondary Schools*. A report of her Majesty's Chief Inspector of Schools, London: OFSTED.

Office for Standards in Education (OFSTED) (2003) *Excellence in Cities and Education Action Zones: management and impact*, London: OFSTED.

Radford, J. (2000) 'Values into practice: developing whole school behaviour policies'. *Support for Learning*, 15(2), 86–89.

Richards, I.C. (1999) 'Inclusive schools for pupils with emotional and behaviour difficulties'. *Support for Learning*, 14(3), 99–103.

Rutter, M. *et al.* (1979) *Fifteen Thousand Hours: secondary schools and their effects on children*, London: Open Books.

Schweigert, F.J. (1999) 'Moral behaviour in victim offender conferencing', *Criminal Justice Ethics*, (Summer/Fall), 29–40.

Tett, L., Munn, P., Blair, A., Kay, H., Martin, I., Martin, J. and Ranson, S. (2001) 'Collaboration between schools and community education agencies in tackling social exclusion', *Research Papers in Education*, 16(1), 3–21.

Visser, J., Cole, T. and Daniels, H. (2002) 'Inclusion for the difficult to include', *Support for Learning*, 17(1), 23–26.

Watkins, C. and Wagner, P. (1995) 'School behaviour and special educational needs – what's the link?' in National Children's Bureau, *Discussion Papers 1, Schools' special educational needs policies pack*, pp 53–72, London: National Children's Bureau.

Watkins, C. and Wagner, P. (2000) *Improving School Behaviour*, London: Paul Chapman.

Wright, C., Weekes D. and McGlaughlin, A. (2000) *'Race' Class and Gender in Exclusion from School*, London and New York: Falmer Press.

Ysseldyke, J.E. and Christenson, S.L. (1987) 'Evaluating students' instructional environments', *Remedial and Special Education*, 8(3), 17–24.

PART 1
District and community level

Chapter 2

Restorative justice in schools

Belinda Hopkins

Introduction

This Chapter explores the potential of a restorative approach in school in addressing challenging or disruptive behaviour and conflict wherever that may occur in the school community. It suggests some steps for introducing restorative philosophy, skills and interventions into a whole school initiative. It describes the initiatives that are already being piloted in certain schools around the UK and some of the issues that are arising from these projects. Finally it highlights current challenges to development and possible solutions and ways forward.

Restorative justice in schools – the potential

In broad terms restorative justice constitutes an innovative approach to both offending or challenging behaviour which puts repairing harm done to relationships and people over and above the need for assigning blame and dispensing punishment (Wright, 1999). Restorative justice is defined not in terms of those who are to blame 'getting their just deserts' but as 'all those affected by an "offence" or incident being involved in finding a mutually acceptable way forward'. In this context the 'offenders' or wrongdoers are also recognised as having been affected and therefore involved in finding the way forward. This approach to justice challenges many notions deeply embedded in western society at least, and enacted in many homes, schools and institutions. These notions include the idea that misbehaviour (however that is defined by those in authority) should be punished, and that the threat of punishment is required to ensure that potential wrongdoers comply with society's rules. Howard Zehr (1995) refers to the shift from retributive justice to restorative justice in the arena of criminal justice as a paradigm shift. It may be that a similar paradigm shift is needed in a school setting if relationship and behaviour management are to be developed along restorative lines.

Restorative justice is considered here in three distinct ways: as a set of processes and approaches; as a set of skills; and as a distinctive ethos and philosophy.

The processes and approaches are the most public face of restorative justice and include all formal or informal interventions which have as their aim to put things right, to 'repair the harm' as it is often phrased, after some behaviour or event which has adversely affected people. In this context 'to put things right' means that the needs of as many of the people involved as possible have been addressed. These interventions, including mediation, conferencing and healing circles, share certain essential steps. Everyone affected by a behaviour, a conflict situation or a problem, has the opportunity to talk about what has happened, explain how they have been affected by it, describe how they are currently feeling about the situation and what they want to do to repair the harm caused. An important element in this intervention is that it is voluntary. The success of the processes depends in large measure on the willingness of people to take part and engage.

These interventions require certain skills on the part of the facilitators or mediators and, it could be argued, will be helped considerably if these same skills are being developed in all members of the community likely to be involved in an intervention. These skills include remaining impartial and non-judgemental, respecting the perspective of all involved; actively and empathically listening; developing rapport amongst participants; empowering participants to come up with solutions rather than suggesting or imposing ideas; creative questioning; warmth; compassion and patience.

These skills are informed by an intention, namely the importance of the underlying ethos that encompasses the values of respect, openness, empowerment, inclusion, tolerance, integrity and congruence. This last is crucial in developing a whole school approach to restorative justice for it is saying, in simple terms, 'walk the talk'. In other words the key question becomes 'Is everything we do here at this school informed by this ethos, these values and a philosophy which gives central importance to building, maintaining, and, when necessary, repairing relationships and community?'

Restorative justice does not have the monopoly on such an approach in schools. Those educationalists who espouse a humanitarian, liberal child-centred approach will recognise much of what has been said about ethos and skills (Porter, 2000). However, in the application of these skills and ethos, restorative justice may be offering something new, especially in developing a behaviour management policy.

Classen (2001) refers to the first of a set of principles of 'Restorative Discipline' (*sic*) which he has developed with his wife Roxanne and which have been incorporated into the behaviour management policy of the school in which she works:

> Misbehavior is viewed primarily as an offense against human relationships and secondarily as a violation of a school rule (since school rules are written to protect safety and fairness in human relationships).

Claasen acknowledges the importance of rules but suggests that sometimes the real purpose of rules is ignored and the focus becomes the fact of rule breaking rather than the human factors beneath the rule breaking.

> In the community when someone violates a law, we call it a crime. In schools, when someone violates a rule, we call it a misbehavior (*sic*). If a misbehavior is observed that isn't covered by a rule yet, we usually write a new rule. Rules are very important and helpful since they help everyone to know what behavior is not acceptable in that school community. Rules also prevent, or at least reduce, arbitrary punishment because the rules are published for everyone to know and members of the school community can appeal to the rules if it seems that they are being punished arbitrarily.
>
>   Where this becomes a problem is when the primary focus of a discipline program is on the rule violation and because of that, the human violation is ignored or minimized. Since the purpose of establishing rules is to provide for a safe, fair, just, and orderly community, it is important that this underlying reason is not lost in our effort to be sure we follow the rules.

A second point emphasises the difference between a common approach to dealing with conflicts between young people and one that tries to use mediation principles. The intention of the former is to 'get to the bottom of the matter', to sort out who did what and who is to blame. Once the person to blame has been identified this person can be 'dealt with' according to the sanctions policy of the school. This is not to say that such a sanction may not also include attempts at conciliation between the youngsters in conflict, but often this might mean an enforced and insincere apology.

   A more restorative approach would be to use the principles of mediation in which both or all sides of a dispute are invited to explain what happened from their perspective, to express how they are currently feeling about the incident and then to be invited to explore a mutually acceptable way forward. Many teachers will say that they use this approach and there are certainly many natural mediators in schools. However the approach is undermined if people are less than impartial in their body language, tone, phrasing of questions, or summing up of the events, or when someone is unable to resist the temptation to offer suggestions or express an opinion about the nature of the behaviour. These are all issues that can be identified in training, when people are encouraged to try mediating in practice scenarios, with feedback from colleagues on their mediation skills.

Introducing restorative justice into a school

The emphasis on involving the school community in resolving conflicts is predicated on the notion that those in the community want to repair harm and that they have the skills and the opportunities to do so. It is useful to think of a whole school approach as one that not only repairs harm in the event of conflict and inappropriate behaviour but also one that builds and nurtures relationship and community in the first place (Johnston, 2002, p. 14). This is a useful starting point when introducing restorative justice into schools, perhaps at a staff training day. I have found it useful to invite participants, in four groups, to consider what is already happening in their own schools to:

• build and nurture relationships
• develop relational skills in themselves and their students
• repair the harm done to relationship in the event of conflict or inappropriate behaviour
• develop their own and their students' skills to engage in these repair processes.

Figure 2.1, in its blank form, is used to initiate debate, and the four groups report their findings. The results of group discussion highlight what is already happening in the school and also where the gaps are. The filled-in version can be used to compare what is already happening in a school with what might be possible if a whole school approach is sought.

Often restorative practices build on the initiatives already in place in a school and can be seen as a natural development of where many schools are already or are moving towards. The approach dovetails nicely with developments in Active Citizenship and the commitment by many schools to the Healthy Schools Programme, which emphasise creative conflict management as part of a healthy school. The concern to reduce exclusion and tackle bullying can also be addressed by such an approach, and this is where some initiatives are already being successful.

Current initiatives in the UK

In the last few years there have been several initiatives in the UK involving some aspects of a restorative approach. Most of these have involved outside facilitators offering restorative conferencing to schools in the event of a bullying incident or when exclusion is being considered. Conferencing is the name given to a process involving as many people as possible who feel directly affected by an incident of conflict or by inappropriate or even offending

	RESTORING (repairing harm done to relationships and community)	**RELATING** (developing/nurturing relationships and creating community)
P R O C E S S E S	**A) undisputed responsibility:** • restorative conferencing • family group conferencing • victim/offender mediation • sentencing circles **B) disputed responsibility, conflict, mutual recrimination:** • mediation • peer mediation • healing circles • no-blame approach to bullying	**including:** • Circle Time for staff (for planning, review, support and team building) • Circle Time for students • school council • circle of friends • peer counselling and mentoring • whole school development of relationship management policy (cf. behaviour management, which tends to be student-focused)
	RELATIONSHIPS	
S K I L L S	**skills include:** • non-violent communication • active non-judgemental listening • conflict transformation • developing empathy and rapport • having difficult conversations • restorative debriefing after critical incidents • understanding and managing anger	**skills include:** • emotional literacy • developing and maintaining self-esteem • valuing others explicitly • assertiveness • acknowledging and appreciating diversity • constructively challenging oppression and prejudice • connecting across differences

◄——— much overlap ———►

Figure 2.1 Restorative and relational process skills

behaviour. It resembles mediation in that the same steps are followed in which everyone has a chance to say how they have been affected by the incident, how they were feeling, how they feel currently and what can be done to repair the harm and make things as right as possible. Some conference practitioners will differentiate the process, which takes place with all involved sitting in a circle, from mediation. The debates about whether the processes are similar and what the underlying theories are which underpin the approach will continue for a long time to come. The debates are not directly relevant to this chapter but it is important and sad to acknowledge that in a field which promotes conflict management and mutual respect there is conflict about what restorative justice is and how it should be developed (Johnston, 2002).

A project in Nottingham, a partnership between Nottingham Education Authority and Nottingham Police, began with offering conferencing in school settings with cases of bullying and harassment and has now been extended to peer buddying. Anecdotal evidence suggests that the people directly involved have benefited from the process, the inappropriate behaviour has been reduced and all sides have been able to move forward more positively.

Comments from education professionals, following training in restorative conferencing, include remarks such as:

> The techniques can be used for major and minor issues: it should be used in all schools.
>   I have seen nothing as relevant in years.

A deputy head involved in using conferencing and restorative principles in her primary school comments:

> The conferences that we've held have been a very positive experience. Children now ask if they can have a conference to sort out problems.

Interestingly this school now trains the young people themselves to run conferences, in the same way that an increasing number of primary and secondary schools are using peer mediators to help resolve conflicts in the playground – another element of the restorative jigsaw in itself.

By far the most important voice, however, is that of the young people themselves. Reflections from the Nottingham project include remarks such as:

> Thanks for organising the conference. Amy sits next to me now and we've sorted it out.
>
> (Girl aged 10)

> It was good because we talked about it.
>
> (Boy aged 5)

Comments from one of the six secondary schools involved in the project include:

> I thought that the Restorative Justice Conference was good and it made me make friends with K ... It was good how we had our parents there, and it made me think how I should behave. The agreement was a good idea and I have still got it.
>   (Year 10 girl who had been bullying someone else)

There is great enthusiasm for using restorative approaches in schools in the Thames Valley where the Thames Valley Police have been in the forefront of promoting restorative measures for dealing with youth offending. In Oxfordshire the local education authority, in partnership with the Youth

Offending Team and the Thames Valley Police, are sponsoring a two-year project aimed at promoting a whole school restorative approach to conflict and inappropriate behaviour. Many police school liaison officers throughout the Thames Valley are using restorative conferencing regularly to deal not only with offending behaviour but also with conflict and bullying in schools.

In January of this year a new project began in Devon, instigated by the Devon and Cornwall Police. This project is using Youth Affairs Officers in six secondary schools to run conferences when needed in the school to which each officer is attached. I have been involved as a consultant in this project and have produced guidelines for enabling the Youth Affairs Officers and the teaching staff to further develop the restorative ethos in the school. My recommendation has been that there needs to be congruence between the way the Youth Affairs Officers deal with serious cases of disruption and the way more minor incidents are dealt with by teaching staff on a day-to-day basis. Initial feedback from this project is positive and encouraging.

Other initiatives include one in Brixton in which non-teaching representatives from several schools were trained in the conferencing process by police officers with a view to developing a restorative approach in their respective schools. The impact of this training on their schools is currently being evaluated. It will be interesting to compare the impact of this project with one in Berkshire where twelve teachers from one secondary school have been trained in the conferencing process. This project is also currently being evaluated.

Interest in the potential of restorative practices in schools is growing and more and more initiatives are being started. For example, the National Association for the Care and Resettlement of Offenders (NACRO) has advertised for a project worker and the Youth Justice Board is offering large sums of money for innovative projects in this field. A partnership of several police authorities (Thames Valley, Nottingham, Surrey, Devon and Cornwall (combined), and possibly Northern Ireland) together with Crime Concern, Mediation UK and Transforming Conflict, is organising a series of 'Restorative Practices In Schools' Travelling Road shows around the country over the next 18 months. A training package for teachers in restorative skills is in the pipeline and being piloted this summer. It will provide experiential practical training in one-to-one challenging situations as well as mediation and conferencing skills.

There is a general appreciation that developing restorative practices in a school is not simply about offering conferences in situations where harm has been caused. The more holistic approach and the potential to enhance the whole school community by relating in a different way is recognised by most people who are familiar with restorative justice (Quill and Wynne, 1993; Johnston, 2002).

Challenges

Effecting change in a school culture is not without its challenges. Interestingly, in both the Thames Valley and in Nottingham a similar story is emerging – that whilst there is undoubted benefit to the individuals involved in conferences most of the time, the school community as a whole remains largely untouched by the process and the philosophy behind it.

As a practitioner and a consultant working in the field of restorative justice in schools I would suggest that the major factors militating against the development of a whole school restorative approach are shortage of time and pressures from conflicting priorities. The shortage of time is in relation to the time available in the school day for dealing with issues in a restorative manner as well as the time available for training, support and review of practice. There are similar pressures on the Initial Teacher Training programmes, which leave little or no room for preparing new teachers in relational and conflict management skills.

There are also issues of relevance and openness to change. Some projects have begun by using outside facilitators, in some cases police officers, to run conferences in the event of extreme behaviour. Although such facilitators may themselves be aware of the wider potential of the approach they have not found it easy to reach the wider school community. For example, in some cases teachers have been understandably cautious about police officers working in school on behaviour management issues. Conversely, in extreme situations where staff welcome outside support, the risk then is that they feel disempowered and are left thinking that the skills of a mediator or a conference facilitator are too difficult for them to use themselves.

A final challenge is to ensure that the ethos and principles of restorative justice are embraced at every stage of the process. Unfortunately there are already examples of the process being imposed on unwilling participants or facilitated by inexperienced facilitators who try to threaten participants or impose their views. There is a significant risk of re-victimisation of those already badly affected by wrongdoing in such cases. Careful preparation of all parties in a conference or mediation is vital to the success of such interventions.

Ways forward

Shortage of time and pressure from other priorities are not to be dismissed. However in my experience these obstacles tend to dissolve once a school community is convinced a restorative approach can make a difference. Dealing with conflict and inappropriate behaviour restoratively takes time initially but greatly reduces the total time that such situations usually take. One part of a whole school approach – peer mediation – greatly reduces the time teachers need to spend on playground conflict for example. In fact, in time such a project, in conjunction with active citizenship and conflict management skills being developed during Circle Time, can greatly reduce playground and classroom conflict anyway. Challenging and distressing incidents have a tendency to send ripples far beyond those immediately involved and bad feeling and bitterness can fester. A restorative approach can bring all of these feelings out in the open and hopefully everyone can move on in a positive frame of mind.

Shortage of time for training, ongoing support and review are real issues, but again I have found that, once convinced, a school finds time and funds for the initiative and can be creative in finding time for training. It is fair to say that most projects are still in their infancy so the question of the necessary ongoing support and review remains an open one.

The question of how to effect behavioural change within a school is complex and the key, to my mind, is in finding common ground and using restorative principles from the beginning. If those affected do not want to take part then the issue needs to be dealt with in a different way. However enthusiastic senior management or governors might be in restorative justice – and as news spreads many such people want information and in-service training – the project will not be successful unless the majority of the school community is on board. By the community I would include teaching staff, support staff, students, governors, parents, administrative staff, lunchtime staff and caretakers, and this list is not exhaustive. It would seem crucial to consult as many people as possible before embarking on a project and use as many channels as possible to communicate what the project is about. Ideally a steering group comprised of representatives from at least the above mentioned groups would oversee the whole project. A second ideal would be to develop training capacity from amongst these groups so that there is not continued reliance on outside training and support. Whole school involvement is at the heart of effective school improvement (Brighouse and Woods, 2000). This is congruent with the restorative values of respect, inclusion and empowerment and the belief that those with the problems are those most likely to find and embrace the solutions.

It is early days to report on how restorative approaches have impacted on school communities. However, elements of the restorative jigsaw are already well known and highly regarded. Circle Time is gaining popularity in the primary school and beginning to be used at secondary level as a way of increasing students' social and emotional awareness and confidence. Peer mediation is becoming better known and both primary and secondary schools are recognising the value of this process. The next step is for the ethos and values of these two processes to imbue every aspect of school life, and for mediation to be a natural part of every adult's repertoire when dealing with conflict or inappropriate behaviour at school.

Enthusiasts of the approach, and I am clearly one, believe that restorative practices in schools can transform existing approaches to relationship and behaviour management. We believe that building and nurturing relationships is at the heart of a successful and happy school. Repairing the harm done to relationships in the event of conflict and inappropriate behaviour is the next priority. In such an environment people are more likely to want to work, more likely to achieve and less likely to be or feel excluded. The vision is an optimistic one. For real change to occur there will need to be time and resources allocated to restorative projects and, however willing a school is to commit itself to change, it may be that support at a higher level is needed.

It is true that there are often too many conflicting pressures for teachers to see how they can embrace restorative practice effectively. Restorative justice is being advocated enthusiastically by many in the criminal justice world, including the Youth Justice Board and the police. It is to be hoped that soon the links that restorative practitioners are making in school and community settings will be made at government level. If there were support from the Department for Education and Skills (DfES) and the Teacher Training Agency (TTA), initial and ongoing training in restorative and relational skills could become more widely available and seen as fundamental in creating an effective learning environment. Time in the school day for such an approach could be made and scope given for reconsidering existing behaviour management policies which currently constrain restorative approaches. In time it would be wonderful to think that every child in the country would grow up in a school where they feel safe and where they learn to resolve their own conflicts. It would be a place where their views are heard and appreciated and where inappropriate behaviour or conflict is considered an issue for the school community to address in an inclusive, compassionate manner using a healing circle, mediation or conferencing. There is hope however. These are exciting times for restorative justice: an idea whose time has come.

I would like to give the last word to a Year 7 girl who took part in a restorative conference I facilitated earlier this year. She had been on the receiving end of some bullying behaviour since starting secondary school this year. Present at the conference was the girl, her mother, the girl who had been causing her distress, this girl's father, the police officer to whom the matter had been reported and myself. The conference went well. It became clear to the so-called 'victim' and her mother that their own loving, supportive relatively affluent family situation was what both the so-called bully and her father did not have. Apologies and plans for future friendship and support were made. In the final closing 'go-round' I asked if anyone had anything else they wanted to say and the jubilant original 'victim', clearly visibly relieved and elated, said 'Whooppee!' I think that just about sums it up.

References

Brighouse, T. and Woods, T. (2000) *How to Improve your School*. London: Routledge Falmer.

Claasen, R. (2001) *Whether crime or misbehavior, restorative justice principles provide guidance on how to respond*. Fresno, CA: Center for Peacemaking and Conflict Studies, Fresno Pacific University. Available online at: www.fresno.edu/dept/pacs

Johnston, G. (2002) *Restorative Justice – Ideas, Values, Debates*. Cullompton: Willan Publishing.

Porter, L. (2000) *Behaviour Management in Schools*. Buckingham: Open University Press.

Quill, D. and Wynne, J. (1993) *Victim and Offender Mediation Handbook*. London: Save the Children/West Yorkshire Probation Service.

Wright, M. (1999) *Restoring Respect for Justice*. Winchester: Waterside Press.

Zehr, H. (1995) *Changing Lenses*. Scottdale: Herald Press.

Chapter 3

Culturally responsive school and community partnerships to avoid suspension

Mere Berryman and Ted Glynn

This text is based on a case study written for *Matauranga Motuhake* (Wilkie, 2001), an NZCER report on special education for Māori to the Ministry of Education.

Introduction

In their statement of intent (Ministry of Education, 2003a), the New Zealand Ministry of Education sets out two key goals that they are committed to from 2003 to 2008. These are:

- Reducing systematic underachievement in education
- Building an education system that will enable all New Zealanders to fully participate in the 21st century.

In relation to these goals, and specifically for Māori students, Durie (2001) has identified three broad goals if Māori are to participate successfully in education. These goals are to:

- live as Māori
- participate successfully in the global community
- enjoy a healthy lifestyle.

Research into the most effective and appropriate learning contexts for Māori students, that has been controlled and legitimated by Māori, is a crucial component of meeting these goals.

This intervention involves three Year 7 and 8 Māori students who experimented with marijuana at their school. Their story is told reflectively through the personal narratives of a grandmother, the teachers of these students and a member of the senior management team. The response of these people (both Māori and non-Māori) to this contemporary global problem was to seek and determine solutions collaboratively in ways that reflect traditional Māori cultural beliefs, values and practices. A community elder invited people from the homes of these students and from the school to a hui whakatika (a meeting seeking solutions) in the school. At this meeting all members involved in the incident, including those responsible for determining solutions, helped to plan an intervention that ensured these students remained at school and continued with more effective two-way communication and support from their homes and from their school.

Historical background to Māori participation in the education system in New Zealand

The Treaty of Waitangi was signed in 1840 on behalf of the British Crown and the Tangatawhenua (indigenous Māori people) of New Zealand. The Tangatawhenua interpreted Article One from this Treaty as promising them partnership, Article Two as promising them tino rangatiratanga (protection or control) over taonga katoa (all treasures) and Article Three as promising them participation and benefits (Durie, 1992). As the Tangatawhenua, Māori saw the Treaty as a charter for power-sharing in the decision making process for the people of this country and understood that by signing the Treaty they would maintain the right to determine their own future and the future of further generations of Māori.

Despite Māori expectations and the promises implicit in the signing of the Treaty, Māori relations with non-Māori historically have not been one of partnership. Māori have endured political, social and economic domination by the Euro-centric majority culture as well as marginalisation through biased legislation, educational initiatives and policies (Bishop & Glynn, 1999). Education under sovereign control was once understood as the means to assimilate Māori students into European culture and society (Codd, Harker & Nash, 1990). A report that highlighted the extremely perilous condition of Māori participation in education (Hunn, 1960) resulted in education reforms and policies such as multiculturalism and biculturalism that were intended to improve education for Māori. However, these and many other mainstream education initiatives have failed adequately to address any aspect of the problems facing Māori students (Spoonley, 1993; Ramsay, 1972) and at the same time these initiatives have continually emphasised the negative features of

Māori knowledge and culture (Barrington & Beaglehole, 1974). One result of this interpretation of Māori participation from a deficit position has been the failure of many Māori to achieve in the education system organised and provided by the majority culture (Bishop, Berryman, Richardson & Tiakiwai, 2001). This situation has led to Māori being blamed for their perceived inadequacies, and in turn has generated self fulfilling prophecies of Māori students' failure (Bishop et al., 2001).

The Treaty of Waitangi Act in 1975 saw the relationship between Māori and the Crown, as detailed in the Treaty, finally recognised by statute. Despite this, Māori as an ethnic group continue to be highly over represented amongst New Zealand students experiencing learning and behavioural difficulties in state schools (Jacka, Sutherland, Peters & Smith, 1996; Donnelly, 1998; Bishop, 1996; Ministry of Education, 2003b). In comparison with non-Māori students, the rate of suspension from school for Māori is three times higher and 38% of Māori students leave school with no formal qualifications as compared with 19% non Māori (Ministry of Education, 2001). These factors contribute to high Māori unemployment or employment in low paid work and, consequently, the over-representation of Māori in many of the negative indices of the wider community beyond school.

Both Ladson-Billings (1995) and Sheurich and Young (1997) contend that where schools practise standard pedagogical methods which are culturally incongruent with the pedagogical practices of the minority culture, then they are practising institutional racism. In New Zealand this practice has been so pervasive that many of the current generation of grandparents and parents have never learned to speak and understand the Māori language, nor have many acquired a thorough understanding of traditional Māori knowledge and cultural practices. Socio-cultural perspectives on human learning emphasise the importance of the responsive social and cultural contexts in which learning takes place as key components to successful learning (Vygotsky, 1978; McNaughton, 1995). For many Māori the social and cultural contexts have changed dramatically and become obscured as the result of successive generations of education dominated by the majority culture. Therefore it is important to note Kawagley and Barnhardt's (1997) conviction, synonymous with the thinking of many Māori elders, that traditional cultural values, beliefs and practices have an integrity and validity that is as relevant today as it was for past generations. It is incongruous however that the dominant culture continues to provide the majority of professionals who determine who and what the problem is, as well as provide the guidelines for special as well as conventional education (Macfarlane, 1998). Possible consequences of culturally inappropriate interventions for youth at risk range from low self esteem, interruption to academic learning, prolonged suspension, school drop-out, delinquent activities, mental or health problems (Willms & Sloat, 1998) and learning situations that marginalise rather than include the student in learning. If educational professionals are truly concerned with students and their learning then it is crucial that they operate a system that is more responsive to the beliefs and cultural practices of their students (Bishop & Glynn, 1999; Dimmock, 1995) and their students' families.

Collaborative storying

This chapter presents a case study told through the process of narrative enquiry or collaborative storying. Storying is a traditional cultural practice preferred by many indigenous people for the maintenance and passing on of knowledge. Researchers (Te Hennepe, 1993; Bishop, 1996; Bishop 1997; Smith, 1999) warn however that many indigenous people are no longer prepared to accept their stories being defined and reconstructed in the language and culture of mainstream educators or researchers. Socio-cultural perspectives on research emphasise the importance of the relationship between those conventionally labeled 'researcher' and 'subject', rather than on maintaining the distance between them. Further, they highlight the significance of the social and cultural contexts in which that research takes place (Glynn, Berryman, Atvars, Harawira, Kaiwai, Walker & Tari, 1997). Narrative inquiry as an approach that aims to maintain the integrity of the story and the storyteller can address some of Māori people's concerns about research into their lives.

Bishop (1996) defines narrative inquiry as a research process where inquiry is based on a series of interviews from which transcripts are made. Transcripts are then used and re-used at subsequent meetings as the basis for joint validation and further inquiry through reflective discussion. In this way, interviews become part of a mutually constructed written record of the narration. The response to the inquiry is based on a co-constructed narrative. Bishop uses the image of a spiral. He explains that participants, in the process of jointly constructing meaning through spiral discourse, repeatedly revisit the research topic. Narrative inquiry therefore results from autonomous partnerships during which time cultural processes are used and appropriate solutions and aspirations are co-jointly identified. Used in this way narrative inquiry recognises that the people and their communities are a meaningful part of the research process (Bishop, 1996) with validity in their own ways of knowing and sharing knowledge (Te Hennepe, 1993; Cole, 1998). It also recognises that the way traditional researchers have operated in the past needs to change.

In order to become more collaborative and less impositional, Heshusius (1994) challenged researchers to strive to seek acceptance by, and participation in, the consciousness of those whom they are researching. Researchers should, Heshusius maintains, try to participate in the consciousness of the storyteller rather than ask the storyteller to participate in their own consciousness. Heshusius (1994) sees participatory consciousness leading to a point when the *'reality is no longer understood as truth to be interpreted but as mutually evolving'* (p. 18). When people are of like mind they can go beyond narrative inquiry and co-construct collaborative stories that will maintain the integrity of the people, their knowledge and their culture. A grandmother and some teachers who had worked with her grandson tell the story below.

The situation

The intervention described here involved one Māori language syndicate (group of classes) within a large mainstream, urban intermediate school (Years 7 and 8). This school successfully managed to avoid suspending or expelling three Māori students who were found to have used marijuana on the school grounds and in school time. Teachers begin the story:

> We had never had an incident such as this in the school and as a school we had just been through Assertive Discipline. This most likely meant that the parents would be rung and the students suspended. They could end up down the road, lucky to get back into the education system on an even footing again. This incident could mean a black mark against their reputation for the rest of their schooling.
>
> I can remember thinking that the option for the school was to suspend, possibly expel these students, and what would that do for the boys? It would only put them in the community – labeled, and the label would not be that they had smoked marijuana, the label would be that they had got caught. And so we could actually be exposing them to more of the same and more reason to participate. So we really had thought long and hard about wanting to protect the boys and wanting to send some strong messages back to their home communities, or in fact the school – our whānau (extended family) community, our class, our syndicate community as well.

The two teachers involved believed that the boys had the potential to do well and that suspension and/or redirection to another help agency would not necessarily provide the best outcome:

> We felt that these kids had potential and for this to happen – who knows – it could start a downward spiral. One of them had amazing potential for leadership in the future. Both boys had come a long way in our lead-up to the cultural festival – they had learned taiaha (actions involving the use of a wooden fighting staff). One had a leadership role in the haka (originally a cultural dance performed prior to engaging in battle) and he had become something of a role model to the others. He had been a problem for us, leading up to that, and the cultural group had given him mana (personal prestige or self worth), given him an avenue to put his energies into, and he responded to the kapahaka (cultural performance) really well. I can remember one of the boys was in Form 1, and he stood out.

Action

The teachers consulted with their *kuia* (respected female elder) who was the unit *kaiarahi i te reo* (expert Māori language assistant), and a highly respected member of the local *iwi* (tribe) and local community. They also consulted with the school management. Following the advice of their *kuia*, this group decided to hold a *hui whakatika*, a meeting that would take place in a Māori context, following Māori protocol that was aimed at seeking worthwhile solutions for all parties (Macfarlane, 1998). Together with the three students and their *whānau* (immediate and extended family) they would seek participation in collaborative decision-making within the supportive cultural context provided by the *hui* (traditional meeting).

The senior teacher recalled:

> I have to take my hat off to that principal because he had a lot of aroha (personal regard and respect) for our kids as well. I explained what had happened and I promised that we would have a meeting with the boys on Monday morning and that I would have one family member for each of the three boys at that meeting. While this action was in line with Assertive Discipline, because we had never had an incident of this kind in the school before and no procedures were already in place, I suggested that maybe the people at the meeting could come up with a solution that could meet everyone's needs.

The first step was to talk with their *kuia* and decide who needed to be involved, then to meet with these people in order to plan the way ahead, and the senior teacher remembered:

> The boys had been told that either they tell their parents or whānau and you get them here on Monday or I will come and I will do it for you. During that weekend I also contacted the families and our kuia in preparation for our hui.
>
> (Senior Teacher)

The meeting was held in the room designated as the syndicate *whare wānanga* (house of learning). The three boys each had at least one family member who attended the meeting. The meeting began with *mihimihi* (greetings) then *karakia* (prayer) that asked for guidance and support. A cup of tea was shared before the *kaupapa* (agenda) of the meeting was jointly set. This involved defining the problem. It was agreed that while the boys had contributed to the problem of smoking marijuana in the school grounds, they were not the problem. However, they could contribute to the solution. All members of the group took part in this exercise and were able to make suggestions and voice any concerns. This was not an easy exercise and at several points the debate was heated. Once a solution was found that was agreeable to all parties, including the boys, a way forward was then decided. This involved developing an implementation plan, then defining and agreeing to individual roles and responsibilities. When this had happened a *kaumātua* (tribal elder) present concluded the *hui* with *karakia*.

A senior classroom teacher and a grandmother together recounted what happened:

> Because each of the boys and their whānau were Māori, it was important that we conducted that meeting according to Māori protocol. It was also important for me that our kuia was there because I didn't know exactly what was going to happen or what was going to come out of that meeting. I believed that she would guide us to maintain the integrity of the meeting and at the same time keep us, and the kaupapa of the meeting safe.
>
> (Senior Teacher)

> It was a hard meeting: nobody knew what the outcome was going to be. When we arrived we knew we were going to talk about what had happened and we were going to try and come up with a resolution but we didn't know what it might look like.
>
> (Classroom Teacher)

> I can remember a dad in particular; he didn't think he should be there: he thought that the school should deal with it and he was actually I think quite angry that he had to come down. They had their baby with them too.
>
> (Senior Teacher)

> Yeah we came up with all sorts of crazy suggestions. I made one suggestion that was to give them a bald head and that guy that you talked about said, 'that's the in thing'. I didn't know that. I felt that it would be a good idea because when we were kids if our brothers did anything naughty they were given a bald head.
>
> (Grandmother)

> They talked about possibly having a kaumātua spend a lunchtime with them to talk about kaupapa Māori (themes), tikanga Māori (cultural beliefs and practices) … and that holistic well-being. We didn't go into that meeting thinking that this is what we want to come out of it. We ran our thoughts past the whānau, and they ran their thoughts past us. So it was a combination of ideas.
>
> (Classroom Teacher)

The collaborative solution was to impose a three-day period of in-school suspension. The boys continued working in their syndicate classrooms but worked on individual learning programmes that had been speedily and specifically designed for them. Different members from the families took turns to support the three boys and the syndicate staff on each day of the suspension. The individual learning programme was developed around positive Māori role models and drew largely on articles and advertisements from a well-known New Zealand magazine that is written around Māori themes and published by a Māori team. All essential learning areas in the New Zealand national curriculum were addressed through this theme.

Each lunch time for the three days of the suspension the three boys would, having invited a whānau member to join them, attend a presentation given from one of three specialists so that they could become more accurately informed about the effects on the body of smoking marijuana. Each presentation and question session was held in the whare wānanga and was conducted following appropriate Māori protocol. The presenters included a youth aide officer, a *kaumātua* who worked with youth and a medical person who worked with drug rehabilitation. All presenters were Māori. At the end of the three days the boys were returned to their normal classroom programme. The teachers and Grandmother talk about the three-day period of in-school suspension:

> We made a space at the back of the classroom so each boy sat just apart from the rest of the class. We spread the boys out through the syndicate so that each of the teachers had one of the boys sitting down the back but we never talked to the other children about what had happened. They all knew but nobody talked about it, it was sort of an unwritten, an unspoken word. It was an amazing experience, to see the rest of the students, distance themselves from the boys but still be there for them, still awhi (support) them. They knew that they could help them through just being there. The adults rotated around the boys and around the classrooms. The boys had lunchtime and morning interval but their days and their timetable were at different times, in this way they were isolated from the rest of the students all day. Not only did they have a different timetable they had a different programme.
>
> (Teachers)

> I admired the way the children supported those boys. They didn't judge them or anything and I know that they helped them to actually bear what happened in those four days.
>
> (Grandmother)

Outcomes

Whānau members were a critical part of the intervention and the subsequent successful outcomes. Supported by their whānau, their teachers, and all of the other students from the syndicate, the boys remained in school with little disruption to their learning programme. Because the role model learning unit created so much interest amongst the three students at risk, it was further developed and continued with all other students in the syndicate. All groups learned from the process, the outcome was seen by all to be just and appropriate for the misdemeanour and more importantly none of the groups (school, student or *whānau*) lost *mana* (personal respect/prestige). Some years later, interviews with some of the whānau members indicated that they had faith in the solutions that had come out of the *hui* and that they felt their contribution was valuable and had been valued.

> Give those children a chance. Have a meeting and use that in-school suspension programme. Work with the whānau to sort out a solution. I think it should be set up

in all schools to protect the children's future and I think it proved to myself and a lot of people that we talked to back home that good teachers didn't just say you're a nuisance. They say I want to help you. We came out of that meeting with a shared understanding of what was going to happen, and we all understood our roles, what our roles would be to make this work.

   I guess it was that point of equal respect wasn't it because we respected them, they respected us back and being fair is very important to those kids. Treating everybody fairly. Those kids were pretty thankful.

   But people paid what they were due. You know it was, it was a very respectful process.

(Grandmother)

The boys all finished college up to at least the end of the fifth form year. The youngest of the three boys successfully finished his sixth form year having competed in top college sports and cultural teams throughout his secondary schooling. For these boys no repeat incidents such as this occurred throughout their schooling.

Discussion

The principal and syndicate teachers recognised that if the solutions were to be worthwhile for these students and their whānau then students and whānau needed to be a major part of the solution setting. Whānau, students, teachers and management collaborated in order to develop and implement changes. These changes to classroom organisation, to student learning tasks and to teaching strategies ensured that students' school learning continued. They had also set a precedent. Here was a workable and respectful response to Māori students at risk. Participation of kaumātua ensured that the students, their families and their culture were central to the solutions that were developed.

Factors aiding success

Four features crucial to pre-European Māori discipline have been identified (Olsen, Maxwell and Morris, 1994). First, there is an emphasis on the whole community reaching consensus through collaborative decision-making. Second, the outcome needs to be acceptable to all parties rather than merely isolate or punish the offenders. Third, and upon an implicit assumption that there may have been problems in more than one context, it is important to examine the wider contexts of the misdemeanour. Finally, there is more emphasis on the restoration of harmony rather than with the wrongdoing. These four core functions of consensus, reconciliation, examination and restoration are implicit in the traditional Māori discipline model and are essential to an effective school conference or *hui* (Macfarlane, 1998).

Participants interviewed all mentioned the importance of keeping everyone's *mana* intact. Drewery, Hooper, Macfarlane, McManemin, Pare and Winslade (1998), theorising and writing about the interactive dialogue that is required if suspension is to be avoided, also highly value a quality or principle that they term the *psychology of mana*. Tate (1990) asserts that *mana* goes beyond personal magnetism to being a force that brings about change. Macfarlane (1998) adds that a leader with *mana* is much more likely to succeed in enforcing the limits, monitoring the situation and maintaining sound relationships.

Leaders such as this looked after the participants in this *hui whakatika*. Initially the principal and teaching staff recognised the importance of the expertise within *whānau*. They were then supported by *kaumātua* who ensured that all of the appropriate traditional practices and protocols, including those implicit in traditional Māori discipline, were employed throughout, in order to ensure the safety of all and the ultimate success of the intervention. This intervention showed what could happen when the majority culture is more responsive to seeking solutions from and with minority culture groups. The reassertion of Māori cultural aspirations, preferences and practices, that was led, supported and legitimised by *kaumātua*, resulted in more effective participation and learning (Bishop & Glynn, 1999). This participation led to greater benefits for all participants, for educators, for families and for these three Māori students at risk of suspension from an education system that is set by the majority culture.

References

Barrington, J. M. & Beaglehole, T. H. (1974) *Māori Schools in a Changing Society*. Wellington: N Z C E R.

Bishop, R. (1996) *Collaborative Research Stories: Whakawhanaungatanga*. Palmerston North: The Dunmore Press.

Bishop, R. (1997) Māori people's concerns about research into their lives. *History of Education Review*, 26 (1), 25–41.

Bishop, R., Berryman, M., Richardson, C. & Tiakiwai, S. (2001) *Te Kotahitanga: Experiences of year 9 and 10 Māori students in mainstream classrooms*. Final Report prepared for the Ministry of Education, Wellington: Ministry of Education.

Bishop, R. & Glynn, T. (1999) *Culture Counts: Changing power relations in education*. Palmerston North: The Dunmore Press.

Codd, J., Harker, R. & Nash, R. (eds) (1990) *Political issues in New Zealand education,* 2nd edn. Palmerston North: The Dunmore Press.

Cole, P. (1998) *First nations knowing as legitimate discourse in education.* Presented N Z A R E Conference, Dunedin.

Dimmock, C. (1995) Restructuring for school effectiveness: Leading, organising and teaching for effective learning, *Educational Management and Administration,* 23 (1).

Donnelly, B. (1998) *Making education work for Māori; Te whakamahi i te mātauranga mō te iwi Māori.* Report in Consultation Te Pürongo mō ngā whakawhiti whakaaro.

Drewery, W., Hooper, S., Macfarlane, A., McManemin, D., Pare, D. & Winslade, J. (1998) *School, Family and Community Group Conferencing.* Proposal to the Ministry of Education. Hamilton: University of Waikato.

Durie, M. H. (1992) *The Treaty of Waitangi in New Zealand Society.* Department of Māori Studies, Massey University.

Durie, M. H. (2001) *A framework for considering Māori educational advancement.* Hui Taumata Mātauranga, opening address. Turangi/Taupo. Department of Māori Studies, Massey University.

Glynn, T., Berryman, M., Atvars, K., Harawira, W., Kaiwai, H., Walker, R. & Tari, R. (1997) *Research, training and indigenous rights to self determination: Challenges arising from a New Zealand bicultural journey.* Paper presented at the International School Psychology XXth Annual Colloquium, *School Psychology – Making Links: Making the Difference,* Melbourne, Australia.

Heshusius, L. (1994) Freeing ourselves from objectivity: Managing subjectivity or turning toward a participatory mode of consciousness. *Educational Researcher,* 23 (3), 15–22.

Hunn, J.K. (1960) *Report on the Department of Māori Affairs.* Wellington: Government Print.

Jacka, S., Sutherland, B., Peters, M. & Smith, L. (1996) *Te kupenga: Children adrift in the truancy crisis.* Research report to the Ministry of Education, Wellington.

Kawagley, A. & Barnhardt, R. (1997) *Education Indigenous Place: Western Science Meets Native Reality.* Fairbanks: University of Alaska.

Ladson-Billings, G. (1995) Toward a theory of culturally relevant pedagogy. *American Educational Research Journal,* 32 (3).

Macfarlane, A. (1998) *Hui: A process for conferencing in schools.* University of Waikato. Paper presented at the Western Association for Counsellor Education and Supervision Conference, Seattle, U.S.A.

McNaughton, S. S. (1995) *Patterns of Emergent Literacy: Processes of development and transition.* Melbourne: Oxford University Press.

Ministry of Education (2001) *Educational statistics for July 1, 2001.* Wellington: Ministry of Education.

Ministry of Education (2003a) *Ministry of Education statement of intent 2003 > 2008*. Wellington: Ministry of Education.

Ministry of Education (2003b) *Ngā haeata mātauranga, annual report on Māori education 2001/2002 and direction for 2003*. Wellington: Ministry of Education, Group Māori.

Olsen, Maxwell & Morris, (1994) Māori and youth justice in New Zealand. Youth Law Review, 1994:8 (July–September).

Ramsay, Peter D. K., (1972) *Māori schooling: Issues In New Zealand Special Education*. Trentham: Wright and Carmen Ltd.

Scheurich, J. J. & Young, M. D. (1997) Coloring epistemologies: Are our research epistemologies racially biased? *Educational Researcher* 26 (4), 4–16.

Smith, L. (1999) *Decolonizing Methodologies: Research and indigenous peoples*. London: Zed Books Ltd./Dunedin: University of Otago Press.

Spoonley, P. (1993) State: policy and practice. In *Racism and Ethnicity*, 2nd edn. Auckland: Oxford University Press.

Tate, H. (1990) The unseen world. *New Zealand Geographic*, 5, 87–92.

Te Hennepe, S. (1993) Issues of Respect: Reflections of First Nations Student's Experiences in Postsecondary Anthropology Classrooms. *Canadian Journal of Native Education*, 2 (2).

Vygotsky, L.S. (1978) Interaction between learning and development. In *Mind in Society: The development of higher psychological processes*. London: Harvard University Press.

Wilkie, M. (2001) *Matauranga Motuhake*. Wellington: New Zealand Council for Educational Research.

Willms, J. & Sloat, E. (1998) *An Outcome-Based Model for Evaluating Programmes for Children at Risk*. New Brunswick: Atlantic Centre for Policy Research.

Chapter 4

Behaviour support in secondary schools: what works for schools?

George Head, Jean Kane and Nicola Cogan

Introduction

In Scotland, England and Wales, the rise in numbers of pupils excluded from school has provoked considerable concern amongst policymakers and professionals in education and beyond. In this chapter, we present the experience of one education authority in reducing the number of exclusions from its secondary schools. The first part of the chapter describes the background to the exercise. In the second part, we offer the education authority's findings in terms of the methods used and their effectiveness. The final part of the chapter offers a brief discussion of these findings and some implications for the next stage of the research.

Background

In recent years, the Scottish Executive Education Department and its predecessor, the Scottish Office Education and Industry Department, have supported local authorities to pursue government policy on social inclusion. Central to this policy is educational inclusion. Through its programme for social inclusion *Social Justice: A Scotland Where Everyone Counts* (1999), with its milestones and targets, the Scottish Executive set a target of a one-third reduction in school exclusions and made available to education authorities funding to pursue that target.

One education authority in the west of Scotland took advantage of this scheme to enhance its existing behaviour support initiative at the start of the 1998 school session. The initiative was aimed at the authority's 21 secondary schools and the funding from the Scottish Office was used to pay for extra teaching pointage for each of the schools. This pointage was to be used specifically for the reduction of exclusions but each of the schools was free to pursue that aim as it saw fit, leading to a variety of approaches to behaviour support across the education authority.

In terms of structures, for example, some schools chose to use the extra staffing to address exclusions directly by allocating it to a specific teacher whose remit would become, wholly or largely, behaviour support. Other schools decided to enhance staffing within guidance and pastoral care in the hope of reducing exclusions through increased monitoring of behaviour and pastoral support. The range of ways of working with young people were just as diverse and were not dependent upon particular structures of behaviour support. This article offers an account of those strategies and an indication of emerging judgements of their effectiveness.

Methodology

To judge the effectiveness of the project, the education authority and its schools wanted to address four questions:

- What is working?
- Where are systems not working?
- What else is needed?
- Is this aspect of behaviour support providing value for money?

In November 1999, the education authority approached the writers and asked them to evaluate the initiative over a three-year period. In order to answer the evaluation questions, four criteria were developed through consultation with the school and education authority representatives and members of the evaluation team. All concerned would know the evaluation was working if:

- There was a reduction in the number of exclusions.
- There was increased provision of support for pupils.
- There was an increase in appropriate staff development.
- Pupils, parents and schools reported positively.

The discussion which follows is based upon data from the first year of the evaluation. Those data had been collected by the education authority from its 21 secondary schools. Each school had been asked to identify six pupils receiving extra support as a result of their referral to behaviour support services in the school. Schools were asked to consider two pupils for whom it was envisaged that intense support would be needed, two for whom a moderate amount of support would probably be adequate, and two who would require little support. The intention was to track each of these pupils through the three years of the evaluation by asking schools to report annually on a standard form known as the *case study form*. Schools were also asked to report on each year's behaviour support activity on a second form known as the *annual report form*. Using the 21 annual reports and the 126 case studies, the education authority hoped to unearth a continuum of experience for pupils, parents and staff. It was also the intention to track the case studies and developing behaviour support provision throughout the three-year period of the project.

In the event, 116 case study forms were returned, giving information about:

- attendance rates
- the referral procedure
- reason(s) for exclusion
- agreed plan of action, timescale, nature of support
- current level of attainment
- involvement in behaviour support.

All 21 secondary schools in the education authority returned the annual reports, offering information on the nature of behaviour support and perceptions of its effectiveness. Responses were organized under six main headings:

- ways in which behaviour support was accessed in the school
- management and structure of behaviour support
- methods of support used
- effectiveness of each method
- attitudes to behaviour support
- staff development.

Both the case study form and the annual report form had sections where respondents could make open comment. In most cases, both sets of forms were completed by one person, usually the member of staff responsible for behaviour support.

Findings

Rates of exclusion

With regard to the first criterion, information from Scottish Educational Establishments Management Information Systems (SEEMIS) provided two sets of statistics: the total number of openings (half-days) lost through exclusion and the total number of incidents leading to exclusion (see Table 4.1). The SEEMIS figures indicate a moderate success rate for the initiative during its first two years. Secondary school exclusions had been reduced by more than 22% between 1997 and 1999.

Table 4.1 SEEMIS data: secondary schools

	1997	*1998*	*1999*
Total openings lost	21567	19770	16751 (–4816 or –22.3% on 1997) (–3019 or –15.3% on 1998)
Total exclusion incidents	2548	2542	2195 (–353 or –13.8% on 1997) (–347 or –13.7% on 1998)

However, the target-setting approach to reducing exclusions has been criticized (Cooper et al., 2000; Munn et al., 2000; Parsons, 1999) as leading to superficial and short-term approaches to the problem of exclusions. Indeed, national exclusion statistics published in 2000 and 2001 (Scottish Executive Education Department, 2000; 2001) indicate that target setting had no positive impact at all on exclusion rates across Scotland. Between 1999 and 2000, exclusions rose by 4%, giving rise to reports that the Scottish Executive would cease its use of a target setting approach to reducing exclusions (Buie, 2001).

The question is worth asking, then: within a target setting approach, what did this education authority do to achieve a reduction in levels of exclusion?

What schools did

The annual reports from the 21 secondary schools gathered information about the nature and effectiveness of behaviour support. Questions were asked about:

- the range of methods used to support young people with SEBD
- the effectiveness of each of those methods.

School respondents were asked to score each method on a five-point scale.

The most frequently used methods were those deployed outside the ordinary classroom: one-to-one support and small group work. The behaviour support teacher used available time to work with individuals or small groups in ways which might or might not have been related to the curriculum.

Sometimes, young people brought materials with them from their subject classes and continued to work on the same activities as their peers but with increased levels of teacher support. Issues were raised here about the subject-specific nature of the secondary school curriculum and the inability of behaviour support teachers to provide teaching informed by understanding of core concepts and skills. On the other hand, there was recognition of the importance of providing curriculum continuity for pupils.

At other times, the individual and small group work related to personal and social development, using counselling and therapeutic approaches. These were seen as broadening the range of strategies traditionally available to secondary schools, with their emphasis on pedagogy and curricular structures. Comments on staff development within the annual reports indicated that it was in the area of counselling that schools identified the greatest need to develop new skills. The high level of use of such approaches suggests that, at least initially, schools wished to develop support on levels other than the curricular.

There were three strategies specified which were designed to support pupils through the ordinary timetable without extraction to a behaviour support base. Of these three, cooperative teaching was the most commonly used with 71% citing it as a strategy. Two further methods of classroom support (target setting and monitoring, and daily behaviour assessment sheets) were used by fewer than half of the respondents. Cooperative teaching is an approach commonly used by learning support teachers in Scotland. Its policy origins are in the Warnock Report (DES, 1978) and in the HMI Progress Report (SED, 1978) where it was endorsed as one of four 'new' roles for remedial teachers, signifying a shift in the way learning difficulties were conceptualized. The difficulties were seen as residing within the curriculum rather than within the pupil. No longer appropriate, then, was extraction from the classroom and the remediation of pupils experiencing learning difficulties. Instead, energies would be devoted to the development of the ordinary curriculum through close classroom cooperation between learning support and class teachers. The use of cooperative teaching in the project described here reflected the desire on the part of those involved in behaviour support to change not just the young person, but the curricular and pedagogical context in which the young person was learning.

The number of respondents citing liaison with parents as a method used (52%) is perhaps surprisingly small. Evidence coming from other sources in the evaluation suggests that this might reflect the great difficulties secondary schools report in developing partnerships with the families of this group of pupils in particular. Work elsewhere (Hamill and Boyd, 2001; Lloyd et al., 2001; Riddell and Tett, 2001) has considered the challenge of developing effective inter-agency working to draw families into a support network for young people in danger of exclusion. What is more surprising, given the attention paid (in policy and in research) to inter-agency working, is that schools did not cite joint working as a 'strategy'.

The range of methods used across the sample of schools and within a large number of individual schools suggests a pragmatic approach to supporting pupils with SEBD. On the one hand, it is viewed as something best directed towards individuals experiencing difficulty (through one-to-one sessions or in small groups); on the other, it is constructed as support for teachers in the context of the classroom and the curriculum. The variety of responses favoured by schools reflects awareness of the diverse range of difficulties experienced by pupils and a desire to develop a similarly broad range of approaches within each school.

With regard to perceptions of effectiveness, cooperative teaching received the strongest endorsement from respondents with 93% rating it as either effective or very effective. The two most frequently used methods, one-to-one support and group work, were both rated as effective by 60% of respondents but group work was the only method to be classed as ineffective (by 7% of respondents).

These figures suggest that 'effectiveness' in relation to a reduction in exclusions is perceived as being about more than retention under the same roof as other young people. Instead, it seems that behaviour support is understood to be, at least partly, about the development of ethos, curriculum and pedagogies better to provide for diversity (Watkins and Wagner, 2000).

It is argued that schools provide more effectively for all pupils by creating a better ethos (Munn et al., 2000). This enterprise relates to creating supportive relationships amongst children, staff and parents and nurturing positive attitudes towards the school and its aims. Very different rates of exclusion in schools are likely to be explained by factors such as teachers' understandings of children's lives, their empathy with them and their fundamental values in relation to inclusion. 'Strategies' in themselves will not achieve the fundamental shift in values which is needed but some strategies enable schools to be critically reflective of their provision overall.

Curriculum and pedagogy, too, will have a bearing upon the extent to which young people with social, emotional and behavioural difficulties are able to participate in the life of the school (Watkins and Wagner, 2000). Much of the broader literature on inclusion relates to the notion of young people as stakeholders in the organization, both shaping and being shaped by the context in which they are learning (Ainscow et al., 2000). Participation is viewed as more than formal (and sometimes tokenistic) involvement in management or decision-making processes. Rather, participation is about partnership in learning itself, through engagement with the core processes of shared planning, negotiation of aims, design of tasks and activities, and formative and collaborative assessment of progress.

The site where school inclusion/exclusion happens is the classroom. In rating cooperative teaching so highly as a strategy, all of the schools in the project recognized classroom experience as important to pupils' sense of commonality with others. However, they also recognized, in the range of strategies they adopted, that different young people required different forms of assistance towards greater participation.

The model of inclusion described above demands very flexible ways of working for learners and for teachers. Again and again, schools noted their desire for 'flexibility' to enable appropriate responses to young people and their view that behaviour support offered some scope to make choices about appropriate support strategies.

Conclusion

The data gave insights into the different models of behaviour support which were emerging as the project progressed. These models existed on a continuum from behaviour support as a separate and distinct strand in school provision (very often in an identifiable place) to behaviour support as permeating all aspects of learning, teaching, curriculum and pastoral care. The aspirations of all schools, however, were to develop more flexible ways of working whatever the choices regarding strategies.

This sense from schools that inclusion requires schools to have 'room for manoeuvre' reflects a broader view that the flexibility required for schools to do well by all children may be irreconcilable with the emphasis on outcomes as the measure of school and teacher effectiveness. Schools interpret the drive to raise attainment as a concern with results and report difficulty in educating children with very challenging behaviour whilst, at the same time, raising levels of attainment through the target-setting approach. Indeed, some commentators attribute the rise in exclusions to the prevailing influence of 'market systems' on education (Cooper et al., 2000; Hayden, 1997; Stirling, 1996):

> The introduction of published league tables of examination results and other indicators of performance in schools has created a climate less likely to be sympathetic to children not only producing no positive contribution to these indicators, but who may also prevent others from doing so. (Hayden, 1997, p. 8)

The flexible approach to supporting some pupils did not necessarily result in a loosening of the tight structures within which most children received their education. There may be a contradiction in responding to some in highly responsive ways whilst maintaining the majority in rigid curricular systems.

The range of strategies was wide but each school had been in a position to make choices about the nature of behaviour support. The resulting sense of ownership over the project felt by schools would vindicate the education authority's decision to devolve to schools the responsibility for designing strategy in accordance with each school's perceptions of what was needed. Ultimately, this factor, rather than any one approach, may have been responsible for the success in reducing exclusions within the allotted timescale.

Views given were wholly positive about the project. This was not surprising, perhaps, when all schools had been allocated additional staffing as a result of their participation and when there was a desire to retain that staffing.

A further phase of the evaluation will focus upon gathering the views of pupils, parents and teachers not directly involved in behaviour support. The researchers anticipate some methodological and ethical difficulties here. Schools have reported their frustration at recognizing the value of working with families and yet finding themselves most often unable to fulfil that aim. The views of pupils themselves will also be difficult to obtain, and, when gathered, may be coloured by the pupils' perceptions of the researchers and their relationship to the school. Nevertheless it is hoped that this further work will provide some basis for understanding the perspectives on behaviour support of pupils, parents and subject teachers.

References

Ainscow, M., Booth, T., Black-Hawkins, K., Vaughn, M. & Shaw, L. (2000) *Index for Inclusion: Developing Learning and Participation in Schools*. Bristol: Centre for Studies in Inclusive Education.

Buie, E. (2001) 'Discipline Goes to Top of the Class', *The Herald* (Glasgow) 20 June.

Cooper, P., Hart, S., Lavery, J. & McLaughlin, C. (2000) *Positive Alternatives to Exclusion*. London: Routledge Falmer.

DES (1978) *Special Educational Needs: The Warnock Report*. London: HMSO.

Hamill, P. & Boyd, B. (2001) 'Rhetoric or Reality? Inter-Agency Provision for Young People with Challenging Behaviour', *Emotional and Behavioural Difficulties*, 6 (3), 135–49.

Hayden, C. (1997) *Children Excluded from Primary School: Debates, Evidence, Responses*. Buckingham: Open University Press.

Lloyd, G., Stead, J. & Kendrick, A. (2001) 'Hanging On In There': A Study of Inter-Agency Work to Prevent School Exclusion in Three Local Authorities. London: Joseph Rowntree Foundation, National Children's Bureau.

Munn, P., Lloyd, G. & Cullen, M.A. (2000) *Alternatives to Exclusion from School*. London: Paul Chapman.

Parsons, C. (1999) *Education, Exclusion and Citizenship*. London: Routledge.

Riddell, S. & Tett, L. (2001) *Education, Social Justice and Inter-Agency Working: Joined-Up or Fractured Policy?* London: Routledge.

Scottish Executive (1999) *Social Justice: A Scotland Where Everyone Counts*. Edinburgh: HMSO.

Scottish Executive Education Department (2000) *Exclusions from School 1998/1999: News Release*. Edinburgh: Scottish Executive.

Scottish Executive Education Department (2001) *Exclusions from School 1999/2000: News Release.* Edinburgh: Scottish Executive.

SED (1978) *The Education of Pupils with Learning Difficulties in Primary and Secondary Schools in Scotland.* Edinburgh: HMSO.

Stirling, M. (1996) *Government Policy and Disadvantaged Children: Exclusion from School: Inter-Professional Issues for Policy and Practice.* London: Routledge.

Watkins, C. & Wagner, P. (2000) *Improving School Behaviour.* London: Paul Chapman.

PART 2
School level

Chapter 5

A whole-school approach to behaviour change at Tennyson High School, 1998–2003

Compiled by Colin McCall from information provided by the school

Context

Geographical location

Tennyson High School is situated in Mablethorpe on the east coast of England. It has a population of 6,000 but this almost doubles in the summer time with the influx of holiday-makers. Although the area provides over 10% of the vegetables eaten in England, the principal industry of the area is tourism. The area is popular as a retirement location; hence the majority of the population is over 50. However, there has been a steady influx of young families into the area and this has created a significant number of young people. Until comparatively recently, housing was very cheap, making this a popular area for those seeking to leave the Home Counties. In 2003 this started to change with house prices rising steeply.

The standard of housing is generally good, but the absence of good health facilities (2 doctors in the town and no dentist), a poor public transport service, a road service which is notoriously slow and has the highest accident rate in Europe, and little industry other than tourism puts the wards of Mablethorpe and the district high on the Index of Multiple Deprivation.

Crime is not a serious problem in comparison with urban areas, but there are more offences per 100 head of population in the district than in the county. The increase in the number of offences has exceeded all comparators in the last year for robbery, burglary and theft from vehicles.

In health, the area has a higher incidence of accidents per head of population than the county regional and national rates.

There are no post-16 education facilities in the town. The drop-out rate is low, but this hides the number who do not enrol on courses initially because of the poor transport provision. The number staying on into education post-16 is one of the lowest in the county, although the trend has been an upward one since 2000.

Principal social and cultural factors

Education is not a high priority amongst a significant number of families in the area. Turbulence in the student population is higher in the local secondary sector than for other secondary provision in the country. It is currently running at around 32% per year and in 2000/2001 was 39%. Many families come to the area because they enjoyed a summer holiday and consider it a good place to live. However, the lack of access to services does not support those families who need help.

Key features of the student population

The school is a secondary modern in a selective area. Approximately 40% of the students pass the 11-plus and go to the local grammar school. The mean score of each student cohort at the school on annual CATs tests is below the national average. Many children do not take the 11-plus, and have low self-esteem as they see themselves as failures; they work alongside those who have failed the 11-plus and also often feel rejected and 'failing'.

The situation in 1998

In 1996, the school was inspected by the Office for Standards in Education (OFSTED) and, following a poor report, was placed in 'Special Measures'. Poor behaviour was one of the major causes for concern, as well as leadership and learning. Features of poor behaviour included lack of attention and disruptive behaviour in the classrooms, poor behaviour in the corridors between lessons and at breaks and lunchtimes, and excessive noise in all parts of the school. The atmosphere was seen as unsupportive of student learning and this was felt to impact on academic results at all levels.

A number of contextual issues were pinpointed by staff:

• There were significant social, economic and cultural factors at work.

- Educational aspirations were restricted by local perceptions, turbulence, the presence of selective schools and the rural patterns of communication.
- The baseline problem was poor behaviour. This was influenced by critical factors in the school environment interacting negatively with students' general lack of commitment to learning.

From this analysis it appeared that the focus for change had to be a whole school approach.

Intervention

Initial steps

One of the key issues was to find a way to address the disruptive behaviour. The Head of Upper and Lower School visited a local secondary school that was using Assertive Behaviour Management (Canter and Canter, 1992) and, following a series of meetings, the technique was first piloted during the summer term for Year 7 only. At the end of the trial period, it was perceived to be successful and, following whole school in-service training for staff (INSET) at the start of the following autumn term, the whole school adopted the approach. The main features included:

- a behaviour points system;
- positive rewards;
- known and publicised sanctions;
- greater consistency in the application of the principles of Assertive Behaviour Management.

The behaviour points system was designed so that all students started the day with five behaviour points, one for each lesson of the day. These were only deducted if the individual student's behaviour was unacceptable. At the end of each term, there were five prizes to the value of £100 for each year group. Students were allocated an entry into:

- Platinum draw – no behaviour points lost;
- Gold draw – 1 behaviour point lost;
- Silver draw – 2 behaviour points lost;
- Bronze draw – 3 behaviour points lost.

The prizes for each year group included a portable stereo system, camera, 'Walkmans' and vouchers and were distributed on the last day of each term.
    At the same time, an isolation room was operated where class teachers sent students who misbehaved to do their work. Senior members of staff supervised

this arrangement. This proved effective in removing poor behaviour from classrooms, but did nothing to modify that behaviour.

Although these measures had some success, a HMI inspection in spring 1999 still heavily criticised the behaviour around the school. From reflections on the measures already taken the staff suggested that:

- It was necessary to look within and beyond the school for ideas on how to proceed.
- Any adopted behaviour management system had to rest on active teamwork.
- The school needed to pilot preventative measures.
- Time out from normal lessons left the classroom learning environment unchanged.
- Staff should continue to engage in review and INSET focused on promoting more positive behaviour.

Next steps (a): September 1999 forward

By September 1999, a new Headteacher had been appointed. His simple philosophy was that improved behaviour in classrooms would result in enhanced results. Staff were supportive, as they had always been. However, there were numbers of students whose behaviour had caused serious concern over a long period and exclusions followed, either fixed term or permanent. The local education authority (LEA) agreed not to force the school to take excluded students from other schools while it was still in Special Measures, despite there being capacity.

In the previous term, hand-held radios had been bought by the school and staff were instructed not to remove disruptive students from the classroom, nor to send them to the Head's office, but to contact the school office for a member of the senior manager team (SMT) to go to the classroom. One of the main advantages of this system was that students were not roaming the corridor where no-one had control, and where they could further disrupt or harass other classes or members of staff or leave the premises. The isolation room was discontinued as it was perceived to serve no useful purpose. At that time, there would be, on average, about five SMT call-outs during each lesson for disruptive students. SMT would either remove the student and allow them to work in isolation outside an office, sit with them in the lesson to calm them down, or sometimes simply have a quiet word in the corridor or in the classroom to guide the student back into a work ethic. In addition, the Headteacher discussed behaviour in full school assemblies in detail, with the view that students needed to take control of their own behaviour, something that was not apparent in a large number of classes. Equally, good behaviour was praised, and highlighted in new weekly 'achievement assemblies'.

These measures had a positive impact but there were still too many incidents of disruptive behaviour that interrupted learning in all years. Consequently 'Behaviour Books' were introduced in the following month. Carried from lesson to lesson by the students each day, they contained a form list, a column for each lesson, and a page of codes related to unacceptable behaviour, for example, talking, chewing, refusing to co-operate. If a student misbehaved and the behaviour was not sufficiently serious to warrant a removal, the behaviour book logged the code and was collected by the form tutor at registration at the end of the school day. The student whose name had a code next to it automatically lost a behaviour point.

The new system worked in the lower school but not where classes were taught in ability sets in the core subjects. It depended on form tutors ensuring that the book was sent out at the start of the day, and the student remembering to collect it at the end of each lesson. The latter situation was not always the case, and some behaviour books were lost for periods at a time. Overall, however, this measure made an impact on behaviour.

In March 2000, HMI removed the school from 'Special Measures', commenting on the improved behaviour of the students. Steps had been taken to promote more explicitly a *culture* that recognised good behaviour and rewarded it, whilst not ignoring significant aspects of indiscipline. The senior management team were now more directly involved in support and sanctions. But further challenges were to follow. In the months following the March inspection, many parents had opted to send their children to neighbouring schools, rather than one in Special Measures. Student numbers were down to the extent that the school was operating at 70% capacity and staff–student ratios were favourable. Though removal from Special Measures was a distinct relief, there was acknowledgement that the underlying issue remained active and that favourable staff–student ratios arising from the special circumstances would not remain.

Next steps (b): after 'Special Measures'

Work continued on behaviour both at individual levels and at whole school level and there was no significant change to the overall strategy at this point. Clearly, the school had to move forward and all the staff worked to the end that behaviour, though better, needed further improvement. In the months following the removal from Special Measures, numbers started to climb, and in the following September the Year 7 cohort was the biggest for some years. The number on roll had exceeded 300 in advance of the LEA's predictions and Year

7 moved from a 2-form entry to a 3-form entry. This alleviated the pressure on classes of 30.

September 2001 saw some significant milestones that all impacted on behaviour:

- The Year 7 cohort climbed to 81, almost twice the number of two years previously;
- The number on roll in the school was 371, a rise of 37% in two years;
- 6 staff had been promoted in the previous term, and there were recruitment difficulties in the core subjects, 2 staff being appointed on the day before the term started;
- 1 member of staff was not appointed and the school had to employ supply teachers to cover the vacancy until it was filled – a duration of a term and a half in total;
- A further mobile classroom was added to the site, providing some additional teaching space but not the much needed specialist accommodation;
- There was increasing additional pressure on classroom space as classes grew; the original classrooms were not designed for the demands of the 2000 National Curriculum and limited students' movement to gain access to resources;
- The timetable resulted in some poor lesson-allocations that significantly influenced the behaviour of some groups.

A revised system was put into place and it was decided to record the students who were removed, the lesson, the time, the member of staff and the reason for removal. This would allow SMT to monitor the incidences of disruption and highlight any specific concerns. Furthermore, students were asked to complete a sheet that required them to reflect on their behaviour and the effect that it had had on the remainder of the group and the teacher. Once complete, it was expected that the sheet was taken home and signed by the parents, so involving them in the process.

In October, disruptive behaviour peaked again with, on one day in late September, 12 lesson-removals taking place. The staff agreed that urgent action needed to be taken.

On examination the timetable had not proved as effective as expected. For example, it was apparent that some groups were taught two of their three mathematics lessons on the last period of the day. In addition, one particular Year 8 group contained a number of students whose behaviour was a focus of concern, because classroom learning was being seriously compromised. The Head rewrote the timetable. Once the upper school timetable was written, he ensured that the Year 8 core timetable was taught at different times of the day, in an attempt to modify behaviour. This took effect in January 2002 and had an immediate impact. This particular group settled better to work, and it was unanimously agreed that the new timetable was largely responsible for this change. Other changes that had been made to the timetable in the upper school contributed to a calmer atmosphere. It was also important to achieve this as, in the first week of term, the dates for the follow-up OFSTED Inspection were announced. A week prior to the inspection the last remaining vacancy was filled and the school was once again with a full complement of staff.

At this point there was a general view that:

- Promoting positive behaviour is a continuous process.
- It has to run alongside ever changing internal and external influences.
- It requires ongoing reflection and review.
- The review must look at school systems as well as students' responsiveness.

Next steps (c): OFSTED again

One of the questions in the Headteacher's form for OFSTED that year related to *turbulence* in the student population. It was the first time that turbulence had been measured. When the Registered Inspector read the figures, he queried them as being rather high. However, he was quickly assured that they were correct, and 39% turbulence across all years had a significant impact on the life of the school. At the same time, a local Primary Headteacher provided a report produced by the Birmingham Advisory Service (BASS) on the effects of turbulence on schools. It cited behaviour, learning and attendance as the key issues related to a turbulent school population. This put many aspects of the challenging behaviour in the school into context and it started some research on exclusions in the school, and the percentage of students who had not commenced with the school at the start of Year 7. Not surprisingly, a greater proportion of students who arrived late to the school were excluded or were disruptive in the classroom.

Next steps (d): the Improving Behaviour Project

A chance conversation between the Chair of Governors and the Headteacher one evening in 2000 sparked a rush of creativity, and a momentum that has not slowed down since. The conversation was on the subject of alternative methods of getting young people switched on to learning. It came at a time when the partnership between the secondary school and the town's only primary school was developing rapidly. The decision was made to share a block of Standards Fund for inclusion to provide a drop-in centre each Monday morning for the parents of students in both schools, to share a cup of tea/coffee. A range of professional staff were available for informal consultation; these included a trained counsellor, a member of the Emotional and Behavioural Support Service (EBSS), a health visitor and the school nurse. In addition, there was the opportunity to develop family literacy, this being a significant weakness in the area. The idea did not catch on however, despite some liberal publicity in both schools.

A joint INSET day had been discussed and this was finalised on the subject of Circle Time (Mosley, 1998). Although at the time an essentially primary school activity, the secondary school staff had welcomed the idea warmly at a staff meeting. Hence the following March, all the staff of both schools gathered together for a day with Jenny Mosley.

The enthusiasm that this generated was tremendous and it was felt by both Headteachers that there were other initiatives that could be undertaken in both schools in a bid to raise the social and emotional maturity of all of the students. Further informal meetings followed and by December 2001 a draft project had been put together, aimed at bringing together all the external agencies to work in unison with students and their families in a bid to raise self esteem, literacy and educational ambitions. The cost was £250,000 a year for three years. A research element was built into the costings to provide essential data for monitoring and evaluation. However, funds were not forthcoming despite bids to many charities.

Undeterred, both heads kept the idea of the project alive and sought ways to launch it, in part if necessary.

In July 2002, 12 months of funding was secured and from this Circle Time (Mosley, 1998) across Key Stages 2 and 3 (Years 4–9) was launched. The main aims were:

- To deliver Circle Time four times a week for five weeks to groups of six students at the beginning of each day;
- To provide a drink and toast at the start of each session;
- To sell the idea using Family Liaison Workers, not employed at the school for any other purpose;
- To include all family members at the same time so that all brothers and sisters experience Circle Time together;
- To keep records on the progress of the students involved using data from Goodman's 'Strengths and Difficulties' questionnaire.

Circle Time was launched in November 2002. It is much more difficult to timetable this in a secondary school. The initial cohort were suspicious of the activity. However, the second and subsequent cohorts were really enthusiastic and initial data from observations of student behaviour shows a marked improvement in the attitude, maturity and learning of the students involved.

Provided that funding is available, it is intended to continue this in the future. Feedback to date suggests that the involvement in Circle Time has increased the willingness of the children to co-operate, both in school and at home, and to care for each other, not engage in conflict.

Assertive Behaviour Management

The second joint INSET day between the two schools aimed to devise something that was common to both schools so that when students progressed from one school to another the expectations were seen to be the same within Assertive Behaviour Management (Canter and Canter, 1992). Although for some of the secondary school staff this was a revision session, it was very well received. On the following day staff worked at revising the school code of conduct. In the first week of term, all students debated the issue and made some interesting and valuable comments. As a result, the new code of conduct was adopted in the second week of the autumn term of 2002. It is in every classroom in the school, and both schools have adopted the same font and style for its presentation.

In addition, from this session, the protocol for lesson removals was standardised and published and reinforced to every student. A new departure was the revision of the 'incident form', used to record incidences of poor behaviour around the school. The original form, in use for some years, required staff to note the incident in as much detail as possible. In line with current thinking, the new form had a number of tick boxes in a bid to cut down the workload needed. The form was well received but the amount of photocopying required for a single sheet of paper was overly bureaucratic and there was confusion as to who had which copies. Pastoral meetings debated the issue in a bid to come up with an improved system. Staff suggested amendments to the form and these resulted in the current version. 'Green sheets' are now well-known to students. They have been modified further to report on positive behaviour also, or for conveying information that will be useful on the student's file. The routine is:

- A green sheet is given for a serious breach of the school discipline code or for a fourth warning in the classroom about disruptive behaviour. The behaviour point is lost on the third warning.
- Three green sheets automatically trigger a letter home.
- Five green sheets automatically trigger a three-day fixed-term exclusion; work is set and is handed in on the re-admission date when a Pastoral Support Plan (PSP) is agreed.

In addition:

- A green sheet is given for every removal from lesson by the SMT. Three green sheets earned in this way triggers a three-day fixed term exclusion; work is set and is handed in on the readmission date when the Pastoral Support Plan (PSP) is agreed.

However:

- A negative green sheet can be redeemed if two positive sheets are earned from the same teacher in subsequent lessons.

The published routine is:

1 Warning ignored – name on board.
2 Behaviour continues – one tick next to name.
3 Behaviour continues – second tick on board and behaviour point is lost.
4 Behaviour still continues – green incident sheet is completed.
5 Behaviour still continues (despite five actions by the teacher) – Senior Management are called to remove the student.

With such a positive response to this INSET day, the heads invited the facilitator back for a second day the following September. He was asked to judge the progress the schools were making and found significant improvements in students' behaviour and learning. On reflection it was clear to the staff that:

- The school had had to make immediate changes and look to wider community-based initiatives to secure a stronger partnership.
- Some changes are rapidly successful, others require the right time and tide.
- The role of 'critical friends' in advising and reviewing practice has been a significant positive influence.
- External review provides both affirmation of achievement and guidelines for the next agenda.
- The determination of the school staff to march on in the face of adversities and set-backs is instrumental in ensuring the continuation of a team approach.

Reflection and review

The changes in the management systems of the school for behaviour were a result of a shared vision about where the school needed to be, if standards were to rise whilst in Special Measures. The removal of Special Measures did not diminish the quality of the vision; rather it sharpened the focus even more as staff were determined that never again would the school be put through such a difficult time. This made change much easier to manage, although consistency was always an issue. This is nothing new in schools; but as staff were prepared to negotiate with, rather than confront students, positive results were seen more quickly; it has to be recognised however that the time for negotiation has to be limited. The immediate result is to avoid confrontation, a feature of the school during the early inspections.

The effect of the 'green sheets' has been quite startling. Students responded very positively as they were handed responsibility for their behaviour. The number of exclusions was initially high but this has quickly dropped. The school can now name those students who regularly disrupt lessons and they are a small number. The net result is a calmer school where more effective learning takes place as the majority of students who wish to learn are allowed to do so. One of the reasons suggested for the rapid acceptance of this method of recording behaviour was ownership from the outset by staff and students. The key was to inform students about cause and effect, and the sanctions that would be applied. Once applied consistently, there was little room for manoeuvre, and students could not play one member of staff off against another. Staff were surprised also with the positive reaction from the majority of parents. They considered that in the case of five green sheets they had been warned in advance that the exclusion would come with two further incidences of disruption. In some cases, this was enough as parents increased their involvement. The exclusions that follow from five green sheets are not always immediate, with two–three days' notice being given. This allows the parents to make any necessary arrangements for child-care or time off work, and allows staff time to gather work so that the students' education is not being seriously compromised and they have plenty to do at home. Parents see this as working together, a powerful tool in education. Students know exactly what will happen once they accrue the five sheets and they know what steps will be taken in the classroom before the green sheet is given.

The broader infrastructure: the involvement and impact of external agencies

Mablethorpe is a popular seaside resort, but it is close to no other major centre of population, and does not support any education offices in the town. This puts it at a major disadvantage when outside agency involvement is requested or required urgently. It seemed, looking back through school records, that the involvement of the agencies was minimal because of a perceived lack of problems in a quiet seaside town. However, this hides the truth of a desperate need for services in such a context. If this were not enough, the problems of recruitment down the east coast are well recognised in the county and the district, but this does not make it any easier to attract or recruit the right staff.

The Emotional and Behavioural Support Service exists to support those students who are experiencing difficulties in school related to behaviour. Many of these are at risk of exclusion, either fixed-term or permanent, and the school did not have the resources to employ its own staff for this purpose. It relied therefore on the LEA. This provided outreach in 1999 for a day a month. However, in 2000 this dropped to half a day a month and then there was no service for 6 months in 2001–2002 as there were vacancies that could not be filled. It was at this time that the parents of a permanently excluded student successfully appealed against the head's decision. The appeals panel stated that the school had not made use of all the available services. They ignored the fact that the LEA did not have the personnel available, but the student was re-instated.

All this adds to the pressure of keeping a balance and showing all students that there is fairness and equality. Other students perceive someone 'getting away' with something and emulate the act. This is the challenge that faces all schools when support services are not available.

The Educational Psychological Service is budget-driven and this forces the school to prioritise its list of students who need attention. Priority has to go to those students who need extra help and time at Key Stage 4 (Years 9 and 10), whereas early intervention has a longer-term beneficial effect.

It was these problems and challenges that drove one section of the Improving Behaviour Project, as it envisaged the two schools having access to EBSS on at least two days each week, an educational psychologist for a day a week at least and a full-time education welfare officer to deal with the high incidence of absence, both unauthorised and condoned. However, it is the level of involvement that the schools were desperate for, and still request. Given that level of commitment, it would be possible for the agencies to work together and to work with local health personnel, if necessary, to provide a comprehensive support service for the families, many of whom do not know where to access the services, and if they did, do not have transport to get there. For example, a mother with two highly disruptive children was referred to a support agency as an emergency case. On arrival, they gave her an appointment four weeks in the future. That did nothing to overcome her concerns, and nothing to modify the children's behaviour in school. Their education is compromised, as is that of those around them if they remain in the classroom. To date there has been no concerted work between the agencies although the school has managed to gain more time from two of the three services. Those services need to be on hand. Rural schools have as much need as urban schools, a fact that is not recognised by Central Government funding mechanisms.

It is clear that the teacher and school can do much to understand and change behaviour, but they cannot always be maximally effective if other aspects of support are not contingent and sustained. Currently opportunities to plan and construct multi-agency responses to significant behavioural needs remain at the level of aspiration rather than actuality.

Collaborative working arrangements that extend beyond the school are a critical element in both prevention and amelioration. The best framework for promoting positive behaviour is that which arises from, and is formulated by, a whole community response.

The future and what it holds: continuing challenges

Young people have always challenged the rules of institutions. The challenge for the future is to be one step ahead of the students whilst relating well to parents. The latest challenge facing the school was that of facial piercings. Although not acceptable as part of school uniform, some students had started to wear these, sometimes openly in order to challenge the authority of the school; others concealed it behind a plaster. It was decided at the start of a new school year to tackle non-uniform rather more stringently, giving students ten schooldays to obtain the correct uniform, or stay at home. However, staff agreed that there should be zero tolerance with regard to facial piercings. On the first day, two students were threatened with being sent home. The word spread quickly and the piercings disappeared. The situation was handled calmly and conflict was avoided.

The senior management team (SMT) will continue to monitor the behaviour through its current processes but will also seek to refine and develop other methods. Staff will need to be aware of legislation and the effects of increasing litigation; procedures will need to be re-examined and revised as necessary and changes in society will need to be taken into account.

Schools and individual teachers are often self critical when students' behaviour deteriorates. It is sometimes too easy to lose sight of the gains that have been made by sound policies being fairly and equally applied in a consistent, quiet and non-confrontational manner. To achieve this in the future continues to be our goal.

Summary

This case study has drawn together a range of issues that surround difficult behaviour and one school's response to it. It has indicated the stages in moving forward along the interrelated dimensions of improving the school's systems and developing more positive student responsiveness. The school's achievements serve as 'indicators for reflection' rather than advice to be followed to the letter. What is revealed is 'real practice' rather than suggesting an ideal of 'good' or 'effective' practice.

There are many lessons to be drawn from the work so far. Some of these are:

- Any behaviour that is challenging or disruptive involves attributes of the individual, the operation of peer norms and the influences of home, the school, and the wider social context. It is important to see both the whole perspective and the distinctions between these interacting elements.
- Invariably the school's response has to be a range of interventions. Whilst these have to be appropriate to the way in which the nature of the difficult behaviour is conceptualised, they may also need to be 'best fit' trial-and-error procedures as the school better understands and utilises pupils' responsiveness.
- It is as important to reflect upon and modify deficiencies in the management of behaviour in the school's environment and systems, as it is to clarify and understand the fuelling effect of any child's difficult or distressing circumstances.
- A central underpinning is to work towards a whole-school environment that is conducive to good ethos and discipline.
- Attention must be paid to positive behaviours and to mechanisms that enable students to visualise the nature of their unacceptable behaviour and its short-term and longer-term consequences.
- Despite the potential for recurring difficulties and setbacks, it is important for the school to work towards stronger than average ties with other neighbouring schools, parents and local community agencies.
- The value of internal and external review is that it can show the progress that has been made as well as highlighting the continuing challenges and needs.

References

Canter, L. and Canter, M. (1992) *Assertive Discipline: positive behaviour management for today's classroom*, Santa Monica, California: Lee Canter and associates.

Mosley, J. (1998) *The Whole School Quality Circle Time Model*, Trowbridge: All Round Success.

Chapter 6

The education of black children: why do some schools do better than others?

Maud Blair

Introduction

The literature on the schooling and education of black[1] children in Britain is extensive. With few exceptions (Channer 1996; Nehaul 1996, Blair and Bourne 1998), most of what has been written has focused on issues of underachievement, over-representation in suspensions and expulsions, early drop-out rates in the USA etc. This focus on the negative is not at all surprising. Black parents over the years have campaigned for better education for their children, have run their own supplementary schools to improve their children's chances, have tried to influence policy and practice in schools and have generally been vocal and active in their attempts to challenge discriminatory and unfair practices faced by black children and to reverse the continuing high levels of under-performance of black children in public examinations. Writers on the subject have tried to share their understandings of the nature and causes of these disadvantages, but despite the research, the community campaigns, the efforts of multiculturalists and antiracists, little seems to have changed over the decades and black and other minority children continue on aggregate to underperform in standardised tests compared to their white peers (Gillborn and Gipps 1996).

A number of theories have been put forward to explain this situation. One explanation, the cultural dissonance explanation (Driver 1979), holds that white teachers[2] do not understand the cultures of black children and therefore misinterpret their behaviour and impose sanctions more frequently or more harshly on black children leading to conflict and disaffection with school. Black children in a white racist society are deemed, therefore, to suffer from low self-esteem, especially if the curriculum either does not reflect their cultures and interests or these are represented negatively in curriculum materials (Green 1982). Another theory, closely allied to cultural dissonance, is that teachers do not understand the learning styles of black children and therefore the teaching and learning experiences of black young people are negatively affected. For black children to succeed, it is argued, it becomes necessary for them to reject their own black identities and think and act white (Fordham and Ogbu 1986; Fordham 1996). There is also the argument that black children are aware that the job market does not operate in their favour and so they see little point in putting a lot of effort into academic work (Ogbu 1988). Others have sought explanations in the children themselves, arguing that certain 'racial' groups are intellectually inferior to others (Jensen 1969; Eysenck 1971; Herrnstein and Murray 1994) or that black children behave more badly and are therefore justifiably placed in lower academic sets (Foster 1990). But the explanation that has been widely put forward both in Britain and in the USA is that racism – structural, institutional and individual – has been the main cause of the negative experiences of schooling of black and other minority children. In Britain, researchers have pointed to the disproportionate levels of reprimands and disciplinary measures that are routinely taken against black children in the classroom (Tizzard *et al.* 1988; Mortimore *et al.* 1988; Gillborn 1990; Wright 1992; Connolly 1995), and in particular the unfair and unjust manner in which black students are disciplined.

> Perhaps even more significant than the frequency of criticism and controlling statements which Afro-Caribbean pupils received was the fact that they were often singled out for criticism even though several pupils of different ethnic origins were engaged in the same behaviour … In sum, Afro-Caribbean pupils were not only criticised more often than their white peers, but the same behaviour in a white pupil might not bring about criticism at all.
>
> (Gillborn 1990: 30)

That black children were more likely to be placed into lower sets and streams was also observed (Foster 1990; Wright 1987). Although Foster argued that black students deserved their placement in lower sets because of their higher incidence of poor and disruptive behaviour, the evidence in favour of the racism and discrimination explanation has been overwhelming.

Some writers, however, have also argued for a more complex understanding of the political and social positioning of black children in schools (Rattansi 1992; Scott-Jones 1996) and of black males in particular (Noguera 1997). Referring to the (damaging) effects of discrimination on black students which some writers have highlighted, Scott-Jones declares that

There is no recognition (by some researchers) of the possibility of a range of reactions to discrimination on the part of students. There is no acknowledgment of the possibility that some students respond to discrimination with an increased determination to do well in school.

(Scott-Jones 1996)

Scott-Jones further argues that the way schools are organised may not be suitable for adolescents, especially those transferring from elementary to middle/secondary school. Others have pointed to the way that schools neglect the role of peer group pressure on adolescents as well as the importance of taking account of the adolescent's natural desire for independence at a time of confusing emotional and physical changes associated with growing up (Cullingford and Morrison 1997; Hargreaves *et al.* 1996; Measor and Woods 1984).

The factors which exist to complicate and confound our understanding of the educational experience of black students, therefore, are many and varied. In an attempt to answer the question posed in the title of this paper, I will argue that there are essentially three major factors which allow some secondary schools in Britain to succeed with black students where others have failed. The first is an understanding by the adults in the school of the *political and social concerns* of their students, and the willingness and courage to address these, however uncomfortable or difficult. Teachers need to know and understand their students individually in order to assist their daily interactions and cater for them as individuals, and also as members of groups in order to be familiar with some of the wider issues that affect students as members of the wider society. The second is adult understanding of and empathy with the *needs and concerns of adolescents*. There is a need for teachers to be in tune with the particular age-group of students they teach in order to cater appropriately for them. The third is the school's willingness to *work with parents as genuine partners* in the pursuit of a socially and academically rewarding experience for students. In their attempts to understand their students as individuals, teachers need to form *meaningful* partnerships with parents, partnerships which recognise that parents are the primary carers of children, and, especially where the teachers are white, that there are issues which affect minority ethnic group students' lives which they cannot grasp unless they deliberately seek that knowledge. Parents are well placed to provide that information.

The focus on black students in this chapter comes from the belief that if a school is willing to address honestly the issues that beset minority ethnic groups (for example black or Gypsy Traveller students) it is more likely to embrace the issues that exist for dominant groups, whereas schools that take a 'colour-blind' approach are more likely to interpret students' needs as meaning white students' needs, an approach which not only misses the diversity and complexity of students' lives, but also marginalises them (Blair and Bourne 1998). Instead of creating a warm and welcoming environment for black and minority ethnic group students and their parents, 'colour-blind' schools are more likely to develop a 'racially hot' environment marked not only by resentment and conflict but by disaffection and, more likely than not, 'underachievement'. Education in such schools is, for black communities, no longer, as Noguera states,

> ...the most viable path to social mobility, (but) serves as a primary agent for reproducing their marginality. (1997: 220)

In order to illustrate my theories, I draw on research evidence from a study carried out by the Open University during 1997 for the Department for Education and Employment (DfEE). Most of the examples are drawn from one of the 18 schools which were involved in the study.

A school that is successful for black students? Like finding a needle in a haystack

School effectiveness has been defined in the literature in measurable terms to mean success in standardised test scores, and more precisely in secondary schools in Britain, to mean acquiring grades A* to C. In seeking schools where students performed well in standardised tests, we began in our study by drawing on the Office for Standards in Education (OFSTED) lists of the General Certificate of Secondary Education (GCSE) results and highlighted those schools which not only performed well in the league tables, but also had a workable figure of a minimum of 10 per cent of black students. The study also covered Bangladeshi and Pakistani students, but this paper focuses entirely on black students largely because the school from which I draw my examples had less than 2 per cent students of South Asian origin. The issues for these groups of students (important though they are regardless of the numbers in the school) also differ in some important respects from those of black students, though my general theories outlined above apply to all students whatever their ethnic group.

Having selected schools which appeared on the OFSTED lists to be academically successful, we visited these schools in order to ascertain the level of success of the black (and South Asian) students. It was not so surprising to us to discover that schools which seemed on the face of it to be successful, were in fact only successful for some of their students. There is an assumption in the literature that an effective school is likely to combine a number of important factors. These are that the school has strong leadership, is well-organised, the staff are united and share a vision, there is a positive ethos, and that there are high expectations of students (Smith and Tomlinson 1989; Nuttall and Goldstein 1989; Reynolds and Cuttance 1992). Smith and Tomlinson (1989) concluded that a school which was 'effective' was likely to be effective for all its students, including minority ethnic group students. However, many so-called 'effective' schools operate in a 'colour-blind' manner which assumes that all students have the same needs and are affected by the same issues. One school in our study, which would qualify as 'effective' by the criteria above, provides an interesting example. A brief look at the ethos and the question of academic success serves to illustrate the point.

In relation to the school ethos, the level of negativity that existed in this school amongst the black students, and amongst the black boys in particular, indicated that their concerns were either not known or not heeded. The students were so pleased to be able to talk about what schooling was like for them, that a group of them asked for a further interview after school because, after my one hour with them in which they gave several examples of racism, especially by specific members of staff, one boy declared that I had not 'heard the half of it'. This state of affairs was not confined to this one school alone but existed for nearly all the black boys interviewed and a significant number of the girls in all the schools, with the exception of the one, Northern Catholic School, from which I draw my examples of 'success'.

Academically, black girls in the school given in the example above appeared, on the face of it, to perform as well and sometimes better than their white male and female peers. However, even this was deceptive. When the category 'black girls' was further broken down into the different ethnic groups (African, African-Caribbean, 'mixed-race'), we found that a school which seemed successful for all black girls was in fact only successful for African and dual ethnicity ('mixed-race') girls. African-Caribbean girls did not do well. The general impression in Britain is also that African students, male and female, generally do well and sometimes better than white students in public examinations. In this apparently successful school (and others), black boys (including African boys) achieved significantly lower grades than their white peers. Furthermore, this level of 'underachievement' was not confined to that one year but, according to the figures, or to the headteachers' statements, applied to at least two or three years previously. This situation was no different for our exemplar school (Northern Catholic) except in the question of steady improvement of black students' results. In this school, black girls from different ethnic groups did well and although the results for the black boys were still by and large lower than for other student groups, they had shown steady improvement over the previous three years. In the year of the study, black girls achieved on average the highest scores for science, followed by black boys, and black boys came second to the white boys in mathematics.

There were therefore no schools in our study which could be said to be equally successful for all their students, least of all for the black students. We decided therefore, that rather than search for the proverbial needle in the haystack, we would examine the factors that led to the steady progress by black students in Northern Catholic School. The school was no different in size from two other Catholic schools (approximately 700 students and approximately 30 per cent black students) and only different in class composition from the one mentioned above, which had more African, dual ethnicity and middle-class black students. It was not by any means a 'highflying' school in terms of its position in the national league tables. It is at any rate commonly accepted that league tables do not and cannot measure accurately a school's actual achievement because of the complexities of schooling, of the environment and because of the diverse concerns of schools. As we state in Blair and Bourne (1998: 69),

> 'good systems' do not necessarily by themselves guarantee successful attainment for all groups of students, nor do league table measurements currently take into account value-added factors and the hard work put in by teachers who want to provide a curriculum that is relevant to a very diverse student intake.

League tables which tell us the percentage of students who obtained high grades in their examinations do not tell us *which* students received these grades and can therefore mask the failure of schools in relation to particular groups of students. A factor which stood out for Northern Catholic School was that there was a qualitatively different response from the black students at this school about their experience of schooling, and as mentioned, black students were making more progress academically than in any of the other schools with a comparable intake.

How a school can make a difference

On the whole, schools in Britain have not succeeded, despite attempts by the multicultural and antiracist movements, in creating environments in which black students as a whole feel the sense of belonging which comes with acceptance of who they are. But in order to accept and respect students' identities, it is necessary to know them and to understand them. This seems to be a particularly tall order in an environment which is ethnically, linguistically and religiously diverse. However, it is this overall student-centred culture and philosophy within the school that is at the root of 'effectiveness' for all students. To achieve such an environment requires a culture change which goes beyond well-meaning policy or statements of intent. Changing a school's culture cannot be done overnight but requires courage and patience, and most of all a deep sense of commitment and a genuine desire to provide equality of opportunity for all students. This last point is a particular challenge at a time in British education when greater tensions are being created between the personal and social needs of students and what Hargreaves *et al.* (1996: 6) describe as the 'traditional, judgmental, fact-centred systems of assessment and evaluation'. In the following sections I describe those issues which were found to be essential for creating a positive learning environment for black students.

Understanding the issues and concerns of black students

An examination of the literature which focuses on issues of 'race', ethnicity and education in British schools reveals an interesting and important fact – that black secondary school students, regardless of where they are in the country or what school they attend, seem to speak with one voice about the nature of their experience of schooling. Our own interviews with black students confirmed what many researchers have documented: that black students feel they are unfairly treated by teachers (i.e. 'picked on'); they believe that teachers often operate with racial stereotypes which are demeaning; that this outlook on the part of teachers affects their attitudes to black students; that teachers have low expectations of them; that teachers discriminate against them; that they do not treat them with respect; and (a complaint common to all students) that teachers do not listen to them, and also that teachers always 'stick up for and support each other' (Wright 1987, Mac an Ghaill 1988; Gillborn 1990; Mirza 1992; Connolly 1995).

Listening to and respecting students

At Northern Catholic, the school decided that in order to deal with the serious problem of black student alienation it was important to listen to the grievances that were brought to them by students, and then find strategies for developing a culture which created a positive learning environment for black students. Listening to students meant actively attempting to understand things from their point of view. The headteacher listened to both the perspective of the students and that of the teachers about what they thought caused the poor behaviour and poor relations within the school. It was important for the students to know that the headteacher would not always 'stick up for teachers', especially when they were wrong. Complaints of racism were never dismissed as a symptom of the 'chip on the shoulder', but were properly investigated and, especially where a teacher had been unaware of the racial nature of their actions, this was explained so that the teacher could see the effects of their actions on the students. This non-judgemental approach was found to be necessary because of the complex nature of racism which can sometimes be unintended, unconscious and unacknowledged (Mac an Ghaill 1988; Gillborn

1997). In contrast, in another school, the black student who reported to the headteacher that he had been treated by his teacher in a racially discriminatory way was questioned about his own attitudes to school, told about his history of poor behaviour and then accused of 'reverse racism'. There was in this school a high level of disaffection amongst the black students, especially the boys, who were also disproportionately affected by exclusions.

An aspect of listening to students and respecting their point of view related, at Northern Catholic, to the manner in which information was gathered and used. It was not enough to have a mission statement which pronounced equality of treatment for all. It was important, as the deputy headteacher stated, that it was made clear to students that they would be believed unless, after investigation, the facts proved to be different. This approach was just as supportive to teachers, who realised that this was not a licence for students to make false accusations or try to gain an advantage, but was inherently about creating a fair and just system. If teachers respected students' rights to be heard, and in the process learnt about the issues that affected students and why, this was more likely to improve relationships within the school than an approach which was authoritarian and dismissive of students' concerns. Teachers were thus encouraged to reflect on their words and actions to understand how these were viewed by students. They were also encouraged to discuss with students rather than immediately resort to punishment when certain types of behaviour were unacceptable. In this way, a culture of mutual respect was developed and one in which black students felt assured that their concerns mattered to the school, would be investigated and appropriate action taken. The deputy head stated that:

> The key to good relations in our school is that we take time to listen to students. We give them a fair hearing. If students feel that you will listen to them and investigate things properly, and sometimes you spend a lot of time listening to something you knew all the time, but the bottom line is, they know you will listen to them.

Respecting student cultures

One of the concerns that black students have is that their histories are excluded from what is considered to be valuable knowledge in the school curriculum. Not only is it excluded, moreover, but what exists is sometimes found to be eurocentric or racist. The restrictions placed on the school curriculum by the demands of the National Curriculum inhibit attempts by schools to place the histories and cultures of minority ethnic groups within the mainstream academic subject area. The feeling of marginalisation of black students was recognised at Northern Catholic, and attempts were made to meet this concern by the introduction within the Personal and Social Education (PSE) programme of a six week course in Afrikan Studies which was taken by all students in the school. This was later followed by a six week course of Irish Studies to reflect another major ethnic group in the school.

The initial introduction of Afrikan Studies was, as can be expected, controversial and greeted with less than enthusiasm from some members of staff and parents. It clearly required courage and perseverance, not only in ensuring that the course was introduced but in gradually persuading staff that it was important and useful. The strategies that were used for addressing staff concerns are discussed below.

Understanding and responding to adolescents

Hargreaves *et al.* (1996) contend that secondary schools have not traditionally been responsive to the needs of adolescents or taken heed of changes in the wider society. A factor that is often omitted in research, and certainly one that seems to be absent in teachers' dealings with black students, is that their identities go beyond the question of 'race' or ethnicity to embrace those factors which they share with all young people, namely, the fact of growing up. It is often assumed that when individual black boys misbehave, it is a factor of their 'race' rather than of their adolescence. It seems likely that this would lead teachers to treat black students differently from white students and explain the pervasive feeling amongst black young people that they are treated unfairly. It is also assumed that in order to create a positive learning environment for black young people, one need only address questions of racism and discrimination and ignore the need to understand black young people *as young people*.

A vital component of teacher education should be to help teachers understand the ways and the needs of adolescents. Many writers have pointed to this phase of development as being particularly difficult for the young people themselves. Adolescents, as Hargreaves *et al.* (1996) put it, 'are complex, diverse, and unpredictable'. These characteristics are part of young people's attempts to grow and become more independent. Writing over 20 years ago, Curtis and Bidwell (1977: 41) stated that,

> although some parents and teachers are sensitive to the ways they assist youth to achieve independence, much opinion seems to be critical of the struggle for independence. This is surprising since this ultimate independence is necessary for the continuance of society.

In many schools, this quest for independence is punished rather than harnessed for the benefit of the young people themselves and the school. In some schools in our study, however, staff showed sensitivity and an ability to engage constructively with the dilemmas of youth. They understood the

pressures of the peer group and attempted to work with this rather than
condemn it. In these schools, suspensions and expulsions were few or non-
existent because staff took an approach which was empathetic rather than
hostile towards young people.

Head of year (Southern International School):

> We very rarely permanently exclude. A student would have to have done something
> horrendous for it to get to the stage of a permanent exclusion. It's very rare, for
> example, in a case of violence, for students to go home not having made up. We talk
> through problems with students and help them find alternative ways of dealing with
> situations.

At Northern Catholic, the head of the school understood and responded to
what one headteacher described as 'the fantastically strong stereotypes in the
society of what people think black boys are like'. These stereotypes included
the belief that where black boys were gathered in a group, there were likely to
be drugs or they were preparing to do something antisocial like 'mugging'; that
black males are violent and threatening; that they have no interest in education
and therefore 'underachieve'; and generally that black males spelt 'trouble'.
The headteacher of Northern Catholic School made it clear to the black
students that she understood what they had to face, and assured them that
such attitudes towards them by teachers would not be tolerated. But, whilst she
offered her full support to the students, she also tried to ensure that they took
responsibility for themselves and others around them. It was made clear, for
example, that a change in the school culture could not occur without their full
co-operation and contribution. Furthermore, not only were they encouraged to
take responsibility for themselves, but also to play their part in the community,
for example, helping to organise a youth conference.

There was thus an understanding that black students were not only adolescents
with all the problems of adolescents, but that they were adolescents who were
situated differently from their white peers both within the culture of the school
and of the wider society. It was wrong therefore to compartmentalise their
experiences into either 'race', or youth; it was necessary to see and appreciate the
complexity of their experiences as young-black-males/females. In their dealings
with all adolescents, the school worked with peer group leaders to provide
examples for others in relation to both behaviour and academic achievement.

> We work through individuals to reverse the trend amongst boys which says that to be
> an achiever is not cool. One African-Caribbean boy … is a very bright boy but became
> more involved with the social side of life and was underachieving. So I called him and
> told him he was turning out to be the equivalent of a 'dumb blonde' – tall and good-
> looking but with nothing. He's very popular with the girls. I asked him if there was a
> particular girl that he liked and he said, 'Ella'. So I said, 'She's not going to want you
> if you are not going to be of a similar academic status. Your good looks aren't going to
> last forever. You can't get through on that charm and that smile. The kind of girls you

like are not going to be interested if you're on the dole.' He knew exactly what I meant. He didn't like to be compared to the dumb blonde. Now he's one of our role models and we have great hopes for him.

The headteacher's appeal to the young man's masculinity is clearly problematic in its ignorance of the dynamics of both gender and disability, and is an issue that needs to be resolved. The point being made here, however, is that it was recognised that giving students equality of opportunity was not a question of 'take it or leave it'. Adolescent boys, with their need for peer group approval and facing the challenge that working hard at school is 'soft', are unlikely to take up opportunities for extra classes or revision work. One teacher pointed out that boys of this age tend to be 'immature learners' and need to be given extra encouragement to take up such opportunities. This also applied to students who were alienated or had other reasons for not taking up opportunities where they occurred. Often, it was the personal interest shown in such an individual by a teacher that could make all the difference.

> **Student:** (Mrs B.) called me to the office the other day and she says, 'I've seen a spark and I don't want it to die. You've got the ability and you can do it. Do you mind me mentoring you? When you get your coursework, show me; when it's finished, show me.' She wants to monitor everything – my attendance, my punctuality, and I will gladly go along with that because I know that she is doing it because she really cares. She is a really good teacher.

Partnerships with parents

As stated at the beginning of this chapter, black parents have been engaged in an ongoing struggle to secure the educational rights of their children in British schools. One reason for this ongoing struggle has been the failure of schools to relate to minority ethnic group parents with respect, and the tendency also to hold stereotypical attitudes towards them. Discussions with black parents reveal very similar concerns to those of their children (Blair and Bourne 1998). Parents have complained about teachers making assumptions about their personal characteristics on the basis of stereotypes about black people. Teachers sometimes assume that black parents are aggressive and this makes them feel intimidated, thus hindering their ability to relate to black parents. One parent stated:

> Most (black) people were born in this country, went to school in this country, and half of these teachers, we used to play with them. So why are they finding us so aggressive?

Amongst the stereotypes held by teachers is an assumption that black parents are not interested in their children's education because they do not always attend 'Open Evenings' where parents meet with teachers to discuss the children's progress. Such arrangements, say parents, are often a waste of time because teachers do not give them quality information about academic progress but focus on behaviour, or else they report that the children are 'doing fine' when this is not reflected in the children's work.

> Usually when I go to Parents' Evenings, it's like, 'Well, she is doing fine'. It is such a generalisation. I want specifics, and they don't seem to be able to give me specifics. You know, I'll say, 'How is she doing in the particular subject?' and they say, 'Fine'. I mean that is why a lot of us are walking the streets because everything was 'fine' at the Parents' Evening.

Parents also report being 'fobbed off' by the school when they want to take up a concern, and that when they do go to the school, they are treated with disrespect not always by the teachers themselves, but sometimes by reception staff. Parents talk about being 'talked down to' by teachers and generally treated, on the basis of their colour and class, as second-class citizens.

How do schools that are 'successful' for black students avoid these mistakes? As with students, the most effective ways of gaining the parents' support and co-operation was to listen to their concerns, consult them about and give them a voice on important issues, both pastoral and academic, and perhaps most importantly, show them respect by acting on their concerns and not merely involving them in a tokenistic way. At Northern Catholic School, an Association of Black Parents and Parents of Black Children was formed. They met in the school and discussed the issues relating to the education of their children, issues which they wanted to take up with the school. These were then reported to the headteacher, or, through the governor representative, to the board of governors. Availing the parents of the school in this way, and then taking up their concerns, also helped to create an environment in which previously disempowered parents felt more confident to join the school's governing body and take an active part in decisions made about and for the school. The headteacher also made it her business to try to understand the issues for the black communities by involving herself in community affairs and getting to know the communities from which the students came. She forged strong relationships with people in the black community. Through this personal education, she understood that her role in the education of black students did not begin and end at the school gate. She understood that black people, young and old, were subject to police harassment and intimidation and she was sometimes called upon by black families to vouch for their children's character where these children came before the law. She also helped and advised parents to find legal support where students in the school were called before the criminal justice system. This intimate understanding of the political issues which beset the lives of the students and their parents gained this headteacher the respect and trust of the black parents. One parent said this of her:

(Black) parents have the confidence to come to her as a friend. She is seen as a friend in arms, struggling together for the good of their children.

The general policy in the school towards the parents was to have a genuine 'Open door'.

> We say to parents that if your child comes home with something and you are asking yourself, 'Should I ring the school?' We say, 'Ring. Don't think anything is too trivial'. We encourage parents to be open, to see if there is anything about the work, the quality of the work, is there too much work, or is there something about the way the teacher may have treated the child in class. We are open enough to say, 'come in and tell us'.

The parents were also closely consulted and involved in policy decisions. When the school was drawing up its anti-racist policy, leading members of the black community were asked to comment on the draft produced. This was then circulated to all parents with children in the school for further comments, then given to the school's governing body for endorsement, before it was finally written up. A similar procedure was taken for the anti-sexist policy.

The interest in the lives and concerns of the black students was an indication of this headteacher's concern for all the students in her school, a concern which was well demonstrated in the support she gave to an 'at risk' Irish boy who finally left school with good credentials. This approach was quite different from that of headteachers in other schools where issues of concern to black students and their parents were often considered 'too sensitive' (see also Hayden 1997), or attempts to address them were seen as 'pandering to minority interests'. What was generally not recognised in schools was that the disadvantaged position of minority group students was part of the wider systemic disadvantages which are experienced by members of minority groups. Instead, the tendency in schools was to blame students and their families for any failures, and to avoid critical thinking or reflection about the school's role in creating or perpetuating such 'failures'.

Strategies for involving teachers in school change

Attempting to change a school is a difficult and slow process because, as Hargreaves *et al.* state,

> educational change is not just a technical process of managerial efficiency, or a cultural one of understanding and involvement. It is a political and paradoxical process as well … educational change which promises to benefit all students … threatens many entrenched interests.
>
> (Hargreaves *et al.* 1996: 163)

General change is difficult enough, but entrenched interests are particularly threatened when the type of change required involves an examination of and deep reflection on one's own beliefs and value systems. The half-hearted and sometimes failed attempts in the 1970s and 80s to implement multicultural and antiracist education bear witness to this difficulty (Troyna, 1992). But change is difficult because it is also about

> transforming sophisticated relationships not simple behaviours, in complex classroom situations and organizational systems, whose purpose and direction are politically compounded and contested.
>
> Hargreaves *et al.* 1996: 168)

At Northern Catholic, the headteacher recognised the potential difficulty of convincing teachers that change was needed, and that this change had to embrace the whole philosophy and culture of the school and not just the disciplinary measures taken against misbehaving students. She was convinced that not only were there gross injustices being perpetrated against the black students with particular reference to the black boys, she was sure that no single strategy would be sufficient to change the climate of hostility and conflict in which the black students and teachers were engaged. She needed to be sensitive to the grievances brought to her by the black students as well as take account of the sensitivities of teachers whose very identity as professionals was threatened.

The strategy adopted embraced both multicultural and antiracist methods. On the one hand, a course on Afrikan Studies was introduced, initially outside school hours and attended voluntarily by students, and then as part of the compulsory Personal, Social Education (PSE) programme in which all students took part. This strategy, which was interpreted by some teachers and parents as favouring black students, met with some opposition. To address this, meetings were organised in order to discuss the basic philosophy of the school and to gain a unified understanding of what equality of opportunity meant in practical terms. It was also explained that unless the issues which affected the black students could be effectively tackled, the relationships in the school would continue to affect negatively the whole of the school community, and black students would continue to 'underachieve' in relation to other students. The headteacher stated,

> I've been quite outright in saying that whatever strategies we use to help black students raises the achievement of the white students and of the whole school because if there is a social problem, it helps to change the atmosphere.

Teachers were encouraged to discuss their fears and misgivings and to ask questions in a climate of openness and honesty in a non-judgemental environment. Parents too were invited to express their feelings and to come to the school if they had questions or wanted to discuss the implications of the Afrikan Studies programme. Alongside the implementation of the Afrikan Studies programme, teachers received in-service education on issues of equality of opportunity.

Another strategy was to get teachers and students to define together what they wanted from their school. As a Catholic school, Year 9 Tutors and their students (12–13 years olds) took 'retreats' together every year, and this was an occasion for all to learn about better communication, conflict resolution, the school's educational and moral mission, and for teachers to get to know their students and 'bond' together outside the normal routines and environment of the school. Out of these meetings and 'retreats' emerged a Code of Behaviour for the whole school and one which applied to the staff as much as it did the students. This Code of Behaviour defined what was acceptable and not acceptable behaviour and, importantly, provided guidelines for resolving difficulties in a respectful and conflict-free environment.

The process of gaining the co-operation of teachers was a long and, according to the headteacher, a hard one. It took six years before she began to feel that there was much more of a united front in the school. The black students were given assurances that racism and unfair treatment against them would not be tolerated and that they had the ear of senior management in the school if they had any grievances. All parents were given the assurance that if their children had a serious grievance, this would be heard by senior management, and together with the parents, the complaint would be investigated and something would be done about it.

The political rationale for addressing the concerns of groups and not only of individuals was explained to the teachers, who were informed that such action applied to all students regardless of ethnicity. These combined strategies, and the headteacher's perseverance in the face of sometimes very strong opposition, finally seemed to pay off so that it was the teachers themselves who were at last able to appreciate the benefits of the more peaceful environment in which they were working. Black students began to feel confident that the one issue which most affected them, that of being racially discriminated against, would at last be taken seriously. A further benefit, which the open discussions and the ability to engage with controversial and difficult subjects allowed the school to do, was to address the issues that affected adolescents as adolescents without the clutter of racial stereotypes. The level of mutual trust that developed enabled the school to introduce changes that were of benefit to the whole school community. Teachers were able to develop an understanding of not only black students' needs but the needs of all students, and to experience the benefits of this for their own teaching.

Conclusion

The case of Northern Catholic High School is an illustration and not a template
for what can be done to change the schooling experiences of black students.
Every school operates within its own context and with its own set of problems
and issues. That the problems faced by black students in British schools are not
confined to specific areas of the country, and that they are just as likely to apply
in situations of low as well as high black student population, have been well
demonstrated in research. The example of Northern Catholic should therefore
offer some encouragement. Black students need to know that they are not only
welcome and wanted in the school, but that they will be treated fairly, their
cultures will be respected, the political issues that beset them as black people
will be understood and form part of the school's sensitivities and
responsibilities toward them. They need to know that their particular needs
will be recognised as complex and comprising their ethnic and 'racial' identities
as well as their needs as 'children' or young people, but also that their
differences will be appreciated.

A major criterion in achieving this kind of positive environment for black
and all students is teachers who are willing to learn and genuinely understand
the issues that affect their students.

Hargreaves *et al.* (1996: 6) state that

> Change is most effective, not when it is seen as a problem to be fixed, an anomaly to
> be ironed out, or a fire to be extinguished. Particular changes are more likely to be
> implemented in schools where teachers are committed to norms of continuous
> improvement as part of their overall professional obligations.

Regretfully, changes relating to 'race' and ethnicity are usually regarded as 'a
problem to be fixed' and 'an anomaly to be ironed out'. This was undoubtedly
the case for many teachers at Northern Catholic. What was needed was not
only strong and determined leadership and a clear vision of what was right for
the school, but enough teachers who were committed 'to the norms of
continuous improvement' to create the momentum for change and provide the
support needed for this to be effective. The extent to which the united
'Catholic' philosophy helped the process is open to speculation. The most
important 'mission' was that of ensuring that none of the students who
attended this school, and none of their parents, should feel in any way
marginalised or discriminated against. To achieve this requires from any senior
management in a school the ability to throw off the 'baggage' of assumptions
that we all carry and which play such an important part in influencing how we
see others and how we relate to them (see for example Sleeter 1994).

What is needed, as one headteacher said, is the ability to create in a school a
'we' ethos and not an ethos of 'them' and 'us' which divides teachers from

students and black from white. Unfortunately, black students in many schools are consciously or unconsciously experienced as 'Other' (Blair 1994). Changing this situation is the real challenge facing teachers who not only care about their students but genuinely want to make a difference to their lives.

Notes

1 I use the term 'black' here to refer to people of African descent whether they be from Africa or the Caribbean. The term is also used to refer to people of dual heritage where one parent is of African descent.
2 Approximately 98 per cent of teachers in British schools are white. Most black children will therefore be taught by white teachers, and some might never have a black teacher throughout their schooling. In writing about 'teachers', therefore, it is assumed in this paper that the teachers are white.

References

Blair, M. (1994) 'Black teachers, black students and education markets', *Cambridge Journal of Education*, Vol. 24, pp. 277–91.

Blair, M., Bourne, J. with Coffin, C., Creese, A. and Kenner, C. (1998) *Making the Difference: Teaching and Learning Strategies in Successful Multi-ethnic Schools*, London: DfEE.

Channer, Y. (1996) *I Am a Promise: The Schooling Achievement of British African-Caribbeans*, Stoke-on-Trent: Trentham Books.

Connolly, P. (1995) 'Racism, masculine peer-group relations and the schooling of African/Caribbean infant boys', *British Journal of Sociology of Education*, **16**, 2, pp. 75–92.

Cullingford, C. and Morrison, J. (1997) 'Peer group pressure within and outside school', *British Educational Research Journal*, **23**, 1, pp. 61–80.

Curtis, T.E. and Bidwell, W.W. (1977) *Curriculum and Instruction for Emerging Adolescents*, New York: Addison Wesley.

Driver, G. (1979) 'Classroom stress and school achievement: West Indian adolescents and their Teachers', in Saifullah Khan, V. (ed.) *Minority Families in Britain: Support and Stress*, London: Macmillan.

Egglestone, S.J., Dunn, D.K. and Anjali, M. (1985) *Education for Some: The Educational and Vocational Experiences of 15–18 Year Old Members of Minority Ethnic Groups*, Stoke-on-Trent: Trentham.

Eysenck, H.J. (1971) *Race, Intelligence and Education*, London: Temple Smith.

Fordham, S. and Ogbu, J. (1986) 'Black students' school success: coping with the burden of "acting white" ', *The Urban Review*, **18**, 3, pp. 1–31.

Fordham, S. (1996) *Blacked Out: Dilemmas of Race, Identity and Success at Capitol High*, Chicago: University of Chicago Press.

Foster, P. (1990) *Policy and Practice in Multicultural and Antiracist Education*, London: Routledge.

Gillborn, D. (1990) *'Race', Ethnicity and Education*, London: Unwin and Hyman.

Gillborn, D. (1997) 'Young, black and failed by school: the market, education reform and black students', *International Journal of Inclusive Education*, **1**, 1, pp. 65–87.

Gillborn, D. and Gipps, C. (1996) *Recent Research on the Achievement of Ethnic Minority Pupils*, London: HMSO.

Green, D. (1982) Teachers' influence on the self-concept of different ethnic groups, unpublished Ph.D. thesis, cited in Troyna, B. (1993) *Racism and Education*, Buckingham: Open University Press.

Hargreaves, A., Earl, L. and Ryan, J. (1996) *Schooling for Change: Re-inventing Education for Early Adolescents*, London: Falmer.

Hayden, C. (1997) *Children Excluded from Primary School: Debates, Evidence, Responses*, Buckingham: Open University Press.

Herrnstein, R.J. and Murray, C. (1994) *The Bell Curve: Intelligence and Class Structure in American Life*, New York: The Free Press.

Jensen, D. (1969) 'How much can we boost IQ and scholastic achievement?', *Harvard Educational Review*, **39**, 1, pp. 1–23.

Mac an Ghaill, M. (1988) *Young, Gifted and Black: Student-Teacher Relations in the Schooling of Black Youth*, Milton Keynes: Open University Press.

Measor, L. and Woods, P. (1984) *Changing Schools*, Milton Keynes: Open University Press.

Mirza, H. (1992) *Young, Female and Black*, London: Routledge.

Mortimore, P., Sammons, P., Stoll, P., Lewis, D. and Ecob, R. (1988) *School Matters: The Junior Years*, Wells: Open Books.

Nehaul, K. (1996) *The Schooling of Children of Caribbean Heritage*, Stoke-on-Trent: Trentham.

Noguera, P. (1997) 'Reconsidering the "Crisis" of the Black Male in America', *Journal of Social Justice*, **24**, 2, pp. 147–64.

Nuttall, D. and Goldstein, H. (1989) 'Differential school effectiveness', *International Journal of Educational Research*, **13**, pp. 769–76.

Ogbu, J. (1988) 'Understanding cultural diversity and learning', *Educational Researcher*, **21**, 8, pp. 5–14.

Rattansi, A. (1992) 'Changing the subject? Racism, culture and education', in Donald, J. and Rattansi, A., *'Race', Culture and Difference*, London: Sage.

Reynolds, D. and Cuttance, P. (1992) *School Effectiveness: Research, Policy and Practice*, London: Cassell.

Scott-Jones, D. (1996) 'Motivation and Achievement: Implication of Minority Status', Discussion Paper presented at the annual meeting of the American Education Research Association, NY, April.

Sleeter, C. (1994) 'How white teachers construct race', in McCarthy, C. and Crichlow, W., *Race, Identity and Representation in Education*, London: Routledge.

Smith, D. and Tomlinson, S. (1989) *The School Effect: a Study of Multiracial Comprehensiveness*, London: Policy Studies Institute.

Tizzard, B., Blatchford, P., Burke, J., Farquhar, C. and Plewis, I. (1988) *Young Children at School in the Inner City*, Hove: Lawrence Erlbaum Associates.

Troyna, B. (1992) 'Can you see the join? A historical analysis of multicultural and antiracist education policies', in Gill, D., Mayor, B. and Blair, M. *Racism in Education: Structures and Strategies*, London: Sage.

Wright, C. (1987) 'Black students–white teachers', in Troyna, B. (ed.) *Racial Inequality in Education*, London: Routledge.

Wright, C. (1992) 'Early education: multiracial primary school classrooms', in Gill, D., Mayor, B. and Blair, M. (eds) *Racism in Education: Structures and Strategies*, London: Sage.

Chapter 7

The Hikairo Rationale: teaching students with emotional and behavioural difficulties – a bicultural approach

Angus H. Macfarlane

Introduction

In recent years there has been a proliferation of behaviour management philosophies, techniques, and instructional methodologies that has increased the complexity of the teachers' responsibilities and functions (Walker & Shea, 1995). While new information continues to be published on the various perspectives of human behaviour, there is a dearth of material which takes into account the New Zealand context and the bicultural and multicultural composition of its classrooms.

This chapter reports an approach to the management of children with behaviour difficulties and should provide practitioners and student teachers with bicultural guidelines. The approach considers contemporary theories while also embracing the framework of traditional Māori concepts and values. The Hikairo Rationale was the structural base for teachers and learners at Awhina High School, Rotorua, a centre for students with profound emotional and behavioural difficulties. In research carried out in 1995 it was shown that by using the rationale suggested, positive differences ensued in students' attitudes, self-esteem, academic performance, and acceptance of themselves and others. Student re-integration to regular classrooms was higher than in a similar study carried out in 1992 by Brian Burgess, head teacher of the Auckland Activity Centre.

A detailed breakdown of the figures for school suspensions shows that Māori students, with regular monotony, are grossly over-represented. If account is taken of the fact that many Māori students drop out of school at a much earlier age than Pakeha (of European extraction) students, the figures become even more disturbing. The first concern is the question of whether schools are providing special support for Māori and Polynesian students. Many schools make this provision, no doubt. But in too many schools, it seems, the equity principles contained in their charters are often no more than empty promises. This ignorance suggests that there is a second concern, that is, providing special support for teachers in New Zealand schools as they try to make sense of stressful and confusing situations.

This chapter addresses this concern. What is offered here is a rationale which recognises Māoritanga and embraces those philosophies and practices which would be useful in making a difference when dealing with difficult young people.

The paper, 'Māori and Youth Justice in New Zeland' (Olsen, Maxwell & Morris, 1993, cited in *Youth Law Review* July-Sept 1994: p8), illustrates that pre-European Māori discipline possessed four identifiable features:

1. An emphasis upon reaching consensus and involving the whole community.
2. A desired outcome of reconciliation and a settlement acceptable to all parties rather than the isolation and punishment of the offender.
3. The concern was not to apportion blame but to examine the wider reason for the wrong with an implicit assumption that there was often wrong on both sides.
4. There was less concern with whether or not there had been a breach of law and more concern with the restoration of harmony.

Programmes have been developed to help schools reduce bullying and violent behaviour. The Seven Step Hikairo Rationale is so named because of the way peaceful resolution was reached following the Ngapuhi onslaught of Te Arawa on Mokoia Island in 1823. According to Stafford (1967) the Ngati-Rangiwewehi Chief, Hikairo, spoke with such mana and influence that the enemy, under Hongi Hika's leadership, declared that there would be no more killing. On this occasion, assertive dialogue, fundamental assurances, and simple sincerity, brought about a change of attitude in the hostile and aggressive enemy.

In the Hikairo discipline method it is considered that students, Māori and non-Māori, can respond receptively to appropriately delivered aspects of tikanga Māori, and it provides a series of systematic, bicultural procedures for teachers and parents to consider. The Hikairo method endeavours to provide focus and direction without blinding the observer to other issues and approaches, and to the individuality of each case. Useful theories, according to Young (1992) make such provisions.

The traditional Māori value of 'aroha' has a very real place in the model. Aroha does not depict a 'soft' approach. In the context of discipline, aroha connotes co-operation, understanding reciprocity and warmth. The Hikairo programme has these qualities in abundance, and is simultaneously assertive.

Step One – Huakina Mai (open doorways)

Educators must respond to unproductive student behaviour by creating opportunities to establish meaningful relationships before the student's first day in the classroom, or centre, or school. Teachers have to be proactive as well as reactive. Too often teachers react to the narratives associated with a student. Students with behaviour difficulties are 'labelled' as bad, unco-operative, uncouth, deviant, arrogant, aggressive, or a combination of these so-called characteristics. The labels develop into 'stories' about the student which, in the main, precede the student's arrival at a new form level or learning environment. Such a perspective is unfair and unacceptable as it represents a continuity of student disadvantage where the individual is forced to operate under handicap conditions socially, psychologically, and educationally.

The positively reactive teacher chooses to destroy the myths about the student by focusing on the behaviour as the problem, rather than the person. The positively proactive teacher, when learning of the likelihood of a 'storied' student becoming a member of the class or centre, makes arrangements to meet with the student, or makes a telephone call to the student before his/her first day in the new setting. The tenor of the teacher's approach is one of control, affection and faith. Teacher: 'I know you will be starting class with us next week and I just want to let you know that we're looking forward to you becoming part of the whanau [family]. We'll work together a lot, as we want to make this a super year…'

From the outset, it is crucial that the teacher gets to know the students and that the students get to know the teacher's expectations. For those students who, unfortunately, have a *reputation for being difficult*, the opening of doorways must occur in the very early stages.

Part of the Huakina Mai process involves establishing rules. Rules are expectations of how individuals are to behave, and are in place to protect individuals' rights, and therefore by definition are 'fair' (Rogers, 1989, 1990). The Hikairo system perceives the notion of fairness to be integral to the helping process. From the very outset the teacher is encouraged to pledge an oath of 'fairness' to the student. This can be expressed in its most simple form in the following utterance by the teacher, 'I promise you that as long as you are at this school, I will always be fair to you. Always. All I want in return is for you to be fair to me. Do we have an understanding?' This is a profound, sincere way of opening the doorway of trust and acceptance.

A Te Arawa whanaunga and respected leader, Mita Mohi, whose middle name happens to be Hikairo, opens doorways for behaviourally difficult youngsters by co-ordinating mau-taiaha wananga at Mokoia Island, three times annually. The young people, Māori and non-Māori, who attend these wananga are introduced to the traditional Māori arts and disciplines. Before the boat leaves for the island a karakia is recited, followed by mihimihi. Then Mita employs his version of Huakina Mai. He says to the rangatahi, 'ko au ko koe, ko koe ko au'. 'I am you and you are me.' Thus is established a bonding of the highest order. The Huakina Mai approach lets the students know that they are valued by the teacher. It is a friendly approach, consciously planned.

Step Two – Ihi (assertiveness)

Assertive communication, properly employed, is one of the most effective tools when responding to a student's aggressive behaviour. According to Alberti and Emmons (1986) assertiveness refers to behaviour which enables people to act in their own best interests, to stand up for themselves without undue anxiety, to express honest feelings comfortably, or to exercise personal rights without denying the rights of others. Ngata (1993) and Williams (1985) appear to express similar views as they refer to whakapuaki in terms of coming forth, opening out and emerging.

New Zealanders have, in their kaumatua and kaikorero, an ideal model of assertiveness. On the marae, these orators excel in terms of self-expression, honesty, directness, self-enhancement and rendering appropriate content and expression for the person(s) and the situation, rather than the universal perspective. Assertive communication is part of an established order of Māori protocol.

The research carried out at Awhina High School (Macfarlane, 1995) is in tandem with Canter and Canter's (1992) assumption that children want and need clear limits on their behaviour so that they know what they have to do to be successful. In addition, they have a right to encouragement when set standards are achieved.

A Police Youth Aid Officer remarked of the Awhina situation:

> Awhina most definitely makes a difference … with its organised and constructive activities. Without Awhina these young people would fall out of the system entirely.

A former student compared Awhina teachers and systems with his 'other' school:

> They were much more helpful to show you the right way to go, keep you on track five days a week and six hours a day. They understood you better than the teachers at your other school.

These revelations may depict a regimented organisation. Such considerations are contrary to the Hikairo philosophy. The above responses, and numerous others of similar vein, highlight the important differences in attitudes, values and behaviours that exist in different educational organisations. These differences affect the socialisation of children and their attitudes and responses towards teachers and schools.

The former student's response suggests an appreciation of having been given directions within certain limits. The Youth Aid Officer implied that organised and constructive activities were instrumental in making a difference. The Hikairo Rationale proposes a classroom discipline plan designed for all students. The plan can be modified for individuals whose behaviour is not improving under the class-wide plan (Porter, 1996). This approach proposes that the general rules and guidelines are explained to the child with behaviour difficulties before that child becomes a member of the class. Preferably, this task is carried out in the presence of a whanau member, guidance counsellor and significant other(s) such as a special education adviser, psychologist or social worker. This is a key hui (meeting) and the key issue here is sincerity. The opportunity to combine assertiveness with sincerity presents itself on a plate in such a forum as many of the components of assertive behaviour (gesture, facial expression, voice tone, inflection, volume, listening, and content) can all be brought into play. Williams (1985) sees Ihi as a synonym for mana but Marsden gives it a more restricted definition as 'vital force or personal magnetism which, radiating from a person, elicits in the beholder a response of awe and respect' (Marsden, 1975, p.193). According to Marsden, Ihi is an intrinsic quality in human beings, a personal essence which can be more highly developed in some than others. Tate (1990) takes it a step further by declaring that mana is not just charisma but a force that brings about change. Mana can move people. The teacher who has mana or Ihi qualities is far more likely to succeed in enforcing the limits, monitoring the classroom and maintaining sound relationships with youngsters.

Step Three – Kotahitanga (unity)

James Ritchie defines Kotahitanga as 'the Māori political process where consensus is achieved through discussion. By this people are brought together, all personal differences and opinions are aired and, even if they cannot all be incorporated in the final decision, given respect' (Ritchie, 1992, p.57).

Kotahi te kohao o	The needle has one eye
Te ngira e kuhuna ai	But it can be threaded with
Te miro whero	Red cotton
Te miro ma	White cotton
Te miro pango	Black cotton

(Tawhiao, 1858)

New Zealand as a nation is founded on the Treaty of Waitangi, an agreement between two peoples with very different cultures and social systems. Joan Metge (1990) contends that despite strong majority pressure, the Māori people and most other minorities have maintained a sense of cultural identity. While this presents a challenge to all New Zealanders, it has significant bearing on educators. Since Māori children are disproportionately represented as 'behaviour difficulty' referrals, the challenge impacts on special educators in a more pressing fashion.

Until recently, the educational institutions in this country have been grounded almost entirely in the culture of the Pakeha majority where members of the minority groups were expected to know about and go about two cultures, their own and that of the dominant majority. Metge (1990) claims that members of the majority group are typically monocultural, knowing little about the cultures of minority groups, even the Māori. The ultimate challenge to teachers of children with emotional and behavioural difficulties is to strive for *bicultural competence*. The bicultural part of the equation refers to the acquisition of the norms, attitudes, and behaviour patterns of their own and another, or perhaps several other, ethnic groups. Competence refers to the ability to function in two different cultures by switching between two sets of values and attitudes (Phinney & Rotheram, 1987). While it would be too much to ask teachers to achieve bicultural competence, it would be reasonable to ask them to strive for it, for in doing so they may become more appreciative of the indigenous minority and their ways. This means putting the onus on teachers to learn more about things Māori; to explore some of the Māori concepts which could ultimately be some of their most powerful resources in their interactions with difficult children.

Cathcart (1994) lists sixteen superb suggestions for linking the culture of home and school. Among them are using minority culture stories, legends and poetry as the basis for work in language, art and social studies, using the art of the minority culture as a creative stimuli in craft development and appreciation, finding out about the culture's science, health, and natural history, and incorporating these into lessons. At Awhina High School regular units of study were centred on Mokoia Island (history), Mount Tarawera (history, art), The Lakes and The Sea (science) and a three-day marae live-in experience was offered twice a year. The Awhina study revealed that the majority of children with behaviour difficulties had limited knowledge of their culture and ethnicity. Some of these children were 'real hard core', whose antics intimidated their mainstream teachers in the most severe fashion. These same children, however, were capable of developing a spiritual (wairuatanga) attachment to the marae and their behaviour in that environment was impeccable. Perhaps the secret is to transfer some of the marae values and practices, the greatest of which is respect for others and for the environment, to the classroom.

The metaphor for the coloured strands or threads of cotton provides a framework for the Special Education Service's policies and practices for services to Māori. Te miro pango refers to Māori professionals, where possible, working among Māori children. The red thread, te miro whero, refers to the regular centres and programmes which make provision for the support and development of Māori in their operation. Te miro ma, the white thread, encourages Pakeha to seek understanding and awareness of Māori children and their families with special needs (Kana & Harawira, 1995).

Step Four – Awhinatia, the helping process (interventions)

A study carried out in Britain revealed that the behaviour of working class boys is more likely to be found unacceptable in school institutions, and that of working class Afro-Caribbean boys the most unacceptable of all (McNamara & Moreton, 1995). Is there a parallel in the New Zealand situation? Do some teachers see a connection between ethnicity and aggression? Why is it that consistently, over the years, approximately ninety percent of referrals made to Awhina High School have been Māori students? Why, also, are the statistics at other centres for children with behaviour difficulties similar? These questions provide the incentive to consider interventions of a bicultural kind.

Home background and social class are often offered as the explanation for difficult behaviour and as a result a child may be labelled 'deviant'. Galloway and Goodwin (1987) strongly argue that since not everyone from low socio-economic backgrounds has emotional and behavioural difficulties, the two factors cannot be inextricably linked. Even if many deviant children do come from disfunctional homes, or Māori homes, that is not an excuse for difficult behaviour. But there are other factors, some of which are listed below.

Teacher Attitude: The teacher must reach out to the students, respect them, embrace their culture and examine the reality of the situation. Children have their own sets of beliefs which do not necessarily match those of the teacher. If these discrepancies exist then a bridge must be built to inter-connect the paradigms of the teacher and the student.

Classroom Climate: Arguments are emerging which support the notion that children with behaviour difficulties need structure and organisation, self-esteem, and a belief in their abilities to learn (Pierce, 1994). The Pierce study cited Mary Morgan's classroom of at-risk students in the south eastern United States. The classroom ambience, developed through the behaviours and interactions of the teacher, was one in which the threat of failure was diminished. According to Pierce the climate in Mrs Morgan's class had three identifiable components: a classroom *organisation* based on correct standards of behaviour and a sensitivity towards others, a teacher *supportive* of the students, and a teacher who *showed enthusiasm to the students*. In other words, each child was valued.

Teach the Rules: Rules need to be explained so that the students understand them and the reasons for them. They need to be specific.

Devise a Plan: This is necessary when dealing with hostile-aggressive behaviour, and should include a contingency plan, possibly involving another staff member, and the steps involved if the removal of an individual from the classroom becomes necessary.

Secret Signals: These clever cues can be arranged collectively as a class, or individually and confidentially. Here are some examples:

• Student is slipping – tap on the right shoulder by the teacher. This action might be enough to quell a simmering situation. If need be, teacher could add the utterance 'kia tupato'.
• Student is losing control – teacher makes eye contact and holds manaia below the chin while looking at the student. This cue reminds the student that, like the manaia, people are taonga, and there is an acceptable level of behaviour expected at certain times.
• Student is deviating – simply say, 'whakatikanga tou waka'. That is the signal by the teacher to bring the canoe back on course.

Kaupapa or Theme: Having a central theme should be a regular, weekly event. The strength of this strategy is that it can focus and re-focus the students on a particular behaviour which requires application. The kaupapa is best serviced when the selection is made by the students themselves. The kaupapa should be on the wall, highly visible, and written in both English and Māori.

Key Words: A system of key words needs to be devised in a code that only the student and the teacher understand. When the teacher mentions any of the Māori departmental gods (except one), that is a signal that the student is having a good day. However, if the teacher mentions the atua Ruaumoko, the student immediately understands that he or she is on shaky ground. Ruaumoko is the god of earthquakes.

Self-esteem: Most teachers will recognise the fact that children with emotional and behavioural difficulties feel badly about themselves. It has been demonstrated through research that these children have low self-esteem (Lund, 1988; Macfarlane, 1995). Teachers can help children, even those with very negative feedback at home, to change their view of themselves and subsequently to change their behaviour. Classrooms where information about the way we think others see us is shared, and becomes part of the curriculum, are ones where self-esteem can be changed through positive feedback (McNamara & Moreton, 1995).

Self-esteem Māori: In general, people whose lives subject them to many and severe frustrations, are more likely to feel hostile and deprived (Ritchie & Ritchie, 1993). These feelings may either lead to violent outbursts or be reflected inwards to produce feelings of worthlessness and depression. Institutions such as family and school have been known to apply sanctions which play no small role in shaping the behaviour of Māori children. Often frustrated, the child says, in effect, 'I am bad, I am Māori, Māori is bad' and the Pakeha world confirms this later on (Ritchie, 1963, p.183). This study by Ritchie was undertaken three decades ago and education has undergone major changes since then, but the stigma lives on, particularly in the hearts and minds of Māori children who are at risk of educational failure.

New Zealand classrooms, therefore, must project the right amount and type of feedback that will influence the pupils' cultural image and self-esteem. The way Māori youngsters feel about themselves affects their ability to form social relationships with their teachers and their peers. Māori role models should be regularly invited to talk to and share experiences with the children. They should be encouraged to experience the Māori arts in a Māori realm so that they will come to know their Māori heritage, and to like it. It does not matter if the teacher is non-Māori. What matters is the provision of meaningful experiences to enhance the students' self-worth. A commitment to bicultural perspectives leads to reduced frustration where the child says, in effect, 'I am alright, I am Māori, Māori is alright.' At the time of the Macfarlane (1995) study, the colloquial expression for alright was, 'tumeke'. As one boy declared when he had mastered the art of the taiaha, 'Tumeke, bro!'

Step Five – I Runga I Te Manaaki (pastoral care)

Smith (1996) contends that in Britain, it is ironic that at the same time as a growing demand for policies which promote inclusive education is emerging, there has been a rapid growth in the number of pupils excluded from schools because of behaviour problems. In New Zealand the trend is similar.

The Government, for its part, has recognised that truancy, including non-enrolment, is a serious concern, and in its 1995–1996 Budget provided six million dollars over three years for truancy programmes. According to Milbank (1996) the Ministry of Education is aware that truancy is often a symptom of underlying psychological, health, social, family or educational problems. While truancy is one way of 'acting out' their problems, other means include juvenile crime, graffiti, violence to others and themselves, and drug use.

The Ministry of Education Truancy Project has a three-tiered level of action. At the first level the schools are funded to monitor student attendance and to follow up on absences. The District Truancy Services operate as a backup to schools' work, and this level of action is funded jointly by the Ministry of Education and the schools, with some community input. At the national level, the Ministry of Education funds and provides a Non-Enrolment Truancy Service (NETS) which aims to find 'lost' students, and return them to schooling, or another legal alternative.

As anticipated, NETS is beginning to encounter young people who have been excluded from schools, and the schools are not keen to take them back. Difficult young people, it seems, are not wanted by schools, despite the fact that schools are meant to be inclusive, and should provide education for all young people from six to sixteen (Milbank, 1996).

Schools suspend students, or push them out, or students leave because they will not accept a school's rules. All over the country, Alternative Learning Centres (ALCs) are springing up to try to provide some sort of education or training for difficult or disenchanted young people. Many of these ALCs attract a large number of Māori students, and they tend to adopt a philosophy based on Māori concepts and values.

In Tokoroa, the secondary schools have pooled their resources to set up an Alternative Learning Centre which is earning a fine reputation as an effective unit, one that is 'making a difference' for these children. Most of the referrals are Polynesian, the staff has a multi-cultural blend to it, and provision is made, on-site, for the presence of a kaumatua (elder). The mana of kaumatua is a formative strategy in dealing with difficult Māori children. Theirs is a commanding role, in a quiet, reassuring way. Te Runanga o Ngati Pikiao is a proactive iwi (tribe) of the Te Arawa Confederation of Tribes of the Rotorua Lakes District. In December 1996, this iwi established a centre called Hei Manaaki Rangatahi (Looking after our Children). This unit has developed its programme without financial or personnel assistance from local schools. Instead, it relies on the concept of manaakitanga to revive cultural identity and self-esteem in these young people; that is, it is run by Māori, for Māori and non-Māori.

In the event of serious violations of school rules, it is not uncommon for a school to impose the ultimate punishment of suspension or expulsion, thus marginalising the student. Much of the literature on at-risk, marginalised youth suggests that alternative schools can be an effective and efficient way of meeting the needs of these students. Piecemeal programmes simply do not work. The research carried out by Wehlage, Rutter, Smith, Lesko and Fernandez (1989), led them to conclude that in order to succeed with difficult students, alternative centres need to be communities of support. Such

communities are those with which students want to be affiliated and where
they are truly educationally engaged.

The following responses from one student in the Macfarlane (1995) study
reflect the general consensus of the responses from the former students.

On staff at Awhina High School:

> *Always supporting, caring, understanding. Not once did they turn away when I needed help.*
> *Full of aroha for everyone.*

On staff at their previous (referring) school:

> *Too much people to take care of. Didn't take any notice of kids that really needed help…*

On programmes at Awhina High School:

> *Helped me more than any other school I went to. I could understand things properly because it*
> *was more straightforward than any other teachings I've had.*

ALCs, and regular classrooms, must make personal connections. Acceptance
and caring provide a secure and nurturing environment for young people who
may have been quite broken, emotionally, in their lives. The students are
supported to draw on their own resources in order to make choices and accept
responsibility. They need to derive and taste success from their academic,
cultural and sporting experiences as these successes can contribute to their
sense of self-worth and to their sense that they are valuable members of the
school community (Cagne, 1996).

If an analogy can be drawn to what Tate (1990) refers to as violations of tapu,
then deviations in behaviour demands to be addressed through tika, pono, and
aroha – essential tonics in the healing, caring process. Tika refers to justice,
pono to integrity, and aroha to love. These students may not manifest these
qualities as well as most. They are qualities which may have been suppressed
and mangled by experiences of trauma and failure. Hence, they need to be
nurtured, and have models provided by the adults around them.

Step Six – Raranga (the weaving process)

The emergence of respect and consideration from the Manaakitanga section
would have emphasised a shared ownership of the situation. The student, the
teacher and the whanau each have responsibilities to implement and monitor
the strategies put in place to assist the developmental process. For the special
learner, this requires a plan.

The Individualised Education Plan (IEP) is the principal method of
identifying educational needs and planning for students with special learning
needs. The practice is now twenty years old and still, supposedly, in vogue.

The IEP meeting is likely to attract a number of people – practitioners, professionals, family members – who are able to contribute to the development of the plan. For some Māori people the sheer title of the process, Individual Education Plan, can be an awesome encounter. Māori people have retained their Māoritanga and expressed it most vividly through the *hui*. Hui is a general term in Māori for any kind of meeting, usually, but not always, on a marae (Salmond, 1976). It would be advisable, in some instances, to refer to the IEP as 'a hui to discuss the individual's education'.

The Hikairo Rationale encourages diverse and multiple participation at the hui. Māori families work on the principle of inclusive families whereby siblings, uncles and aunts, and grandparents play a role in whanau (family) discussions. Fraser claims that 'that involvement of the whanau can aid the partnership process so that decisions which are collaborated receive maximum consideration from a variety of perspectives' (Fraser, 1995). Some IEP hui have been known to have in excess of twenty people in attendance. While numbers and venues can usually be determined beforehand, it is essential that school staff familiarise themselves with the protocol for the hui, as the proper rituals have a bearing on the mood and level of effectiveness of the meeting.

The hui may be held in the classroom, at the whanau home, or on a local marae. Many secondary schools now have a *marae* and this is an admirable option. While the business of the meeting may be preceded by *karakia* (prayer) and mihimihi (greetings), the deliberations that follow are usually controlled in a more contemporary style, more of the quality of a European meeting. Because Māori people love to laugh, humour can be injected into the discussions. The IEP need not be a sombre affair; rather, it is a celebration to mark the new directions of an individual. In that context, Ginnot (1972) advises that what the teacher tells the parent about the child touches on deep feelings and hidden fantasies. A concerned teacher is aware of the impact of words and will consciously avoid comments that may kill dreams.

Refreshments should be offered after the hui, which is also the opportunity for informal conversation. The student, who has been the centre of attention of the hui, should be included in this small festivity, which is still part of the communal gathering.

The raranga concept, through the IEP hui process, is an essential tool in weaving and strengthening the pattern of the student's behaviour. Reviews need to occur from time-to-time in order to consider the progress in the interim periods. Unsatisfactory progress means that the plan should be revised and the strategies examined. Good progress must be acknowledged by specifying exactly what the student has achieved. Excellent progress is not the domain solely of the gifted student. It is quite in order, therefore, to send a letter of commendation to the whanau of the student with behavioural difficulties. This is a powerful instrument for self-esteem enhancement. As Tate (1990, p.90) contends, 'by continually striving to act with tika, pono, and aroha in day-to-day life, tapu flourishes and mana radiates outward like the ripples of a stone dropped into a pond'.

Step Seven – Oranga (a vision of well-being)

Tungia te ururua	Clear away the undergrowth
Kia tupu whakaritorito	So that new shoots
Te tapu o te harakeke	May emerge

(Henare, D., Comer, L. & Thompson, M., 1991).

The matter of student aggression in schools is as much a health issue as a social issue. Glasser (1975) is in tandem with Māori psychology when he states that a person gains strength by progressing along four success pathways: giving and receiving love; achieving a sense of worth in one's own eyes and in the eyes of others; having fun; and becoming self-disciplined. Failure to proceed along these pathways drains a person's mana (power, authority, prestige). This drainage takes its toll through the individual making irrational choices and ending up in difficulties. Teacher and whanau cannot preach the Oranga philosophy unless they practise it, and understand it.

Understanding Māori development involves considerations of their holistic view of the world. This world view is bound up in history and cosmology which are used to form a picture of 'the way things are'. Māori people do not see the sacred and secular as separated but as parts of the whole. James Irwin (1984, p.6) states that 'Europeans may still tend to see human beings as made up of body, mind and spirit as though these are separate entities which could be dealt with separately'. Irwin illustrates the Māori holistic view by relating these entities as interlinked, like the sides of a triangle, as follows:

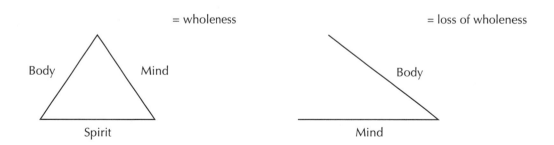

Durie (1994) employs a similar concept when proposing the Whare Tapa Wha model based on the four walls of a house. Each wall is necessary to ensure strength and balance and each represents a complementary dimension of well-being.

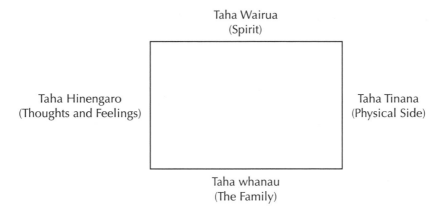

Taha Wairua
(Spirit)

Taha Hinengaro
(Thoughts and Feelings)

Taha Tinana
(Physical Side)

Taha whanau
(The Family)

The addition of whanau to the Irwin model has significant implications in the realm of special education.

If it is difficult to identify the problems affecting a child with behaviour difficulties, teachers are encouraged to take opportunities to know the child better. Sometimes, this involves a better understanding of the cultural background of the child. In dealing with these problems, the teacher may face the added difficulty that Māori children often need special consideration. The Hikairo Rationale proposes that it is not only the children who need special consideration, but their ethnicity also.

Children's ethnic socialisation develops in terms of many levels including the immediate family, the school, the community, and the entire culture (Bronfenbrenner, 1979). Phiruney and Rotheram (1987) consider that there are important differences in attitudes, values, and behaviours which distinguish ethnic groups. Seeking a better understanding of Māoritanga, therefore, is an important challenge facing special educators in Aotearoa New Zealand.

Conclusion

From the time schooling emerged in this country, there have been homogenising functions. Cultural differences have been difficult for educators to handle and accept because they are so values-laden. Majority groups have tended to reject or devalue any cultural style that is not in tandem with their own. The Hikairo Rationale proposes the celebration of diversity by the consideration of some of the cultural values of Māori. In an educational sector where a large number of students are Māori, the role of cultural appreciation enhances the understanding and intervention methods to change the behaviour of the students being served in the programmes. The Rationale does not address the historical influences on that group, such as colonisation and subjugation. Nor does it capitalise on the notions of today's circumstances in Aotearoa being shaped by the events of yesterday (Temm, 1990). Rather, the Hikairo programme offers a series of bicultural strategies and considerations which attempts a synthesis of the integrity of traditional values and some contemporary behavioural principles.

In the Hikairo Rationale a positive attitude from teachers towards emotionally and behaviourally disturbed students is vital if they are to support their pupils in their attempts to change their behaviour. McNamara and Moreton (1995, p.17) add that 'it would be helpful if all teachers could move to an attitudinal position where they can see that some difficulties are caused by school norms and expectations which do not fit with social class and ethnic group behavioural norms'.

Prevention of classroom behaviour problems rests on establishing and maintaining order. A good curriculum backed up by lesson design, good feedback, and incentives for effort are elements that will maintain order (Canter & Canter, 1992). However, it is the teacher's mana that will establish that order in the first place. The point here is that effective special education practitioners express themselves and their work as art. According to Eisner (1994), their qualities of speech, gesture, movement and timing are part of their routine. The complete artist, however, would add cultural competency to the repertoire.

The Hikairo model has adopted a range of approaches in an eclectic manner. It is designed to generate hope in teachers, students and whanau and it embraces the rights of all individuals. The model is a humble one which realises that dazzling success is not easy to achieve in the realm of emotional and behavioural difficulties in the classroom. Sometimes youngsters get hoha (fed up) with being good and the problems will recur. Even Hongi Hika's fighting instincts resurfaced from time-to-time, the ultimate proof, perhaps, that there are no guarantees in behaviour management. However, with passion and persistence, the probabilities of making a difference will improve. It should be remembered that it was Hikairo's assertive, no-nonsense, sincere approach which convinced the Ngapuhi tribe against further aggression. Little wonder that in the Apumoana-o-te-ao-Hou meeting house, Hikairo has a place of prominence.

Nau te rourou	With your food basket
Naku te rourou	And my food basket
Ka ora te iwi	There will be ample
Let each contribute	

Glossary of words not translated in the text

aroha	love, acceptance	mihimihi	greetings
atua	god	rangatahi	youth

awhina	help, support	Ruaumoko	god of earthquakes
hoha	frustration	taiaha	long club
kia tupato	be careful	taonga	treasure
kaikorero	speaker, orator	te ao hurihuri	the modern world
karakia	prayer, incantation	tikanga	customs
kaumatua	elder	wanaga	learning
manaia	bird-like carved figure	whakapuaki	assert
mau-taiaha	art of weaponry	whanau	family
		whanaunga	relation

References

Alberti, R. & Emmons, M. (1986). *Your Perfect Right: A Guide to Assertive Living*. California: Impact Publishers.

Bronfenbrenner, U. (1979). *The Ecology of Human Development*. Milton Keynes: Open University Press.

Burgess, B. (1992). *Referring At Risk Students to Activity Centres*. Unpublished Master's Dissertation: Massey University.

Cagne, A. (1996). Success at Contact: The Argument for Alternative Schools for At-risk Youth. *The Alberta Journal of Educational Research*, XLII, 3, pp. 306–324.

Canter, L. & Canter, M. (1992). *Assertive Discipline: Positive Behaviour Management for Today's Classroom*.: Santa Monica: Lee Canter and Associates.

Cathcart, R. (1994). *They're Not Bringing My Brain Out*. Auckland: Reach Publications.

Durie, M. (1994). *Whaiora: Māori Health Development*. Auckland: Oxford University Press.

Eisner, E. (1994). *The Educational Imagination: On the Design and Evaluation of School Programmes* (3rd Ed.). New York: Macmillan College Publishing Company.

Fraser, D., Moltzen, R. & Ryba, K. (Eds), (1995). *Learners With Special Needs in Aotearoa/New Zealand*. Palmerston North: Dunmore Press.

Fraser, D. (1995). Students With Behavioural Difficulties. In D. Fraser, R. Moltzen & K. Ryba (Eds.), *Learners With Special Needs in Aotearoa/New Zealand* (pp.229–266). Palmerston North: Dunmore Press.

Galloway, D. & Goodwin, C. (1987). *The Education of Disturbing Children: Pupils With Learning and Adjustment Difficulties*. Harlow: Longman.

Ginnot, H. (1972). *Teacher and Child*. New York: Macmillan.

Glasser, W. (1975). *Reality Therapy: An Approach to Psychiatry*. New York: Harper and Row.

Henare, D., Comer, L. & Thompson, M. (1991). In *Ka Awatea: A Report of the Ministerial Planning Group*. Wellington: Ministry of Māori Development.

Irwin, J. (1984). *An Introduction to Māori Religion*. Flinders University, Australia: University Relations Unit.

Kana, P. & Harawira, W. (1995). Special Education Service (SES) Policies and Practices: Services to Tangata Whenua. In D. Fraser, R. Moltzen & K. Ryba (Eds), *Learners With Special Needs in Aotearoa/ New Zealand* (pp.33–49). Palmerston North: Dunmore Press.

Lund, R. (1988). The Self-Esteem of Children With Emotional and Behavioural Difficulties, *Maladjustment and Therapeutic Education*, 5, (1).

Macfarlane, A. (1995). *Constructing Values Education Programmes in a Centre for Special Learners: A Collective Responsibility. Me Whakaputaina te Turanga, Tena Pea Ka Tika*. Unpublished Master's Dissertation, University of Waikato, Hamilton.

Marsden, M. (1975). God, Man and Universe: A Māori View. In M. Kings (Ed.), *Te Ao Hurihuri* (pp.117–137). Auckland: Reed.

McElrea, F. (1994). The Intent of the Children and Young Persons' and Their Families Act – Restorative Justice. *Youth Law Review* (pp.4–9). Auckland: Youth Law Project Inc.

McNamara, S. & Moreton, G. (1995). *Changing Behaviour: Teaching Children with Emotional and Behavioural Difficulties in Primary and Secondary Classrooms*. London: David Fulton.

Metge, J. (1990). *Te Kohao o Te Ngira: Culture and Learning*. Wellington: Learning Media.

Milbank, G. (1996). *Providing Learning Opportunities for Young People*. Unpublished Explanatory Paper, Ministry of Education, Wellington.

Ngata, H. (1993). *English-Māori Dictionary*. Wellington: Learning Media.

Phinney, J. & Rotheram, M. (1987). *Children's Ethnic Socialization: Pluralism and Development*. Newbury Park: Sage Publications.

Pierce, C. (1994). The Importance of Classroom Climate For At-Risk Learners. New Zealand Council for Educational Research. *Set Special, Item 10*.

Porter, L. (1996). *Student Behaviour. Theory and Practice for Teachers*. Sydney: Allen and Unwin.

Ritchie, J. (1963). *The Making of a Māori*. Wellington: Reed.

Ritchie, J. (1992). *Becoming Bicultural*. Wellington: Huia Publishers.

Ritchie, James & Ritchie, Jane (1993). *Violence in New Zealand*. Wellington: Huia Publishers.

Rogers, W. (1989). *Making a Discipline Plan: Developing Classroom Management Skills*. Melbourne: Nelson.

Rogers, W. (1990). *You Know the Fair Rule*. Melbourne: ACER.

Salmond, A. (1976). *Huia: A Study of Māori Ceremonial Gatherings*. Wellington: Reed.

Smith, C. (1996). Special Needs and Pastoral Care: Bridging the Gap That Shouldn't be There. *British Journal of Learning Support*, 11, 151–156.

Stafford, D. (1967). *Te Arawa*. Wellington: Reed.

Tate, H. (1990). The Unseen World. *New Zealand Geographic*, 5, 87–92.

Temm, P. (1990). *The Waitangi Tribunal: the Consequence of the Nation*. Auckland: Random Century.

Walker, J. & Shea, T. (1995). *Behaviour Modification: A Practical Approach for Educators* (6th Ed.). New Jersey: Mosby: Prentice Hall.

Wehlage, G., Rutter, R., Smith, G., Lesko, N., & Fernandez, R. (1989). *Reducing the Risk: Schools as Communities of Support*. Philadelphia: Falmer.

Williams, H. (1985). *A Dictionary of the Māori Language* (7th Ed.). Wellington: Government Printing Office.

Young, M. (1992). *Counseling Methods and Techniques: An Eclectic Approach*. New York: Merrill.

Chapter 8

'One size fits few'[1]: a case study of a school that has defied the constraints of a European education system for Polynesian students

Mollie Neville-Tisdall and Ann Milne

Introduction

This chapter traces the struggle of one low socio-economic New Zealand school to change the inherent institutionalised racism in the education system. The school has faced powerful opposition from Ministry of Education officials as well as principals in neighbouring schools towards its passion to change the structure and content of schooling to meet the needs of its students. Every student in the school, Clover Park Middle School in South Auckland, is from a so-called 'minority' including the indigenous people of New Zealand, the Māori.

Internationally, racism in education is a topic on which many educators are silent in public, and stereotypical in their reactions in private (Pollock, 2001). There is an international sense of inevitability and hopelessness in regard to the achievement of minority students, which is perpetuating a lower class of people of colour (Pollock, 2001). The result is that there have been generations of young people alienated from schools that do not respect their cultures or

---

[1] Ohanian, S. (1999) *One Size Fits Few*. Portsmouth, NH: Heinemann.

treat them and their 'cultural baggage' with dignity. No country can afford to continue to create a disaffected sub-class that has little decision-making power for or ownership of their future.

Most Western countries have spent large sums of money on special programmes for and research on minority students, such as those programmes that proliferate in South Auckland in New Zealand. However, the contention of this chapter is that the education system is treating the serious problem of underachievement among Polynesian students with traditional Eurocentric, patriarchal solutions (Bishop, 1999; Johnston, 1992, 1999; Smith, 1999; Mead, 1997; Rykis, 1999; Walker, 1991; Webber, 1996).

Needless to say, the leaders of 'deficit' programmes for low-decile schools are predominantly European – the Polynesian parents and school staff in one school nickname them 'Beads and Blankets' taken from the jargon of colonial times. This is not to say of course that the leaders of these programmes and the researchers (who are predominantly European) are racist, rather that as Bohn and Sleeter (2000:158) believe:

> It is not because the teachers don't care about the students, but because we all base our interpretations of the world on our life experience
>
> (Bohn and Sleeter, 2000:158)

It is significant that Cummins (2001a:650) in his introduction to the republication of his 1986 paper 'Empowering Minority Students, a Framework for Intervention' in the *Harvard Educational Review* notes there is no improvement in the education of the disadvantaged since he first published his paper fifteen years before:

> There is a deep antipathy to acknowledging that schools tend to reflect the power structure of the society and that these power relations are directly relevant educational outcomes
>
> (Cummins, 2001a:650)

There is an irony, as Johnston and Viadero (2000, cited in Pollock, 2001:10) point out, that we should not focus on the gap between minority and middle class white students; however, he adds, '**unless people act to reduce it**.' The purpose of this chapter is to take a case study of one school in South Auckland, New Zealand that is reducing the gap.

Background

The emphasis of this research is on the Māori ownership of education for their community. However, Clover Park has the same emphasis for all cultures within the school.

Although statistical data for Māori achievement in New Zealand certainly does not tell the full story there would seem to be little cause for complacency and congratulations about the educational realities for Maori in recently released Ministry data:

Table 8.1 Māori involvement in education, July 2000

Percentage of all students enrolled at a school in New Zealand who are Māori	20.1
Percentage of these students who were involved in Māori medium education[2]	18.0
Percentage of these students who were involved in Kura Kaupapa Māori[3]	3.3

Therefore 96.7 percent of all Maori students are educated in mainstream schools. Although Māori make up only 20.1 percent of all the students in our schools, the following statistics show the disproportionate number of Māori students for whom the system is not working:

Table 8.2 Alienation of Māori students 1999/2000

Percentage of all stand-downs and suspensions in 2000	41
Percentage of those students who left school with no formal qualifications in 1999	36
Percentage of all students who dropped out of school in Year 9 in 1999	33.8
Percentage of all students who dropped out of school in Year 10 in 1999.	38.7

(Source: Ministry of Education. *Education Statistics of New Zealand for 2000*)

Clearly there is a need for a different approach to improving outcomes for Māori in our education system. Unfortunately most interventions and initiatives 'focus on norms set by the majority', which 'retain the focus of policy solutions within Eurocentric views and philosophies', and 'continue down the cul-de-sac of deficit theorising' (Bishop & Glynn, 1999).

Johnston (1999) calls these attitudes by Pakeha educators 'Māori-friendly' and notes that there needs to be instead a 'Māori-centred' approach. She points out that Non-Europeans are participating in policy developments 'but only within boundaries influenced and controlled by "Māori-friendly" rules'. Therefore Māori, Polynesians and Asians become marginalised by the mainstream. In other words they have a 'friendly' European system to work within but have no ownership. Johnston suggests that this emphasis on a supportive and non-hostile environment controlled by the Europeans remains

[2] Defined as using Māori as the medium for instruction for more than 12 percent of the time – a minimum of 3 hours per week.
[3] Total immersion Māori language schools set up initially by parents who were concerned that their children's knowledge and use of Māori language and competency in the culture would be lost if they went to an English-medium school. At the time of writing there were 59 Kaupapa Māori nationally.

European as they are effectively able to control the level and manner of Māori involvement. In contrast she suggests that a Māori-centred approach places Māori at the centre – 'it recognises structural and political considerations'. She further suggests that this aims at addressing unequal power relations with inadequate decision-making forums for Māori. A recent government publication for schools, *Better Relationships for Better Learning* (2000), encourages principals and staff to better their relationships with Māori parents by being *'whanau* friendly' – a term regarded as patronising by many Māori.

In conjunction with other leading Māori scholars, Tapine and Waiti (1997:74) write:

> The crisis for Māori is that while there has been a perceived rise in overall educational achievement, levels for Māori have remained unchanged.

Leading Pacific scholars (Paskale and Yaw, 1998) make similar statements about their children's education and opportunities. The result in New Zealand has been that many Maori have withdrawn from the state system:

> into either schools whose philosophies are Māori and supportive, or the Māori initiated Kohanga Reo and Kura Kaupapa Māori schools
>
> (Johnston, 1992:17)

However, 96.7 percent of Māori, who have no access to Māori immersion schools, are still educated in mainstream schools and the purpose of this study is to show how a mainstream school has given ownership of education to the Polynesian community.

New Zealand literature

The research voices used here are predominantly those of Māori and Pacific writers – it is their narrative. As, for example, even today, women's research is largely absent from the international literature so Māori, Asian and Pacific voices are almost silent. Bryant (1998), in writing on Native American concepts of leadership, notes that the history of leadership in the academy is male and white and practices do not address the worldview of other cultures.

Māori and Pacific researchers write and have written within the traditional western paradigm but are now claiming ownership of a research paradigm of their own. Linda Smith, director of the International Research Institute for Māori and Indigenous Education at Auckland University, in her book *Decolonizing Methodologies: Research and Indigenous Peoples* (1999), sums up the attitude of Māori academics:

> It appals us that the West can desire, extract and claim ownership of our ways of knowing, our imagery, the things we create and produce, and then simultaneously

reject the people who created and developed those ideas and seek to deny
them further opportunities to be the creator in their own culture and own
nations

(1999:1)

As seen above, Johnston (1999) calls these attitudes 'Māori-friendly'. Johnston
suggests that this emphasis on a supportive and non-hostile environment
controlled by the Europeans remains European as they are effectively able to
control the level and manner of Māori involvement. She suggests that the aim
should be to address unequal power relations with inadequate decision-making
forums for Māori.

In a statement to the National Middle Schools Conference in 1999, Ann Milne
showed how these differing power relations affect minority students such as
Māori:

> In the third international study of Maths and Science, Māori students performed 26th
> out of 29 countries. Ninety percent of non-Māori students sit our national external
> examination at Year 11 but only 63% of Māori. Suspension rates are three times the
> rate for non-Māori

(Milne, 1999)

In their book, *Culture Counts* (1999, pp.53–4), Bishop and Glynn give a powerful
insight into the key issues for this power imbalance. In summary these are:

• the belief in cultural superiority which makes some feel inferior
• the ideology that 'we are all New Zealanders' and therefore the same and
  those who fail have some personal or cultural deficiency
• the denial of alternative world views
• the denial of the Treaty of Waitangi, which guaranteed Māori sovereignty
• the concentration of all knowledge, pedagogy and the process of
  legitimation of knowledge to one world view
• the perpetuation of minority status for ethnic groups, as change for
  minorities happens only with the support or the veto of the majority.

A strong condemnation of the attitude of many pakeha principals with high
proportions of Māori in their schools is made in a recent *New Zealand Education
Review* (Evans, 2001) and comes from the monitoring group for the Maori
teacher training course, Te Rangakura:

> the attitudes expressed by some principals to matters Māori, their scant attempt to
> pronounce Māori words and overt denigration of Te Rangakura.

(Evans, 2001:4)

The report further critiques the way that these principals complain about the
non-involvement of the Māori parents and community when 'just down the
road the monitoring group would find a school with real commitment to

providing an equal environment for Māori and Pakeha students and big Māori parent involvement'.

Perhaps the most apt and colourful quotation comes from Māori academic Bill Hamilton (1998), who says with some irony concerning the present situation in education for Māori, 'I am feeling optimistic because somewhere amongst the horse shit – there must be a pony'!

International literature

A survey of recent literature, in particular from the United States and Canada, led us to draw two conclusions: firstly, that the problems faced by minorities in other countries are similar to those in New Zealand. Secondly, there is considerable research that supports the changes made at Clover Park Middle School but in New Zealand the bureaucrats are reluctant to take the risk of allowing new policies or modifying the existing structures and systems.

Attribution of blame for failure of minority students

In her exhaustive report on her recent research, Pollock (2001:7) attributes failure of minority students not only to the obvious socio-economic problems but also to the 'racialized expectations' of educators. As she observed in her study, teachers talk about 'all students' achieving while quietly expecting racial patterns.

Cummins (2001a:650) notes that teachers explain failure in terms of family conditions, language and poverty rather than on negative expectations, inappropriate curriculum or inadequate teacher training. However, his findings from extensive research place the blame squarely with those in power who are reluctant to relinquish it and who ignore the research that makes recommendations for change. Driessen (2001:515) says that the one-sidedness of education forcing minorities to 'fit' the existing culture in effect contributes 'to an expansion of already existing differences'.

Like Māori and Pacific and other Afro-American academics, Schlesinger notes the prejudice against the use of home language in the school – a societal discourse that proclaims that 'bilingualism shuts doors' (Schlesinger, 1991:108 cited in Cummins 2001a:654). He asks, 'Do we truly want historically subordinated groups to develop active intelligence and imagination whose outcomes, by definition, cannot be predicted?' As we shall see, it is clear from the reaction of those administering education in New Zealand there is indeed a reluctance to 'take the risk' of developing active intelligence and imagination among Māori and Pacific students.

Methodology

This case study was conducted using naturalistic inquiry, which studies the
culture of an institution within its context over a period of time (Lincoln and
Guba, 1985). Naturalistic inquiry uses qualitative, ethnographic methodology.
This is carried out within the appreciative inquiry paradigm which, as Elliott
(1999) notes, is designed to help research participants to identify their own
achievements. This process can empower people who have always thought
themselves to be disadvantaged. The key data collection innovation of
appreciative inquiry is the collection of people's 'stories of something at its
best' (Bushe, 1998).

The difference between traditional approaches to organisational change and
Appreciative Inquiry can be seen in Table 8.3.

The research site: Clover Park Middle School

Clover Park Middle School is at the lowest decile[4] or socio-economic income
level in the country. Although it has had official status as a four-year (Years 7 to
10) middle school since 1995, the move to retain students longer than the
traditional two intermediate years began in the Māori bilingual unit in 1990.
This initiative was strongly driven by parents who sought continuity of the
language and learning environment developed in the school.

Early changes to the structure of the school addressed the need for students
to study in their home language and culture. This move gave rise to attacks
that this was a form of apartheid. The school was divided into four areas or
units that are multi-levelled, multi-aged and vertically grouped from years 7 to
10. Of the four areas one is rooted in Māori values, one in Samoan beliefs and
the other two are labelled 'general' but one takes in predominantly Tongan and
the other most of the Cook Island and Asian students. Students elect which

Table 8.3 Traditional Organisational Development (OD) Process versus Appreciative Inquiry

TRADITIONAL OD PROCESS	APPRECIATIVE INQUIRY
Define the problem	Search for solutions that already exist
Fix what's broken	Amplify what's working
Focus on decay	Focus on life-giving forces
What problem are you having?	What is working well around here?

(Hammond, 1998, p.2)

---

[4] New Zealand schools are ranked 1–10 on the basis of the socio-economic background of
the parents. Decile 1 is the lowest and decile 10 the highest.

area they will join. The whole purpose is one of cultural validation: to build self-confidence, self-esteem and a positive identity within students grossly disadvantaged within New Zealand society.

There is an integrated and holistic curriculum and an emphasis on the importance of adult–student interaction. Most importantly, home language and cultural practice (whanaungatanga) is the basis for administration, for assessment, pedagogy, and curriculum development and implementation.

Clover Park Middle School has received excellent reports from the Ministry of Education's audit office and received favourable attention from the media, for example, the programme *60 Minutes*. The school's role in helping the students to understand their own cultures and languages and hold their heads high has had a positive effect on student attitudes to learning.

Students are supported to extend their mother tongue as well as become proficient in English and great effort is expended to employ teachers and community members who are fluent in the students' languages. This is a remarkable shift from the endless English as a Second Language classes that most schools promote.

It was clear however from very early in the change process that simply changing the language of instruction was not enough and

> had little positive effect on the achievement outcomes or self-esteem of our Māori students and we were fairly sure this was because the school's overriding philosophy, organisation and structure still followed the monocultural norm
>
> (Milne, 2002: 44)

All respondents in the Clover Park questionnaires – which supplied the bulk of the data presented in this chapter – mentioned their passionate belief in the validation of each culture represented in the school. The school therefore functions as an extension of the home:

> Cultural validation underpins the values of our school. I have never heard blatantly disparaging remarks about our students in this school as I have at other schools – like 'so and so is "so thick", "dumber than dumb" ' – our students are genuinely treated as individuals whose backgrounds are respected
>
> (Neville-Tisdall, Milne and Treanor, 2000b)

New learning is 'built on students' prior experiences', and staff attempt 'to eliminate the "mismatch" between home & school and validating students' cultural beliefs and values in all aspects of school practice and programme'. They recognise that the poverty can create barriers but they 'do a huge number of things in the area of pastoral care, to "balance the books" '.

A key aspect of the school is the sense of genuine affection between staff, staff and students and within the student cohort. The whole culture in the school can be summed up by one of the staff, 'We are a *whanau* now – not many Islands competing for space'!

Te Poho: changes in 2001

Towards the end of 2000, Māori staff, Māori Board of Trustees' members and a core group of Māori parents prepared an application to Te Puni Kokiri[5] for 'capacity building' funding. This was funding made available by the government to help 'close the gaps' for Māori. Although this terminology later became unpopular and was withdrawn from use because of a public backlash, the funding continued and the school was successful in accessing it.

In the Otara, South Auckland community where Clover Park is situated, Māori make up 25 percent of the population. Unemployment is high, 27 percent of families are raised by a single parent and 38 percent of the community receive the unemployment benefit. Where whanau (family) support has broken down and families have become fragmented and dysfunctional it is extremely difficult to access extended whanau support for young people who are at risk of alienation from society. They become statistics in youth crime, health, for example, teenage parenting, youth suicide, and educational dropouts. The end result is a further erosion of capacity to participate in employment and to achieve economic independence.

The risk of alienation from education is particularly high at the emerging adolescent stage and therefore of prime importance to middle school students such as those at Clover Park.

The school has worked hard at providing a context that is relevant for Māori learners. In spite of these efforts Māori students are still at risk. There is unacceptably high condoned absence, and relatively few parents actively support their children educationally. The school has a marae complex (meeting place) which is utilised extensively by the community, but the school still feels it fails to break down the barriers that prevent many Māori parents from feeling comfortable in the school setting. The Māori students are consistently those most at risk of stand-downs and/or exclusion, although the school tries every other alternative before this option. Far greater numbers of Māori students seek or are referred for social work support and intervention and are involved in school disciplinary processes than all other ethnic groups.

While it would be easy to become disillusioned by this situation, it needs to be put into perspective in terms of the national disparities and the economic realities for Māori students. While the national statistics report a 'relatively slow' 1.5 percent rate of growth in the numbers of Māori enrolled in tertiary education in 1998, the real picture for Otara can be found in the report of the Auckland University taskforce for improving participation in tertiary education (Maani and Warner, 2000), which found a 43 percent drop in the number of students entering the university from low-decile schools in South Auckland.

---

[5] The Ministry of Māori Development

The aim of the project, named 'Te Poho',[6] was to build capacity in Māori parents to support students, and conversely, in the staff of the bilingual whanau and the school to support Māori parents and students. Māori staff expressed strongly that the key to social, emotional cultural and learning development of Māori students is the active involvement of both the community of Māori home whanau and school whanau working together with common understandings and goals.

This idea of *reciprocal* relationships is very different from the common school practice, which develops relationships with the community characterised by school needs and demands. Schools ask parents to help, expect them to attend school functions, support the school in ensuring their children follow the rules, behave in ways the school decides, complete school tasks and assignments and ensure they attend every day. How then can we expect dialogue and interaction with families to have a positive impact on young people when the Eurocentric 'rules of the game' are set by the school? Ghuman (1999) emphasises the importance of a two-way process in the development of identity for young adolescents from ethnic minorities:

> The development of coherent identity is likely to be facilitated only if there is a symbiotic relationship between home and school. On the other hand, if young people receive conflicting messages from these institutions and diverse emotional and social demands and commitments are expected, they are likely to be confused in their identity.
>
> (Ghuman, 1999, cited in Ghuman (2002) *http://users.aber.ac.uk/org/pasgch01.html* accessed on 16.03.04)

The concept of symbiotic and reciprocal relationships carries an expectation that this interaction will be *mutually advantageous*. Te Poho was designed to facilitate that process.

In the initial scoping of the project with Māori staff in February 2001 the need to change significantly the basic philosophy of how to interact with parents was a major debate. There was general agreement with the aims of the project that included:

- to establish a forum for ongoing discussion with Māori parents about educational, developmental, social growth of young Māori adolescents
- to provide the school marae as the central location for interaction between Māori parents and school
- to establish and maintain regular contact through home visits, bringing Māori parents into school
- to identify the additional risk factors for specific Māori students and families, e.g. attendance

---

[6] Te Poho was a taniwha of the local Ngai Tai people, who nurtured and fed the people.

- to establish authentic consultation processes that are relevant to Maori whanau
- to break down barriers between Māori whanau and school
- to raise achievement levels of Māori students through ongoing support and active involvement with parents and extended whanau
- to coordinate all interactions and interventions concerning Māori students.

The raising of achievement levels was deliberately placed lower in the list because it was felt that other conditions had to be strengthened first in order to impact on student learning. The question was how could the school do that? At the beginning of the process, Māori staff, key parents and Māori Board of Trustees' members held 'live-ins' on the marae and several hui[7] to encourage thorough reflection and debate. For the Te Poho participants Appreciative Inquiry drove their approach to dialogue with parents. Working from a perspective that valued parents' views and promised to act on these was very different from the deficit assumptions most Māori parents experience. The Project Co-ordinator and a small group of helpers who were past-pupils in the bilingual whanau visited every home of the 83 pupils. They asked the following questions:

1 Name three positive things that have happened in your child's time in Te Whanau o Tupuranga?
2 Name three things you would like to see change about your child's education?
3 What system of communication with a school has worked best for you?
4 How can we improve the ways we communicate with your whanau?
5 Tell us about an activity in your child's education, that **you** have participated in as a parent, that **you** have enjoyed the most.
6 What services that the school provides have been most useful to you as a parent?
7 What improvements or other services would you like to see?

Parents spoke powerfully about their preferences and aspirations. Why should we be surprised to learn that 'one size does not fit all'? Some parents, for example, wanted written, posted communication. Some could rely on their children to bring home newsletters. Others preferred to speak face to face. Why could we not accommodate those preferences?

Responses included:

---

[7] Meetings

Three positive things that have happened in your child's time in Te Whanau o Tupuranga?

My son, Simon, drew a cool picture describing his older brother, Joshua, going fishing, showing the clouds, the sea and the fish. Everything about it was Māori. I am so proud of my son Simon.

The biggest achievement from my girls is that they enjoy going to school. This alone is good.

An activity in your child's education, that you have participated in as a parent, that you have enjoyed the most.

Helping him at night with his homework. Some of the work he shows me I do not understand, but we both do our best to complete the work.

What improvements or other services would you like to see?

Courses (This included parents' courses and more for students after school).

Within the first twelve months of the project all parents had been visited once and telephoned twice as a follow up. Fifty percent of parents responded in writing to parent survey and there was a 13 percent increase in the number of parents attending regular meetings and hui as a result of their involvement in Te Poho initiatives. Staff were able to collate and act in response to parent requests and feedback – in turn enhancing home/school credibility and support. Te Poho has accessed personnel and agencies prepared to act as facilitators and support people (for example, for the variety of wananga, past-student network and so on). The feedback from the home visits has been collated and staff are able now to formulate a planned, structured response to this. This means they are now 'dealing with data' instead of guesswork. Specific changes include a homework centre, posting written communication, mentoring by older siblings, and providing courses for parents. These have included: Helping your child with Maths, Māori language and traditional crafts. Māori staff have also benefited from professional development in community consultation (Appreciative Inquiry) methods.

A significant development, quite unplanned for in the original project design, was to hold a reunion of students who had belonged to the bilingual whanau over the last 15 years. Past pupils heard about the project and demanded they be involved in Te Poho. By concentrating our efforts on parents and caregivers we had overlooked this very important resource, and they were not going to allow us to leave them out. These past students are now very involved with the whanau's activities and are offering their services as helpers and mentors. We plan to build significantly on this welcome involvement.

In 2002, with further, but far less funding, the Project Coordinator and Māori staff and community have prepared a plan for the future of the whanau. This development, based on the school marae, still with the major focus of student learning and appreciative inquiry, has the following vision.

Vision

Project Te Poho is an ongoing commitment to develop the way in which we work with our Māori community. Based in the school's bilingual whanau, Te Whanau o Tupuranga, Te Poho's goal is to develop reciprocal relationships with the wider whanau that are mutually beneficial. This includes offering resources and services to the whanau that are difficult to access for a number of economic and cultural reasons. The lack of these resources is often a barrier to learning for our students and restricts the development of our community. Providing these services will enhance the achievements and learning of our children. Te Poho aims to contribute to the community as a whanau in order to strengthen our relationship with it.

Kia Aroha Marae Strategic Plan 2002

Planned areas of focus include:

• Education Development
• Health Services
• Manaakitanga (Support/Caring for people) Programme
• Community Support and Legal Services
• Funding and Resources.

2002: confronting the system

2002 brought a dramatic change for the school. At the end of 2001 Clover Park hosted the secondary schools Māori cultural competition, Te Ahurea. This was a very large event and preparation involved the whole school and Māori community. As everyone worked together on the marae in the week leading up to Te Ahurea some more recent ex-students arrived to help. We found to our dismay that these students were no longer at secondary school. These young people who had been valued, happy and achieving in Clover Park in Year 10, had become alienated from the environment of the secondary school. Parents of these students, also working at the marae, compared stories and found similar experiences. They formed a deputation to the school to ask the staff to take their students back again.

Rather then see these valued former students lost to education the school took the 15 students and embarked on a struggle to keep them. There was violent antagonism from neighbouring secondary schools, and the Ministry of Education. The common attacks seen in the international literature surfaced in

Auckland. The school was seen as illegally challenging the status quo, failing to provide the children with skills to accommodate to the dominant culture of secondary schools, creating separatism in their language units, emphasising culture at the expense of achievement and, worst of all, breaking the rules of the system! The principal visited the Minister of Education in Wellington to try to get support for the students and, after a tense meeting, managed to secure an agreement to hold the students at Clover Park for one year – subject to agreement from a local secondary school to 'attach' them to their roll. This was refused three times. The Minister then advised the school in March, after the students had been attending daily from January, that he had asked Ministry of Education officials to 'assist parents to place their children elsewhere'.

This meeting took place on 11 March on the school marae. The wharenui (meeting house) was filled with students, parents, extended whanau, kaumatua, and school staff. During the day the senior students, devastated by this news, had been given the opportunity to write letters and to talk about how they felt. The students selected three of their group to speak to the Director. Their choice of speakers surprised staff. One boy, who hadn't been in school since he was excluded for drug use in Year 10, and had been in some subsequent and serious trouble, told them he 'loved this school heaps'.

After the third speaker, a Year 13 girl who told them they had closed down Queen Victoria School[8] forcing her to leave there and now they were doing it to her again, the students broke into a haka.

> It was spine tingling, hair rising on the back of your neck stuff – I've never witnessed a haka like it. Everyone in the whare (except the senior Ministry officials) was not just crying – they were sobbing. The kids took their haka right up in front of them – it was a real challenge, girls screaming defiance, boys so angry but so, so powerful – then our Year 13 girl gave him the letters from every student and told him she wanted him to read every word.
>
> Parents then spoke just as eloquently – voices shaking with emotion saying what it meant to them to have their child back in education, doing homework at night, knowing they were learning, hurrying off to school in the morning because 'Whaea told them they couldn't be late', grandmothers, kaumatua all challenged the Ministry of Education.
>
> A University of Waikato researcher spoke about their research[9] in a range of secondary schools and the significantly different results they found in the narratives of Clover Park's Māori students and offered their support to keep these young people at Clover Park. She said other Māori students are asking for what Clover Park's Māori students already have and the model we have is of value for other schools. MOE (The Ministry of Education) were very impressed with that.
>
> (email from Ann Milne to Mollie Neville-Tisdall, March 12, 2002)

---

[8] An integrated school for Maori girls (owned by the Anglican Church), closed in 2001.
[9] *The Experiences of Year 9 and 10 Māori Students in Mainstream Classrooms: Milestone Report No. 2*. Presented to the Ministry of Education, April, 2002. As yet unreleased.

A working party was formed from this meeting and a compromise reached to enable the students to stay for the 2002 year. A high school out of the area (with a woman principal) has agreed to put the now 13 students on her roll. The only resourcing these students receive is free tuition via the Correspondence School in three subjects only. There is no staffing or funding and Clover Park's Board and staff have agreed to provide from within their own staffing entitlement and resourcing, supervision and support for these students – and to provide Te Reo (Māori language) as a fourth subject.

It has not helped that this arrangement was not finalised with the Ministry until the end of May and students have been seriously affected by this delay. In addition, the Correspondence School format does not provide the opportunity for the school to work in the way they know the students learn best. One has already left in despair and yet another has become pregnant but is going to a school for pregnant school children.

Student voices

One of the authors of this chapter gives an account of her discussion with students in the senior class shortly after they were re-admitted into Clover Park as follows:

> A large light and tidy room – twelve young people look up to greet me. Some are writing, one is reading a Māori story lying on a couch and the rest are working on an assignment on the computer. I know several of them from past visits to Clover Park and I feel comfortable, warm and welcomed. Over three days they behave with impeccable ingrained manners deeply embedded in their cultures. They provide food, make coffee and I feel like a Taonga (a treasure). One day as we were chatting over a meal I suddenly realised with a shock that these stable, secure, confident young men and women are the young people who have truanted, been stood down from schools – maybe have resorted to drugs or petty crime as a reaction to the change from Clover Park to large urban secondary schools.
>
> Over three days I talked with the new Senior Class about their passion to stay at Clover Park or to return to it from other schools. There are 12 young people in the room, eight boys and four girls. Two of the girls and two boys have stayed at Clover Park the rest have returned from secondary schools.
>
> (Neville-Tisdall, unpublished)

The voices below are the voices of senior students, authentic and passionate, as they discuss their experience of pedagogy, discipline and school attitudes towards students in Clover Park and their return to the school. These students also talked about their experiences in other schools, most often in very negative terms. Comments below are included only as they relate to Clover Park, however. A final paragraph summarises Clover Park's principal's observations on the experience and bearing of those who left Clover Park and came back and those who have never left.

Pedagogy at Clover Park

Teachers put in an effort. They are in the same culture and situation as us (Tu).

Teachers expected everyone to pass and do well (Tia).

We had an open plan classroom and all ages worked together like a family (Peter).

The teachers plan their classes (Bob).

We help each other and work together (Tracey).

We're asked not told (Bob).

Teachers can be teachers and whanau at the same time.*[10]

Yeah, everyone's just putting into it. It's like Ms Milne is forever going hard with the senior class. On the computer writing letters or researching things or whatever. She's always on top of it. Not just with work, all round things.*

We're able to help each other with anything. Like um, if someone gets stuck on one bit, you can just go up to someone and if they know it they'll help you out.*

Discipline at Clover Park

Words which frequently came through the data for Clover Park were 'peaceful', 'safe' and 'warm'. Students said they do not misbehave in Clover Park as it is a family and as the older ones in the family they are mentors for the rest of the school. Bullies stopped bullying, truants stopped truanting and the lazy worked hard.

It's disciplined but not over disciplined (Bob).
No hell raising (Bob).
We learn leadership.*
We are given options.*

Attitude of the school to students

Most people are giving (Teok).
We like the different qualities everyone has (Tracey).
We relate with each other.*
Mates and teachers help me out (Teok).

---

[10] Denotes students' voices unidentifiable in the tape transcript

When my Grandfather passed away a few years ago I was in the Kapa Haka group
and we were getting ready for a competition and um, my Mum come and got me and
told the teachers cause we were at a 'live-in' and then a few hours later they turned up
at my Aunt's house where my Grandfather was to help me with the loss of my
Grandfather (Tracey).

Returning home to Clover Park

The 'return home', as several students called their return to Clover Park, was as
important for the parents as for the students: 'Like a magnet to a piece of steel'
(Judah). The students described how happy their parents were that they were
now safe, cheerful and out of trouble. All their parents visited the marae with
the Ministry of Education and regularly attend parents' events.

Walking into school in the mornings is like walking home (Judah).

Like coming home (Bob).

Awesome to be back (Peter).

Nothing could hurt me (Tawhiri).

Well I left here in 2000 and um I went to the same (as previous speaker) school … and
I got into a lot of trouble there and I came back here to my old class and I asked the
teachers to help me out so they helped me out by trying to get me to go back to
school. But I wouldn't. Every day I would come back to here instead of going to the
school. So the teachers helped me out with my Mum and with pulling me out of
that school and getting me back here. And then I just started learning again once I
come back (Judah).

Parents are now happy:

When I was at the other schools it was 'He'll be all right', and now, especially with my
Dad I don't know – he's just been touched by an angel. 'Is your schoolwork all right?'
    Yeah, my whole family is happy cause I'm the longest person, I'm the only person
in my whole family who has made it to the sixth form (Tracey).

All loved coming back to the family or whanau, to the many celebrations and
rituals whether for grieving, leaving, arriving or success. All loved the many
opportunities to celebrate their cultures – every culture – and most of all the
Kapa Haka. Home and school are now a single entity. When they walk out of
the school grounds they go to one of their homes where they talk and listen to
music. They confirm the research finding that successful schools for minorities
are schools that reflect the culture of the students' home.

Those who have stayed and those who have come back

As the days progressed the principal at Clover Park noticed a marked
difference in the demeanour between those who had chosen to stay and those

who had returned from other schools. Half had come back and half had never left. Those who had never left were far more bouncy, cheerful, chirpy and confident. They knew that they would fail to fit into secondary schools. When asked why they stay at Clover Park:

> Because the school up the road – I don't know that school. Bad influence. They're just hoodrats, they're Māori too.*
>
> I wouldn't do school work and don't go to school.*
>
> Cause I don't want to go to another. You just get all the things you need from this school. The students they help you.*
>
> I was worried cause I didn't want to go to another school.*

In marked contrast those who had left the secondary schools would look down so that I could not see their eyes when they talked about the shame of the way they were treated and the way they had reacted. When they described their life in the Senior Class now at Clover Park their eyes sparkled and they looked up falling over themselves to tell the principal how happy they were.

The Ministry of Education Meeting

The students did not want to talk about the marae meeting with the Ministry of Education. When they talked about it they were angry.

> Rage. So much rage (Tawhiri).
>
> They tried to take us away from our school [and] We're not giving up (Tane).

Conclusion

In interpreting the Universal Declaration of Human Rights, Article 26, Clinchy (2001:497) concludes that the diversity among students and the diversity of educational belief and practice make educational diversity and choice absolute requirements of any fair, just and democratic education system. In the same year Pollock claims:

> Racial patterns are never natural orders, and ... thus can and must be collectively dismantled ... We must also forge an urgent language of communal responsibility, for only such a language will unify rather than divide various players in the common task of making such patterns go away.
>
> (Pollock, 2001:10).

Educational achievement is not measured solely on test results, league tables or even numbers admitted to tertiary institutions – although all of these are important. The true outcomes can only be measured by the quality of life of all our citizens. Are they confident? Are they full of dignity and poise? Is their culture understood and respected by all cultures? It is interesting that so much literature, both academic and literary, written by racial and ethnic minorities talks about 'invisibility'. To make us **all** visible and **all** enter into dialogue – we need all children to have 'comparable status and cultural capital' (Hall, 1997b:205).

The students' own words are more thought provoking than those of adults and academics. At one point the students were asked: 'But you just don't seem the sort of people to make and get into trouble?' Students replied:

> It's just the environment of Secondary School.*
> It's just what happens.*

Asked if it happened to everyone, the reply was:

> There was certain people who sort of like the hard work and stuff and those were the people that the teachers liked, but it was kind of stupid cause if you're not helping the people that aren't doing well, how are they ever gonna do well and no one's helping them and they just get worse and worse and no one's looking after them or anything and they get worse and worse. The good people get better and then people drop out. The other fellas are still down the road.*

Bibliography

Bishop, R. and Glynn, T. (1999) *Culture Counts: Changing Power Relations in Education*. Palmerston North: Dunmore Press.

Bohn, A.P. and Sleeter, C.E. (2000) Multicultural Education and the Standards Movement. *Phi Delta Kappan, 82* (7), 156–159.

Bryant, M. T. (1998) Cross-cultural Understandings and Leadership: Themes from Native American Interviews. *Educational Management and Administration, 26* (1), 7–20.

Bushe, G. R. (1998) Appreciative Inquiry with Teams. *Organization Development Journal*, 16 (3), 41–50.

Clinchy, E. (2001) Needed: A New Educational Civil Rights Movement. *Phi Delta Kappan, 82* (7), 493–498.

Clover Park Middle School (2002) *Kia Aroha Marae Strategic Plan*. Prepared by Te Poho Project. Clover Park Middle School.

Cummins, J. (2001a) Harvard Educational Review Classic: Empowering Minority Students: A Framework for Intervention (Author's Introduction). *Harvard Educational Review, 71* (4), 649–655.

Cummins, J. (2001b). Empowering Minority Students: A Framework for Intervention. (Reprinted from *Harvard Educational Review, 56*, (1), 656–673).

Driessen, G. (2001) Ethnicity, Forms of Capital, Achievement. *International Review of Education, 7* (6), 513–538.

Elliott, C. (1999) *Locating the Energy for Change: An Introduction to Appreciative Inquiry*, iv. Winnipeg: International Institute for Sustainable Development.

Evans, S. (2001) Kura Principals Feel the Strain. *New Zealand Education Review*, (November 23), 4–5.

Ghuman, P. (1999) *Asian Adolescents in the West*. London: BPS Books.

Hall, P.M. (1997a) Race, Ethnicity, and Schooling in American: An Introduction. In P.M. Hall, (Ed.) *Race, Ethnicity and Multiculturalism: Policy and Practice*. New York: Garland Publishing.

Hall, P.M., (1997b) The Integration of Restructuring and Multicultural Education as a Policy for Equity and Diversity. In P.M. Hall, (Ed.) *Race, Ethnicity and Multiculturalism: Policy and Practice*. New York: Garland Publishing.

Hamilton, B. T. (1998, January) There Must be a Pony. Paper presented at the New Zealand Educational Administration Society's Biennial Conference, Wellington, New Zealand.

Hammond, S. (1998) What is Appreciative Inquiry? Article published in the *Inner Edge Newsletter*. Thin Book Publishing Co. Retrieved August 1, 2001, from: http://www.thinbook.com/thinbook/chap11fromle.html

Johnston, P.M.G. (1992) *From Picot to School Boards of Trustees: 'Catering for* Māori *Interests'*? (Research Unit for Maori Education, Monograph No. 10). Auckland, New Zealand: The University of Auckland.

Johnston, P.M.G. (1999) In Through the Out Door: Policy Developments and Processes for Māori. *New Zealand Journal of Educational Studies, 34* (1), 77–85.

Johnston, R.C. and Viadero, D. (2000, March 15) Unmet Promise: Raising Minority Achievement. *Education Week, 19* (27).

Lincoln. Y.S. and Guba, E.G. (1985) *Naturalistic Inquiry*. Beverly Hills: Sage Publications.

Maani, S. and Warner, A. (2000) *The Economic Implications of Tertiary Fee Rises in Relation to Student Welfare and the Policy Environment*. Auckland: University of Auckland.

Mead, S. (1997) *Landmarks, Bridges and Visions*. Wellington: Victoria University Press.

Meier, D. (1995) *The Power of Their Ideas: Lessons for America from a Small School in Harlem*. Boston: Beacon Press.

Milne, A. (1999, January) *A Response to Issues of Identity and School Alienation in South Auckland, New Zealand*. Paper presented at the New Zealand Educational Administration Society, Auckland.

Milne, A. (2001) *Te Poho: Thinking Harder about Whanau Involvement*. Paper presented for completion of the Masters of Educational Administration, Massey University, Albany.

Milne, A. (2002) How a Whole School Addresses the Treaty in Action, Thought and Deed, *Waikato Journal of Education, 8*, 43–56.

Milne, A. (2002, March 12) Email to Dr Mollie Neville-Tisdall.

Ministy of Education (2000) *Better Relationships for Better Learning*. Wellington: Ministry of Education.

Ministry of Education (2000) *Education Statistics of New Zealand for 2000*. Wellington: Data management and Analysis Division, Ministry of Education.

Ministry of Education (2001) Māori Education: Some Suggestions from the Research Literature – a Discussion Paper. *The Research Bulletin, 12*, 1–31. Wellington: Research Division, Ministry of Education.

Morris, J. E. (1999) What is the Future of Predominantly Black Urban Schools? The Politics of Race in Urban Educational Policy. *Phi Delta Kappan, 81* (4), 316–319.

Neville-Tisdall, M., Milne, A. and Treanor, G.P. (2000a, September) *Diversity: Moving towards Cultural Validation in Two Low-Decile Schools in Auckland, New Zealand*. Paper presented to the National Middle Schools Association, Washington DC.

Neville-Tisdall, M., Milne, A. and Treanor, G.P. (2000b, November) *Eurocentric to Ethnocentric: The Dynamic Transformation of School Organisation in Two Low-Decile Schools in Auckland, New Zealand*. Paper presented to the New Zealand Association of Research in Education, Hamilton, New Zealand.

Neville-Tisdall, M. (2001) *The Future is Here*. Paper presented to New Zealand Intermediate and Middle Schools Association, September, Auckland.

Neville-Tisdall, M. (2002) Pedagogy and Politics in New Zealand's Middle Schools. *Middle School Journal, 33* (4), 45–51.

Ohanian, S. (1999) *One Size Fits Few*. Portsmouth, NH: Heinemann.

Paskale, A. and Wang Yaw (1998) *Weaving the Way*. (A research project sponsored by the Education and Training Support Agency). Wellington: Education and Training Support Agency.

Perlstein, D. (2002) Minds Stayed on Freedom: Politics and Pedagogy in the African-American Freedom Struggle. *American Educational Research Journal, 39* (2), 249–279.

Pollock, M. (2001) How the Question We Ask About Race in Education Is the Very Question We Most Suppress. *Educational Researcher, 30* (9), 2–12.

Rich, A. (1986). *Invisibility in Academe: Blood, Bread, and Poetry*. New York: W.W. Norton.

Rykis, P. (1999, January) *Whose Playing Field, Whose Rules, Whose Goal Posts?* Paper presented at the New Zealand Educational Administration Society's Research Conference, Auckland.

Scheurich, J.J., Skrla, L. and Johnson, J.E. (2000) Thinking Carefully About Equity and Accountability. *Phi Delta Kappan*, (December), 293–299.

Schlesinger, A., Jnr (1991). *The Disuniting of America*. New York: W.W. Norton.

Smith, L. T. (1999) *Decolonizing Methodologies: Research and Indigenous Peoples.* Dunedin: University of Otago Press.

Statistics New Zealand (1998a) *Samoan People in New Zealand: Pacific Island Profiles.* Wellington: Statistics New Zealand.

Statistics New Zealand (1998b) *New Zealand Now:* Māori. Wellington: Statistics New Zealand.

Tapine, V. and Waiti, D. (Eds) (1997) *Visions for* Māori *Education.* Wellington: NZCER.

University of Waikato (2002) *The Experiences of Year 9 and 10* Māori *Students in Mainstream Classrooms: Milestone Report No 2.* Presented to the Ministry of Education, April. As yet unreleased.

Walker, R. (1991) *Liberating* Māori *from Educational Subjection.* (Research Unit for Māori Education, Monograph No. 6). Auckland, New Zealand: The University of Auckland.

Webber, B. (Ed.) (1996) *He Paepae Korero: Research Perspectives in* Māori *Education.* Wellington: NZCER.

Chapter 9

Evaluating Teacher Support Teams in secondary schools: supporting teachers for SEN and other needs

Angela Creese, Brahm Norwich and Harry Daniels

Introduction

Teaching a complex curriculum to a diverse range of pupils means additional demands on teachers as they work with other colleagues on planning and teaching the curriculum, and managing learning support. Support for learning can take a variety of forms. Help can be to individual children, to small groups or to the teachers themselves. Such teacher–teacher collaborative support has been seen as central to behaviour management approaches (Elton Report, 1989) and an important part of developing improved whole school SEN policies and practices.

This chapter reports ongoing research that looks at the importance of collaborative structures in schools and their relationship to provision for special educational needs. Specifically, it is about the setting up, running and evaluation of Teacher Support Teams (TSTs) in five secondary schools over a period of eighteen months. A TST is an organized system of peer support that consists of a small group of teachers who take referrals from individual teachers on a voluntary basis. The referring teacher brings concerns about classes, groups or individuals in order to discuss and problem solve with their peers. Follow-up meetings are held as necessary. The process is as confidential as the requesting teacher wants it to be.

TSTs are novel in that they are an example of a school-based development designed to give support and assistance to individual teachers. In this way,

TSTs address a significant but neglected area of school development that has the potential to enhance the working conditions of teachers. They involve a sharing of expertise between colleagues, rather than some teachers acting as experts to others. They also provide an opportunity to support students indirectly by supporting teachers. As a form of group problem solving, they have the potential of extending staff involvement in the development of SEN policy and practice (DfE, 1994). They can help focus on the balance between addressing students' needs and bringing about change within school systems (NCC, 1989). TSTs aim to complement existing structures for supporting teachers at work. They are not intended to replace them.

Relevant literature

The role of a collaborative professional culture in schools is an important but under-researched aspect of school effectiveness and improvement literature. What there is, points to the positive benefits of collaborative cultures (Rosenholtz, 1989; Nias, 1989; Fullan and Hargreaves, 1992). However, creating such an ethos can be problematic: professional individualism has been seen as an obstacle to such collaboration and has been attributed to the organizational structure of schools, especially in secondary schools (Nias, 1993).

The literature promotes the idea that schools which aim to develop support structures allowing for professional interaction and shared knowledge with fellow teachers are likely to have positive outcomes. This is partly a question of providing teachers with the opportunity to be reflective practitioners (Pollard, 1988 in Woods, 1993), extended professionals (Hoyle, 1989 in Woods, 1993), or teacher-researchers (Cochran-Smith and Lytle, 1993), but also of allowing the school to reallocate its time and resources as problems are solved in-house.

Teacher collaboration outside of class is less well researched, but includes the work of Hanko (1989, 1990), Mead (1991), the Newcastle educational psychology service (Stringer *et al.*, 1992) and our own work (Norwich and Daniels, 1997; Creese *et al.*, 1997a, 1997b and 1997c). Although differing in focus, this work has developed and evaluated collaborative problem-solving schemes. Study of group peer support systems in the UK and USA shows positive results. American research has indicated that Teacher Support Teams can contribute to a drop in the number of inappropriate referrals to outside services and other benefits (Chalfant and Pysh, 1989; Harris, 1995). Other research which looks at teacher support outside of class focuses on inter-school collaboration, particularly around special needs (Lunt *et al.*, 1994).

This chapter discusses the outcomes of a DfEE funded development and evaluation project which aimed to develop TSTs in five secondary schools and then evaluate outcomes. The aims of this project were:

1. to evaluate the processes of setting up and maintaining Teacher Support Teams in secondary schools;
2. to evaluate the short-term effects and perceived usefulness of TSTs over a period of up to four terms and to compare these effects with those found in primary schools;
3. to disseminate the outcomes of the project to schools through school review and development materials;
4. to link the TST approach to schools' need to develop their SEN policies and practices, as required by the Code of Practice (CoP).

Initiating the TST project

The project began with five schools who opted to participate in the project in response to invitations through local networks. One of these, although still interested in the idea of setting up a TST in their school, did not manage to get started. This left four schools operating a TST with varying degrees of success. These four schools were diverse. The first was an inner-city London school (school A), the second was an outer-city London school (school B), the third, a school in a new town (school C) and the fourth, a grant maintained girls' high school in a small country town (school D). The school that failed to initiate a TST was also another inner-city London comprehensive (school E).

Schools were prepared for the TST process through training led by the project team. The aims of the training were as follows:

- to become familiar with the concepts and principles of school based support teams as providing peer support and meeting special educational needs;
- to design a TST relevant to the needs of the school, based on an understanding of the operational issues and through staff consultation;
- to develop knowledge and skills that are relevant to providing sensitive and practical support in the teams.

In addition to this initial training, TSTs in each school were provided with ongoing support in the form of termly visits from the research team. These meetings lasted for approximately one hour and the TST set the agenda.

Evaluation methods

The impacts of the TST were studied through a combination of qualitative and quantitative data collection methods. Each school was studied as a unique case operating in a wider social context, but within a common evaluative framework which focused on:

- background information about the schools;
- the process of setting up and running TSTs;
- the outcomes and impacts of the TST on the school.

Data were collected at three stages during the project: as a baseline before the introduction of TSTs; during the operation of the teams; and after one year of operation. Semi-structured interviews were designed to cover the topics: response to the TST strategy; resources for the TST; attitudes to SEN in the school; the development orientation of the school; and support for teachers. Seven members of staff were interviewed at each school. These included: the head teacher; a senior teacher; SENCO; two members of the TST; and two classroom teachers. During the operation of TSTs, field notes from support meetings with the TST members and observations of TSTs in operation were recorded. At the end of the evaluation period, semi-structured interviews were conducted again to cover any changes in the areas covered in the baseline interviews. Questionnaires using a mixture of provided and open response formats were designed to assess the perceived impact of TSTs for requesting teachers, TST members, senior teachers and non-requesting teachers. In this way we were able to triangulate the findings by looking at factors both within schools as well as across schools. Further details are available in Creese *et al.* (1997b).

Data analysis

Interviews were coded using categories arising from the interview schedule and the data themselves. Observations of the team at work were written up in considerable detail. These reports provided the researchers with the opportunity to code and analyse the TST meetings and look for patterns across the data. Case logs kept by the teams at each school also provided rich descriptive data on the kinds of problem referred to the team, and the outcomes achieved by the team in collaboration with the referring teacher. The final interviews were held during the last stage of the project. Baseline and final interviews were coded and analysed using the 'Non-numerical, Unstructured Data Indexing, Searching and Theorizing' (NUDIST) programme.

Findings

As there is not enough space to set out the four case studies, the findings will be reported in this chapter in two ways. First we present more detailed data from two of the schools which were selected to illustrate TST functioning in two different kinds of school: an inner-city school and a small town grant-maintained school. Second, we set out ten generalizations which were inferred from the four schools.

Two schools

School A, the inner-city mixed school, has a larger number of students on free school meals and on the various stages of the Code of Practice as well as lower GCSE scores. This contrasts starkly with school D, the small town girls' grant-maintained school, which has lower numbers of children on the various stages of the Code of Practice and receiving free school meals, while also achieving higher GCSE exam results.

In the full DfEE report of this study (Creese *et al.*, 1997b), the interviews with staff members were written up as vignettes which offered rich descriptions of the issues raised by teachers at each school. These vignettes represented a summary of the interviewees' collective perceptions of their school.

The main points for schools A and D are summarized below in terms of:

1. school atmosphere;
2. processes of running a TST;
3. impact at end of evaluation period.

School atmosphere

School A

The TST was established in an atmosphere of distrust and there were obvious tensions between the senior management team and the teaching staff. Those identified too closely with the senior teachers were regarded with a certain amount of suspicion and included the members of the TST who were 'hand-picked' by the deputy head. Moreover, senior teachers were perceived as having favourites among the teaching staff, with those on the outside unable to get support. The school managers were also keen to make changes in the school in order to achieve their priorities and they felt that newer members of staff were more able to make these changes and initiatives. Teachers were perceived by the SMT as either open/not open to change. Provision for pupils with SEN was regarded as a high priority for the SMT, although the changes being made around SENs were also causing a certain amount of tension among the teaching staff. As regards the TST, it was seen as a means of using the localized expertise of teachers for supporting other teachers. But, it was also perceived as a means of correcting the teaching of certain staff members.

School D

Staff, pupils and parents worked within an atmosphere of success. The school was doing well and there was the confidence that goes with that. Teachers were therefore able to admit to any problems they may have within this climate of success. The senior management and teachers were in agreement over the aims of the school. One of these aims was staff development. Staff welcomed the TST as something for them without any hidden agendas. There was an excessive number of applications to be a member of the team.

In summary, the ethos of the two schools contrasted dramatically. School A faced the challenges of pursuing its aims in an atmosphere of social/urban deprivation while also dealing with internal staff tensions. In contrast, school D operated in an atmosphere of nationally recognized success while also operating a cohesive staff development policy reached through bottom up staff consultation and discussions.

Processes of running a TST

These processes will be examined in terms of:

- personnel of team and meeting schedules;
- ongoing support for TST and visit notes;
- cases referred to the TST;
- support for TST in school.

School A

PERSONNEL AND MEETING SCHEDULES: The four team members were selected by the deputy head to achieve 'the right balance' between being approachable and also experienced and creative enough to suggest strategies to other teachers. One team member dropped out in the first term due to pressures of work and was replaced by another. The team consisted of two women and two men. Of these, one was SENCO, one was a head of year, and the other two were class teachers. The team advertised its existence through a staff meeting at the beginning of term. Meetings were held fortnightly during period 2 on Tuesdays.

ONGOING SUPPORT: The issues that emerged from these support visits were about the SEN co-ordinator's role in the TST, the relationship between TST members and senior teachers, and the expectation of the senior teachers for the TST. This team confronted the issue about how much the team should be centred on the SEN co-ordinator's work and how much a wider scope could be taken in supporting teachers generally. The SENCO herself struggled with feelings of guilt at not being able to solve all of the issues raised in meetings. Another issue was the relationship with senior teachers. Although the team felt that the senior management team was supportive of the idea of the team, this support was not evident in real resources to back them. For example, though team members gave up one free period to run the team, they felt that their work was not given priority. No time was assigned to the TST and its members. A third issue was the senior management team's aims for the TST. One of the school's priorities was raising the quality of teaching. The responsible deputy head could see the benefit of having a group of peers in a TST offering advice to colleagues who had difficulties with their teaching. However, because the TST is set up on a voluntary referral basis, she was not able to direct the teachers she had in mind as needing help to visit the team. One of her disappointments with the team was that these teachers were not referring themselves. She therefore saw the team as failing in these terms. This left team members feeling that they were not being fully supported.

CASES REFERRED TO THE TST: The three cases referred in this school were about behaviour and learning issues. One was about an individual boy and the remaining two were issues pertaining to whole classes. These cases were dealt with successfully according to the referring teachers and the TST team.

SUPPORT FOR TST: The final questionnaires showed that 16 non-requesting teachers knew about the existence of the TST in their school. However, 79 per cent (eleven teachers) felt the TST had not become part of the school's structures, with only three saying that it had. Of these 16 teachers, 56 per cent (nine) wanted the TST to continue in the school, while 44 per cent (seven) said they were not sure. Interestingly, there was a mismatch between the views of TST members and senior teachers about the level of support given for the TST scheme. While the four TST members viewed the senior managers as slightly to fairly supportive, the four senior managers viewed their support as fairly to very supportive.

School D

PERSONNEL AND MEETING SCHEDULES: This team started with five members, all women.[1] They were short-listed from volunteers who put their names forward after the idea was introduced at a staff meeting. In selecting the team the deputy head attempted to achieve breadth in terms of teaching experience, pastoral work and curriculum subject areas. Initially there was concern that too many had been selected, though this proved not to be so. By the end of the first year the team had four members, after losing one member through retirement.

Once the team was selected a member visited each of the faculties in the school to advertise the scheme. The joint problem-solving nature of the team was also advertised at that time. This team, which called itself a staff support team, met once a week after school.

ONGOING SUPPORT: Two issues were raised during the two support visits to the schools, opening up school structures and support for staff. The processes of the team over the two terms were described in very positive terms. The TST members and the wider teaching staff at this school saw the TST as fitting easily into current structures in a complementary way. It opened out school structures and allowed individual team members and referring teachers to improve the workings of their own areas of responsibility. Moreover, the TST process was framed as a process which conscientious teachers would use. The TST agenda was clear and transparent to its members and to the rest of the staff as there to support teachers, not to evaluate them.

CASES REFERRED TO THE TST: There were six cases referred in this school, four of these were about behaviour problems; two were about individual girls and two about groups of girls. The remaining two cases concerned one girl with an emotional special need while the last case involved changing whole school policy on supervising the lunch hour. All cases were judged as having been dealt with successfully by the referring teachers and the TST team.

SUPPORT FOR TST IN SCHOOL D: Of the 44 teachers who knew of the existence of a TST, support for the principle of a TST was expressed by 43 teachers. Moreover, this was the only school that teachers perceived the team as having become part of the school's structure – 71.4 per cent saw it as being part of the school; 78 per cent wanted the team to continue, while only 21.4 per cent were not sure. There were no respondents who did not want the TST to continue.

Impact at end of evaluation period

The impact will be summarized in terms of the perceived usefulness of TST, the relation between the TST and SEN provision and the future of TST in the school.

School A

All the team members believed that the TST had been useful for referring teachers. Of particular note, was the outcome of one referral that led to a teacher forum for all those teaching a particular child. The team also commented that it had allowed them reflection time and opportunities to learn new strategies and form new relationships. The senior management team felt that the team had been useful for the team members themselves in terms of their own professional development and for the referring teachers. However, they were disappointed that only confident teachers had used it. The one non-referring teacher interviewed thought that TST was a good idea, but felt that staff saw it as something for certain people. The referring teacher who was interviewed reported that discussion with the team had been extremely useful and had resulted in new and useful strategies.

Team members did not want the TST to be too closely associated with special needs. It was felt that TST should be for the teachers themselves and their professional concerns, not exclusively linked to SEN. The SEN co-ordinator felt that the TST did not work out as they had anticipated, so that it was difficult to associate it with any developments in the SEN policy. In fact, the highlighting of SEN issues in the TST made the SEN co-ordinator anxious. According to other TST members, Individual Educational Plans (IEPs), for example, were not improved through the TST process, as the team did not want the TST to be used for this purpose. Working on IEPs would have given the group too much of a SEN focus.

The future of the TST was in doubt in this school. It was felt that the TST remained a good idea – professional people helping professional people in a non-judgemental, non-inspectorial way. However, one of the biggest issues for the senior management team was teachers whom they had targeted as needing special help, but who did not use it. One suggestion from the deputy head was that it could become worked into current structures, so the heads of departments would have to use it when facing problems around children and teachers. Overwhelmingly, the issue of time as a resource emerged in the final interview data. Not enough time, too much stress and low teacher morale were mentioned over and over again. The school was in flux, with the appointment of the new head instigating changes in the school systems. Ironically teachers recognized that the more pressure there was in the school, the more need there was for a TST. However, lack of resources meant that it was not supported either in terms of time or money. The senior teachers wanted the TST members to convince them it was worthwhile continuing with the scheme, while the TST members wanted senior teachers to provide more support by giving it a higher priority. The future of the team looked in jeopardy because of lack of time and managerial support.

School D

TST members felt that it had been particularly useful in dealing with behaviour issues. Staff viewed it as complementary to the school's other systems for supporting teachers. The members of the TST were seen as very approachable and its presence seen as 'an option not a hassle'. All team members in their other roles (SEN co-ordinator, deputy head, head of year, and head of department) had been proactive in encouraging teachers to use the team. The team worried that not enough people had come and they would have been happier if they were used more regularly.

The SEN co-ordinator had used the TST to present SEN as a shared issue. She did not present herself as somebody who had superior knowledge and had felt that TST meetings had helped her to rewrite IEPs and make them more realistic. The staff saw a future for a TST at the school, but that it needed relaunching. Moreover, some teachers felt that they could only bring very large problems to the team – otherwise they would be bothering their colleagues. Team members said that they would like to move away from this perception. The team also saw a place for heads of faculty visiting a TST to discuss action plans and felt that it helped bring the pastoral and academic aspects together. Although team members all wanted the team to continue, in this school too, time was an issue.

Senior management was seen to be very supportive of the TST and supportive of teachers generally. One referring teacher felt it an appropriate way to cope with teacher isolation in schools.

Generalizations from the four schools

These tentative generalizations about the conditions that support TSTs were inferred from systematic comparisons between the four schools using the general evaluative framework.

Support from the senior management team

Where the TST worked best, as in the small town school, there was active support by the senior management team. This is an example of where TST becomes part of the school's structure for supporting staff as it is worked into the schools' systems. The scheduling of the TST meetings and providing cover for staff is therefore of importance. Meetings held during the school day require cover not only for the referring teacher but also the TST members. In one school, team members themselves covered for referring teachers on a rotating basis. When TST members were expected to use one of their 'free' periods for the TST, they did not feel supported. This was taken to indicate a lack of senior teachers' commitment to the initiative. Meetings held during the timetable were also in need of protection, so that they were not cancelled during times of crisis. Meetings held after school needed to be worked into the meeting schedule so that the TST members were not expected to do additional work. Support for TST also required providing adequate facilities for meetings in the form of a quiet room.

No hidden agenda

Part of senior management's support for TST is clarity about the aims of the initiative. The research team presented TST as a non-evaluative, peer problem-solving forum. Moreover, TST was to be voluntary and confidential. Where this was carried through in two schools, the TST was more successful than in the other two schools in which an additional agenda existed. In one of these schools, for example, the senior teacher had another aim for the TST, which was to improve the quality of teaching for certain teachers who were felt to be failing. The expectation of the TST in this case was as a team to deal with problem teachers, and consequently not as an open forum for problem solving among sympathetic peers.

Consulting teachers about membership of TST

The scheme worked best in the school in which all teachers had the opportunity to apply to be TST members rather than being simply selected. This school held an election for their TST members and found that many more teachers wanted to be members than places were available. Only at this stage did the SMT become involved and members were selected from the list of applicants to reflect representation from academic and year groups. The election also acted as a form of advertising, thus raising the TST profile in the school. In less successful TSTs, senior management either selected the team without consultations or used informal and limited consultation. In the other two schools, where TST operated less well, team membership was voluntary but there were fewer teachers interested in taking part. In the one school where selection was without consultations, it came to be viewed by some other members of the staff as belonging to the senior teachers' 'gang of golden boys and girls'.

Trust and non-interference from senior teachers in the TST

Senior teachers in all the schools spoke of frustration at not knowing what was happening in the TST. However, this played out differently from school to school. In two of the schools, senior teachers attempted to involve themselves directly in the TST process. In one TST, a deputy head tried to make one teacher refer her problem to the TST, but the teacher refused. In another case a senior teacher who was a TST member used information presented at a TST meeting against the teacher during a formal evaluation meeting later on in the year. There was some suspicion that this resulted in the teacher not being promoted. On the more positive side, in the one school with the most successful TST, the head teacher became more comfortable with the initiative as the year went on. The trust shown by the SMT in this school resulted in staff feeling more relaxed about the whole issue of confidentiality.

SENCO as problem sharer not problem solver

SEN co-ordinators differed from school to school in their approach to the TST. In one school in particular, the SEN co-ordinator's role within the TST was played out as problem solver. In this situation she often felt guilty because the TST threw up problems that she felt she had to solve. This had the effect of making her feel that her SEN responsibilities had actually increased rather than being more equally shared. In another school, the SEN co-ordinator saw the TST meetings as an opportunity to share problems and learn about different approaches from colleagues. She played the part of problem sharer where problems became jointly owned and where SEN became a more shared responsibility.

Collaborative and non-collaborative meetings

In one school thought was given to the kind of interactions to be developed in the TST group. Members of the TST became aware of the skill of listening and accepting ideas within a group context. Group processes came to be seen as needing time and attention themselves. Collaborative practices, such as accepting and building on others' ideas rather than competitive practices resulted in the most productive meetings. In another school where TST meetings had worked within a hierarchical framework, team members were less relaxed than in other teams where occupational positions were played down. The groups that worked at emphasizing the value of all members' contributions, including the referring teacher, were observed to be most at ease.

Maintaining a high profile for the TST

Advertising the team regularly was another factor. In one school, members of the team attended department meetings in order to discuss the work of the TST with their colleagues. Other teams put up notices telling teachers about the scheme. Another method was to describe the TST in the staff handbook. Publicizing successful outcomes among the staff was perceived by teams to be a useful approach. However, the issue of confidentiality was important here, as the TST had to protect the confidentiality of the referring teacher, especially when discussing individual cases. In some instances, the kind of referred problem resulted in whole school policy changes, such as, changing a school's behaviour policy. When the outcomes of TST meetings resulted in bringing about a change in policy, the staff were able to appreciate and feel part of this change.

Ethos of the school: formal and informal support systems

The general collaborative atmosphere of the school was very important in terms of the success of the TST. In one school, where tension existed between the senior teachers and the teaching staff, the TST was seen by some as a formal structure in the hands of the management team that could be used to manipulate teachers. In another school, where the senior teachers showed benign support for the TST, the project never achieved a high enough profile for staff to develop an opinion about it. Only in the school where the TST was presented as something for the staff and where teacher support was an overt aim of senior management did TSTs become embedded within the school's structure. However, this is not to suggest that other support systems were not operating in the other schools. For example, in the school where senior management and teachers had an acrimonious relationship, a strong network of informal support systems operated. An informal support system might perhaps be expected in such a climate of suspicion and mistrust. There was a tremendous amount of bad feeling expressed about the senior management as well as feelings of low morale. Informal teacher support was very important in this school.

Improving individual educational plans (IEPs)

Lastly, in several schools the TST was reported as having helped to make IEPs more relevant and applicable for referring teachers. One of the aims of the project was to examine whether operating a TST had a positive impact on the schools' SEN policies and practices, as required by the Code of Practice. In two schools the TST process was judged to have been helpful in making IEPs more specific and meaningful. This is because they allowed teachers the opportunities for talk about issues with colleagues. In some cases the TST led to the review of IEPs and setting more helpful and realistic targets.

Discussion

The comparison of the two schools in this chapter showed the importance of both external and internal factors in the adoption and success of an initiative like the teacher support team one. The small town girls' school was providing for a more advantaged and higher attaining group of pupils than the inner-city school. The approach of the senior teachers to the TST initiative was also different. In the small town school the initiative was seen to be in-keeping with an explicit school development priority on staff development. The TST was seen to combine action relevant to this priority while enhancing SEN provision. The direct involvement of one of the senior teachers in the team also showed the degree of commitment and involvement of senior management in the initiative. In the inner-city school, the TST initiative was supported in principle by senior management but was left to the selected team to show what it could achieve. The school was undergoing much turbulence and senior teachers felt threatened about inspection. There was less of a consensus between the TST team and the responsible senior teacher about the purpose of the team and what could be expected of it. Finding times to meet with requesting teachers was more problematic.

The role of senior management in secondary schools can be seen from this project to be crucial to an initiative like TST. In all four project schools there were some problems over time and this made it difficult to maintain support of the TST kind for teachers to varying degrees, but especially in three of the schools. For them, more immediate, internal and often external priorities had a tendency to be placed first. In two of these schools new heads were appointed during the period of the project. These schools also underwent other changes that had a negative impact on the TST. All four schools had an Ofsted inspection during or just prior to the project. Only in the small town school, described in this paper, did senior management maintain a high profile for TST, and this was the school which was succeding on all other external criteria (GCSE and Ofsted reports) and had the lowest number of children with statements and receiving free school meals. Our conclusions about senior management reflect findings from research and theory based in the school management and improvement literature. Without senior management support, initiatives are unlikely to be protected and will not become embedded and operate successfully (Weindling and Earley, 1987; Torrington and Weightman, 1989; Dean, 1993).

The difficulties encountered in three of the four schools in operating a teacher support initiative as fully as these three teams would have liked can also be seen in the wider policy context. Schools have experienced increasing pressures to respond to major external initiatives concerned, for example, with curriculum, assessment, financial management, inspection and SEN over the last ten years. The central thrust behind these changes has been to raise attainment levels with an emphasis on performance, effectiveness, targets and outcomes. SEN developments following the SEN Code of Practice have similarly been focussed on increased efficiencies and target setting in the form of individual educational plans. Within this culture of schooling, it is often difficult for a school, struggling to respond to its major external demands, to translate a principled support for a teacher support system like TST into the commitment of time and senior management backing that is needed. That this was not problematic in the small town school raises important questions about whether this kind of teacher support system is suited to the needs of struggling schools, like the inner-city school described above. This does not mean that teacher support has to be set-aside in such schools, but that perhaps different kinds of teacher support could be adopted. This position is backed by findings from a national survey we conducted into various types of teacher support in 1000 primary and secondary schools (Creese *et al.*, 1997c). We found that at least 21 per cent of schools were running one or other kind of teacher support system. However, while 60 per cent of these schools set up *ad hoc* gatherings for teachers experiencing difficulties with certain children, only 21 per cent reported running a system resembling what we have called a TST in this project. The low incidence of TST like systems could be because of their relatively high requirements in terms of preparation and time. However, it was also found that a quarter of the schools which reported running any teacher support system, ran at least three forms of support, while one in ten were running six or seven forms. This indicated that some schools specialized in such systems. This might be because staff development and support were important whole school priorities with teacher support for SEN fitting into and adding to this broader commitment. The connection between the adoption of TST and the wider emphasis on staff development in the small town school suggested this conjecture. It is something that needs further research examination.

The internal working of the teams and the perceptions of the rest of the staff were also important features of the TSTs. Teams that were willing and able to listen and learn, as much as talk and offer suggestions, were seen as more successful than those that set themselves up as having definitive answers to problems. The study has also shown the complex interconnections between systems within the secondary schools, such as between the operation of the Code of Practice stages, the pastoral system and the TST. The potential of the TSTs to bridge between these systems was appreciated in each school, but again only in the small town school was bridging partially successful. This was related to the various roles held by the TST team members (head of year, head of department, SEN co-ordinator and deputy head). The TST initiative and principle were well received in all schools, and even where they had difficulties in operating the team fully, teachers maintained their belief in its potential contribution. This replicates what we found in our previous evaluation of TSTs in primary schools (Norwich and Daniels, 1997).

Some of the difficulties in running TSTs were also experienced in implementing our evaluation design. We had planned to assess the impact on teachers who requested support from TST by interviewing them before and after TST meetings. Unfortunately it proved difficult to make contact via telephone with these teachers. Teachers were willing to be interviewed at the start and end of the project, the teams were able to keep logs of their case discussion and team meetings could be observed, but the impact on teachers was more difficult to monitor. Ideally, we would also have liked to monitor change in classes or pupils about whom teachers had requested support. This study needs to be replicated with more schools and with greater access to monitoring the impact of team support on those requesting support and those they teach.

Nevertheless, the project has provided significant insights and some practical recommendations. The project shows that teachers appreciate the value of collaboration as a principle and practice and its contribution to implementing the SEN Code of Practice and to staff development and wellbeing more generally. This means that governors and senior managers need to recognize teacher collaboration and teacher support as an issue and ensure that it has a prominent place in school life. That is, they need to develop a common understanding of how support systems relate to the needs of teachers and their pupils. Senior managers need to understand the implications of this in terms of time, money and management backing. Both informal and formal methods of teacher support and collaboration need therefore to be included in reviews as part of school development planning. The aims of support need to be clarified and the experience of teachers to be drawn upon. One way of gauging teachers' opinions about setting up and running various forms of support, is to use a questionnaire to staff (for an example, see Creese *et al.*, 1997; p. 10). This questionnaire focuses specifically on the TST type of teacher support. A more elaborate questionnaire could be designed to include other forms of teacher support like those we examined in the national survey. Our findings also suggested that SEN policy and practice were improved when based on collaborative problem solving. In schools where the staged system of the Code of Practice and the writing of IEPs is overly bureaucratic, the TST can provide opportunities to discuss problems. It is best that TSTs be promoted as complementing existing schemes, not replacing them. If a school wishes to set up and run a TST, careful planning is needed. Consideration should be given to the membership of the team, publicizing the team, role of team members and the nature of referrals, amongst other factors (see Creese *et al.*, 1997; p. 14 for further details). In secondary schools, perhaps even more so than in primary schools, the complex nature of inter-departmental relationships, pastoral and academic systems and special systems mean that TSTs depend on the commitment of time from the SMT if the team is to fulfil its potential contribution to the school.

Note

1 This is a single sex girls' school. Male teachers make up 19 per cent of full time teaching staff.

References

Chalfant, J.C. and Pysh, M. (1989). 'Teacher assistance teams: five descriptive studies on 96 teams', *Remedial and Special Education*, 10, 49–58.

Cochran-Smith, M. and Lytle, S.L. (1993). *Inside Outside: Teacher Research and Knowledge*. New York: Teachers College, Columbia University.

Creese, A., Daniels, H. and Norwich, B. (1997a). *Teacher Support Teams in Primary and Secondary Schools*. London: David Fulton Publishers.

Creese, A., Daniels, H. and Norwich, B. (1997b). *Teacher Support Teams in Secondary Schools*. DfEE Report.

Creese, A., Daniels, H. and Norwich, B. (1997c). 'The prevalence and usefulness of collaborative teacher groups for SEN: results of a national survey', *Support for Learning*, 13. 109–114.

Dean, J. (1993). *Managing the secondary school* (2nd edn). London: Routledge.

Department for Education (1994). 'The organisation of special educational provision', *Circular 6/94*. London: DFE Publications Centre.

Department of Education and Science (1989). *Discipline in Schools* (Elton Report). London: HMSO.

Fullan, M. and Hargreaves, A. (1992). *What's Worth Fighting For In Your School?* Buckingham: OUP/OPSTF.

Hanko, G. (1989). 'After Elton – how to manage disruption', *British Journal of Special Education*, 16, 140–143.

Hanko, G. (1990). *Special Needs in Ordinary Classrooms: Supporting Teachers*. London: Blackwell.

Harris, K. (1995). 'School-based bilingual special education teacher assistance teams', *Remedial and Special Education*, 16, 337–343.

Lunt, I., Evans, J., Norwich, B. and Wedell, K. (1994). *Working Together: Inter-School Collaboration for Special Needs*. London: David Fulton Publishers.

Mead, C. (1991). *A City-Wide Evaluation of PSG Training*. Birmingham: Birmingham Local Education Authority.

National Curriculum Council (1989). 'Implementing the National Curriculum – Participation by Pupils with SEN', *NCC Circular No. 5*. York.

Nias, J. (1989). *Primary Teachers Talking*. London: Routledge.

Nias, J. (1993). 'Changing times, changing identities: grieving for a lost self'. In: Burgess, R. (Ed.) *Educational Research & Evaluation for Policy and Practice*. London: Falmer Press.

Norwich, B. and Daniels, H. (1997). 'Teacher support teams for special educational needs in primary schools: evaluating a teacher-focused support scheme', *Educational Studies*, 23, 5–24.

Rosenholtz, S. (1989). *Teachers' Workplace: The Social Organization of Schools*. White Plains, NY: Longman.

Stringer, P., Stow, L., Hibbert, K., Powell, J. and Louw, E. (1992). 'Establishing staff consultation groups in schools', *Educational Psychology in Practice*, 8, 87–96.

Torrington, D. and Weightman, J. (1989). *The Reality of School Management*. Blackwell Education.

Weindling, D. and Earley, P. (1987). *Secondary Headship: the First Year*. Slough: NFER-Nelson.

Woods, P. (1993). *Critical Events in Teaching and Learning*. London: The Falmer Press.

Chapter 10

Circle Time: a much-neglected resource in secondary schools?

Marilyn Tew

In this chapter 'Circle Time' (with initial capitals) refers to the Quality Circle Time Model and the strategies used within the circle as devised by Jenny Mosley (1989, 1993, 1996) as opposed to the many other circle-time methods to be found in educational practice.

Introduction

There is an ever-increasing concern from government about standards of achievement. League tables and percentage targets for literacy are the spurs used to provoke greater attainment at all levels of education. Yet, through the years, research has shown behaviour, motivation and learning to be linked to self-perception, personal growth and development (Burns, 1982; Lawrence, 1985, 1988; Maslow, 1962; Rogers, 1969).

OFSTED (Office for Standards in Education) reports have recognized and commented on the contribution Quality Circle Time is making to promoting spiritual, moral, social and cultural development and to developing positive behaviour and relationships borne out of mutual respect and value.

- 'The weekly Circle Time for each class enables pupils of all ages, at their own level, to reflect on aspects of their lives, to discuss moral and social issues and to express with confidence their understanding of right and wrong and their sense of justice. Pupils learn to listen well to others, to be tolerant of other viewpoints and to respect fellow pupils.' (Canberra Primary School, 1995, para. 14)

- 'Circle Time effectively enables pupils to voice opinions and question each other about matters which may not easily be discussed in lessons. They speak openly to one another and their opinions are valued.' (St Vincent's RC Primary School, 1994, p. 12)

Many thousands of children who have been involved in Circle Time meetings in their primary schooling are entering secondary school. These children have been part of schools that have a whole-school Circle Time approach. In regular, weekly Circle Time meetings, they have grasped an understanding of the value of the individual and the notion of consultation. They have learnt to take turns and know that they can speak and be heard. They have a clear understanding of the need for rules and the rewards and sanctions that accompany them. They are in no doubt as to the behavioural expectations of their school community and concepts as esoteric as democracy and citizenship have been experienced through the functioning of their classroom and school environments.

Once in secondary school, what happens to these young people? Do they encounter an environment in which they feel valued and trusted? Do they have the same clear understanding of expectations in their secondary school as they had in the primary? I think that the answer in many cases is a resounding 'No'. Too many young people encounter conflicting messages and a system in which they often feel powerless and without a voice. In an age of rising exclusions, school refusal and absenteeism, something must be done to bridge the 'divide' that so often exists between the philosophies of primary and secondary approaches to personal, social and moral education.

OFSTED seems in no doubt that where time is invested in the process, relationships within the school improve, no matter what the age range of the pupils: 'The excellent quality of relationships within the school is evidence that pupils feel respected and valued. This enables them to reflect positively on their experience of life. Circle Time, an exercise to raise self-esteem, is used by form tutors …' (Warren Comprehensive School, para. 43).

Theoretical background of the Circle

The circle has always been a symbol of unity, healing and power. The use of a circle for conference and exchange of views is ancient and can be found in the traditions of groups such as the North American Indians and Anglo-Saxon monks. It is clear, however, that in the twentieth century, many psychologists have contributed to our understanding of how and why 'circle time' works.

Dr J. L. Moreno (1934, 1946) was the acknowledged forefather of all active groupwork approaches. He was responsible for developing the methods of sociometry, psychodrama and sociodrama, which have directly influenced all experiential groupwork programmes. Moreno's clear understanding of the importance of 'the group' and of social interaction to the development of self makes his work very relevant as to why circle time has the power to contribute to self-concept.

> Mead (1934) and Rogers (1951) have also offered theoretical frameworks which have bearing on the power and effectiveness of circle time. Mead suggested that the behaviour of the individual can only be understood in terms of a social dynamic and therefore the individual act can only be comprehended as part of a whole. Circle Time strategies are designed to help individuals understand their behaviour and the response of other people towards it. They offer a model of helping that acknowledges that the behaviour of an individual child is embedded in the social interactions of her class group. It needs, therefore, to be the class group that works with her to help her become aware of the range of other responses she could choose from. (Mosley, 1996, p. 72)

Carl Rogers extended the phenomenological framework and emphasized the importance of the self within the social world. Young people have a perceived self-concept which can change in the light of new information. The individual has the capacity for self-understanding and the positive ability to reorganize self-structure. His work demonstrated that certain core conditions are necessary in order to facilitate learning: if a teacher can create or provide these conditions, the individual is free to re-examine their perceptions of their social, moral or personal world: 'The therapist/educator must be genuine or concerned ... must possess unconditional positive regard and experience an empathic understanding of the client's internal frame of reference and endeavour to communicate this experience' (Rogers, 1951).

Research by Burns (1982) demonstrates that if pupils are offered respectful relationships and a warm supportive ethos, their social and academic performance will flourish.

In the light of the above research, it becomes clear why the structures, conditions and strategies of the Jenny Mosley Model, if firmly adhered to, have the potential to build self-esteem, encourage the development of self-control and promote empathy and moral awareness in any group of young people.

Circles and PSE (Personal and Social Education)

During the 1960s, 1970s and 1980s, a plethora of initiatives arose out of humanistic and child-centred approaches to education, influenced by the work of Rogers (1961, 1983), Burns (1979, 1982), Button (1982), Brandes and Ginnes (1986), Lawrence (1988), and many others.

PSE is the subject of much debate at government level. In July 1997, the Government brought out a White Paper entitled *Excellence in Schools*. This document proposed an approach to education in which 'education is the key to creating a society which is dynamic and productive, offering opportunity and fairness to all' (p. 9).

Schools and families were recognized as having responsibility to ensure that children and young people learn respect for others and for themselves: 'They need to appreciate and understand the moral code on which civilised society is based and to appreciate the culture and background of others. They need to develop the strength of character and attitudes to life and work, such as responsibility, determination, care and generosity, which will enable them to become citizens of a successful democratic society' (p. 10).

In October 1997, the Green Paper *Excellence for All Children: Meeting Special Educational Needs* followed the White Paper. Section 8 focused on dealing with children with emotional and behavioural difficulties. The government declared their intention of putting their educational principles into practice: 'Schools need to offer a setting where all children are valued and encouraged to behave well, where there are clear guidelines for behaviour, teaching is positive, and where damaged self-esteem can be rebuilt' (p. 81).

So far, however, these words remain as pure rhetoric. In secondary schools, few coherent approaches exist to make the intentions substantial. Yet Circle Time has been shown over and over again to be effective in providing a setting where children:

- are encouraged to behave well;
- are valued;
- experience positive teacher relationships;
- learn to care;
- understand a moral code;
- appreciate the cultural background of others;
- develop strength of character, determination and responsibility;
- take part in a democratic process;
- have damaged self-esteem rebuilt.

The question remains as to why this excellent approach, so successful in primary schools, is not used in secondary school.

The Circle Time Forum

Humanistic psychology and a consequent student-centred approach to learning underpin Circle Time practice. It is rooted in the notion that each individual has worth, individuality and the right to control their own direction. It also requires that the teacher is self-aware and able to create a classroom 'climate' that is supportive and conducive to helping pupils realise their innate self-potential. Circle Time creates an emotionally 'safe' place for pupils to explore what they think and feel.

This model of Circle Time is 'safe' because it is bound by strict groundrules for teachers and children, based on respect, valuing and reflecting back to participants a positive mirror of their selves. Of paramount importance is the rule that no name may be used negatively, thus keeping parents, pupils, teaching and non-teaching staff safe from exposure or ridicule, whilst allowing issues to be discussed and problems solved.

Groundrules for the Circle

- No one may put anyone down
- No one may use any name negatively (creating 'safety' for all individuals including teachers and parents)
- When they speak, everyone must listen
- Everyone has a turn and a chance to speak
- All views are taken seriously
- Members of the class team suggest ways of solving problems and
- Individuals can accept the help or politely refuse it.

Throughout the Circle Time meeting, groundrules strictly apply. Action is taken if someone persists in breaking a groundrule. First a visual warning is given, allowing the person to decide whether to continue to break the rule, or to change their behaviour. If he/she persists in breaking the rule, a short period out of the circle follows. (In my own research, I only had to apply this sanction on two occasions in a nine-week period. Most often the impetus of the activities, peer pressure to keep the groundrules and the nature of the subject matter kept pupils involved.)

Jenny Mosley's model of Circle Time follows a firm structure so that the group moves from warm-up exercises and fun into a round where every person is given the opportunity to speak individually. The respect afforded to an individual and their choices is very powerful in raising self-esteem. For just a few minutes, they are the centre of attention and a whole group of people is listening intently to everything they say. The round progresses to 'open forum' where issues and individual problems are aired and brainstormed, an activity which often leads to an individual or group action plan. The next stage is to celebrate success and finally to end on fun.

The research programme

As part of an M.Ed. degree at Bristol University, I worked with a new intake Year 7 class in an 11–18 comprehensive school of 1400 pupils. Approximately 50 per cent had experienced circle time in their primary schools. The other 50 per cent had no previous experience of this method of learning. I chose Circle Time because it builds on primary practice and is an emotionally 'safe', easy-to-learn teaching methodology which any PSE teacher or form tutor could master. One of my aims was to influence future PSE teaching, so it would be pointless suggesting complicated delivery techniques which busy, overloaded teachers would be unable or unwilling to try out.

My specific aims in using Circle Time for delivering PSE were:

- to cover the PSE curriculum content of the nine-week module,
- to build a 'sense of group' which would affect co-operation and friendships in the class,
- to foster positive relationships between pupils,
- to create a climate of openness that would permit honest discussion of the topics covered and the possibility of changing self-perception,
- to model a teacher role that was facilitative, not authoritarian.

I worked alongside the allocated PSE teacher for this group and in parallel with another Year 7 group. I deliberately chose a parallel group which had a PSE teacher similar in philosophical stance to myself. I interviewed her before we began teaching and we agreed an approach. Both were positive, using as much verbal praise as possible; both were child-centred, using active groupwork, discussion, open-ended tasks and drama techniques such as role-play. In this way, any results obtained were more likely to be because of the circle strategies, than because we had very different teaching styles.

Structures and techniques used

Every lesson followed the same general pattern, though the content and activities changed each week in order to be appropriate to the topic. The five main structures used were:

- Warm up
- Round
- Open Forum
- Celebration
- Closure.

Warm-up games

Designed to provoke laughter and break down the tensions between individuals, warm-up games unite the class and energize the group. Sometimes, though, if there is an excitable feel to the class, the warm-up game can bring focus, calm and concentration. Each game has its own rules which reinforce moral values and foster verbal and physical contact between individuals. They break up friendship groups and cause pupils to sit next to and work with new people for each activity. An interesting aspect of most games is that they create the need for positive eye contact (one of the most significant features of relationship building) between group members. They can also be used to release feelings which are explored later in the open forum.

Rounds

A 'speaking object' is passed round as a visual symbol signifying the right to speak and be heard. (In our case we used a coloured ceramic egg which pupils held in a reverential and slightly dreamy way when they spoke.) In order to keep up a good pace and stop the circle 'grinding to a halt' with the vociferous dominating discussion, rounds are usually scripted with a sentence stem such as 'I don't like it when …'. The majority of people contribute to a round but anyone can say 'I pass' without feeling awkward, and thereby choose not to speak. Every contribution is acceptable and valued, creating a climate of trust and genuine interest. In PSE lessons, the rounds are related to the topic under discussion this week and they can be informed by small group work, paired work or individual worksheets. Rounds are used any time opinion is sought or for evaluation and feedback.

Open forum

At the heart of Circle Time, the open forum enables pupils to develop 'inner locus of control'. Rotter (1966) originated the concept of 'locus of control'. A pupil who has an external locus of control feels that they have little or no control over what happens to them. They are the victims of events and circumstances. Those who have inner locus of control perceive themselves as having control over what happens to them, they are masters of their fate. They believe that they are in charge of their own life; they can make choices and decisions to get what they want; they feel good about themselves; and are more likely to achieve academically. The open forum teaches young people to own their behaviour and so increases their perception of being in control of their own lives and actions. They ask for help with aspects of their life or behaviour and have the power to accept or reject the advice proffered by their classmates. The script is 'Would it help if I ...?' or 'Would it help if you ...?' From the open forum comes an action plan that promotes personal responsibility for behaviour and actions. Various techniques including role-play, scripted drama, discussion and brainstorming can be used as part of open forum. I am constantly amazed at the level of sensitive, generous, creative thinking that young people invest in helping one another during this part of Circle Time.

Celebration

Towards the end of Circle Time, pupils are encouraged to thank group members for their contribution to the group dynamics. 'Thank yous' follow open forum, as an important vehicle for lightening the group atmosphere and redirecting thinking to positive things. Psychologically, it is unsound to leave individuals in 'problem mode', with unresolved issues. Any member of the group can nominate another to be thanked, e.g. a quiet member of the group, or a member with a good sense of humour. This activity involves one-to-one, positive and direct communication. It is to do with giving and receiving compliments and is an important component of building self-esteem and positive relationships. An important point for the group facilitator is to check that everyone experiences a 'thank you' at least once in a course of Circle meetings. Creative nomination categories ensure everyone is included.

Closure

All group experiences need time for closure. Each Circle Time ends with fun and the closing activity might encompass some form of reflection or engender laughter. It is important to provide a 'bridge' into the next activity of the day so a useful closure is a quick round of 'One thing I am looking forward to today is...'.

Results

At the end of the nine-week module, I gave questionnaires to both of the PSE groups. The intention was to see if there was any difference in perception of the lessons or in outcomes in terms of relationships or the sense of 'belonging' within the group. Several pupils then volunteered to be interviewed allowing me to access a fuller range of their opinions.

As a result of analysing the questionnaires, written comments and interview data, it was possible to see some of the differences in perception between the group taught PSE using the Circle Time method and those taught PSE in a student-centred approach.

Q1   Did you enjoy the PSE module of the last 9 weeks?

Ninety-six per cent of the group taught with the circle technique enjoyed the lessons, whereas 87 per cent taught using only the student-centred approach enjoyed the lessons.

Q1a   If you answered 'yes', what made the lessons enjoyable?

Of the group taught using circle time, 43% enjoyed the games; 18% enjoyed the sitting in a circle; 11% found the topics fun, not like 'normal lessons'; 11% found it easier to talk and enjoyed hearing what other people had to say; 8% felt they had a fair share of everything and that everyone had a say; 9% found lessons helpful, easy to understand and enjoyable; and 3% learnt that not everyone is laughing at you. Of the group taught using the student-centred approach only, 38% enjoyed the visiting speakers; 15% perceived the lessons as 'not work' and the topics fun; 12% enjoyed making posters and watching the videos; 6% enjoyed talking and sharing; 6% found the topics new; 6% enjoyed the teacher and no homework; and 3% enjoyed the free gifts from visitors.

Q1b   If you answered 'No', what did you not enjoy about the lessons?

Only one person in the Circle Time group did not enjoy the lesson because 'I know everything and it wasn't much fun'; 13% of those in the other group did not enjoy the lessons: they found them 'boring', or 'had done all the work before'.

Q2   Which topics did you enjoy the most?

The topics covered were: safety, health (including mental health and hobbies), dental health, bullying and being a teenager. The spread of interest was very similar between the two groups.

Q3   What made the topics enjoyable?

The reasons why they found certain topics interesting was also similar in the two groups, though the weighting was different. Seventy-three per cent of the

Circle Time group made reference to discovering how other people think and feel, talking and listening, and joining in activities and games. Fifty-one per cent of the other group made reference to increased awareness and feelings; the other 49 per cent enjoyed making posters or watching videos, or perceived the lesson to be 'fun'.

Q4   What methods (types of teaching) did the teacher use that helped you to understand the topics that you covered?

Teaching methods noted by the Circle Time group were: groupwork, drama/role-play, pairs, games, rounds, practising the skills of learning, visitors, the groundrules, and discussion. Students in the other group noted board-writing, groupwork, videos, posters, worksheets, visitors, and teacher explanation.

Q5   Do you use any of the methods (types of teaching or learning) that you used in PSE to help you in other lessons?

The level of awareness of transferable skills was interesting. The Circle Time group seemed to be much more aware of the learning process and the skills needed to learn. They noted that learning to talk easily was useful in English; that the five skills of speaking, listening, looking, thinking and concentrating that we constantly practice in the circle are useful in every subject area; and that role-play was useful in drama. The other group made very little connection between methods used in PSE and in other lessons. They seemed to be less aware of the process of learning.

Relational interactions

Q6   A list of tutor names
Q7   How many of these people did you know by name before you came to this school?
Q8   How many do you know by name now?
Q9   Write a positive comment next to each of the names describing some way in which you have got to know them.

Questions 6–9 attempt to quantify the increase in relational interactions in the group. Since the rest of the timetable is identical for the two groups, I have attributed any difference in degree of peer-awareness to the explicit relationship-building exercises used in Circle Time.

   Before coming to the secondary school, students in the Circle Time group averaged knowing five people in the group; students in the other group averaged knowing four people in the group.

   After 9 weeks, students in both groups knew the whole tutor group by name.

After the 9-week PSE module, students in the Circle Time group could give detailed personal information on an average of twelve people in the group. Students in the other group could give detailed personal information on an average of five people in the group. There was also a significant difference in the nature of the information. They were asked to make a positive comment that reflected some aspect of the person that they had come to know or appreciate. The Circle Time group had no problem in writing a great variety of information such as 'is a good runner', 'always happy', 'good at listening', 'kind', 'good sense of humour', etc. The other group seemed to find it much harder to find positive comments about character. They tended to record more facts about hobbies and wrote 'works hard', 'quiet', 'likes football', etc.

Q10   How confident do you feel about being able to share ideas in this group? (Very confident, Reasonably confident, Slightly under-confident, Very under-confident)

Of the students in the Circle Time group, 81 per cent felt very confident or reasonably confident about sharing ideas in the group; 19 per cent felt slightly under-confident or very under-confident about sharing ideas in the group. Of the students in the group taught using the student-centred approach only, 78 per cent felt very confident, or reasonably confident about sharing ideas in the group; 22 per cent felt slightly under-confident or very under-confident about sharing ideas in the group.

Q11   How good do you feel about being part of this tutor group? (Very good, Reasonably good, Not very good, Not at all good)

Ninety-five per cent of the students in the Circle Time group felt very good or reasonably good about being part of this tutor group. Ninety-two per cent of the students in the other group felt very good or reasonably good about being part of this tutor group.

It should be remembered that the teacher working with Group B was a highly experienced PSE teacher. She employed positive methods of classroom management and motivated by encouragement. The class engaged in groupwork activities and a considerable amount of discussion. This accounts for the high percentage of pupils who were comfortable to share ideas in the group and who felt good, or reasonably good about being part of this group. Despite the skill level of the teacher in Group B, Group A still scored higher, a fact that I would attribute to the strength of the Circle Time structures and strategies, not to the skill of the teacher/facilitator.

Interviews conducted amongst pupils indicated that the Circle Time group had gained considerable insight from the experience of learning PSE this way.

• 'The circle helped everyone to take part because in my old school when we did PSE we used to sit in rows in desks and in the circle we could see everybody and it was much easier to talk. You didn't feel that you had to turn round all the time, you just looked across the circle; much easier.'

- 'I think it did help build friendships because you learn that a lot of people share the same views as you, so you find new friends.'
- 'I liked passing the egg around and voicing our opinions. I thought it was cool how people had different opinions about different things.'
- 'I know people more intimately, so I get on better because there were some people I thought I didn't want to be friends with but when I got to know them, I found out I really liked them and I enjoy being friends with them.'
- 'I think the "thank yous" make people feel nicer inside because if you really help someone and they say "Oh thanks" you think they are a bit ungrateful really. But when they say "Thank you" in the circle, and say it in front of loads of people it makes you think "Yeah, they are so grateful for what I did". It just makes you feel so much better.'

The pupils' perception was that Circle Time had been a worthwhile activity and a relevant method for teaching PSE. They felt that they had benefited from the lessons individually and as a tutor group. Learning methods acquired during Circle Time were seen as relevant to other contexts and the pupils seemed to be much more aware of the learning *process*. Rogers (1983) argued the difference between 'teaching' and 'learning'. Significant learning 'combines the logical and the intuitive, the intellect and the feelings, the concept and the experience, the idea and the meaning. When we learn in that way, we are whole' (p. 20).

Teachers' attitudes to PSE taught through Circle Time

I began using Circle Time in registration with Year 7 groups. I run six 20-minute sessions and include themes of friendship, co-operation, the community, feelings and self-awareness. Even in these short sessions the tutors and myself have noticed an increase in self-confidence of some students. … It is intended that tutors will continue to use Circle Time with their tutor groups throughout their school lives, thus providing them with a forum for problem solving and building self-confidence.

C. Atherton, Cranford Community School

The teacher that I worked with in my research was in the position of being able to compare the work that I did with her usual approach to the same topics. She made the following observations about PSE taught through the circle.

I think it was a relaxed approach. It made people think a lot more about each other. I don't think it got as much detail about PSE topics, but that might not have mattered, depending on what the aim was. The main thing was it got them to know one another and their attitude to one another was much better.

> I think the circle increased the number of friendships and relationships in the group. They had opportunities to discover more about one another and more 'in depth' things than in normal discussion. They also sat next to different people all the time because of the way in which the circle worked. The games mixed them up, then 'apples, oranges' and move on two chairs constantly changed the pairs for paired work. They did not have a chance to get into friendship groups and stay there as they do in lessons sat at desks. I think that really helped them to find new people and get to know them.
>
> I found the egg the best bit. I especially liked the way in which the pupils took part and were willing to say what they thought. It was very powerful and the circle creates its own atmosphere.

Not everything was wonderful however, and she voiced some of the misgivings that teachers have in relation to this kind of group work, and particularly to the circle:

> There were several occasions when I felt quite vulnerable. It is not usual for me to tell pupils anything about myself in a discussion. I would normally get their opinion, but not give mine. In the circle, when the egg came to me, I had to say something about myself and I found that quite difficult at first, but I thought it was good.

This teacher also voiced her initial scepticism about some of the activities of the circle. She thought that pupils would consider the games 'beneath them' and was both amazed and pleased when she saw how involved they became and how much they evidently enjoyed the lessons.

Implications

Drawing together some of the findings of this research, we find issues that have implications in our education system, particularly in secondary schools.

1. Tutors or PSE teachers can make a difference to how the pupils in tutor groups view themselves and relate to one another. Student-centred methods of teaching PSE have a positive impact, Circle Time techniques are even more effective. In raising self-esteem, we will raise pupil confidence to tackle new situations, raise expectation and, in the long-term, raise performance: 'Many theories of self-esteem point out that if an individual becomes part of a group they trust and feel safe in, then the group can open up to that individual a new, more positive view of their self' (Mosley, 1993, p. 58).

   Circle Time also breaks down the 'in group, out group' power bases that young people establish in tutor groups. The games and activities constantly mix up the working groups and establish common links across the subgroupings of the class. Individuals and groups are perceived in many different lights, making it much harder for 'cliques' to maintain their mystique.

2. There is a conflict between PSE course content in terms of the information students need (particularly in relation to sex and drug education, aspects of healthy living and work experience) and the process. So many PSE programmes become bogged down in content at the expense of process. There may well be an argument for allocating content to subject areas such as science and careers, while concentrating on the relevant personal processes in PSE or tutor time. *A whole-school approach would ensure liaison between subject areas and the pastoral teams.*

3. Some teachers feel under-confident and insecure with tutorial and PSE programmes. For a Circle Time programme to work, tutors would have to practise the skills needed to run circles effectively. Mosley (1996, p. 36) lists the skills as:

    *   The ability to listen well.
    *   The ability to be honest sometimes about your own feelings and thoughts.
    *   The ability to use good eye contact and show emotional warmth and empathy.
    *   The ability to recap what pupils have said and reflect it back to them to show you have understood.
    *   The ability to notice and thank pupils for the skills focused on in Circle Time: i.e. thinking, looking, listening, speaking and concentrating.

4. Pupils are in no doubt that they value the Circle Time meeting and the opportunity it gives to develop relationships and explore issues relevant to their world.

5. In order for teachers to feel confident with any PSE teaching, INSET is needed and a commitment to widespread PSE in initial teacher training. This research indicates that Circle Time is a powerful technique in the secondary school, just as it has proved to be in primary education. It is an underpinning process through which much of the current PSE curriculum could be explored. Yet, as with any initiative, without government backing to provide funding for the required training and resources, the situation with regard to PSE in secondary schools is likely to remain unchanged.

Conclusions

There have been many great initatives to improve PSE teaching and to make the design and delivery of a balanced course easier. There seems to be considerable conformity over the content of a pastoral curriculum, however it is delivered. It is the process of delivery that lacks coherence, the very process which is often of greater value in personal, social, behavioural, moral and spiritual development than the content.

In recent years, research by Howard Gardner (1993) into the concept of 'multiple intelligences' has furnished a growing recognition of the importance of developing relationship skills and emotions in education. Gardner's work paved the way and Goleman (1996) added greater credibility with his book *Emotional Intelligence* in which he cites work that seeks to bring emotion within the domain of intelligence. Social intelligence is both distinct from academic abilities and a key part of what makes people do well in the practicalities of life. When researchers tried to define intelligence in terms of what it takes to lead life successfully, they came up with abilities in five main areas:

- *Knowing one's emotions* – self-awareness, recognizing feelings and the ability to monitor them – important in decision making and valuing one's own decisions
- *Managing emotions* – handling feelings so they are appropriate – necessary for dealing effectively with the setbacks of life
- *Motivating oneself* – marshalling emotions in the service of a goal – essential for paying attention, mastery, creativity and stifling impulsiveness
- *Recognizing emotions in others* – empathy, a fundamental 'people skill' – a necessary skill for the caring professions
- *Handling relationships* – the skill of managing emotions in others – renders it possible to interact smoothly with others.

At the same time as this research is unfolding, concern over behaviour in schools, teenage pregnancy, parenting and other social issues has increased interest in self-esteem, emotional education, communication and relationship skills within the school setting. Education Minister, Estelle Morris, talks about relationship as the 'fourth R'.

Society is making increasing demands on schools to educate for life so that young people are able to cope in today's world. We ignore the process of emotional growth and personal, social development at out peril. Teachers increasingly find themselves educators against the backdrop of crumbling institutions such as family, church and the concept of stable relationships. How can they 'secure for all pupils opportunities for learning particularly likely to contribute to personal and social development' if they are not provided with the time and the training to do so? Perhaps we should leave the final word to a pupil in a Year 7 class in one of our secondary schools:

> 'I think if you just sit down at tables and on chairs and discuss things it doesn't really work. It doesn't have as much effect, but if you sit in a circle, you can see everyone, you can see them talking and hear them really well, you don't have to turn around, so you concentrate more.'

References

Brandes, D. and Ginnes, P. (1986) *A Guide to Student Centred Learning*. Oxford: Blackwell.

Burns, R. (1979) *The Self Concept*. London: Longman.

Burns, R. (1982) *Self Concept Development and Education*. London: Holt Saunders.

Button, L. (1982) *Group Tutoring for the Form Teacher*, Two books: *Lower Secondary (1), and Upper Secondary (2)e*. London: Hodder and Stoughton.

DfEE (1997) *Excellence in Schools*, London.

DfEE (1997) *Excellence for All Children: Meeting Special Educational Needs*, London.

Gardner, G. (1993) *Multiple Intelligences: The Theory in Practice*. London: Fontana Press.

Goleman, D. (1996) *Emotional Intelligence*. London: Bloomsbury.

Lawrence, D. (1985) 'Improving reading and self-esteem', *Educational Research* 27 (3), pp. 194–200.

Lawrence, D. (1988) *Enhancing Self-esteem in the Classroom*. London: Paul Chapman Press.

Maslow, A. H. (1962) 'Some Basic Propositions of Growth and Self-actualisation Psychology' in A. W. Combs (ed.) *Perceiving, Behaving, Becoming*. Washington, DC: ASCD Year Book.

Moreno, J. L. (1934) *Who Shall Survive?* New York: Plenum Press.

Moreno, J. L. (1946) *Psychodrama* (2nd revised edn). New York: Beacon House.

Mosley J. (1996) *Quality Circle Time*. Cambridge: LDA.

Rogers, C. (1951) *Client Centred Therapy*. Boston: Houghton Mifflin.

Rogers, C. (1961) *On Becoming a Person*. Boston: Houghton Mifflin.

Rogers, C. (1969) *Freedom to Learn: A View of what Education Might Become*. Columbus, Ohio: Charles E. Merrill.

Rogers, C. (1983) *Freedom to Learn for the Eighties*. London: Merrill.

Rotter, J. B. (1966) 'Generalised Expectancies for Internal versus External Control of Reinforcement', *Psychology Monographs* 80, pp. 1–28.

Chapter 11

Bullying at school: the no-blame approach

Lorraine Demko

Introduction

Bullying at school affects an estimated 1.5 million young people, making it probably the most underrated problem in Britian's schools today. Bullying can cause mental health problems which may affect people long after their school days are over. Pupils' academic success may also be at risk if they feel threatened and intimidated.

Persistent bullying may be verbal, physical or psychological, or a combination of these. It can include kicking, shoving, name-calling, intimidation or torment, as well as the fear of being bullied. Apart from making the victim miserable, bullying can lead to bedwetting, nightmares, faking illness, truancy, physical injury and, in extreme cases, to suicide.

There is, however, no evidence to suggest that the conventional method of tackling bullying – punishment of the bully – is effective. A new and somewhat controversial method of tackling bullying in schools – the no-blame approach – is therefore being promoted by Eastern Surrey Health Commission to see if it can reduce the incidence of bullying behaviour, and encourage the victims to tell others what has happened.

Research carried out by Peter Smith of the Department of Psychology at the University of Sheffield, for the Department for Education (1994), showed that most victims do not tell anyone. The no-blame approach is controversial because it rejects punitive ways of dealing with bullying behaviour, in favour of a non-punitive approach. Eastern Surrey Health Promotion believes that if punitive ways of dealing with bullying worked, bullying would not present such an enormous problem.

Group dynamics

The no-blame approach is a whole-school approach. It relies on group dynamics and the empathy of the group members. The method puts the emphasis on the effects of bullying on the victim's feelings and emotions, rather than on the ins and outs of what occurred. You do need to know who was involved in the bullying incident. Instead of being punished, bullies are involved in looking at how their actions have affected the victim.

The approach was developed by Barbara Maines, an educational psychologist in Avon, and George Robinson, Director of Studies at the West of England University (1991a,b). When implemented effectively, research has shown that it will reduce bullying to extremely low levels (1994).

The aim of the Surrey project was to introduce schools to the no-blame approach. This project was funded by the Department of Public Health in Eastern Surrey Health Commission, in response to the report on the ChildLine Bullying Line (La Fontaine) on the incidence of bullying reported in independent, day and boarding schools.

This chapter reports the findings of the pilot study into the implementation of the no-blame approach. After the pilot was completed, 12 independent schools in the East Surrey area adopted the no-blame approach using the process developed as a result of the pilot.

Aims

My aim was first, to find out the extent and type of bullying taking place in a boys' preparatory school; second, to identify the most appropriate strategy to help the school to deal with it, and third, to evaluate the success of the strategy. In the summer of 1993, a questionnaire was distributed to 148 pupils aged seven to 13 attending a boys' preparatory school. The questionnaire was anonymous, but boys could sign it if they wanted. Any boy who signed the questionnaire was followed up by the school. The aim of the questionnaire was to identify where bullying was taking place, what form it took and how pupils wanted the school to intervene. The results obtained were also used later to help assess how much the incidence of bullying had fallen since the beginning of the project.

More than 80 per cent of pupils said that a little bullying went on in the school and more than half had actually experienced bullying. More than 80 per cent said they would speak to someone if bullied: almost three-quarters of the sample said they would speak to parents and almost half said they would talk to their friends. More than a third of the sample said they were worried about being bullied at school.

When asked what the school could do to stop bullying, more than a quarter of the pupils suggested punishment, more than a third recommended intervention by the school, fewer than a quarter wanted more staff on duty and about one in seven suggested that bullies should be expelled.

Staff from the school and from Eastern Surrey Health Promotion discussed various options (Maines and Robinson 1991a, 1991b; Elliott 1991). One possibility was to organize bully courts, which use peer pressure to change the behaviour of the bully. Another was to introduce a suggestion box in which pupils would place ideas about what punishment would be appropriate. The disadvantage to this scheme is that teachers have no control over what suggestions are made, and this may lead to retribution by the bully.

The third option was the no-blame approach. As described in *Stamp out Bullying* (Maines and Robinson 1991b), it involves implementing seven steps:

(1) Take an account from the victim – who must be really listened to. The circumstances in which the bullying took place are not important, but its effects are. Note the feelings expressed, and allow the victim to elaborate at length, through talking, pictures and writing.
(2) Convene a meeting of all those involved in the bullying – to include no more than eight people. Those attending should include the chief instigators and observers or those who colluded by failing to intervene. The victim should not be present at this meeting.
(3) Explain that there is a problem for the victim and clearly describe the distress caused by the bullying.
(4) Instead of attributing blame, state that you know that members of the group are responsible and can do something about it.
(5) Ask all the group members if they can make suggestions on how they could help. Do not extract a promise of improved behaviour.
(6) Arrange to meet the group a week later to check progress.
(7) Throughout, convey your belief that the young people are not bad, that they are capable of kind behaviour and that they will help the victim.

The deputy head of the school thought that the no-blame approach complemented existing codes of practice within the school and would work well with existing lines of communication between pupils, teachers and parents. The school therefore decided to implement the approach.

Its first step was to organize small discussion groups with pupils to talk about what it would feel like to be bullied, what they would do if they were bullied or saw someone else being bullied. At this stage, only the deputy head had received training on the no-blame approach. At these meetings, teachers explained how the no-blame approach works. They stressed that bullies would not be punished and that victims would receive support and advice from one of two teachers appointed to deal with such problems.

Building on work already done at the school and the data from the questionnaire, the school developed a policy on bullying which was circulated to the head, deputy head, the director of studies and the school governors before being disseminated to staff, pupils, parents and governors. It included sections on the following:

- Our aim for your son.
- Definitions of the bully and the victim.
- Where does bullying take place?
- The results of the survey.
- Procedure for incidents for pupils, teachers and parents.

The school appointed two members of staff to deal with bullying incidents and to liaise with all other staff on such problems. The policy was implemented in September 1993.

Evaluation

In the spring of 1994, two terms after introduction of the policy, a second questionnaire was administered to the same 148 pupils to evaluate its effectiveness. The results of this questionnaire showed that, while there had been some reduction in bullying, the school had not fully implemented the approach. More than half of the pupils felt that the incidence of bullying had reduced. A quarter felt that it was the same. Almost half of the pupils said they had been bullied in their class or year, and that they had talked to someone about it. More than half of those who said they had been bullied had not talked to someone about it. Just over half said their class or tutor group teacher had not talked to them about bullying. A similar proportion said they would like to spend more time talking about and looking at bullying in more detail.

The evaluation highlighted the need for more preventive work and better communication within the school to ensure that pupils, staff and parents understood the approach and felt confident about using it. For example, it was felt that not all bullying incidents were being reported, and that bullying was still occurring in the playground, although staff had increased their vigilance.

The main problem appeared to be that by the time the message about the approach reached the pupils and teachers (via the deputy head), it was greatly weakened. Staff had no clear understanding of how the approach worked, or the philosophy behind it. Many pupils said that they had not been informed about the approach. The school therefore decided to set up a working party to plan half-day training sessions for pupils.

Lack of success

The no-blame approach was not totally successful in this pilot project because of several factors. These included:

- Lack of training for all members of the teaching staff on issues related to bullying and the no-blame approach.
- Lack of clear objectives in the planning of the work on bullying which was carried out with the pupils.
- Lack of training for parents on issues related to bullying and the no-blame approach, including the need for parents to co-operate with the school's policy on bullying. Parents should not advise their children to tackle the bullies themselves: by definition, the victims do not have the skills or resources to deal with the problem and could end up feeling even more helpless.
- There was little uptake of the support that was available from the health promotion unit, the educational psychology department or the school nursing service.

To help other schools, the head, deputy head and the director of studies drew up recommendations with the support of the health promotion unit on the best way of implementing the no-blame approach. These are as follows:

- Provide a comprehensive training programme with clear objectives for the whole school community. This should enable the school to implement the no-blame approach as part of a whole-school response to bullying behaviour.
- Hold an awareness-raising day, looking at issues around bullying and the no-blame approach.
- Provide INSET training by an experienced practitioner on the no-blame approach to all teaching and support staff.
- Make use of consultancy services to schools, so that the school has professional support when developing its own anti-bullying policy.
- Plan and support work with the children on increasing awareness of and understanding the process of bullying, for example, through drama, art and poetry.
- Explore what it is like to be a bully and to be a victim and demonstrate that bullying is not acceptable to the school.
- Hold parents' workshops to inform and train parents on the no-blame approach.
- Hold follow-up workshops, to enable teachers to share their experiences and models of good practice within their school.

Conclusions

The pilot study showed that if the no-blame approach is to reduce bullying, the whole school must be committed to it. A cascade of information on its own cannot give a clear understanding of how this approach to bullying is best implemented or of the group dynamics involved in bullying. Before teachers, or anyone else, can understand the effects of bullying, they need first to understand the pain and suffering to enable them to empathize with the victims. The pilot has shown that if teachers are to achieve this, schools need to receive adequate training, advice and support from appropriate professionals.

Teachers need to have clear and achievable goals if they are to reduce bullying behaviour. Following the pilot study, the health promotion unit now adopts the model described above when introducing new schools to the no-blame approach.

Feedback from parents whose boys were at the school where the pilot project was conducted has been very encouraging. Parents were informed by a letter that accompanied the anti-bullying policy that the school has been a front-runner in addressing bullying behaviour and reassured that if they report an incident of bullying, the school will deal with it swiftly and effectively.

The school involved in this pilot project has now adopted the new procedure for implementing the no-blame approach.

References

Department for Education (1994) *Bullying: Don't Suffer in Silence: An Antibullying Pack for Schools*, HMSO, London.

Elliott, M. (Ed.) (1991) *Bullying: A Practical Guide to Coping for Schools*, Longman/Kidscape, London.

La Fontaine, J., *Bullying: The Child's View – An Analysis of Telephone Calls to ChildLine about Bullying*, available from Turnaround Distribution Ltd, 27 Horsell Road, London N5 1XL.

Maines, B. and Robinson, G. (1991a) *Michael's Story ... the No-blame Approach*, Lame Duck, Bristol.

Maines, B. and Robinson, G. (1991b) *Stamp out Bullying*, Lame Duck, Bristol.

Maines, B. and Robinson, G. (1994) 'The no-blame approach to bullying', paper presented to the British Association for the Advancement of Science, Psychology Section, September.

Chapter 12

Learning support units (LSUs): a modern miracle or an old wolf in older sheep's clothing?

Bob Sproson

Introduction

In this chapter I look at the origin of learning support units (LSUs) in England and identify the view of the Department for Education and Skills (DfES) of what an LSU should be and do.

> LSUs (learning support units) are an important element in the Government's drive for behaviour improvement in schools. There are now in excess of 1,100 around the country and the number is growing steadily
>
> (Chris Gittins, 2002, in a letter to LSU managers and headteachers of secondary schools with an LSU)

I then attempt to consider my own experience of the reality of these aspirations. Finally I reflect upon my own experiences as Manager of 'behaviour support' to secondary schools in my own local education authority and of responding to LSU financing.

LSU origins and purpose:

The beginnings of LSUs lie within the Excellence in Cities initiative launched by the UK government in 1999 and at the time of writing they are a key element of the government's inclusion and improved behaviour agenda. From the outset the Department for Education and Employment (DfEE), renamed the

Department for Education and Skills (DfES), has seen LSUs as something new. They were not to be a re-emergence of the old 'remedial' departments. On no account were any young people to receive their whole education within an LSU, nor were they to be 'placed' therein for a lengthy period of time. The stated intention from the outset has been that LSUs were not to be 'sin bins', although a TES headline hailing their development (26th April 2000) reads: '1000 sin bins to curb the unruly'. Neither staff nor students were to see an LSU as a place where bad children are sent. Even more importantly, bad children were not to be sent there permanently.

Alan Thompson, a DfEE official, set out clearly in an annex to a Standards Fund Circular (2000) what should not be tolerated in LSUs. The following are listed as 'barriers to success':

- the centre being seen as separate or exclusively concerned with SEN;
- long term student placements which result in difficulties in reintegration;
- minimal involvement of subject teachers;
- a lack of opportunity for the centre to influence the work of the school;
- a lack of clear entry and exit criteria.

He envisaged LSUs as small, probably having a maximum of ten students at any given time, staffed by trained full-time staff or teachers released part-time from other duties. There must be absolutely clear referral criteria and no student's 'length of stay' should exceed two terms. All pupils must have targets set and communicated within a device such as an IBP (individual behaviour plan) and the following performance indicators were to be used:

- reduction in the number and frequency of incidents leading to a punishment being imposed;
- reduction in the number of fixed term and permanent exclusions;
- improved rates of attendance;
- improved educational attainment of pupils referred.

Baselines and targets were to be set to show 'the extent to which the LSU is expected to reduce the number of, for example, exclusions and increase the rate of attendance'.

In summary LSUs were intended to:

- enable schools to provide short-term teaching and support programmes to meet the needs of difficult to manage (my term, not the DfES') students;
- keep disaffected students in schools whilst addressing the behaviour management difficulties which they present and enabling them to reintegrate full time (reduce exclusions);
- minimise the difficulties caused to staff by the most difficult to manage students without recourse to exclusion.

The last bullet point harmonises with a statement made by Estelle Morris, the then Secretary of State, at a 1999 headteachers' conference when she stated that there was no contradiction between the government's stated aim to raise standards of behaviour and attainment and its drive to maintain 'difficult and disaffected' pupils within mainstream classrooms. She left promptly at the end of her address without taking questions.

   These original aims and aspirations for LSUs are adapted in the DfES (2002) document 'Guidance for Establishing and Managing LSUs'. Although the general view of how LSUs should be utilised is little changed, there is now the clear direction that they should be bespoke and developed according to identified needs within each school. LSUs should:

- be designed to meet the needs of *carefully selected* pupils (my italics);
- be an integral part of a whole school behaviour and inclusion policy;
- be developed through a whole school behaviour audit (this is new);
- provide targeted support for specific priorities within the school's behaviour and inclusion strategy.

Despite the individual nature of each LSU there should remain features which are common to all in order to achieve desired outcomes. Key features remain much as those envisaged by Alan Thompson, although they are now expanded. I have listed 23 such features:

1. it is part of whole school policy;
2. it is supported and regularly reviewed by senior management;
3. there is clear line management;
4. it is recognised by pupils and parents as an asset to the school, helping those with difficulties;
5. all teachers and support staff are involved and aware of working principles;
6. the role of the LSU is tightly defined as a raft of intervention strategies;
7. LSUs are seen as 'centres of excellence'. Staff provide training to other staff;
8. responsibility for referral lies with a designated senior manager;
9. referrals are never made outside of agreed procedures;
10. the referral process is evidence-based and formulates 'treatment' in the form of an IEP or other plan;
11. referred students' social interaction during break and lunchtimes is 'organised';
12. pupils work to targets agreed with parents and success is regularly celebrated;
13. there is a separation of LSU students from those excluded from lessons as an emergency;

14. regular (even daily) contact is maintained with parents/carers and form tutors/pastoral staff;
15. there is an identified programme of learning which addresses 'individual difficulties' and includes teaching to improve numeracy and literacy and directed work on social and emotional literacy;
16. teaching is always aimed at reintegration to mainstream classes;
17. teaching is adapted to the 'styles elsewhere in the school' and styles 'appropriate to the pupil';
18. there is always planned and phased reintegration;
19. pupils should be able to return for extra support if they 'regress', but this is strictly controlled for times 'that are agreed by everyone';
20. there is regular monitoring and evaluation through the collation of recorded data;
21. there are strong multi-agency links to encourage 'good family working';
22. wide use is made of other trained and vetted adults;
23. pupils all view the LSU as a place for 'rigorous learning' which 'supports pupils in mastering the challenge of school and raises their self esteem and motivation in a caring and positive atmosphere'.

Potential for sources of these aspirations

I applaud the intention that schools should attempt to cater for and support difficult to manage students and that LEAs have a role to play in ensuring that schools do that. However, the assumptions underlying the stated aims and functions of LSUs raise a number of issues that warrant discussion.

The very fact that LSUs are for 'specially selected' students is significant. I take 'specially selected' to mean not that the students are selected on the basis that they are the most difficult to manage within the schools, rather that they are selected as being like the hero, Morgan, in the 1968 film, 'A Suitable Case for Treatment'. Thus there will be those who are difficult to manage, not suitable for treatment, who must tread other paths, presumably leading elsewhere.

LSUs are intended mainly for difficult to manage students, students who have a propensity to behave in ways which adults, and often peers, find intimidating, threatening or strange and yet the insistence must be upon high standards of behaviour within their confines. I am not seeking to suggest either that it is fine for students to 'misbehave' or that we should not seek to attain high standards, but, unless my experience is exceptional, young people who inhabit an emotionally arid domestic world will act out their anger at times during the school day. There is real confusion within the inclusion rhetoric here. This rhetoric spreads right through the range of provision for students who are difficult to manage and is fuelled by the drive for standards and the needs of target-setting. Just as doctors achieve far better results if they treat patients of basically sound constitution who do not smoke, eat a healthy diet and exercise, so teachers do so with students well fitted, emotionally and intellectually, to education.

Learning support units are not intended to support students who require 'specialist provision'. There are inclusionists who would argue that such specialist provision should simply not be required. Certainly, however many places are made available, students appear to fill them, and then there are always more students requiring specialist placement. This may be an argument for not providing any discrete provision or it could be utilised to support the view that it is only society's insistence that all young people attend the institution of school that creates the need for discrete specialist provision for some.

I have a degree of sympathy for both views. I currently, however, believe that we delude ourselves that we can enable/empower/support/train/ cajole/bribe/make almost all young people behave in a manner that is acceptable within mainstream schools. LSUs, and other specialist provision for students who are difficult to manage, are all required to meet targets which relate to learning outcomes and improved behaviour and attendance. Put simply, the best way to run a school that can meet government success criteria is not to have any students in it who are difficult to manage. We are always trying to approximate to mainstream, to replicate what is available there, and to monitor progress against similar criteria. Thus local education authorities end up with students who do not fit anywhere. Currently we have examples of specialist independent provision called anything but schools so that they will not be inspected within a schools framework in order that students who choose not to 'respond to support' can be 'hidden away' by LEAs responsible for their education. No-one wants Office for Standards in Education (OFSTED) inspectors to arrive and find students who have been referred into a particular provision because of their long proven propensity to behave 'inappropriately' doing just that!

My point here is simply that within this tight DfEE/DfES definition of LSU provision those students who present severe management difficulties cannot be catered for, thus in schools where staff practice is good, even excellent, one wonders for which students the LSU will provide. Perhaps they should target those students who want to learn, but find the hustle and bustle, the size, the noise of mainstream education intolerable. Such students may have the potential to achieve well in terms of attendance and attainment, provided that they are not squeezed back into the hurly-burly.

Secondly there is confusion as to whether referral to the LSU is punishment or support. It is formally described as the latter. However, a legitimate reason for referral is return to school post-exclusion which is clearly a punishment. Placement in an LSU therefore may be seen to constitute part of this form of punishment also.

Thirdly there is a notion of short-term cure here, in the idea that is conveyed of 'revolving door' PRUs. Take the students out for a while, develop some skills, work on self esteem and they are fit for mainstream. My experience leads me to believe that support of whatever kind often needs to be longer term than this and the dangers described in the next point are clear. There is an acknowledgement that training and support from LSU staff should be utilised to modify mainstream practice to make it more inclusive of a broader diversity of students. Many mainstream teachers find the notion that they might alter their behaviour to accommodate a young person very difficult, however.

Fourthly, for students with little investment in mainstream education and little perceived chance of 'achievement' there may be little motivation to leave the LSU after the maximum two terms. I sat with a student in a local LSU who, despite the DfES's guidelines that students should not access the whole of their learning experience within an LSU, spent a whole term attending the LSU solely. When I broached the notion of going back to mainstream lessons, he told me quite clearly, and with no hint of antagonism or unpleasantness, that if we tried to make him go back, he would simply go and find the headteacher and swear very loudly at him. That would ensure referral back to the LSU. He liked it there, he felt a sense of personal achievement and he had little intention of giving it up. A situation like this presents a school with a dilemma, whether to refuse to allow the student to remain in the LSU beyond the prescribed two terms, in which case exclusion or a 'managed move' appear the only remaining options, or break the rules and allow the student to remain in the LSU.

Lastly, the greatest difficulty facing LSU staff is the differing perceptions of stakeholders:

- LEAs may have devolved the funding to schools but they retain a monitoring role and will need to show that progress has been made against the prescribed performance indicators.
- Senior staff may share that view or could see the role differently.
- Some mainstream teaching staff may simply want respite from certain students with minimal referral criteria to the LSU.
- Parents may have a variety of views, as will support staff and students.

It is my experience that the same dilemmas face the new LSUs as faced many of the 1970s and 1980s remedial departments, special schools, and all other specialist provision. The question is whether LSUs exist to:

- take a few students away or support and improve mainstream practice;
- protect the greater good of the community by removing unwanted students because those students have an equal right to a high quality educational experience;
- be supportive or isolationist and punitive units.

Some parents/carers will shift heaven and earth to get their charges admitted, others will fight tooth and nail to keep them out.

Personal experience within one local education authority

My personal experience of LSUs in the LEA leads me to identify a number of practical issues in relation to their functioning. Among these are resourcing and what constitutes evidence of 'success'.

Resource issues

Ongoing government funding for LSUs is not guaranteed.

Following our first allocation of money through the Standards Fund of 2000–01, my local education authority set about identifying appropriate schools in which to develop LSUs. Complex mathematical computations were performed to identify the schools with the greatest need. Once funding was split between schools only two received sums that allowed them to make any accommodation available for the work. A further seven schools have received up to £28,000 per annum to staff and resource the provision. Given that the minimum staffing for an LSU is considered by 2002 (within the DfES guidance) to be, 'a full time LSU manager and a classroom assistant', and that, with oncosts, and any sort of management responsibility allowance the LSU manager will cost the employer around £32,000, then it is clear that these schools have not been fully funded by the support provided to them. There is even more concern now that the LEA and headteachers have been notified that grant 201 (School Inclusion: Pupil Support) which funds LSUs will cease from 2003–04. The DfES is looking to LEAs and schools to maintain these from 'general funding'. Few schools will wish to place provision for difficult to manage students at the top of their list of priorities. Unless funding is ring-fenced for students who can be infuriating and tiresome and time-consuming, it will never survive competition from other 'bidders' under general funding. This does not bode well for the future of LSUs.

Addressing government success criteria

In order to address success criteria in the current OFSTED inspection framework I have to evaluate the work of my service. In terms of practice there have been some excellent pieces of work carried out in LSUs especially when that has linked in clearly with the work of behaviour support teachers. I need to back up 'good news stories' with figures and show how we have worked with schools to develop successful and innovative LSU provision. I can certainly show that we have worked hand in hand with schools and can provide case studies of students who have remained within mainstream who would otherwise have been excluded. We also have data from interviews with parents, students and staff which show how highly valued some of the LSU provision is and how much particular students feel they have progressed. There is hardly a negative comment within the data. The problem is that I have no evidence that any of this work has reduced the numbers of students requiring 'education otherwise than at school' (EOTAS), or that the number of days lost to exclusion has significantly reduced. Although the data collection exercise produced much that is positive, the evidence that LSUs have managed to 'cure' students and move them back away from the need for support within two terms is not clear. There have been some examples of this, but largely students like what they get and are determined to hang on to it. Also many students have loved having LSUs as a near-permanent base. Well laid reintegration plans have rarely worked.

Of the schools funded through the Standards Fund grants only two are continuing to run what is instantly recognisable as an LSU. Of those, one is currently undergoing significant recruitment difficulties and has had to close the LSU through lack of staff. We do intend to re-open, but the remit of the LSU will be significantly altered when that happens. The other school is running a successful Key Stage 3 (students aged 11–14) programme that is:

- working very closely with our EOTAS providers to create bespoke programmes for students,
- supporting some very difficult to manage KS3 students in a whole variety of ways,
- having a small but discernible influence upon the practice of some 'mainstream' staff.

The unit has been staffed from the outset by two very talented and committed support staff who bring huge amounts of care and energy to their work. Staffing has latterly been augmented by the full-time attachment of a senior member of staff as manager. This LSU will undoubtedly continue. As yet there is little reduction in referral levels for EOTAS, but there is evidence that that may come. There is evidence of improved attendance on the part of referred students and ample evidence that student behaviour within the LSU is very good. It remains a struggle to have 'two term turnarounds'. The staff's experience is that students require ongoing support to 'survive' in mainstream. This unit is well supported by senior management and this has meant that simple 'dumping' of students has not been allowed to take place. Those very senior staff who ensure that this does not happen visit the LSU 'informally' on occasions.

There is a further success story. In one of the county's village colleges there exists a senior management team which is wholly committed to the notion of inclusive education. Through the creative use of LSU funding they have set up what we call an LSU. A small number of students do move from here into the mainstream and a further small number access some mainstream lessons whilst being based in the 'LSU'. The vast majority of students (thirty plus), however, attend the LSU full time, just as they might attend an offsite pupil referral unit (PRU). The curriculum is substantially different from mainstream as is the ethos. The inclusion ethos is shared, at least by senior management, and the emphasis is upon preparation for post-16 next step rather than reintegration to mainstream during compulsory education. There have been visits from HMI leading to complimentary feedback. This 'LSU' 'works' for its students, but comes nowhere near to meeting the DfES criteria.

Conclusion

To summarise, from experience my feelings about LSUs are as follows.

In schools where teachers practise effectively and, by definition, respectfully of students, there is little requirement for an LSU as described within the DfES guidance. When 'carefully selected' students are supported in such a manner, our experience has been that they do attend better, are happier, both at school and at home, and generally have a much 'nicer' time. I am not convinced that learning outcomes grow enormously, or that students will allow themselves to go back full-time into 'the mainstream'. LSUs, by definition, will not maintain the most difficult to manage students within schools unless they are adapted in the way described above, which strictly moves them outside the LSU remit. Genuine reflection brings me back to my core belief. Education is always a human process. Effective practitioners make good or bad systems work and enable vulnerable and/or difficult to manage students to find a handhold on the face of the mainstream cliff. The best of systems without creative, warm, committed, caring practitioners will fail. No matter how we try to dress all this up, some teachers succeed with nearly all students, no matter what. Some only succeed with the chosen few. Some barely do that.

References

DfES (2002) 'Guidance for Establishing and Managing LSUs'. DfES.

Gittins, C. (2002) 'Letter to LSU managers and headteachers of secondary schools with an LSU'. DfES.

Thompson, A. (2000) 'Annex C to Standards Fund Circular (Supplement) 24(b) Secondary School Learning Support Units'. DfEE.

Chapter 13

Nurture Groups: the research evidence

Paul Cooper[1]

Introduction

This chapter deals with Nurture Groups, which are a form of educational provision for children with Social, Emotional and Behavioural Difficulties (SEBD). The specific focus of the chapter is an exploration of the body of research that provides insight into the effects of Nurture Groups on the social, emotional, behavioural and educational functioning of children with SEBD. After a brief account of the history of Nurture Groups and their theoretical and organisation features, particular attention is given to the University of Leicester Nurture Group Research Project.[2] This is a national study of the personal, social and educational outcomes associated with NG placement that took place in the UK between 1999 and 2001.

Nurture Groups 1970–2003: theory and development

Nurture Groups (NGs) can be defined as a school-based learning environment specifically designed for pupils whose difficulties in accessing school-learning are underpinned by an apparent need for social and individual experiences that can be construed in terms of unmet early learning needs

---

[1] Key statistical sections of this paper are based on work carried out in collaboration with Dr David Whitebread, Faculty of Education University of Cambridge

[2] Research staff on the project were Ray Arnold, Eve Boyd, Jane Lovey, Janie Butler and Kris Neilson. The project was funded by the Nuffield Foundation.

(Bennathan and Boxall, 2000; Boxall, 2002). The key insight here is that for some children the developmental processes associated with early attachment needs are incomplete when they reach the statutory age of school enrolment.

This means that the guiding theory of Nurture Groups is that many children who exhibit emotional and behavioural difficulties often experience emotions and exhibit behaviours that are deemed inappropriate to their age range. Normal infant behaviour, it is argued, is characterised by extreme egocentrism, and a concomitant disregard for the needs and feelings of others. In order to progress from this state to the level of social competence that is required in the standard infant school classroom, the individual has to go through a nurturing process that equips them with the ability to meet their individual psychological needs through social interaction, through means that are compatible with the needs of others (Maslow, 1970). This process is essential to healthy psychological development in general, since without such progress individuals will be severely impaired in their ability to understand and regulate their behaviour, form relationships, and communicate with others. The process is also vital in laying the social and psychological foundations for learning as conceptualised from a socio-cultural perspective (Vygotsky, 1987 edn.; Bruner et al., 1966). Thinking about Nurture Group practice has been strongly influenced by Bowlby's attachment theory (Bennathan and Boxall, 2000). In this way NGs can be located in the tradition of developmentally informed types of provision (Bennathan and Boxall, 2000) such as Feuerstein's (1969) 'Instrumental Enrichment' Programme and the High/Scope programme (Berrueta-Clement et al, 1984; Sylva, 1986; Sylva and Ilsley, 1992).

The NG is designed to provide pupils with an educational bridge to permanent and full-time placement in mainstream classrooms. This is achieved by combining features of a caring home environment with formal curricular demands. One of the crucial elements of the thinking underpinning NGs addresses directly the important distinction between the NG and family setting. Whilst NGs contain many of the features of a family setting (i.e. soft furnishings, kitchen and dining facilities) the preferred group size, according to the originator of NGs (Boxall, 2002), should have a lower limit of ten pupils (the upper limit is 12). Educationally, this is designed to give the pupils the experience of involvement in group activities, and to enable the teaching of group participation skills that will be necessary for successful engagement in a mainstream classroom. This measure also helps prevent the development of inappropriate child–adult attachments that might challenge the parent–child relationship. These aims are further supported by the requirement of the classic NG model that NG pupils remain on the roll of a mainstream class, attending for registration in the mornings and participating in mainstream class activities for at least one afternoon per week, and more during the period of phased reintegration that is sometimes deemed appropriate for returning pupils. Rather than attempting to mimic or usurp the parent–child attachment relationship, NGs are intended to produce a form of educational attachment. That is, within the confines of the educational setting, children are encouraged to develop trusting and caring relationships with adults which are carefully focused on enabling pupils to learn and practise pro-social skills and engage in the challenges of formal curricular tasks.

Practical insights from Attachment Theory are exploited in a number of ways. The two adults are always present, and their patterns of interactions with one another are designed to model positive social interaction and cooperation. For example, it is common in NGs for the staff to engage in conversations with one another in full view and hearing of the NG pupils, and, in so doing, illustrate patterns of discussion, debate and collaborative decision making. The daily routine within the group is explicit, uniform and predictable. NG staff engage in intensive interaction (Nind, 1999) with individual pupils, at appropriate times throughout the NG day, and this is balanced with periods of group instruction. The 'classic' (see below) NG day is structured in accordance with the standard school day. The social and developmental targets for individual pupils are devised on the basis of psychometric assessment of their developmental needs and functioning (the Boxall Profile) (Bennathan and Boxall, 1998) and educational assessments. Individual learning tasks are determined on the basis of staff perceptions of pupils' current needs in relation to this data.

NGs are not a new form of educational provision. They were devised by Marjorie Boxall, an educational psychologist, who set up the first groups in ILEA in the early 1970s (Bennathan and Boxall, 2000). Having gone through an initial period of popularity, which lasted for the best part of a decade, NGs dwindled in numbers, with many of the original groups being closed down (Bennathan and Boxall, 2000). In 1998 a national survey found fewer than 50 groups in the UK (Cooper et al., 1998). Current (unpublished) evidence (NGN, 2003) identifies over 300 groups throughout the UK. This figure reflects only those groups that have registered with the NGN. Even at 300, this represents a 600% increase over five years. An informed estimate places the current number of groups in the region of 1,000 (Marion Bennathan, personal communication).

Preliminary to the current study

Preliminary to the current project, a survey of NG provision in England and Wales was carried out (Cooper et al. 1998).

An important finding was that there were 4 basic variations of the NG theme. These variants can be characterised in the following ways.

Variant 1: the classic 'Boxall' NG

These groups accord in all respects with the model established by Marjorie Boxall (Boxall, 2002; Bennathan and Boxall, 2000). The 'Boxall' NG represents an inclusive form of educational provision, involving the temporary and part-time placement (usually 9 out of 10 half-day sessions per week) of pupils in a setting designed to meet their specific developmental needs and promote their educational progress. In this model, pupils who attend the NG are exclusively selected from the mainstream roll of school in which the NG is located. In order to maintain the pupil's sense of belonging to the school as a whole, the pupils remain on the roll of a mainstream class throughout their time in the NG. The NG pupils register with their mainstream class every morning, and are collected by NG staff after the registration period. For one afternoon per week pupils from the NG attend lessons with their mainstream class, whilst the NG staff engage in record-keeping activities and meet with parents. The main purpose of the NG placement is to enable pupils to return to mainstream classes full-time. This normally takes place after three or four school terms, though, where appropriate, this can take place after one or two terms. Initial placement, target setting and the monitoring of pupil progress are facilitated through the use of the Boxall Profile. This is a normative diagnostic instrument designed to measure developmental status as well as social, emotional and behavioural functioning.

In order to facilitate opportunities for intensive interaction between adults and pupils, two adults, a teacher and Teaching Assistant are required to staff groups composed of between 10 and 12 pupils.

The NG provides an holistic curriculum, incorporating the National Curriculum with a curriculum designed to address social, emotional and behavioural factors underpinning academic learning. Each school day is organised around a regular and predictable pattern of events that include formal curricular activities, based on the National Curriculum, combined with free play and social activities (such as the daily 'breakfast').

Variant 2: new type NGs

Variants of this type are based on the principles underpinning the classic model but differ in structure and/or organisational features from the Boxall groups. One way in which the second variant differs is in terms of the amount of time pupils spend in these groups, which, in mainstream schools, can vary from half a day to four days per week. Other versions of this variant may serve a cluster of schools, rather than a single school; be located in a special school, or take the form of an off-site unit. One LEA covering a large geographical area has created a 'travelling NG', which moves from school to school. They may also vary in terms of the age range catered for. Classic groups cater for KS 1 and KS 2 pupils, whereas New Variant NGs sometimes cater for KS 3 pupils. Regardless of organisational differences, however, these groups retain core structural features, such as small group size, and being staffed by a teacher and TA, and they adhere to the core principles of the classic approach in terms of developmental emphasis and the holistic curriculum.

Variant 3: groups informed by NG Principles

These are groups which sometimes bear the name 'Nurture Group', or are claimed to be variants on the NG concept, but which often depart radically from the organisational principles of classic and new variant NGs. They may, for example, take place outside of the normal curricular structure of the schools where they are located, taking the form of lunch-time, break-time or after-school groups. Or they may take the form of 'havens' or 'sanctuaries' that can be accessed by pupils at different times. The groups may be run by a single individual or a non-teaching adult (such as a TA, mentor or counsellor). The activities that go on in these groups will tend to focus on social and developmental issues but will tend not to have the academic emphasis of the classic and new variant groups.

Variant 4: aberrant NGs

These are groups which bear the name 'NG' or are claimed to be variants on the NG concept, but which contravene, undermine or distort the key defining principles of the classic NG. These will be groups that can be found in any of the above configurations but will lack an educational and/or developmental emphasis in favour of control and containment.

The significance of variation

The first two variants might be seen as genuine NGs. The third variant often provides important social and emotional support for pupils, though is in danger of being peripheral. The fourth variant is potentially dangerous, by promoting a distorted image of the theorised NG.

The effectiveness of Nurture Groups: evidence from a national research study

The study reported by Cooper and Whitebread (2003) set out to assess the effectiveness of NGs in promoting positive, social, emotional and educational development. The study focused on variants 1 and 2 (see above) and measured: (1) the effects of NG in promoting pupil improvement in the NG, (2) the extent to which these improvements generalised to mainstream settings, (3) the impact of NGs on whole schools, and (4) the impact of NGs on parent-child relationships.

The full results of this study are available in the report prepared by Cooper and Whitebread (2003), and a number of publications are currently being prepared based on this. The current chapter offers a brief account of some of the key findings.

Samples

A group of 359 pupils (71.5% males; mean age: 6 years 5 months) attending NGs were studied. A further 187 pupils (matched to a random sample of NG pupils) were studied, composing 4 comparison groups: (1) 64 pupils with Emotional, Social and Behavioural Difficulties (ESBD) attending NG schools; (2) 65 pupils without ESBD attending NG schools; (3) 31 pupils with ESBD attending schools which do not have NG provision; (4) 27 pupils who do not have ESBD attending schools that do not have NG provision.

Data gathering tools

Levels of Social, Emotional and Behavioural Difficulties (SEBD) were assessed and monitored for all the participants using the Goodman Strengths and Difficulties Questionnaire (SDQ) (Goodman, 1999; 1997), which was completed by *mainstream teachers,* and relates to pupils' behaviour as observed in the mainstream classroom setting. This is a 25-item behaviour screening questionnaire that measures 5 subscales: hyperactivity, conduct problems, emotional symptoms, peer problems (these 4 subscales contribute to a Total Difficulties score) and pro-social behaviour.

In addition, students attending the NGs were assessed using The Boxall Profile (Bennathan and Boxall, 1998) (completed by *NG teacher*). This is a detailed normative, diagnostic instrument (Bennathan and Boxall, 2000), which can be used to measure a child's level of emotional and behavioural functioning, including behaviour associated with academic engagement.

Addressing pupils' behaviour

Parent perceptions were accessed using questionnaires, a semi-structured telephone interview, and face-to-face semi-structured interviews. The children's perceptions were accessed using a face-to-face informant-style interview.

NG and mainstream staff perceptions were collected using questionnaires and semi-structured interviews.

Findings based on quantitative data

What are the effects of NGs on pupils' social, emotional and educational functioning?

Table 13.1 reports the changes in Goodman's Total Difficulties scores over the 4 terms that they were measured for the whole sample of NG children, control group 1 (the comparison group of children with SEBD in the NG schools, but who remained full-time in the mainstream classes), and control group 2 (the comparison group of 62 children without SEBD attending the NG schools).

Table 13.1 Goodman's Total Difficulties SDQ Categories and Mean Scores for Nurture Group (Term 1: n = 359; Term 2: n=301; Term 4: n=115) and Mainstream Children with SEBD (Term 1: n = 64; Term 2: n= 64; Term 4: n=42), and without SEBD (n = 62)

	Nurture Group Pupils		Mainstream Pupils with SEBD		Mainstream Pupils without SEBD	
	No.	%	No.	%	No.	%
Term 1						
Normal	43	12	10	15.6	61	98.4
Borderline	60	16.7	8	12.5	1	1.6
Abnormal	256	71.3	46	71.9	0	0
		(88)[1]		**(84.4)**		**(1.6)**
Mean SDQ Score	19.33		17.83		2.65	
Term 2						
Normal	98	32.6	16	25.0	58	93.5
Borderline	55	18.3	13	20.3	4	6.5
Abnormal	148	49.2	35	54.7	0	0
		(67.5)		**(75.0)**		**(6.5)**
Mean SDQ Score	15.68		15.69		3.31	
Term 4						
Normal	40	33.3	11	26.2		
Borderline	13	15.0	11	26.2		
Abnormal	62	51.7	20	47.6		
		(66.7)		**(73.8)**		
Mean SDQ Score	15.33		14.62			

Goodman SDQ scores: 0–11 = Normal; 12–15 = Borderline; 16–40 = Abnormal
[1] bold figures in brackets indicate sum of abnormal and borderline percentages

In spite of attrition problems the overall picture indicates that improvement in social, emotional and behavioural functioning (as observed by mainstream teachers when the pupils are in mainstream classrooms) was greater for the children in NGs than it was for the children in the same schools who were not attending NGs. Although NG children started with generally poorer Goodman SDQ scores, they improved more quickly than the children in the same-school mainstream SEBD comparison groups (see Table 13.1). Repeated measures analysis of variance, however, found that, although the improvement rate for NG children was significantly greater than that for the non-SEBD controls, the difference in improvement rates between the NG children and same-school SEBD control group children was not statistically significant. It is also clear that whilst behaviour improved for both NG and SEBD-same-school controls between Term 1 and Term 4, the period of greatest improvement for both groups is between Terms 1 and 2.

Established vs New NGs

However, a clear difference emerged between Group 1a children in established NGs and the Group 1b children in newly established groups. When we focused on the pupils who attended the longest established groups (i.e. those which had been in existence for more than 2 years prior to the commencement of the study), and compared their progress with mainstream controls over the first 2 terms, we found their rate of improvement to be greater than that of the total NG sample (see Table 13.2).

Thus we can see that at the point of entry into these established NGs, 91.8% of the NG children were reported to be not within the normal range as measured by the SDQ, as opposed to 84.4% of the matched mainstream SEBD children. However, within a year this had reduced to 65.9% for the NG children (a gain of just under 26%), but only to 75% (a gain of about 10%) for the mainstream group. This time the difference in rate of improvement between NG pupils and both sets of controls was statistically significant.

Children with SEBD in mainstream classes in established NG schools (control group 2) vs Children with SEBD in schools without NGs (control group 4)

Further confirmation of the effectiveness of the established NGs emerged when we compared the performance of the pupils with SEBD in mainstream classes in established NG schools, with the performance of a matched group of mainstream pupils with SEBD in schools that did not have a NG: we find major differences in pupil progress over two terms (see Table 13.3).

Addressing pupils' behaviour

Table 13.2 Goodman's Total Difficulties SDQ Categories and Mean Scores for pupils from established Nurture Groups (i.e. Groups founded 2 years or more prior to study) (n = 220) and Mainstream Children (with SEBD n = 64; without SEBD n = 62)

	Nurture Group Pupils		Mainstream Pupils with SEBD		Mainstream Pupils without SEBD	
	No.	%	No.	%	No.	%
Term 1						
Normal	18	8.2	10	15.6	61	98.4
Borderline	40	18.2	8	12.5	1	1.6
Abnormal	162	73.6	46	71.9	0	0
		(91.8)[1]		(84.4)		(1.6)
Mean SDQ Score	19.92		17.83		2.65	
Term 2						
Normal	75	34.1	16	25.0	58	93.5
Borderline	41	18.6	13	20.3	4	6.5
Abnormal	104	47.3	35	54.7	0	0
		(65.9)		(75.0)		(6.5)
Mean SDQ Score	15.30		15.69		3.31	

Goodman SDQ scores: 0–11 = Normal; 12–15 = Borderline; 16–40 = Abnormal
[1] bold figures in brackets indicate sum of abnormal and borderline percentages

Table 13.3 Goodman's Total Difficulties SDQ Categories for Mainstream Pupils with SEBD in established Nurture Group schools (n=64) and in schools without Nurture Groups (n=31)

	Mainstream Pupils with SEBD in NG schools		Mainstream Pupils with SEBD in non-NG schools	
	No.	%	No.	%
Term 1				
Normal	10	15.6	2	6.5
Borderline	8	12.5	3	9.7
Abnormal	46	71.9	26	83.9
		(84.4)[1]		(93.6)
Term 2				
Normal	16	25.0	0	0
Borderline	13	20.3	6	19.4
Abnormal	35	54.7	25	80.6
		(75.0)		(100)

Goodman SDQ scores: 0–11 = Normal; 12–15 = Borderline; 16–40 = Abnormal
[1] bold figures in brackets indicate sum of abnormal and borderline percentages

There was no statistically significant difference between the total Goodman SDQ scores of pupils in the schools with NGs and those in schools without NGs at the beginning of Term 1. After 2 terms, however, there was a highly significant difference. This was a consequence of the fact that not only had the pupils in NG schools improved from a mean rate of 84.4% falling into borderline or abnormal ranges, to 75%, but the pupils from the schools without NGs had actually declined in their mean performance, with their combined borderline and abnormal scores increasing from 93.6% to 100%.

This pattern was repeated in terms of improvements on the Goodman Pro-Social scale, which showed a significant difference between scores for the two groups. However, this time, the non-NG pupils' mean performance improved, as well as that of the NG school pupils, though the latter group's rate of improvement was significantly better.

While once again the difference in scores at the start of Term 1 were statistically not significant, the difference in scores at the end of Term 2 had become significant. The main difference resided in improvement in scores falling into the abnormal range, with the number of NG school pupils in the abnormal range improving by 15.7%, compared with 0.1% improvement for the non-NG school pupils.

Boxall Profiles

Boxall Profiles relating to pupils' performance in the NG setting were completed for NG children by their NG teachers at the start of Term 1, and the end of Terms 2, 3 and 4.

These profiles showed significant improvement between Terms 1 and 2. The Boxall categories reflect many of the areas covered by the Goodman SDQ. In addition, one of the 'Developmental Strands' of the profile deals with processes relevant to engagement with the learning activities and the curriculum. The strand labelled 'Organisation of Experience' is divided into 5 sub-strands: 'gives purposeful attention'; 'participates constructively'; 'connects up experiences'; 'shows insightful involvement', and 'engages cognitively with peers'. The significant improvements noted on these items indicate that after two terms in the NG pupils, in general, were better placed to engage effectively with learning activities in group situations.

Highly statistically significant improvements occurred between Terms 1 and 4 on all Boxall scores. However, differences between Term 2 and 4 scores were on the whole less significant. This supports the findings of the Goodman data, to some extent, and indicates that improvements in behaviour were most marked in the first two Terms. An important additional finding here was that significant improvements on the sub-strand 'organisation of experience' continue between Terms 2 and 4. This suggests that whilst improvements in social, emotional and behavioural difficulties tended to be most marked in the first two terms, improvements in behaviour associated with engagement with learning tasks continued, for NG pupils, beyond this and into Term 4.

Qualitative data gathered from the teacher, parental and child interviews also supported this finding, with children, teachers and parents identifying improvements in children's social, emotional, behavioural and academic functioning (see below for further details of qualitative evidence).

The differential impact of NGs

In order to examine possible differential impacts on different groups of children a cluster analysis was carried out using initial SDQ scores of all SEBD children. The purpose of a cluster analysis is to find patterns of connection between different items on the questionnaires used. When applied to the Goodman SDQ data, this approach revealed five distinctive patterns among the presenting difficulties identified by mainstream teachers. The five clusters were:

1. pupils who presented mainly social and emotional problems (i.e. pupils who showed high levels of 'emotional symptoms' and 'peer problems' on the SDQ);
2. pupils who exhibited global problems (i.e. pupils who showed high levels of problems across all the SDQ categories: 'emotional symptoms', 'conduct problems', 'hyperactivity', 'peer problems' and poor 'pro-social behaviour');
3. pupils who exhibited mainly disruptive behaviour problems (i.e. pupils whose SDQ scores showed high levels of 'conduct problems', 'hyperactivity', 'peer problems' and poor 'pro-social behaviour');
4. pupils whose SDQ scores indicated mainly problems of a mainly 'anti-social' type (i.e. pupils who were borderline on the 'emotional symptoms', 'conduct problems', 'hyperactivity' and 'peer problems' sub-scales, and were abnormal in their scores on the 'pro-social behaviour' sub-scale);
5. pupils whose score highlighted 'hyperactivity' (i.e. pupils who scored in the borderline on 'conduct problems' and in the abnormal range on the 'hyperactivity' sub-scale).

It should be noted that this analysis was carried out with pupils from the Group 1a cohort of NG pupils (i.e. those attending the most established groups). This sub-group was chosen for the analysis because of its relatively high level of successful performance in terms of improvements on Goodman scores. Further analysis of other sub-groups will be carried out subsequently.

An examination of the Boxall Profiles of the cluster groups is also helpful in describing these apparently different and relatively distinct groups.

The Boxall scores for all groups represented high levels of difficulty compared with the general population of children in these age groups. Clusters 2 (Global problems) and 3 (Disruptive behaviour) are reported to be experiencing the most widespread difficulties, emerging as relatively high compared with the other NG children in three and four of the Boxall scales respectively. Cluster 1

(Social/emotional) scored highly in 'self-limiting features' and Cluster 4 (Anti-social) in 'unsupported development'. Cluster 5 (Hyperactive) did not evidence relatively high levels of difficulty in any of the Boxall scales compared with the other NG children. This is in spite of the fact that there are a number of items on the Boxall Profile that relate directly to hyperactive-type behaviour.

A second round of Boxall Profiles completed by NG teachers at the end of the academic year show consistent improvement for NG children in all areas for all SDQ Clusters.

However, SDQ scores completed by the children's mainstream teachers at the beginning of Term 1 and the end of Term 2 show differential improvement between SDQ Clusters for NG children in comparison with mainstream SEBD children.

Cluster groups 2 (Global problems) and 3 (Disruptive behaviour) show significant improvement overall. However, for Group 2 there was no difference in the improvement between the NG and Mainstream children, whereas the children in Cluster Group 3, who were in a NG, showed significantly greater improvement than those in Mainstream. For Cluster Group 4 (Anti-social) there was no significant improvement overall. However, this masks a significant difference between the children in NGs, whose SDQ Scores improved, and those in mainstream, whose Difficulties appear to have worsened. Cluster Groups 1 (Social/Emotional) and 5 (Hyperactive) showed no significant improvement between Term 1 and Term 2 whether they were in NGs or Mainstream classrooms.

The differences in performance recorded by the Boxall and SDQ instruments suggest that for some pupils the gains made whilst they were in the NG were generalised to the mainstream, whilst for others (notably, children in the hyperactive and social/emotional clusters) there was no substantial generalisation.

How do differences between NGs affect pupil progress?

Findings from Multiple Regression Analysis

Multiple regression analysis sets out to identify, from a statistical standpoint, the relative importance of individual factors on outcomes (i.e. in this case, pupil performance as recorded by Goodman and Boxall scores). A range of variables believed to have a likely influence on differences in performance between NGs was generated largely on the basis of the analysis of qualitative data. The following statistically significant findings were generated:

1. *Proportion of week spent in NG.* The difference between Term 1 and Term 2 SDQ Total Difficulty scores among NG pupils was predicted by the

proportion of time during a week that pupils spent in the NG, suggesting that the higher the proportion of time spent in the group, the greater the improvement over the first 2 terms.

2. *Make up of group.* Differences in SDQ scores over four terms were predicted by two variables: percentage of acting out pupils in the group, and whether or not the NG teacher had been replaced during this period. The positive influence of having more acting out clusters is consistent with the finding, reported above, that these clusters (Clusters 2, 3 & 4) tend to perform better in terms of improvement on the Goodman SDQ scores.

3. *Stability of NG staffing.* The finding that change of NG teacher accounts for 23.4% of the variance in total SDQ scores over 4 terms highlights the importance of stability for longer term NG pupils.

4. *English fluency.* Predictors of differences in scores on the Boxall Profiles between Terms 1 and 4 were (for Diagnostic Profile scores) fluency in English at the time of entry to the NG. The importance of fluency in English is perhaps accounted for by the fact that NG practice is characterised by intensive verbal interaction between staff and pupils. Qualitative evidence suggests that the majority of children improve in their fluency during their time in the NG. The current finding suggests, as one might expect, that children with an initially higher level of fluency have an advantage throughout their time in the NG.

   With regard to the Internalisation of Controls sub-strand (i.e. the sub-strand most closely associated with academic engagement), over the 4 terms, 30.4% of the variance in scores is predicted by fluency in English, and proportion of week spent by NG pupils in the NG accounts for 23.2% of the variance in scores. Again, as with the SDQ regression analysis, the importance of the amount of time pupils spend in the NG is emphasised. Taken together, these findings begin to point to the likely conclusion that NGs which depart from the classic NG arrangement, whereby pupils spend 90% of the week in the NG, are reducing the probability of success for their pupils.

5. *Institutional quality (as determined by OFSTED inspection reports).* The final finding is that, over two terms, 33.7% variance in the Diagnostic Profile Scores is accounted for by institutional quality. This finding points to the importance of whole school factors as an influence on the performance of pupils in NGs. The implication here is that the better the quality of SEN provision and behaviour management practices in the mainstream of the school, the shorter the amount of time required for successful placement in a NG.

Findings based on qualitative data

Qualitative data was gathered from interviews with parents (n=139), teachers and LSAs (in NGs (n=70) and mainstream (n=90)), Head Teachers of NG schools (n=36), and pupils (n=227). Data was gathered through interviews and questionnaires, as well as through 11 case studies of individual groups, which were carried out after the main data collection phase was completed. What follows is a brief summary of the major findings, presented in relation to the relevant research questions.

What is the impact of NGs on the mainstream schools they serve, in terms of NG staff perceptions and mainstream staff perceptions and practice?

When asked about the whole-school impact of NGs there are a number of common themes emerging from interviews. In particular, NG staff members were very clear about the need for clarity about the nature and purpose of the NG and its role within the school. Central here was a concern to communicate to mainstream colleagues the importance of having what was seen as a relatively small group of pupils (maximum of 12), 'balanced' in terms of having a range of pupils with externalising and internalising emotional and behavioural problems being catered for by two full-time staff who exploited the opportunities created by the favourable staff–pupil ratio for modelling and sharing of tasks by two staff working closely together. Careful planning and liaison were needed in relation to full-time reintegration of pupils. The view was repeatedly expressed that the success of the NG was perceived to be associated with the extent to which staff throughout the school shared a common view of the nature and purpose of the group. The importance of this being communicated to parents was also stressed. From the perspective of NG staff, pupil entry criteria for the NG were very important. This was linked to effective target setting and monitoring of progress through the use of the Boxall Profile and other standardized instruments (e.g. the Goodman SDQ). It was clear that many of these factors posed a potential for conflict within the school as a whole, where there would often be a demand for placements in the NG that could not be met owing to the upper limit set on the number of pupils to be catered for in the NG at any one time. The quality of communication between staff within the school, and with parents, about these issues was, therefore, seen as a major issue by all parties and crucial to the careful planning and liaison between NG and mainstream staff in relation to the monitoring and full-time mainstream reintegration of pupils.

Mainstream staff were highly positive about the value of NGs to schools as a whole. A questionnaire asking teachers to assess the impact of NGs on their school was sent to 90 mainstream staff and returned by 87.8% (n=79). Returns indicated that 46% (n=36) believed that the NG had a strongly positive impact on the school, whilst 50% (n=40) believed that the NG had at least some positive impact on the school. Only 4% (n=3) felt that the NG has had no impact on the school, and no mainstream staff suggested that NG has had a negative impact on the school.

Mainstream teachers cited a number of features relating to positive impact. Many of the issues mentioned in this regard concerned teachers' ways of thinking about and dealing with pupils with emotional, social and behavioural problems. Generally, there was consensus that the presence of a NG contributed to the development of more 'nurturing' attitudes and practices throughout the school, which were reflected in positive changes in the ways in which teachers talked and thought about children, particularly in relation to an understanding of SEBD. This was attributed to the developmental insights terms that are central to the NG approach. Teachers commented, for example, on ways in which such insights enabled them to feel more confident in dealing with certain kinds of behavioural problems in terms of pupils' needs, rather than in terms of their own failures as pupil managers. This helped them to overcome feelings of helplessness that often accompanied such problems in the classroom prior to having a NG in the school. An accompanying factor here is the view expressed by many mainstream teachers that the NG, by virtue of the fact that it temporarily removed a number of difficult pupils from mainstream classrooms, created more opportunities for mainstream staff to focus on the needs of pupils with SEBD who remained in the mainstream.

There was also evidence, from interviews with Heads, that the presence of a NG helped contribute nurturing principles to whole school policies. This was often related to amendments to school behaviour policies that took on more of an emphasis on unmet need as an underlying cause of problems, rather than on punishing deviant behaviour.

What are pupils' and parents' perceptions of and attitudes towards NGs?

There was a strong relationship between parents' views of the NG and its perceived effect on their child's social, emotional, behavioral and educational functioning. The vast majority of parents believed that the NG placement had a positive effect on their children in all of these areas. More than half of all parents interviewed cited improvements in their children's behaviour, academic attainment and enjoyment of school. These improvements were held in contrast to their children's earlier mainstream experience, and the belief was commonly stated that these improvements would have been unlikely to occur had the child remained in mainstream. Where parents were dissatisfied, this was commonly related to perceived lack of progress, or the belief that their child should have access to the NG for a greater proportion of the week. Some parents were anxious and resistant to the idea that their child should be returned to a full-time placement in the mainstream. A strong theme to emerge from parent interviews was the high value they placed on interactions with the NG staff, and their belief that these staff had developed unique and positive insights into their children.

Pupils interviewed reflected many of the positive views already expressed by staff and parents. Their responses drew particular attention to the quality of interpersonal relationships in the NG and their fondness for the NG staff. Another prominent theme in pupil responses was appreciation of the regularity and predictability of NG routines. Particular routine activities that were singled out for comment were 'breakfast' and snack times, and opportunities for free play and a choice of activities that occurred at certain times during the NG week. These were seen as distinctive and desirable features of the NG which were not available in the mainstream classroom. Similarly, the quietness and calmness of the NG environment was often contrasted with the more frenetic atmosphere of the mainstream classroom. This sense of calmness was associated with opportunities to work at the individual pupil's preferred pace. Pupils indicated that this atmosphere helped them to avoid becoming frustrated and marginalised in ways that occurred in the mainstream classroom. This situation was further aided by the speed of adult response when pupils required help. Finally, pupils commonly commented on the pleasantness of the physical environment of the NG, and their sense of ownership of the NG, and pride at being identified with the NG.

Discussion

On the basis of the current study NGs appear to have added significantly to positive work that mainstream primary schools do with SEBD pupils. An unexpected finding is that schools with NGs appear to work more effectively with pupils who have SEBD who do not attend NGs than schools where there is not a NG on site. Schools that have NGs achieve significantly higher gains for pupils with SEBD (both in the NG and in the mainstream) than schools which do not have NGs. In fact, in the current study, whilst mean rates of improvement in social, emotional and behavioural functioning were observed over four terms in NG schools (and most markedly in terms 1 and 2), mean scores for matched pupils in schools without NGs declined over terms 1 and 2. Both quantitative and qualitative data point to the strong possibility that the presence of an effective NG adds value to the work that schools do with the wider population of children with SEBD. The qualitative data in particular indicates that mainstream staff develop more 'nurturing' approaches to pupils on the basis of their interactions with NG staff. These interactions are supported by the tangible benefits accrued by NG pupils from their placement in the NG, which are reflected in their mainstream performance as observed by mainstream staff.

The complexity of factors involved in promoting the kind of institutional change suggested by these findings is immense. For example, we do not have data on the antecedent conditions in NG schools. It might be assumed that there was a state of readiness in these schools that encouraged staff to perceive both the need for additional provision for children with SEBD and a philosophical bias towards the NG approach. Having said this, it is clear from the firsthand testimonies of both NG and mainstream staff, that classroom practices were influenced by the active presence of a NG and the communication among staff that went on around this presence. There are two factors, mentioned by mainstream staff, that were claimed to contribute to this positive effect. The first was the dilution of SEBD problems in classrooms facilitated by the removal of pupils attending NGs. The second was the set of theoretical insights that were shared with and adopted by mainstream staff, based around NG practices. This suggests that NGs are capable of providing impetus for school improvement akin to the approach described by Munro (1999). As Munro noted in his study, the combination of sound theory and practical interventions seems to have achieved more than one might expect from either a theoretical or practical intervention alone. It is a hypothesis worthy of further investigation that mainstream staff in NG schools were able to incorporate developmental insights in their practical theorising and teaching, because these insights were delivered in the context of the management of real pupil cases. This suggests that the emphasis placed by staff on the NG as a 'whole school' initiative is a powerful aid to school development and individual staff development.

An important aspect of the NG effect, as measured by Goodman and Boxall data, is that improvements in social, emotional and behavioural functioning do not seem to improve significantly after term 2; however, significant improvements in behaviours associated with engagement in educational tasks continue into the 3rd and 4th terms. For pupils in NGs that have been established for 2 years or more, these improvements are of a statistically significant level, when compared with the improvements experienced by mainstream SEBD controls. This suggests that the effectiveness of NGs improves over time, as NG staff and the school as a whole become more expert in working with the NG approach. This adds further support to the idea that NGs, when properly introduced, contribute to staff-development. The more intensive experience of NG staff, it would seem, leads to increased competence over time.

Another factor affecting the success of NGs includes the amount of time pupils spend in the NG over the course of a week, with larger periods of time predicting higher levels of mean improvement. This applies throughout the period of placement. It is possible, however, that the longer-established groups might be able to compensate for limited time through well developed patterns of co-ordination between the NG and mainstream.

The nature of children's difficulties and the balance of groups also appear to be important factors. NGs appear to produce significant gains across a wide range of difficulties, in both SEBD and educational terms. When they are in the NG, pupils presenting with internalising and acting out patterns of behaviour show impressive rates of improvement. When they are in their mainstream classes, however, it is the children who have exhibited high levels of acting out behaviours initially who seem to generalise their improved behaviour to the mainstream setting. Children who present with mainly social/emotional problems, and exclusively hyperactive behaviour, do not generalise the improvements made in the NG to the mainstream setting. This complex finding may be open to a number of different interpretations. One likely explanation is that the NG provides intensive social learning experiences that equip children who lack self-regulatory strategies with appropriate skills. On the other hand, pupils whose difficulties reside primarily at the level of unresolved emotional difficulties, or in the form of congenital problems with impulse control (e.g. as in the case of AD/HD), will have these difficulties catered for in the NG (and hence will make positive progress there) but will continue to be vulnerable to ubiquitous features of mainstream classrooms (e.g. relatively higher levels of stimulation; lack of individual attention; more complex daily routine; greater emphasis on pupil self-regulation) which in turn stimulate their dysfunctional behaviour patterns.

The wider implications of these findings give us pause for thought about some of the taken-for-granted features of many mainstream classrooms. As was noted in the introduction to this chapter, the NG provides a setting highly conducive to the application a social-constructivist approach to pedagogy. The fact that some pupils are enabled, after a relatively brief period of time in the NG, to generalise the social-emotional and academic engagement improvements accrued in the NG to the mainstream is encouraging, but it begs many questions. The findings of the study by O'Connor and Colwell (2002), for example, suggest that whilst the general improvement is maintained over the long term, there is some deterioration in performance in certain areas. This might be taken to suggest that there are features common to mainstream classrooms that continue to be aversive, even to those pupils who are able to generalise improvements to the mainstream setting. For other pupils, notably those with primarily emotional difficulties and the symptoms of hyperactivity, the mainstream environment appears to be continuously aversive. These findings could be interpreted to suggest that for generalisation and maintenance of effects to be optimised pupils who have had a successful experience of NGs continue to require some additional support of a type that reflects key features of NGs that are not easily replicated in the standard mainstream classroom. These features are likely to include the high level of individualised interaction that takes place between staff and pupils across a range of social and academic activities, the small group size and the relative simplicity and predictability of the daily routine. If this is so, it implies the need for a careful review of certain fundamental assumptions underpinning the ways in which mainstream classrooms are structured and organised.

As a way forward in thinking about the direction that such developments might take, we might look to the qualitative data provided by this study. This data supports the conclusion that key stakeholders in schools (i.e. mainstream teachers, NG staff, heads, parents, and pupils) value NGs for the opportunities they create for effective engagement with SEBD and learning problems. A crucial factor here is the sense of empowerment and optimism that stakeholders associate with NGs and the tangible effects they accrue. These positive attitudes help staff, parents and pupils to identify paths towards positive development through their engagement with the NG approach. This suggests that NGs provide an approach which many teachers are able to integrate into the practical theorising underpinning their pedagogy. Only when such integration is possible can innovation produce practical outcomes.

Summary and conclusions

Statistically significant improvements were found for NG pupils in terms of social, emotional and behavioural functioning. NGs which had been in place for more than two years were found to be significantly more effective than groups which had been in existence for less than two years. Pupils with ESBD in mainstream classrooms improved in behavioural terms significantly better than pupils with and without SEBD attending schools that did not have NG provision. The greatest social, emotional and behavioural improvements took place over the first two terms, whilst improvements in behaviours associated with cognitive engagement in learning tasks continued to improve into the third and fourth terms. There were differential effects in relation to the type of problem presented by pupils. Pupils with global SEBD difficulties, anti-social and mainly disruptive behaviours tended to generalise improvements accrued in the NG to mainstream settings. Pupils with primarily social-emotional problems, and pupils whose major presenting problem was hyperactivity, although they improved in the NG, tended not to carry this improvement over to the mainstream.

A further important finding is that NGs appear to have the capacity to influence positively the ways in which parents interact with their children. This study sheds new and interesting light on this important area, but requires far deeper scrutiny in future research.

This study suggests that NGs are a highly promising form of provision for young children with a wide range of SEBDs. There is also good evidence to suggest that successful NGs contribute to the development of the 'nurturing school' (Doyle, 2003). The failure of certain sub-groups of pupils to generalise improvement to the mainstream may be taken to highlight the context-dependent nature of certain kinds of pupil difficulty, and suggests the need for attention to be given to promoting the opportunities for nurturing approaches in mainstream classrooms.

References

Bennathan, M and Boxall, M (1998) *The Boxall Profile*, East Sutton: Association of Workers for Children with Emotional and Behavioural Difficulties

Bennathan, M and Boxall, M (2000) *Effective Intervention in Primary Schools: NGs*, London: Fulton

Berrueta-Clement, J R et al (1984) *Changed Lives: the Effects of the Perry Pre-School Programme on Youths through Age 19*, Ypsilanti, MN: Monographs of the High/Scope Press

Boxall, M (2002) *NGs in School: Principle and Practice*, London: Paul Chapman

Bruner, J, Olver, R and Greenfield, P (1966) *Studies in Cognitive Growth*, New York: Wiley

Cooper, P, Arnold, R and Boyd, E (1998) *The Nature and Distribution of NGs in England and Wales*, Cambridge: University of Cambridge School of Education

Cooper, P and Whitebread, D (2003) *The Effectivenes of Nurture Groups*, Unpublished Research Report, University of Leicester

Doyle, R (2003) 'Developing the nurturing school: spreading NG principles and practices into mainstream classrooms', *Emotional and Behavioural Difficulties*, 8(4): 253–267

Feuerstein, R (1969) *The Instrumental Enrichment Method: an Outline of Theory and Technique*, Jerusalem: HWCRI

Goodman, R. (1997) 'The Strengths and Difficulties Questionnaire: a research note', *Journal of Child Psychology, Psychiatry and Allied Disciplines*, 38(5): 581–6.

Goodman, R. (1999) 'The extended version of the Strengths and Difficulties Questionnaire as a guide to child psychiatric caseness and consequent burden', *Journal of Child Psychology and Psychiatry*, 40: 791–801.

Maslow, A (1970) *Motivation and Personality*, New York: Harper Row

Munro, J (1999) 'Learning more about learning improves teacher effectiveness', *School Effectiveness and School Improvement*, 10(2): 151–171

Nind, M (1999) 'Intensive interaction and autism: a useful approach?' *British Journal of Special Education*, 26(2): 96–102

O'Connor, T and Colwell, J (2002) 'The effectiveness and rationale of the "NG" approach to helping children with emotional and behavioural difficulties remain within mainstream education', *British Journal of Special Education*, 29(2): 96–10

Sylva, K and Ilsley, J (1992) 'The High/Scope approach to working with young children', *Early Education*, Spring

Vygotsky, L S (1987) *Collected Works*, New York: Plenum

PART 3
Classroom level

Chapter 14

The language of behaviour management

Bill Rogers

Introduction

The language of management, and of discipline, operates in a dynamic relationship. Developing skill in this area does not simply involve a series of words, phrases or sentences. If it is our *intention* to discipline with respect and confidence, that intention needs to come *through* the language. Only then will our language be relationally dynamic.

Being assertive (for example), when it is called for, requires some skill in communication and control over one's non-verbal behaviour but it is the *intention to assert* one's needs, or rights, or to protect someone else's needs, feelings, and rights, that really signals assertive behaviour. Assertive behaviour also needs to be context appropriate. Assertion often means we communicate with a firm, resolute, unambiguous tone and manner, matched by confident (non-aggressive) body language. In this sense the *skill* of assertion is 'conscious' and not simply the outcome of reactive feelings. Assertion is not about winning: it's about establishing and affirming fair rights and needs.

The language framework developed in this chapter is not formulaic; it is meant to give some conscious focus, and some utility, about management and discipline language when developing a personal discipline plan.

Key principles and skills of the language of management and discipline

1. Keep the corrective interaction *unintrusive* wherever possible. For example, we can manage such behaviours and issues as calling out, lateness, leaning

chairs, uniform misdemeanours and students without equipment with 'low' intrusion (a brief non-verbal cue, an incidental direction, a rule reminder). By keeping most correction 'low' intrusion, we keep a pleasant, positive tone to classroom life so that when we need to be *more* intrusive (as context may demand) such intrusions will be seen to be significant. These are times when our first response to a student's behaviour needs to be highly intrusive, but that is the exception (reserved for hostile or aggressive student behaviour).

2. Avoid *unnecessary* confrontation (this includes embarrassment, *any* sarcasm, any sense of continued hostility or looking threatened). Humour (repartee, the *bon mot*, the witty Pythonesque turn of phrase ...) can defuse and reframe tension and lift the spirits of teacher and student alike. Sarcasm invokes hostility and resentment – why wouldn't it?

3. Keep a respectful, positive tone of voice wherever possible.

4. Keep the language itself positive where possible:
   - *'when–then'* is more invitational than *'no,* you can't, *because* ...';
   - avoid *overuse* of 'shouldn't', 'mustn't', 'can't', 'won't' and interrogatives such as 'why?' or 'are you?';
   - avoid pointing fingers or gesticulating when making a corrective or assertive point – use an 'open hand' when emphasising;
   - be brief where possible (avoid *long* directions or reminders about behaviour).

5. Re-establish working relationships with the student as quickly as possible. Even a brief return to a student's desk to ask how their work is going is enough. Often a pleasant manner and a brief encouraging word will help.

6. If you need to communicate appropriate frustration – even anger – do so assertively rather than aggressively:
   - keep the assertive statement brief;
   - focus on the primary behaviour or issue;
   - avoid servicing 'secondary behaviours';
   - de-escalate any residual tension.
   If we need to communicate annoyance or even anger (where necessary and appropriate), we can do so in a professional manner consistent with our feelings.

7. Follow up on issues that matter *beyond* the classroom context. This emphasises that you, the teacher, care enough to make clear and sort out the issue of concern with the student.

A framework for management and discipline language skills

Many of these skills are set out here (in summary form) to highlight the 'least-to-most intrusive ...' nature of management and discipline language.

Tactical ignoring

The teacher selectively attends to student when on-task, tactically ignoring aspects of secondary behaviour.

Tactical pausing

The teacher briefly pauses in a spoken direction or reminder to emphasise attention, and focus.

Non-verbal cueing

The teacher supplies a cue that carries a clear (unspoken) message, reminder, or direction.

Incidental language

The teacher directs or reminds the student without directly *telling* them: e.g. 'There's some litter on the floor and the bell is going to go soon ...' (i.e. you know that I know that I'm encouraging you to pick it up). In this approach the teacher describes reality and allows the student to process the 'obvious' expectation: e.g. 'This is quiet reading time' to students who are whispering to each other. Sometimes it will be appropriate to combine the description of reality with a behavioural direction: e.g. 'This is quiet reading time now (the incidental). Read quietly inside your heads. Thanks' (the behavioural direction: teacher taps own head). It is very effective from upper primary level onwards.

Take-up time

This refers to the teacher refocusing eye contact and proximity after having given a direction or reminder.

Behavioural direction

The teacher directs a group or individual by referring, directly, to the expected or required behaviour: e.g. 'Jason (...), Dean (...), facing this way, thanks'. Behavioural directions are appropriate for communicating the *required* behaviour, as when students are talking while the teacher is talking and the students need to be facing the front and listening.

- Focus on the expected or required behaviour.
- Use verbs/participles (rather than negative clauses): e.g. 'facing this way and listening ...' rather than 'Don't talk while I'm talking please', which only tells the student what we don't want them to do.
- Finish with 'thanks', or 'now' if the student/s vacillates and prompt attention is necessary.
- Keep the direction or instruction brief: 'Michael (...), Troy (...), sitting up and hands in laps – now' to infants. In this example, 'now' is said firmly but not sharply.

Rule reminder

The teacher briefly reminds the class group, or individual(s), what the rule is: 'We have a rule for asking questions'; 'Remember our rule for safe scissors ...'. The teacher does not need to *spell out* the rule each time. Rule reminders can also be given through a question: 'What's our rule for...?'

Prefacing

The teacher focuses on a positive issue before engaging discipline. For example, the teacher sees students being a bit silly at their table. Walking over, he has a chat about the painting they are working on. As he turns to leave he adds, very quietly, yet firmly, as he scans the group, 'Remember to use the paints thoughtfully'. This approach is effective when one has a positive working relationship with the class. It sets the discipline within a *relational focus*. It is obviously more effective in the on-task phase of the lesson and in non-class settings. I have also found it helpful, sometimes, to direct a student aside (from his immediate peers) to then have a brief disciplinary chat. The distraction, early enough, may stop a subsequent disruptive pattern of behaviour.

Distraction/diversion

The example in 'Prefacing' is a typical 'distraction'.

The teacher notices that a student is folding a worksheet during the instructional phase of the lesson, and says, 'Damien (...), the worksheet will be easier to read *un*folded. You'll need it later'. Calm, *not* sarcastic, the teacher then gives take-up time.

Direct questions

The teacher uses an imperative form of question rather than an 'open' form: e.g. 'what', 'when' or 'how' rather than 'why' or 'are you'.
    'What are you doing?'
    'What should you be doing?'
    'What is our rule for...?'
These sorts of questions direct responsibility to the student rather than asking for reasons. Direct imperatives focus on a student responding to their *present* responsibility rather than looking for reasons *why* they are not behaving considerately or responsibly.
    'We need you to do your work in a way that doesn't create a problem for ... How are you going to do that ...?' to a Year 10 student engaged in time wasting and noisy off-task behaviour.

Directed choices

A 'choice' is given by the teacher within the known rules or routine: 'Yes you can work on the drawing when you've finished the diary writing' ('when ... then'; 'after ... then'). In this sense, the choice is expressed as a *conditional* direction: 'We'll organise a toilet break when I've finished this part of the lesson'. All choices given to a student are, in a sense, conditional. They refer back (one way or another) to the rights and rules and responsibilities.

'Choice'/deferred consequences

Here the teacher makes the consequences of *continued* disruptive behaviour clear within a choice: 'If you cannot work quietly here ... I'll have to ask you to work separately ...' (to two noisy students).
    'If you choose not to put the personal stereo away I'll have to ask you to stay back after class [or ...] to discuss your behaviour'.
    This assumes that, earlier, the teacher would have reminded the student about the rule and (if necessary) given the student a choice to '... put the personal stereo in his bag or on the teacher's desk'.

Blocking, partial agreement, refocusing

Blocking is a strategy whereby a teacher blocks out a student's procrastinating argument.

A teacher directs two students to face the front and listen (during instructional time). They whinge, 'We're not the only ones talking …!' The teacher blocks their avoidance whingeing by gesturing with an open hand, palm facing out, towards them and *repeats* the direction. In effect she is saying, 'I'm not interested in *why* you were talking, or who else was talking. Hear the direction and face the front and listen'. In this she is redirecting to the main issue (at *this* point in the lesson) and avoids over-servicing the secondary behaviour. It is normally helpful, having blocked the procrastination, to give take-up-time and reclaim group attention.

There are occasions when students whine and whinge, for example when infants try to explain who took whose toy. The teacher firmly, kindly but firmly, blocks: 'Michael (…), Troy (…). Stop' (hand gesture). 'I'll listen when you use resonable voices.' It can help to then tune in to how they are feeling and then focus: 'What is our rule for …?', or 'How can we sort this out so that…?'.

Partial agreement

The teacher deals with the student's procrastination or avoidance by *partially* agreeing with the student (where appropriate) and refocusing back to the rule or required task.

A teacher reminds a student (who is chewing gum) of the rule. The student challenges by saying, 'But Mr Scroggin lets us chew gum in his class'.

Instead of arguing, the teacher *partially* agrees, 'Maybe he does'. The teacher *then* redirects, 'In this class the rule is clear. The bin is over there, thanks' (the incidental direction). At this point it is often helpful to give the student some take-up time.

Assertive comment/direction/command

There are degrees of assertion in one's language and voice. Fundamentally when we assert we are making our rights (or others' rights) clear in a decisive, firm, non-aggressive way: 'That language is *unacceptable* here. We have a rule for respect. I expect you to use it'. Firm, non-aggressive eye-contact, a clear, calm voice and directed, focused, language are at the heart of assertion. Our confident 'calmness' also affects the other person's calmness and the audience, who feel the ambient tension.

Assertion enables our professional skill to strongly emphasise expectations without getting into a heated argument or slanging match. If the student argues, block and refocus.

Commands

When giving commands, keep them short, and establish direct eye contact: 'Michael (...)!' The first word should be sharp and louder; to gain *attention*. 'Michael (...)', bring the level of the voice *down* as eye contact is established, and cue the command in a firm, decisive, assertive voice: 'get down off the table – *now.*' In a fight situation, if the names of children aren't known, use the loud generic attentional command, 'Oi (...)!, Oi (...)!' – then a firm assertive voice, 'Move away *now.*' Use non-verbal cues to indicate the students should separate. Direct the audience of peers away and immediately send for adult assistance. It is preferable to give commands only in those situations where unambiguous, *immediate* stopping of disruptive behaviour is warranted. We also need to be able to back-up our commands if a student refuses to obey. Our back-up should consist of a school-wide time-out plan, involving adult support, assistance that can be invoked as quickly as possible in a crisis.

Obviously, we cannot plan for every contingency. These key principles are the underlying framework of the way we communicate and relate in our teaching and management.

The key language skills are suggestions of the sorts of things one can say in typical management and teaching contexts. The language 'forms' can serve as *aides-mémoire* to give some prepared focus.

Settling the class outside the classroom

> As I approach 8D, in the corridor, I scan the students arriving. Some have US-style 'baseball' caps on, some wear sunglasses, a few are still eating, a couple of students towards the back have mobile phones in their hands, a couple of students are listening to personal stereos, a couple of boys are 'testosteronically bonding', and so on.

There are sensible reasons for corridor settling and age-appropriate lining-up: the brief settling signals (by the teacher); a change of pace, place, space and purpose in terms of group behaviour.

I find it helpful to comment briefly on hats, personal stereos and any testosteronic bonding or pushing *before* directing the class group inside.

> Firstly a brief, group-settling direction as I scan the group or line.
> 'Settling down folks ... (...). Thank you. Morning, everyone – just before we go in (...)! I notice several students with hats on ..., Ben (...), Lucas (...), Marcus (...).'

This brief description of reality is often enough to make the issue of 'hats-off' clear without directly *telling* the students. Sometimes it is enough just to give a non-verbal cue (hand-to-head) for caps off.

'Down the back, I can see mobile phones (…). We're going into a learning environment …' Giving a non-verbal cue to the lads listening to personal stereos, I add, 'We're going into the classroom. Remember the rule about personal stereos. Thanks.' Re-scanning the whole group, 'Looks like we're ready folks. When you go in, remember to…'

It can help Day 1, Session 1 (and the next few sessions), to emphasise our expectations about seating and settling once inside the room. With infants I find it helpful to ask them, 'What do we need to do when we go inside our class?' and then fill the gaps in their forgetfulness as necessary.

This corridor-settling does not take long but it *prefaces* the teacher/student expectation about purposeful behaviour on the other side of the classroom door. In time, the outside-settling should become a habit so that all that is necessary is a *brief* line-up, or grouping, before moving into the classroom.

It is worth discussing with colleagues how they normally settle a group prior to classroom entry: what sorts of things they do and say, and why.

The first three minutes

The first three minutes are important in any lesson. The teacher has to both *initiate* and then *sustain* group attention.

Obviously the teacher needs to allow a little time for the students to take their seats (or sit on the carpet) during which time the teacher needs to convey that he or she is purposefully waiting for the class to be seated ('eyes, ears this way') and ready to begin.

It will help to have a brief discussion with each new class, in the establishment phase, concerning the basic expectations about classroom entry and settling at their work area or desk. Such settling varies with subject area, of course. In drama it may involve having shoes off, against the wall and sitting in a semicircle; in an information technology (IT) room it may mean finding a seat, turning to face the front and sitting, waiting. The main thing is to have a workable routine that will enable 25–30 students to settle smoothly and consciously attend to group instruction/teaching time. Students also need to know that their attention (in the first three minutes) is expected ('eyes, ears at the front, thanks', 'hands in lap' at infant level).

It can help (at upper primary and middle school) to establish and maintain a reasonable target time for group entry, settling, having relevant materials and being ready to engage in group learning. A reasonable target could be, say, 1–2 minutes. This target time is set as a class target, and encouraged and reviewed over the first half dozen lessons or so (Pearce 1997).

Cueing for attention in some classes may mean students go straight to an activity, as in English, where students file in, take their seats, quietly get out the class novel and read for, say, five minutes. Some schools still direct students to stand behind their seats quietly at the beginning and close of each lesson. Carried through positively, even this can be a useful cue. There are a range of non-verbal cues to establish group attention in the instructional phase of the lesson.

Managing distracting and disruptive behaviour during the instructional phase of a lesson

The typical disruptions that can occur during the instruction phase of a class lesson can range from rolling on the mat and hiding under tables through to those annoying pockets of private chats while the teacher is seeking to engage and teach the class.

The most common disruptions in this phase of the lesson tend to be: talking while the teacher is talking; cross-talking across the classroom; calling out to the teacher; lateness; leaning chairs and motoric restlessness; fiddling with stationery; and clowning (attention-seeking behaviours). Most of these behaviours tend to be exhibited in the establishment phase of the year as students test out their relationship with each other, with the group and with their teacher.

When exercising discipline in a whole-class, whole-group context it is important to be aware of what we do and say such that we avoid alienating the cooperative students. In this part of the lesson or activity, anything we do or say, in discipline terms, has an immediate audience effect beyond the individual (or small group) that we address. For example, if we are overly confrontational we create a tone, an emotionally palpable tone, that can hinder motivation and cooperation. While there are some occasions when a brief, unambiguous communication of frustration and anger is appropriate, most of the time, when we are dealing with the sort of disruptive behaviours noted earlier, it is important to be respectfully positive. Being positive, confident and *appropriately firm* are not antithetical concepts.

'Thanks' is to be preferred rather than 'please'. 'Thanks' carries an expectation of what is directed rather than a request (please).

Sometimes private natter, or talking while the teacher is talking, is *unfocused* student behaviour rather than *disruptive* student behaviour. Either way the approach noted above keeps the discipline least intrusive (p. 199–200).

If the description and direction is focused on an individual (or several individuals) it is important to preface with the student's name(s): 'Dean (...), you're fiddling with the window blinds' (the description of student behaviour). '*Facing* this way and *listening*, thanks.' 'Facing ...' and 'listening ...' *behaviourally* direct the students to the expected behaviour.

Behavioural directions

When using behaviour directions it is helpful to focus on the required or expected behaviour, briefly and positively wherever possible (p. 201–2).

'Dean (…), you're calling out [the descriptive element]. *Hands up* and *waiting* thanks [the *behavioural* part]' is in preference to 'Don't call out …' or 'Why are you calling out …'. Equally unhelpful is the question 'Are you calling out?'

Students coming into class late

A student comes into class late. The teacher walks over to the door and asks, 'Are you late?' It is surprising that the student doesn't answer, 'Course I'm late!'

If the teacher asks, '*Why* are you late?' it sounds (particularly if the teacher is frustrated) as if the teacher is interrogating the student, when in fact the teacher may only want a reason. Does it matter, at that point in the lesson, *why* a student is late? Trying to get answers, and reasons, at the classroom door only feeds (in some students) incipient attention-seeking or even power provocation. Of course we need to address the issue of the student's lateness, but it is unnecessary to dwell on the lateness in front of the class.

When students are late it is always helpful to welcome them, briefly and positively, especially in the first few lessons. We won't know, initially, if a student is late because he or she is lazy, disorganised or time-wasting, or if there are home-related issues (relevant to late arrival for Period 1).

Teacher: *[Welcomes student at the classroom door.]* Welcome (…). It's Tony, isn't it? *[Teacher is still learning names. He puts his hand out to shake hands with Tony. Tony frowns, looks a little tentative – not expecting this approach. The teacher, briefly and politely, acknowledges Tony's lateness.]* You're late. There's a spare seat over there – next to Carlos. *[The teacher doesn't tell Tony to sit there: he describes the obvious reality. He focuses on the important issue at this point in the lesson: direct the student to be seated and get on with the lesson.]*

Student: I don't sit there … I sit down the back with … *[He's less defensive with this teacher, but still procrastinates.]*

Teacher: Those seats are taken, Tony … *[The teacher could add, 'And if you'd been here on time you would have had your bleedin seat!' … He resists the temptation!]* We can organise a seat change later. *[This adds a (future) choice, defusing any residual tension. At this point the teacher redirects his eye-contact away from Tony, turning to re-address the class; he scans his eyes across them.]* As I was saying folks … *[Resuming his lesson flow, as if Tony will (naturally) sit down where the teacher has incidentally directed. He does – he walks across to the seat in a slightly exaggerated, posturing, way and flops down. The teacher tactically ignores this residual secondary behaviour keeping his focus – and the class's attention – on the lesson.]*

He follows up with Tony later, at the end of the lesson, for a brief chat about the student's lateness. If the student is persistently late (three times over several consecutive days) he will take the lateness issue further with the year advisor to see if there is a pattern across other classes.

When students are late

- Welcome the student.
- Acknowledge (briefly) the lateness.
- Direct (incidentally where appropriate) student to a seat.
- Give take-up time.
- Resume the flow of the lesson or activity.

Discipline in the establishment phase of the lesson

- Scan, focus, scan (avoid maintaining eye contact for too long with any one individual or small group).
- Keep language brief.
- Use positive language where possible.
- Focus on specific behaviour (when disciplining) or focus on the relevant rule.
- Avoid arguing with students – verbally block or partially agree and refocus back to the rule or main issue.
- *Tactically* ignore non-verbal secondary behaviours wherever possible and wherever appropriate. If a student's secondary behaviour is also inappropriate, or disruptive, address if briefly and refocus the student(s) back to the expected rule, or behaviour.

Non-verbal cue-ing

Many disruptive behaviours can be addressed – even nipped in the bud – by a non-verbal cue.

> A couple of students are leaning back in their chairs as the lesson begins. The teacher pauses in her delivery and verbally cues the students, 'David and Liam (…)'. They look towards her. She cues non-verbally by extending her thumb and three fingers down to indicate a chair with four feet on the floor. When she initially established this class cue she communicated both the verbal and non-verbal aspects of the cue to associate the idea of chair legs 'on the floor'.

Non-verbal cues minimise the need for the teacher to verbalise the required behaviour every time. This is particularly helpful in early years classes.

Typical cues are:

- The teacher crosses his or her index fingers then beckons with the right hand to indicate facing the front to cue for 'cross your legs and face the front'.
- The teacher raises one hand, and covers his or her mouth with the other to indicate 'hands up without calling out' (to students who call out in class discussion time). Some calling out can be *tactically* ignored if the teacher is confident in such an approach but a non-verbal cue can act as a *brief* reminder without disturbing the flow of the activity too much.
- The teacher puts one hand over the other and pulls it in to the chest to indicate 'keep hands and feet to yourself'. This is an important cue for restless, touchy infants.
- The teacher touches one eye with a forefinger, then an ear, and uses a beckoning hand to the front of the room to indicate 'eyes and ears this way now'.
- The teacher holds up a thumb and forefinger a little distance apart to indicate 'use your partner-voice, thanks'. This is an effective reminder/direction during on-task learning time as the teacher is moving around the room. He or she may be working at one table and can remind a table group nearby by cueing across the room. I have used this reminder cue countless times in secondary classrooms.
- A similar cue I have used for years is the thumb and two fingers turning down, rotating an imaginary volume control (old-fashioned technology that one!).

As with any discipline strategy it is important to avoid any unnecessary tension. If the cue above were given with a jerky, thrusting hand and a glare and a big sigh from the teacher it would hardly be seen as a *simple* reminder!

When using a non-verbal cue for the first time it will be important to associate the meaning of the cue by giving both the non-verbal cue and the spoken reminder/direction.

Eye contact

Eye contact can engage attention, show interest and indicate intent. A stare, however, can create ambiguity if unaccompanied by verbal direction. Too long a stare may reciprocate, in some males, a perception of hostility or threat. Dodge (1981, 1985) has researched attributional bias in aggressive children, observing that aggressive boys *selectively* attend to the available cues in their environment, with a perceptual and attributional bias towards aggressive intent in the other party.

As teachers we can avoid unnecessary hostile attributions with such pupils by considering proximity, and following eye contact with a brief direction or reminder; avoiding unnecessarily extended eye contact; giving take-up time; and avoiding unnecessary win-lose perception by how we frame language – i.e. using appropriate choices.

Tactical ignoring

Tactical ignoring is a difficult skill. It is a *conscious* decision not to attend to some student behaviours such as sulking, sighing, eyes to ceiling, the 'hang-dog look', the wry mouth and frown when you direct students to do something really difficult like go back to their seats, or put their hands up without calling out, or put their pens down while you're talking to the class!

Tactical ignoring is also a form of non-verbal communication to all students (not just the student you are *tactically* ignoring). It demonstrates that the teacher is focused on the main issue and it further avoids overly reinforcing attentional secondary behaviours e.g. 'Don't you raise your eyes to the ceiling like that …!' 'Why can't you do something without sighing? What's wrong with you?'

We obviously should not ignore behaviours that the students know should not be ignored: any repeated and loud calling out, or butting-in that affects a teacher's right to teach; any verbally rude or defiant language; any hostile or aggressive behaviour.

Take-up time

I was teaching a Year 10 class, as a mentor teacher, and as I scanned the room during on-task learning time I noticed that a student had what looked like a novel on top of his exercise book. I walked over.

'It's Damon, isn't it?' It was my first session with the class and I was still learning names.

He looked up (not attempting to close the book). 'Yeah – it's Damon.'

'I notice you've got a book there, a novel? What's it about?'

'It's about a serial killer,' he said, looking up with a grin.

'Well, let's hope he's not after a teacher,' I said (and meant it). This brief chat is a form of prefacing prior to some task refocusing. I thought it best to focus on the task.

'How's the work going?'

'It's boring,' replied Damon.

'It may well be boring, Damon, but it's our work for today. Do you know what to do?'

My tone was pleasant, expectant of cooperation. He sighed, leaning back. 'Yeah, sort of.'

I gave a brief reminder of the task, pointing back to the board and adding, 'By the way, the novel. I'd like you to put it in your bag or if you like you can leave it on my desk till the bell.' He grinned back. 'I'll come back and check on your work a little later, Damon.' This was the discipline part of the brief engagement. The walking away, at that point, allowed some take-up time for the student and also gave a task refocus. With older children it only escalates unnecessary confrontation to take, or snatch, the distracting item. Similarly, if a directed choice is given to the student (as above) to stand there, waiting, until they put the item away also creates unnecessary tension.

Take-up time can also convey trust in the student that he or she will respond appropriately. It allows some face saving in potentially tense situations. It is important to go back to the student later to check if they are back on task and also to briefly re-establish the working relationship.

An aside on uniform misdemeanours

> A young girl is wearing a ring in class. A present from her father, it has a sentimental almost 'Linus-like' psychological comfort for her. New to this school, she comes across a teacher who notices this major crime and asks her to hand it over. The girl is both upset and very frustrated.
>
> 'No. No way.'
>
> 'Give it to me. … now.'
>
> The teacher repeats his command and puts his hand (palm out) to indicate he expects her unquestioning compliance.
>
> 'No!' the girl clenches her fist. She (quite naturally) doesn't know if she'll ever get it back. She mentions that the teachers in the other classes hadn't said anything.
>
> 'Right. You're on detention.'

This may sound like a manufactured example, but it isn't. True, the teacher concerned may not have known the girl's psychological attachment to the ring. True, the teacher may be seeking to be vigilant about the uniform/dress code. The problem is he has not tuned into the girl's welfare as part of the discipline process and he lacks any skill in managing natural adolescent behaviour. He seems only concerned about the pettifogging application of the rule. He may also hold demanding, absolutist views about control and vigilant teacher discipline.

> In another class at the same school a teacher comes up to a student wearing a ring during on-task time.
>
> 'Rachel, that's an attractive ring.'
>
> The girl has a brief chat with her teacher.
>
> 'You know the rule about rings?' (The teacher's voice is quiet. She is keeping it low key).
>
> 'But other teachers haven't said anything,' the girl frowns.

'Maybe they haven't, Rachel, but the school rule is ...' The teacher partially agrees and refocuses to the school rule. The teacher gives a non-verbal signal to the student's pocket indicating for the girl to put it away in her pocket. The girl owns her behaviour. Relaxed vigilance.

End of story. If the girl refuses a fair directed choice like this, the teacher knows the issue is probably an incipient power struggle and will defer the matter to an out-of-class follow-up. If the teacher catches her with the ring on again in a school like this the issue may occasion a stay-back session to emphasise the rule.

If you ever happen to teach in a school that promotes a confiscation policy on rule-breaking jewellery, at least give the dignity of assurance of returning it the same day. I've known 'power-merchant' teachers to keep rings and non-dangerous *objets d'art* until the end of term! That is simply psychological harassment. It always staggers me that some students will easily hand such items over. In schools where students do not evidence unquestioning compliance to teacher control such an order ('Hand the ring over') would be laughed at.

More than personality

I have heard teachers observing some of their colleagues' behaviour management practice with the disclaimer, 'Oh, it's just their personality. That's why they can get through to those students'. While personality is important, if they observe more carefully, they will note that these colleagues are also aware of their own non-verbal communication and the impact of their global set of behaviours on others. They will note that these teachers are conscious of their management and discipline language.

There are skills that can enhance personality and aid positive communication: increasing positive congruence between what we communicate (content), how we communicate (non-verbal tone), timing (when we intervene) and why we choose to communicate this way at all (our values and our aims).

As in all reflective teaching we should, essentially, consider the *effect* of our behaviour on others and trust that they will do likewise (no new message this, just a difficult one).

Following up with students beyond the classroom setting

There are a number of reasons why we will need to follow-up with students beyond the classroom:

- To clarify an issue relating to class learning (homework or misunderstanding about class work or a student getting behind with their work). In this case the follow-up is normally to emphasise empathetic teacher support. There should not be any emphasis on punishment for students who are currently struggling with classroom learning, or work/task assignments.
- To initiate a discussion about a concern regarding the student's behaviour.
- To follow through with any *deferred* consequences. A typical example is when a student has left a mess and has made no effort to clean up. At primary level teachers sometimes use deferred consequences for students who have made no effort to complete classwork.
- To initiate a process of mediation with students who have exhibited conflict behaviour in class time.
- To initiate detention or formal stay-back procedures.

When following-up with students in an out-of-classroom setting:

- Consider whether a follow-up or follow-through session is merited in the first instance.
  At secondary level it is often difficult to follow-up issues between classes (especially during a six-period day!). Sometimes one can manage a *brief* word of follow-up after class and sometimes that may be enough. If the issue is important enough, though, it is worth directing the student to come to a later meeting (e.g. during the lunch break). In that brief moment after class we won't be able to go into the details; it will be enough to make the appointment.

Ethical probity

When conducting any one-to-one teacher-student stay-back session, it is crucial to be sensitive to ethical probity, particularly with a male teacher and female student or vice versa. It will help in any extended one-to-one sessions to have a colleague of the opposite sex present in the room (abstractedly working on their work programme) while conducting the follow-up.

- Whether the follow-up is a brief chat, a task based consequence (i.e. cleaning up mess left), an interview with a student or even a detention it is important that the teacher emphasise the certainty rather than the severity of the consequence.
- Tune in briefly to how the student is (probably) feeling at this point – they probably want to be outside with their mates, and may be really annoyed, even angry, or possibly even anxious. By briefly tuning in we humanise the follow-up while retaining consequential certainty. 'You're probably feeling annoyed that I've asked you to stay back after class [or to have this meeting

at lunchtime, or …]'. Our tone and manner here (as so often in discipline transactions) are really important. If we sound as if this follow-up session (however short in terms of time) is some kind of win for the teacher, the student will probably define the issue in those terms as well.

- Focus specifically on the student's behaviour, or the issue of concern you have as their teacher: 'I'm concerned about what happened in class when …'.

  If it is a task-related consequence it is enough to direct the student(s) to the task-requirement: 'Bradley, when the work area is tidy (be brief and specific) then you'll be ready for recess …'. With task-focused consequences it can help to refer to the class routine/rule: 'In our class we leave our work areas tidy …'.

  In helping to *specifically* focus on a student's disruptive behaviour it may be appropriate to mirror the student's behaviour (Rogers 1997). When mirroring the teacher briefly acts out the typical, characteristic, disruptive behaviour of the student (i.e. calling out, frequent seat leaving, loudness or talking while the teacher is talking) and even their 'secondary' behaviours.

  When mirroring behaviour in this one-to-one context:
  — ask permission of the student: 'I'd like to show you what I mean when I'm referring to you calling out …'; 'Do you mind if I give you a brief demo of how loud you often speak in class …?'; 'Let me show you what I see you do when you push and pinch others when you're sitting on the mat in carpet time [this to an infant student]';
  — keep the actual mirroring brief;
  — avoid the impression you're getting some Machiavellian satisfaction out of showing the student how annoying or stupid they are;
  — having mirrored the student's typical classroom behaviour, physically step back (as it were) from the kinaesthetic re-creation;
  — refer back to the mirrored behaviour to further clarify the issue of concern: 'So *that's* what it looks like when you…';
  — with older students it can help to invite a response: 'So how many times do you think you call out like that?'

  Mirroring is an attempt to illustrate and clarify a student's characteristic disruptive behaviour and to enable teacher–student dialogue. It is used in the context of teacher support, to help the student own and change their pattern of behaviour.
- Where appropriate, invite the student's right of reply. This can be verbal or written. Ask questions that will enable the student to focus on their behaviour in the light of what happened (to occasion the staying back) and refer back to the basic rights and responsibilities in the student behaviour agreement. In this the teacher is making the important point that, in some way, the student's behaviour has affected someone else's rights.

The basic questions we can ask are: 'What happened …?'; 'What rule or right was affected by your behaviour …?'; 'How do you see what happened, and how do you feel about it?'; 'What can you do to change things … fix things up … sort things out … make things better …?'. These can even be presented as a written proforma. We could call this proforma the '4W' form, after the four questions prefaced 'What…?'.

Some supplementary questions when involving a student in a longer follow-up session can include:

— 'What do you want to happen – for you?'
— 'What do you think will happen if you … [keep reacting in class like …; be specific]?'
— 'What can you do so that others can get on with their work without … [make reference, briefly, to the student's current behaviour]?' 'What can you do so that others can feel safe?'
— 'How can I, and your other teachers, help you to … [be specific about the key behaviours necessary to change for the student to get some success back into his classroom learning and social engagement]?'

The spirit and tone in which these questions are asked are crucial. If they are asked in a provocative, confrontational way they will (obviously) create the very resentment and resistance the teacher is seeking to refocus with the student.

The emphasis with all extended follow-up on issues of behaviour is to enable the student to become more self-aware (with regard to their behaviour).

The outcome of these questions should be some understanding, even some plan, that will increase the student's sense of self-monitoring and regulating behaviour.

If the student does not respond to *supportive* questioning, or even refuses to cooperate, the teacher can still make the following points clear so the student is as aware as possible of what needs to change:

— 'This is what I see, and note, about your behaviour …[be specific].'
— 'It isn't helping you when you … [be specific].'
— 'This is what you'll need to do if you want to change your behaviour so that you can … [be specific].'

Allow take-up time for the student to respond to *each* issue raised, and assure the student of your willingness to support them in making a behaviour plan.

• Another approach when working with students who present with resistant patterns of behaviour is to explore, with them, their likely goals behind their behaviour in terms of attention and power.

Some students will frequently use the line (even whine) that 'I can't …': 'I can't do the work …'. A firm, supportive, focusing can often help:

'Perhaps you can't do the work:
— *because* you're not facing the front and listening during the teaching time…;
— *because* you haven't got your pen, ruler and pencil ready to start…;
— *because* you haven't read through the task [assuming their reading skills are proficient – if they're not we should always find creative ways to adjust the task as well as extend their thinking]…;
— *because* you're easily distracted by sitting near Dean…
So let's make a plan to … [address the can'ts]'.

A plan can then be developed that will incrementally build up academic survival skills and behaviours to enhance the student's learning.

> As with all communication with students in situations where there is natural, ambient, tension:
> - calm yourself before trying to calm the student;
> - avoid rushing the dialogue (allow some time for student response);
> - be aware of your open, non-confrontational, body language;
> - avoid crowding their personal space;
> - keep the focus on the primary behaviour or primary issue of concern (avoid pointless arguing);
> - refer to the student behaviour agreement;
> - keep a supportive, invitational, tone wherever possible.

- With task-based consequences it is enough to direct the student to the task, give them some take-up time and check for task completion.
- Separate amicably. I've heard teachers raise the strained-relationship stakes by having the unnecessary last word: '… and if you pull that stunt again I'll…!!'
- Track the student in terms of ongoing disruptive behaviour. If the follow-up session sees no discernible change in the student's behaviour or attitude it will be worth checking with other colleagues (through the team leader/year advisor) to see if this behaviour is *typical, frequent,* or *characteristic* across the year level and across classes. If there is typical, frequent disruptive behaviour in such cases it is wiser to have a year-level, whole-staff approach to working with the student.

Bibliography

Dodge, K. A. (1981) 'Social competence and aggressive behaviour in children', paper presented at Midwestern Psychological Association, Detroit, Michigan, USA, May.

Dodge, K. A. (1985) 'Attributional Bias in Aggressive Children'. In P. C. Kendall (ed.) *Advances in Cognitive Behavioural Research and Therapy* 4. Orlando, FL: Academic Press.

Kyriacou, C. (1986) *Effective Teaching in Schools*. Oxford: Basil Blackwell.

Pearce, H. (1997) 'Groupwork in the classroom'. Unpublished notes.

Rogers, B. (1997) *Cracking the Hard Class: Strategies for Managing the Harder than Average Class*. London: Paul Chapman Publishing.

Chapter 15

Improving classroom behaviour

C. Watkins and P. Wagner

Introduction

Making sense of classrooms and classroom behaviour

It often seems that the classroom is one of the most talked-about contexts there is, at the same time as being one of the least understood. There is a great deal of simplified talk about what goes on in classrooms, much of it based on unrecognized assumptions. Such simplification becomes a significant problem when we consider how to improve classrooms, as simple prescriptions usually have little impact on them. We need ways of approaching classroom change which are equally as complex as the context.

If you were to select a person at random on the number 31 bus, and ask him or her to tell you how teaching should be organized in classrooms, the frightening fact is that you might receive an answer. Such an answer would be based on the fact that the person was once a pupil in a classroom. It might also reflect some of the media commentary about teaching, much of which is stimulated by the rhetoric of government and its agencies. These two perspectives have a worrying similarity in that both of them over-focus on two aspects: the first is the teacher, and the second is what they dislike about the teacher's performance. Such myopia does not get us far.

In this chapter we will build an alternative and more comprehensive focus on understanding the classroom situation and its effects, both on teachers and on pupils, before offering a range of frameworks for thinking about experiments to improve classroom behaviour. These frameworks are not offered as a set of prescriptions, but as some lines of action which depend on the diagnosis of the existing difficulty. The chapter finishes with some thoughts about broader methods of ensuring healthy classrooms.

Our perspective in this chapter is not that of the prevalent 'inside the person' explanations – neither for pupil nor teacher. Rather, we intend to recognize the importance of the context of behaviour, as in the chapters which precede and follow this one. An example of context in concrete terms was given by the Governor of a New York prison who was worried about the amount of fighting between inmates. The strategy of 'change the person', by putting fighters on a bread and water diet, seemed ineffective, as was the more liberal version of talking to fighting inmates to persuade them into better behaviour. The problem was finally solved by calling in a bricklayer, who rounded off the walls at the junctions of corridors – these had been identified as the situations where fighting broke out, when poor visibility led to surprise encounters. Perhaps this example is over-concrete, as it focuses so much on the physical aspects, and we know that situations are more than that. So, before we examine some of the specific and observable aspects of classrooms, it is also important to consider the meanings which may be attributed to this context.

Images of classrooms

It is interesting and illuminating to ask yourself and to ask your colleagues the following question: 'What situation that is *not* a classroom is most like a classroom in your view?' In our experience this brings forward important trends and particulars. Many people find the question difficult to answer, which may reflect the uniqueness of the classroom situation in our society. Trends we have observed include that teachers in primary schools are more likely to answer 'a family' than are teachers in secondary schools, while the latter are more likely to offer situations such as theatre, or church, thereby reflecting the performance and audience aspects, and the traditional approaches to audience control. We suggest that teachers with these images of classrooms are more likely to engage in one-to-many interactions, expect to be listened to because of their role, and see their job as conveying a message. On the other hand, a different image was conveyed by a teacher in a Richmond school who answered 'an office': he described a situation where everyone came in each day knowing their roles and working relations, and what they aimed to achieve. Again a teacher who answered 'a restaurant' brought to attention her view of offering pupils a range on the menu, and indeed of changing the menu over time. Another teacher who answered 'an aeroplane' not only highlighted the physical aspects in her school where the desks had been placed in pairs, but also the role aspects of the hostess answering the call bell in this setting. Finally, a student teacher who wrote an essay likening classrooms to prisons, with no hope of alternatives, failed the course!

Clandinin (1985) describes a teacher's image of 'the classroom as home' showing how this embodies personal and professional experiences, and how in turn the image is expressed in her classroom practices. Bullough (1991) has shown how metaphors reflect conceptions of teaching, and how these evolve through student teaching, maintaining motivation on the journey. Connelly and Clandinin (1994) illustrate how the telling and writing, retelling and rewriting of teachers' and students' stories results in changes in teaching practices, while Bullough and Stokes (1994) explore the analysis of personal teaching metaphors as a means of facilitating professional development.

Teachers are major orchestrators in making classrooms into whatever they become, and within some broad trends, the variety of what they construct is considerable. The usefulness of identifying one's image of a classroom goes beyond mere illumination. It can be a route to significant improvement. If teachers are given the time and support to unearth their current images, they may also see good reason to move on to other images which are more sympathetic to the teacher role, more enhancing of pupil autonomy and more appropriate to the twenty-first century. Transformational change does occur on occasion, especially if a teacher's preferred image of classrooms is at stake. A teacher we met in Birmingham told us that she had changed her approach to teaching overnight: on being asked how she became the exception to the rule about classroom change being generally slow, she said that in her case a 'pupil pursuit' of a class she taught led her to vow that she would never again contribute to such a passive picture for pupils. She decided to pursue her preferred image of a classroom much more actively after that experience.

Understanding the classroom context

The classroom is measurably one of the most complex social situations on Earth. This statement is not made in order to mystify anything: quite the opposite – it makes sense of why simplistic approaches to classroom improvement do not work. For example, the tendency to focus on the teacher and to use oversimple descriptions of teachers does not fit the facts. Decades ago Ryans (1968) applied multiple psychometric measures to a sample of over 6,000 teachers and related them to assessments of their classroom work. Teachers receiving a uniformly high assessment of their classroom behaviour turned out to be those with the highest frequency of involvement in avocational (non-work) activities (Ryans, 1968, p. 393). There are two responses to these findings: one is to say 'Yes I can explain why teachers who do more at the weekends perform better in classrooms...' the other is to say that such studies took a too-personal focus on the teacher, and missed the point by not analysing the context. If you only focus on the teacher, you will get spurious perspectives.

Instead we use the fact that all our behaviour relates to context. This principle, often forgotten, may be summed up by the statement: $B = f(p.s.)$. Behaviour is a function of the person and the situation. Each human being has a unique profile of responses and approaches which vary across the situations he or she meets. A teacher who behaves in one way in classroom A may not do so in classroom B, and not in the staffroom, or at the pub. Sadly when a difficulty arises, all the focus may be on classroom A, rather than on the variety, range and exceptions. Similar considerations apply to pupils whose behaviour varies in important ways across learning situations and social situations in and out of school.

So if we intend to focus on the context where teachers and pupils spend most of their school time, and in which the majority of difficulties in most schools are experienced – the classroom – it will be important to recognize some of the unique and influential aspects of that setting. The following derives from the work of Walter Doyle (1980; 1986a; 1986b; 1990).

Characteristics of the classroom situation

1 *Classrooms are busy places.* Teachers can be engaged in 1,000 interactions a day, sometimes more. It is very difficult to name a comparable job on this dimension: perhaps air traffic controllers cope with comparable complexity, although their job makes less personal demands. Teachers make a non-trivial decision in the classroom every two minutes. One result of this for the teacher can, of course, be tiredness, especially for the beginner teacher or, if they do not find means of coping with the busyness, stress.

This feature also draws to our attention the fact that because events happen fast teachers learn to act fast: their appraisal and decision-making in classrooms is rapid. Even so, every event cannot be reflected on in depth, so the development of *routines* is another feature of classroom life which helps cope with the busyness of the situation. Some routines may embody poor practice as far as pupil learning is concerned, but the classroom situation makes such demands for routinisation.

For the pupils in this busy environment it is apparent (and confirmed by numerous classroom interaction studies) that the amount of individual attention they receive with the teacher in a day is likely to be only a few minutes and probably highly interrupted. The way in which we conceptualize learning in classrooms must take this into account by not implying that pupils learn only when interacting with teachers. The social skills of this busy situation are key to pupils being able to make the best of it: they have to get used to being one of many, especially when it comes to adult attention, and this can demand extra skills of being able to wait, or finding other sources of help. We often feel that more explicitness about these social skills and their development would relieve many difficulties in classrooms.

2 *Classrooms are public places*. This statement is meant in two ways. First, classrooms are public in the general sense that many people have a view or opinion on classrooms and how they ought to operate. Second, classrooms are public in that a teacher's and a pupil's behaviour is generally highly visible to all the other members in the event.

The implication of the first is that the teacher is at the centre of a number of people's expectations – parents, colleagues, head, local authority, central government and, of course, pupils. In the unlikely event that these various expectations are in broad agreement with each other, the teacher will probably feel strongly supported in her or his job. It is more likely that disagreements exist and the teacher feels in a state of 'role strain'. Resolving role strain can be accomplished in a number of ways, each with its own costs and benefits – a classic has been the strategy of isolating role performance from view by the conflicting parties: this leads to the phenomenon of classroom as a castle, with paper over the windows to the corridor.

The implications of the second sense of publicness are various: teachers may feel that they are 'on stage' to some degree and have to develop an approach which blends the public and the personal. Teachers may act towards one pupil with the intention of affecting others in the audience – the 'ripple effect' – but mainly teachers adopt a focus toward groups of pupils (whole class or less). This group focus grows out of the imbalance in numbers in the classroom and also serves to cope with the busyness of the situation.

Pupils learn to experience much public evaluation of their work and behaviour and they adopt a variety of strategies in the face of this: strategies to work out what answer teacher wants, strategies to assess whether teacher is being fair in her or his evaluations, especially when they are public, and so on. Some studies suggest that teachers give public evaluations of pupils every few minutes. Pupils learn to be treated as a member of a group which is not always of their choosing, and in turn may adopt a group approach toward affecting other – including, on occasion, their teacher.

3 *Classroom events are multidimensional*. There is a wide variety of purposes, interests and goals represented by the different personnel in a classroom. The teacher may have thoughts about the staff meeting this evening, or the mortgage: the pupils may have thoughts about what is on television or what

someone said to their friend. In the middle of this, teaching and learning takes place. Personal–social aspects of pupils' and teachers' lives are always affecting classroom life.

Even when we focus on the learning dimension alone the statement still applies. The classroom contains a multiplicity of information sources – books, worksheets, displays, other visuals, as well as all the verbal and non-verbal behaviour of teachers and pupils – and these sources generally do not all refer to the same thing. The information from multiple sources is sometimes incompatible, and sometimes inconsistent, so that skills of selection are crucial for learners. This skill is even sometimes required in order to handle the ambiguities in a learning task.

For the teacher an implication is that they need to manage events on a multiplicity of dimensions: knowing subject, appraising students, managing classroom groups, coping with emotional responses to events, establishing procedures, distributing resources, encouraging thinking, keeping records and so on. With these tasks all affecting each other the result may feel overwhelming on occasion. Effective teachers accept and mediate this multidimensionality. Sometimes they engage it explicitly in their classroom management, through references to what they are aware of going on elsewhere, and sometimes in their subject, through links to daily life.

For pupils this multidimensional environment means that on the occasion when they intend to engage in academic work they need to display considerable skills in selecting what is salient information and what is not, especially when attempting to identify the demands of a task. These are not usually the skills which are referred to when identifying academic achievement.

4 *Classroom events are simultaneous.* The multiple events in the classroom do not occur in a step-by-step fashion but simultaneously, especially from the teacher's point of view. One group is happily working away, another group wants attention for something, and meanwhile someone is climbing out of the window. Teachers attend to numerous aspects at the same time: the pace of work, the sequencing of pupil contributions, the distribution of pupils attended to, the accuracy of pupil contributions, the development of the argument and so on, while at the same time monitoring work involvement levels, other pupil behaviours and external events.

This has at least two implications for teachers. First, it is important to exercise the skill (at least apparently) of being able to monitor more than one aspect at once. This is sometimes described as the 'eyes in the back of the head' phenomenon. Second, it follows that teachers may exercise a choice as to which aspect to respond to and which to ignore. The style of operation of this choice can have critical effects and can make the difference between a 'smooth' teaching performance which gives rise to a purposeful climate, and a 'lumpy' performance where the teacher seems controlled by events and appears to be 'chopping and changing'.

For the pupils the simultaneity of classroom events is not such a salient phenomenon since they may not intend to have a perspective on the whole situation and its events. However, the fact that it is salient for teachers can be exploited very effectively by those waiting for teacher's back to turn. Some pupils quickly learn the skills of avoiding teacher's monitoring.

5 *Classroom events are unpredictable*. In such a busy, multidimensional environment it is not possible to be in a position of predicting the course of events with a fine degree of accuracy. Despite teachers' proper professional attempts to predict how this group might respond to the material, or how long it might take, they know that there will be surprises, so they generally become skilled in recognizing and tolerating unpredictability.

Disruptive effects are easily generated by interruptions: the external ones (the window cleaner, the snowstorm) and the internal ones (the projector breakdown, the tannoy announcement). Routines in classroom life can be viewed as one attempt to engender predictability and reduce ambiguity. Nevertheless teachers perforce must be able to tolerate high levels of ambiguity in classroom life.

Pupils also have strategies for coping with unpredictability: their seeking every detail of what is expected in a task, searching for the answer teacher wants, requesting low-risk predictable tasks, and making teacher predictable through stereotype and labelling are examples. They all serve as attempts to reduce ambiguity.

This analysis helps us realize that the nature of classrooms demands that teachers exhibit high-level skills, an ability to interpret situations and orchestrate learning. They often cannot describe these aspects, and sometimes feel hesitant to do so lest 'it divides them from the layperson'. But their professionalism is founded on this complexity.

It also helps us recognise the poverty of those views which portray the classroom as a simple cause-and-effect situation, which offer a simple teacher-centered view, and which seem to imply that there is a prescription for successful teaching in all contexts. These views are common, but are positively dangerous as a basis for improving classrooms. They lead respectively to teachers feeling de-skilled when simple add-ons do not work, to classrooms not being places where students develop the skills to take responsibility for their learning, and to the creativity of the system being depressed. This can lead to teachers passing on prescriptions, which can in turn depress student performance.

This understanding of the classroom setting, its demands and constraints, accounts for other important phenomena. It helps us appreciate that teachers exchange, use, even create new practices daily as they face and resolve problems in the classroom. Large-scale programmes and curricula probably represent a small proportion of the everyday changes which teachers are making in their classrooms. Teachers decide whether their practices are valid from a range of bases, from personal feeling to scientific, with a tendency toward the former – the intuitive practitioner, feeling his or her way through. They are involved in recipe collecting and exchanging, traded on the basis of 'what worked for me' and 'what feels right'. The working assumption is that one practitioner cannot tell another something: they can only exchange experiences. Although teachers may seek information from a range of sources, this is highly dependent on availability and accessibility: peers in the same school become the most credible.

When it comes to improving classrooms from the perspective of difficult behaviour, this perspective also sets us up to examine more about the situation and how it is orchestrated than about individual incidents. Here we will consider significant differences in style of management, but before we do that it is instructive to register some widespread trends.

Surveys of teachers' views of troublesome behaviour in classrooms have been conducted in various phases and various places. Wheldall and Merrett (1988) surveyed 198 teachers in the West Midlands, asking them to identify the most troublesome behaviours from ten categories provided. Forty-seven per cent elected 'talking out of turn' (hereafter referred to as 'TOOT') followed by 25 per cent choosing 'hindering other children' (HOC). For the most frequent troublesome behaviour, the results were similar: TOOT 55 per cent, HOC 21 per cent, with no other category above 10 per cent. When asked about the most troublesome behaviour of the particularly troublesome individuals, the results were TOOT 33 per cent, HOC 27 per cent. Houghton, Wheldall and Merrett (1988) surveyed 251 secondary teachers in the same area: the most frequent and troublesome classroom misbehaviours were TOOT 50 per cent and HOC 17 per cent. A modified survey of 70 nursery teachers found 55 per cent of teachers listing 'not listening', and concluded 'In nurseries where the work is much less formal, the same type of behaviours are seen to be troublesome to teachers' (Merrett and Taylor, 1994, p. 293)

Further afield, in St Helena 50 returns from first and middle school teachers showed most disruptive behaviour: TOOT 42 per cent, facing away from work 25 per cent. The most common misbehaviours were TOOT 43 per cent, facing away from work 16 per cent. In particularly troublesome children, TOOT was most disruptive and most frequently occurring. (Jones, Wilkin and Charlton, 1995). In Singapore 89 primary schoolteachers rated the most disruptive behaviours as talking 26 per cent, and disturbing others 21 per cent, although interestingly 15 per cent chose nothing.' The most commonly occurring misbehaviours for these teachers were: talking 42 per cent and facing away from work 13 per cent (Jones, Quah and Charlton, 1996).

In a similar vein, research carried out for the Elton Report (Gray and Sime, 1989) analysed questionnaire results from 2,500 secondary teachers and 1,050 primary teachers in England and Wales. Of the problem behaviours which teachers experienced, TOOT was again top of the list: 97 per cent of each group reported it occurring at least once during the week, with 53 per cent of secondary and 69 per cent of primary teachers reporting its occurrence at least daily. Further, TOOT was identified as the problem behaviour most difficult to deal with, and when asked to consider a particularly difficult class, the most difficult behaviour was TOOT. The same questionnaire was returned by 156 junior primary and 621 primary teachers in South Australia (Johnson, Oswald and Adey, 1993). The most common discipline problems were TOOT 30 per cent, HOC 38 per cent, and idleness and work avoidance 33 per cent. When asked to report on a difficult class, the behaviours which were difficult were the same.

The similarity in these results is striking, notwithstanding some interesting differences. What is the problem with TOOT? Why do teachers across the world report it with such regularity? There are two main response to these questions. The first is to address the behaviour, and to start with the most difficult pupils (who interestingly are not reported as displaying different types of difficult behaviour), and develop a method with them of reducing the behaviour. This is the behavioural approach, as most recently described by Anderson and Merrett (1997). Leaving aside for a moment the question of who will staff such a specialized intervention, the track record of behavioural approaches raises some doubts when implemented in the classroom: Bain, Houghton and Williams (1991) report that the frequency of the targeted teacher behaviour, such as 'teacher encouragement', can return to near-baseline levels after the intervention ends. Corrie (1997) adds an extra doubt about this approach, by demonstrating that the frequency of TOOT varies in classrooms, and by studying the classroom situation in which it occurs she found that different teachers had different views of that situation, their roles, their approaches to the group, to learning and so on. It was not to be reduced to a consideration of 'teacher skill'.

So an alternative response to the above surveys is to say that they tell us something important about the typical classroom situation, around the world. This would require us to consider the role of talk in classrooms, and how it may be best utilized in the service of learning, teachers' views on this, the organizational perceptions of classroom talk, and the degree to which the classroom curriculum encourages, supports and develops talk.

The reactive classroom is not effective for improving behaviour. As before, we take being proactive to mean anticipating potential difficulty, thinking ahead rather than waiting for problems to arise. In contrast, being reactive means only responding to current problems, and planning a response once they have arisen.

Many approaches focus on aspects of the teacher's response to unwelcome behaviour. These latter often reflect the question which may be heard in many unstructured teacher conversations about classroom difficulty: 'What do I do if...?' or 'What do you do about...?' The inherent risk is that of casting the teacher in a response-led role, which is an ineffective strategy in the classroom situation. It is a case of closing the stable door after the horse has bolted.

Responses to events do not provide the answer. They set the teacher on the back foot and can initiate a pattern of the teacher being run by events rather than of orchestrating purpose and momentum in the class-room. What is more, responses of the short variety do not work. Clarke *et al.* (1981; Gay and Parry-Jones, 1980) undertook a detailed analysis of the internal structure of disruptive incidents in classrooms, detailing the actions which initiated and terminated the incidents. The analysis demonstrated that 'soft' and discursive strategies were four times more likely to lead to an exit from the incident than were hard commands. O'Hagan and Edmunds (1982) demonstrated that apparently successful attempts to control disruptive conduct by intimidatory practice may have deleterious consequences in other ways, for example, on pupils' inclination to truant. So when we raise some aspects of teachers' responses later in this chapter, it is with recognition of their secondary importance to the wider aspects of classroom management.

The most effective element in reducing general classroom disruption is the teacher's skill in planning activities. This implication is supported by research findings such as those of Kounin (1977), whose extensive and detailed studies showed that the action which teachers took in response to a discipline problem had no consistent relationship with their managerial success in the classroom. However, what teachers did before misbehaviour occurred was shown to be crucial in achieving success, through a preventive focus which reduced difficulty. The teacher's ability to manage the classroom group through planned activities is a key element in developing constructive behaviour patterns.

So, with these contextual points in mind, we turn to consider difficult behaviour in classrooms and its improvement. For the reasons given we will not adopt reactive approaches, and will not fall into another available trap of focusing on deficits in teachers' 'classroom management skills'. There is not a meaningful consensus on what these are, and as Corrie (1997) has shown, any focus on the teacher would be better served by considering their knowledge and conceptions of classrooms. Instead we take a first step of clarifying the picture of the difficulty.

Diagnosing classroom difficulty

Many 'solutions' which are proposed for difficult behaviour in classrooms are not based on a diagnosis of the situation. They are favourite solutions which may work but may not. For example, one source of advice' may suggest that a teacher becomes more 'positive' and rewarding, another may propose that the differentiation of tasks needs attention, while another may want to alter the social relations. The list could easily go on, but we must ask the question, 'What is the basis for the advice?' In many cases it is an enthusiasm transferred from another situation, or in some cases it is an enthusiasm for a particular model for fixing a classroom. Given what we recognize about the complexity of the classroom, any advice which pre-selects a single aspect for focus is likely to work only as a matter of chance. Instead of this, we need to develop a way of being clearer about the difficulty and of matching the advice to that clearer picture. We will call this 'diagnosis', although we do not wish to stimulate medical connotations and the idea that a single organic cause will be found. Given the complexity and connectedness of classrooms, an 'accurate' linear diagnosis will not be forthcoming, but a narrowing of the focus will be achieved.

There are probably a number of dimensions along which classroom difficulty could be addressed. Given the importance of context in behaviour, we have chosen to order things in terms of how widespread in time and space the difficulty is. So diagnosing the *extent* of difficulty will develop a clearer focus. We recognize that this does not always happen in everyday conversation about classroom difficulty, since teachers are not practised in being specific. 'That class was awful today' is a comment which many of us will have heard (and may have used), but such a comment does not necessarily reflect an accurate analysis of the pattern of behaviour, and is likely to be an overstatement of the position. Given this, it is valuable to be more specific about the extent of difficulty, with the caveat that exaggerated comments are often delivered in the staffroom at break-time, where it is not necessary to initiate immediate action (other than to continue stirring the coffee).

The challenge is to adopt a form of diagnostic thinking which will support us in spotting the patterns in the difficult behaviour.

The following questions attempt a starting diagnosis, and lead on to ideas and frameworks which may be useful in thinking about improvement of the behaviour patterns.

Is there a *particular* disaffection in this classroom? In other words is it restricted to particular times, places or persons?

If Yes, does the disaffection relate to:

1 Particular sorts of teacher–pupil interactions. Examine skills in handling conflict, avoiding escalations.   (sections A to G)

2 A particular *classroom* context.

  Analyse the physical, social and psychological features of this classroom.   (section H)

3 Particular *activities*.

  Analyse the design and message of these activities.   (section I)

4 A particular *subgroup* of pupils.

  Analyse the role of this group within the class and the roles of key members within the group.   (section J)

If No, is there a general disaffection in this class? In other words does it seem to involve most people and most occasions?

If Yes, does the disaffection relate to:

1 The *curriculum* offered. Is it appropriate for this class?

  Do pupils feel they achieve something valuable?   (section K)

2 The *profile of activities*. Is it engaging?

  Are pupils involved in the activities?   (section L)

3 The *responsibilities* in this class. Are they developed and shared?

  Are pupils involved in planning?   (section M)

4 Classroom *rules*. Are they agreed, understood, accepted and used?

  Are pupils reviewing the success of this class?   (section N)

5 The *climate*. Does it need review and improvement?   (section O)

6 The sense of *community* in this classroom. Is it positive?   (section P)

The sections which follow contain various suggestions for action (and inaction) on the part of a classroom teacher experiencing difficult behaviour. But at the outset let us be clear:

• Not all of these suggestions will be appropriate for your situation.
• Not all of these suggestions will be appealing to you as a teacher.

- Not all of these suggestions will 'work' – especially if we take that to mean producing obedience.

Anyone who felt they had to do all of what follows would be overwhelmed straight away. But if you use these suggestions to set off trains of thought about the situation you know and find difficult, and if you professionally select and modify the suggestions to your own situation, there may be some value gained. Clearly a series of considerations and possible lines of action is not a workbook of recipes.

If you let the diagnostic questions above lead you to some sections rather than others, then the order of the sections which follow is unimportant. They are certainly not in order of importance. Beginning with the most immediate considerations, what to think about and do in a difficult interaction, might appear to promote a 'What do I do if they do X?' mentality, which is exactly the sort of reactive approach which does not work. Somewhat better would be to ask the proactive question 'How can I create a classroom where these things don't happen?', which is considered in the latter sections. These later suggestions are not any less immediate because they appear later – we can start changing our classroom climate tomorrow, for example. Nevertheless we put incidents first, in order to speak to the concerns of the teacher, perhaps tired and frustrated, who has a focus on particular individuals and incidents – let us consider them first before moving to the wider scale and equally immediate matters of classroom patterns and classroom community.

Frameworks and ideas for improving classroom behaviour patterns

The first few sections have a common theme: how a teacher can develop their choice of response to a difficult incident, as opposed to feeling that they have to react in ways which are not improving the situation. It is not surprising that in the busy classroom situation, quick reactions are made: the problem arises when these contribute to the escalation of a troublesome incident. We all find ourselves in situations where we feel we have little choice, but by thinking about the situation and the message we most wish to convey a new range of alternatives can develop.

A. Styles of responding

Consider the following classroom situation: Timothy grabs Rosemary's ruler and appears to hide it from her.

Consider the following options for the teacher:

(1) 'Timothy, stop being childish and give back Rosemary her ruler.'
(2) 'Timothy, we ask before borrowing in this classroom.'
(3) 'Timothy, you're quite able to get on with your work, so return Rosemary's ruler and let her do the same.'

These three simple options have both similarities and differences. They are similar in that they all indicate to Timothy that the teacher has noticed his behaviour and decided it is inappropriate. In that sense they may all serve to mark a boundary on behaviour. But they also have differences:

(1) has elements of judging the person, negatively.
(2) points to an agreement previously made.
(3) refers to roles and responsibilities in learning.

The impact of these different styles, if generalized over time, can be quite marked. Style (1) can be counterproductive in terms of improving behaviour because it may build up resentments: it may be the style of the 'deviance-provocative teacher' (see section G). Style (2) can be effective if it is set against a background of making and reviewing agreements regarding classroom behaviour. Style (3) makes the important link with what we aim to achieve in classrooms; it reaffirms our purpose.

But style (1) is quite prevalent in our classrooms. The most frequently occurring teacher comments are very brief: 'Stop it' and 'Shut up!'

B. Teachers' ways of conveying to pupils that behaviour is inappropriate

When things are going well, the communication between teachers and pupils is complex and reflects shared meanings which have developed between them. For example, the teacher who, without looking up from the work she is checking with a pupil, says 'someone's being silly' and two pupils at the back of the room stop the behaviour they are involved in – because they know and can interpret the informal rules of that classroom. On another occasion in another classroom, the same comment might be ineffective as the teacher has not built up shared meaning with a class with the result that their ways of conveying the inappropriacy of behaviour are not successful.

Hargreaves, Hester and Mellor (1975) identified the following 11 teacher strategies:

1 Descriptive statement of the deviant conduct: 'You're taking a long time to settle down'.
2 Statement of the rule which is being invoked: 'Rulers aren't for fighting with', 'When I'm talking no one else talks'.

3 Appeal to pupil's knowledge of the rule: 'You know you're meant to write it in the book'.
4 Command/request for conformity to the rule: 'Shut up', 'Put that away'.
5 Prohibitions: 'Don't', 'Stop that'.
6 Questions: 'Are you listening?', 'What's going on over there?'
7 Statement of the consequences of the deviant conduct: 'I won't bother to read if you go on like this', 'Someone will get hurt if this equipment is left lying here'.
8 Warnings and threats: 'I'm going to get annoyed', 'You'll be in detention', 'I'll send you to the head'.
9 Evaluative labels of the pupil and her or his conduct: 'Stop behaving like a baby', 'Don't be daft'.
10 Sarcasm: 'We can do without the singing', 'Have you retired?'
11 Attention-drawers: 'Sandra!', 'girls!', '5C!'

If we ask the question 'Are some of these strategies more effective than others?' we have to recognize that all of them can be effective in some situations in the short term. However, strategies 2 and 7 are worthy of our attention since they achieve two goals: they signal that the behaviour is unwanted and they communicate the rule which the teacher sees as being broken. As such they are likely to have the most effective long-term contribution, especially in a classroom where the communication of informal rules seems to have been ineffective.

Within this theme we do not want to convey an image of successful classrooms as rule-bound environments: neither pupils nor teachers find that motivating, and the occasions when rules are relaxed are often memorable for building relationships. One of pupils' criteria for judging teachers is 'can he have a laugh?' (Gannaway, 1984). However, breaking rules is most meaningful when someone knows what the rule is that is being broken.

C. Responding to aggression – assertively

Aggression may come in a number of forms – verbal, indirect, and so on. Direct physical aggression towards a teacher is comparatively rare: reported and recorded non-accidental injuries involve one-third of 1 per cent of teachers (see data cited in Department for Education and Science, 1989).

When faced with direct aggression, the two main responses are 'fight' (returning the aggression) or 'flight' (non-assertion). These may seem natural or, indeed, sensible in evolutionary terms. However, their cumulative effect in a classroom is unlikely to promote a constructive set of relationships. It is possible to develop a new response – learning to respond to aggression assertively. In this mode a teacher can retain more control of his or her own behaviour, and therefore go beyond the more basic 'fight or flight'.

When people start to consider and develop more assertive responses in their repertoire, two connected things become noticeable. First, their predictions – they often predict that they will get a violent reaction to their assertive response. This is inaccurate, as anyone who goes beyond this fear to experiment with assertive responses will tell you. But this fearful prediction can stop a few people ever reaching the experimental stage. This is the second point: our predictions shape our range of behaviour – this can be limiting, as implied above, or it can be in an expanding fashion, where our predictions support a wider range of action options. It is useful, therefore, to practise identifying one's own predictions, especially those small 'inner voices' which speak in moments of difficulty.

Professionals who behave confidently and who give the impression that things are under control are less likely to be assaulted or to witness assaults (Poyner and Warne, 1988).

D. How can I get myself to react less?

Adopting a more calming inner dialogue will help to ensure that difficulties do not escalate, and is part of becoming less reactive. This takes practice. Here it is worth considering the very fast sequence which occurs when we are faced with any incident. It starts with the lower part of the brain firing off some very quick feelings. Then follow, we hope, the higher parts of the brain which bring in a range of considerations and previous experiences. Finally, we decide what to do and act. As Goleman (1996) has clarified, emotionally intelligent behaviour operates a sequence as shown below:

Figure 15.01 Three stages in emotionally intelligent behaviour

The problem with some of our reactions is that the 'think' stage is bypassed, so that what we do is driven by what we feel.

There are various approaches to reducing our reactivity. We could:

- deliberately make more of a gap between the Feel and the Do:
  - count to ten (or less)
  - consider more than one option.
    It can be useful to be open-handed about this, saying what is going on as

you are doing it, for example: 'I'll count to five now, and consider whether it would be best to do X or Y.' This can be very effective for demonstrating that you retain control – of yourself first and of your role.

- spot the inner voices which make you most reactive, i.e. the thoughts which serve to perpetuate feelings rather than move on from them. Examples which might keep you stuck in reactive mode could include:
  - 'That Terry is a mean little blighter.'
  - 'He's always trying to take advantage of me.'
  - 'She shows no respect for me or for anyone.'
- Occasionally try something counterintuitive to break the pattern:
  - 'Wayne, what a nice pair of shoes, are they new?'
  - 'Nigel, I want you to walk round the classroom shouting.'

Brown (1986) has indicated how there are occasions when being paradoxical with a pupil actually stimulates them to exercise more of their self-control.

E. What the pupil says next

There are some classic responses which pupils give when teacher has suggested they are doing something inappropriate. These were identified in the 1950s by Sykes and Matza (1957) and remain alive and well now:

- 'It wasn't me', 'It was X's fault' (denial of responsibility).
- 'We were only having a laugh', 'It didn't hurt' (denial of injury).
- 'It was only Y', 'He deserved it' (denial of the victim).
- 'I bet you've done it', 'You let Z off' (condemning the condemners).
- 'It was important to show him ...' (appeal to higher loyalties).

There are various ways in which you might perceive these responses, each of which could lead you to different paths for your next response:

- as 'excuses'
- as testing you out
- as the sort of responses which self-respecting people give when accused.

What will our next response be? Here are three types of possibilities:

- *Escalate*? For example, 'Don't give me those excuses' or 'Don't speak to me like that'. There is good evidence that such responses do lead to matters escalating. Créton, Wubbels and Hoomayers (1989) and Admiraal, Wubbels and Korthagen (1996) have highlighted the vicious cycles when teacher and pupils symmetrically intensify each other's behaviour. Remember that giving hard commands can lead to hard responses from pupils.

- *Hostile*? 'You should be ashamed of yourself.' Well, let us hope that shame is not what pupils take away from their classroom experience. This sort of response does not give the pupil room to save face, and to wind down when they have been playing the wind-up game with teachers. As Rogers (1992) points out, students who seem to want the last word are often concerned about how they manage in front of their peers.
- *Passive*? 'Why are you doing that?' That is a question to which there is no real answer, and we do not want it anyway. We want the difficulty to reduce and constructive working relations to resume. Asking this sort of question can give pupils a wonderful opportunity to sidetrack you with lots of creative answers to your question.

Preferable to these three responses is something which is both assertive (not aggressive) and non-escalatory, something which brings attention back to the important matters of the classroom and productive relations for learning. Perhaps 'That's as may be – now let's get this activity done'.

Some of the skills in asserting yourself, as described by Dickson (1982) are:

- give a clear statement of what you want: 'I want you to return to your table.'
- stick to your statement, repeating it as necessary.
- deflect the other person's responses, the ones which may undermine your statement, for example irrelevances or argumentation, perhaps by prefacing your restatement with a short recognition of their view: 'I've heard your reason for looking at the fish, but I want you to return to your table.'

Rogers (1992) suggests that pupils often engage teachers in 'secondary behaviour' which diverts the teacher from their original concern of resuming activity. This could be any number of things: a grunt, a glance to a peer, a question – the potential is considerable. In this context assertiveness is appropriate, remembering that it is not about getting your own way but about practising clear communication within the rights and responsibilities of one's role.

F. Managing conflict

Conflicts will happen, in classrooms as much as anywhere else. Conflicts are endemic in school life: that is not necessarily a problem – it is the way we handle them that matters. One of the most important orienting points is not to confuse conflict with aggression: such a view can lead to conflicts being swept aside or denied. Different sorts of conflicts you might meet include: (1) conflicts within yourselves, you want to carry on talking with a pupil at break and you also want to get some coffee; (2) conflicts between yourself and someone else, the class wants to see part of the video again but you want to move on; (3) conflicts between other people, some pupils are arguing about whose actions led to the experiment failing. It can be useful to clarify to yourself which type of conflict you are experiencing. Here we will comment on type (3) then (2).

When teachers find that difficult behaviour in a classroom is expressing conflicts between pupils, they sometimes say that they feel at a loss for how to improve matters. There are a number of background features which help to reduce conflict and to advance pupils' personal-social development (see, for example, Katz and Lawyer, 1994):

1 *Co-operation*. Helping children to work together and trust, help, and share with each other.

2 *Communication*. Helping children learn to observe carefully, communicate well, and listen to each other.

3 *Respect*. Helping children learn to respect and enjoy people's differences and to understand prejudice and why it is wrong.

4 *Expressing themselves positively*. Helping children learn to express feelings, particularly anger, in ways that are not destructive, and learn self-control.

5 *Conflict resolution*. Helping children learn how to resolve a conflict by talking it through.

When managing conflicts between others:

- Get the parties to talk in a structured way – one at a time – taking turns to speak and to listen.
- If appropriate, get both parties to take more distance on the situation by writing down how they see it.
- Get them to make suggestions for how to end the conflict.
- Treat it as a practical problem-solving exercise, rather than a moral lesson: 'what can we do to solve this?' rather than 'I want you to apologise right now'.
- Make sure that each person's proposal for resolving the conflict is put in clear practical terms, and that the other person has had a chance to indicate whether they agree to the proposal (Bach and Wyden, 1968).

A conflict ends when each person has aired their views, and they have questioned each other enough to ensure that this airing has been properly achieved.

G. The deviance-provocative teacher and the deviance-insulative teacher

This is an idea about how teachers may vary in their handling of difficult incidents. We all vary, so it is not an idea for putting us into fixed categories.

When we are a deviance-provocative teacher (Jordan, 1974), we *believe* that the pupils we define as deviant do not want to work, and will do anything to avoid work. It is impossible to provide conditions under which they will work, so the pupils must change. Disciplinary interactions are a contest or battle – which we must win.

When we are a deviance-insulative teacher, we *believe* that these pupils really want to work, but that the conditions are assumed to be at fault. These can be changed and it is our responsibility to initiate that change. Disciplinary interactions relate to a clear set of classroom rules which are made explicit to the pupils.

The deviance-provocative teacher is unable to defuse situations, frequently issues ultimatums, and becomes involved in confrontations, whereas the deviance-insulative teacher allows students to 'save face', and avoids confrontations.

Thus the deviance-insulative teacher has some beliefs and responses which make up a 'virtuous cycle' in which behaviour goes well. Whereas the deviance-provocative teacher has some beliefs and responses which make a 'vicious cycle' in which behaviour does not go well.

In lessons managed by the deviance-provocative teacher, deviant pupils are neglected other than for the many negative evaluative comments made about them. Pupils are referred to higher authority when they refuse to comply – which they do. The deviance-insulative teacher avoids favouritism, or other preferential treatment in lessons.

H. Skills in managing the classroom context

Creative teachers display many skills. Those included in the following framework relate to the particular complexities of the classroom which were outlined at the start of this chapter.

Teachers managing the classroom situation are:

1 managing the physical setting – layout, seating, resources, etc.
2 managing the social structure – groupings, working patterns, etc.
3 managing the psychological setting of the classroom:
    a handling the timing and pacing, developing effective routines;
    b giving a personal yet public performance, with a focus on group participation;
    c being aware of the multiple dimensions of classroom life, and showing it;
    d managing more than one event at the same time, ignoring as appropriate;
    e recognizing and tolerating the unpredictable nature of classroom life.

This framework of headings can be useful on those occasions when it seems that difficult behaviour is associated with a particular classroom. As a precursor it can also be useful to think about our broad profile of skills.

Here we use the term 'classroom' deliberately, since teachers sometimes tell us that they experience most difficulty in a particular room. 'They're fine during the rest of the week – it's just when we get into that room.' In this case it is useful to analyse the features of the classroom which this framework highlights:

1   *Physical setting*: layout of furniture, positioning of seats, resources, lighting, display, etc. (for a literature review see Weinstein, 1979). Do any of these seem linked to the difficulty? If so, can you experiment with some aspect? We have seen groups of teachers deconstruct and reconstruct the physical design of a classroom, rearranging everything which moves, in order to support the patterns of behaviour they seek. Managing the physical setting is one of the teacher's key skills, but not always exercised: they often de-skill themselves by saying that someone else would not like a change on this front – the cleaner, the colleagues, even the pupils.

      The physical setting of a classroom also carries messages about ownership and purpose of that place. Review these in a classroom where difficulty is occurring. Are there positive signs of pupils and purpose in this room?

2   *Social structure*: the groupings of pupils, patterns of working together, rationales given, etc. (also the subject of a later review by Weinstein, 1991).

      Classroom life is about being in groups, yet this aspect is often not analysed or developed. Broadly speaking, classrooms can be effective with any social structure in which a range of groups are used for learning and in which pupils learn about being in a group. Groupings which carry signs of devaluing some pupils (for example, so-called ability grouping) can lead to worsening patterns of behaviour. If you think that a particular way of grouping is related to difficult behaviour, you might consider a range of modifications. One teacher gave each pupil a playing card as they entered the classroom: large groups could be formed using the suits, small groups using the card values. This also carried the message that it was important to be able to work with anyone in the class. Regrouping of pupils can be quickly carried out by allocating a letter to each person in the current grouping and then composing new groups on the basis of the letters. The element of randomness is also useful as it demonstrates that teacher does not have some secret basis on which to rig the groupings. Teachers who involve pupils in thinking about groupings in this way will usually find that the groups work better.

      The rationale for working in groups might be poorly communicated in some classrooms: reiterating that it is for getting on with the learning and for getting on with each other is necessary. Reteaching the skills of working together can be important.

3 *Psychological setting*: this is mainly managed through the type of activities in the classroom and the way they are conducted. Teachers actually manage activities rather than students, and as Doyle (1990, p. 351) remarks, 'if an activity system is not established and running in a classroom, no amount of discipline will create order'. Specific activities will be reviewed in the next section.

a) The busyness of the classroom is managed through timing and pacing of activities. Too few activities can lead pupils to seek diversion: too many can get them confused. The transitions between classroom activities can be unstable periods which need effective orchestration. They are well handled when preceded by some advance warnings: 'There are three minutes before we return to the whole group', 'We've been working on this experiment for ten minutes now so you should be about half-way through'.

b) The publicness of classrooms can create difficulties if it becomes exaggerated. In other words if everyone's behaviour, and especially any difficult behaviour, becomes the heightened focus for public attention. It is constructive to have private interchanges in the classroom, including with those pupils whose behaviour concerns you. Positive communications such as praise are more effective if handled privately. The sense of the classroom being a stage for everyone's performance declines as the relationships in a group develop, and as the focus returns to learning activities not persons.

c) The multidimensional nature of classroom life needs recognition. Those teachers who try to keep the rest of life firmly outside the door operate less effective classrooms. Instead of operating defensively in that way, the challenge is to acknowledge the rest of life and link it to the learning. This may mean giving a few moments to something which you know is engaging pupils' attention, and seeing what can be learned before moving on to the classroom agenda. More broadly a curriculum which has been related to the life experiences of pupils is a hallmark of authentic pedagogy, in which pupils are challenged to think, and to apply academic learning to important, real-world problems. Pupils who receive more authentic pedagogy learn more, regardless of social background, race, gender (Newmann, Marks and Gamoran, 1995).

d) The simultaneity of classroom events demands a key skill from the teacher, that of selective ignoring. Effective teachers are effective at deciding what to overlook. They give a 'smooth' performance, which maintains a sense of momentum, and conveys the sense that they are steering the events. By contrast, the teacher who does not use such skills effectively gives a 'lumpy' performance, responding to something here then something there, so that momentum is lost and the events seem to be in control. Perhaps in a classroom where difficulty has developed, a teacher can find their sensitivity heightened towards that difficulty, and as a result exercises the skills of selective ignoring less well. More broadly, there are occasions when our own approaches to managing the classroom constitute interruptions, and disturb the flow in a non-productive way (Arlin, 1979).

e) The unpredictability of classroom life has to be recognized and accepted as well as managed. Teachers are sometimes very effective at conveying the message that unpredictability is to some extent inevitable, which in turn may help pupils recognize this. The skills of turning one's attention away from an interruption, or of learning from unpredicted happenings can be built in the classroom. When it is not recognized or reaches levels for which class members are unprepared, it can be associated with difficult behaviour. Here, the purposes and routines of the classroom might need to be reviewed and re-established for this particular classroom. The process of establishment is usually thought of at the beginning of the school year (Emmer, Evertson and Anderson, 1980), and the process is very illuminating at that time (Ball, 1980; Beynon, 1985), but it may need to be reviewed at other times, especially if patterns of difficulty have arisen.

I. Analysing particular classroom activities

If you have identified that a classroom difficulty relates to particular activities, the next step is to identify whether there is something about the way we construct the activities which might be improved. The basic ingredients of a classroom activity are shown in Figure 15.02.

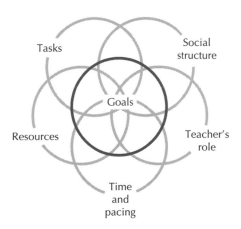

Figure 15.02 Ingredients in classroom activities

Scan the following examples, and see whether you agree that much of a classroom might be portrayed through a focus on features of the activity and situation:

- Brian the drama teacher has a large open space for his room. He arranges chairs in pairs throughout the room and sets the class off on their warm-up task, selling an idea to each other for two minutes while he keeps time. Pupils bring the resource of their out-of-school knowledge. Then groups of four are formed to develop the script for a fantasy advert. Brian uses tight timing for the first half of the lesson, viewing himself as task facilitator and monitor, regularly reminding the groups to use their understanding of influence language.
- Sheila the science teacher has a laboratory with fixed benches and cupboards. Pupils have learned how to use the resources of the room. After a brief introduction with diagrams on the board, they work in small groups to carry out an investigation for about 50 minutes. Pupils occasionally call on Sheila as an extra resource in their problem-solving.
- Andrew teaches languages from the front of a classroom fitted with rows of desks. He uses the blackboard to run a question and answer session for ten minutes: pupils then write the answers into exercise books individually for ten minutes. Andrew sees himself as the sole source of the knowledge which the pupils are gaining.

These brief examples might also remind us that the way in which activities are set up and groups are managed strongly influences the type of control behaviour which the teacher adopts. Bossert (1977) demonstrated consistent patterns in these influences, and the fact that they operated regardless of the individual teacher. Note also how little is said about the goals of the activity in most cases. Yet the element *Goals* is central in keeping the whole activity together and in creating purpose in the classroom. Ames (1992b) and others have noted that very often the goals of classroom activities are not made clear.

J. Thinking about pupils' roles in subgroups

If a subgroup of pupils seems to be associated with difficult classroom behaviour, we often focus on particular individuals, and attribute things to them – 'ringleaders' and so on. However, the most visible members of a group are not necessarily the sources of power and influence in that group. We need to take seriously the notion of roles in groups, treating role as a cluster of behaviours which is meaningful to others. Role relates to context and does not describe all of a person, but to a set of interactions with the role-partners. A leader cannot be a leader without followers, the bully cannot be a bully without victims.

When analysing the behaviour of pupil groups in a classroom, it follows that we will create a more powerful picture by looking at how the various roles relate and interact in the playing out of the behaviour in that group. Systematic ways of describing roles in groups are not easy to find, and everyday descriptions might not lead us forwards. The work of Bales (1970) has proved useful since it found three important dimensions along which the roles people adopt in groups can be described. The first captured the degree to which the person exercised power or dominance in the group: one's position could be upward or downward on this dimension. The second illustrates the degree of liking or the evaluation a person attracts: one's position could be positive or negative on this dimension. The third portrays the degree of contribution to the group tasks: a person may be forward or backward on this dimension. Thus, we have a three-dimensional space into which it is possible to locate the general role style of group members (Figure 15.03).

This conceptual framework can be of direct use as it stands. With practice it is soon possible to array the various members of a group in the space by thinking about their positions on the three dimensions in turn. Bales used these dimensions to identify 26 role types, and Figure 15.04 shows our attempt to fit everyday descriptive words to this systematic description. Note that these are not meant to be agreed descriptions: they are the perceptions which members of a particular group might hold about the roles within it.

Applying this to a group of pupils allows us to see the trends and patterns between them. Sometimes we can see that the difficulty highlights a group of dominant people of different styles: the challenge is to harness their dominance towards group goals. Sometimes we can see a pattern of argumentation between roles: on these occasions it is unlikely that one will relinquish dominance, but it may be possible to teach pro-social skills to both parties.

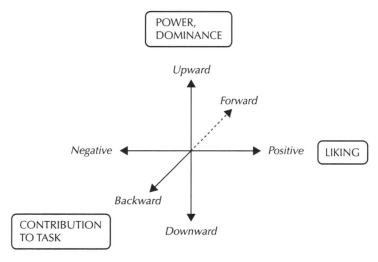

Figure 15.03 Three dimensions along which group roles vary

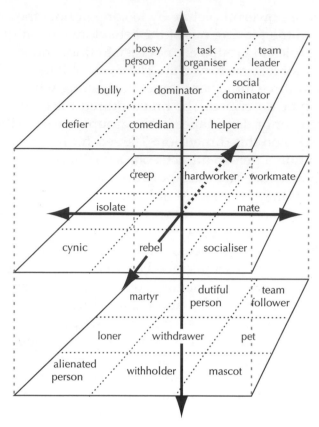

Figure 15.04 Possible group descriptions of role types on three dimension

Sometimes the role which is being played by third parties is passive towards difficulties, and needs to be enhanced in the interests of a positive group. In the secondary school, we may also be able to collect information which identifies pupils' role types in the different groups they are part of for different lessons. The variation in roles displayed can be productive for creating an improved picture in those lessons where difficulty arises.

K. Reviewing classroom curriculum

Some approaches to difficult classroom behaviour do not include any consideration of the curriculum. This is potentially counterproductive. Classroom management is not an end in itself, and our goal is not to have well-managed intellectually sterile settings. What is available for learning in the classroom is a crucial element in the patterns of behaviour which develop there.

When we feel that a class's difficult behaviour is related to them being 'switched off' from the curriculum on offer, we have to be proactive in turning that picture around. In these days of National Curricula and government-specified initiatives, it is easy for any teacher to feel that they have little control over the curriculum in their classroom. But that is to confuse the broad content with the important lived learning relationships which day by day permeate your classroom(s). A proportion of the classroom curriculum relates to the National Curriculum, but only to your own interpretation of how to offer it, and there is a lot more to the classroom curriculum than that.

We can identify three strands, each with aspects that are planned and aspects that are responsive to the events which arise. When disaffection seems general in a class, the questions under the three headings below might generate a focus for work to increase engagement.

L. Looking at the profile of activities and engagement

Sometimes disaffection in a class is related to the profile of activities which may have become narrow or repetitive. Here we need to consider the overall profile of activities in a classroom, and their success in creating pupil engagement and learning.

Perhaps a practitioner's list such as this would help to think about the range of possibilities:

- answering teachers' questions (spoken)
- class discussions
- copying
- dictation
- group work
- individual help and guidance
- listening to teacher speaking
- practical work
- reading
- reporting to the rest of the group.
- research
- role-play simulations
- taking notes
- talking to other pupils
- watching demonstrations
- watching videos
- working in pairs
- writing answers to questions from a book/the board.

Hughes (1997) collected pupils' perceptions of the frequency of these activities, as well as their perceptions of how effective each was in developing learning. The results shown in Figure 15.05 have some similarity with the findings of Cooper and McIntyre's (1993) studies of teachers' and pupils' perceptions of effective classroom learning. These showed that pupils and teachers prioritise active approaches such as group/pair work, drama/role-play, story-telling and drawing. Nevertheless, the reality in many classrooms is that the frequent activities are those where pupils are passive.

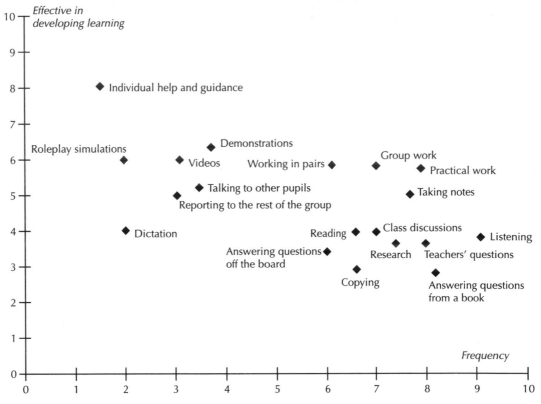

Figure 15.05 Pupils' perception of frequency of classroom activities and their effectiveness in developing learning

Research on the characteristics which lead to engaging classrooms has been summarized under headings with the acronym TARGET (see Ames, 1992a):

Tasks
• Engage personal interest, variety and challenge.
• Help pupils establish short-term goals, so that they view their classwork as manageable, and can see progress.

Authority
- Help pupils participate actively in the learning process via choices and decision-making.
- Help them develop and use strategies to plan, organize and monitor their work.

Recognition
- Recognize individual pupil effort, accomplishments and improvement, and give all pupils opportunities to receive reward and recognition.
- Give recognition and rewards privately so that the value is not derived at the expense of others.

Grouping
- Promote and support co-operative group learning and the skills in peer interaction.
- Use mixed and varied grouping arrangements, helping pupils learn from the experience in different groupings.

Evaluation
- Evaluate pupils for individual progress and improvement: offer feedback and opportunities to improve their performance.
- Vary the method of evaluation and make evaluation private.

Time
- Adjust task or time requirements for pupils who have difficulty completing their work.
- Allow pupils opportunities to plan their timetable, and progress at an optimal rate.

M. Reviewing classroom responsibilities

Sometimes poor behaviour in a classroom is associated with a lack of development in the range of pupil roles. Rather than being engaged in creating a productive climate, pupils can slip back into anonymity, and experiment with other forms of behaviour.

When teachers are thinking about developing the range of roles for pupils, they might think about allocating responsibilities for classroom duties. This is fine as far as it goes, but may be available to only a few and may feel trivial to some. So we should consider responsibility and a range of roles in wider aspects of classroom life. Well-structured work in groups is a potent medium for pupils to learn about roles in working together. Direct work of this sort builds from the allocation of functional roles in the group – reporter, timekeeper, arbiter, etc. Extending from these skills, there needs to be a focus on roles for learning. This often develops from a structured review of how the role felt, what responsibilities emerged and how others in the group viewed the role.

The most crucial responsibility a pupil takes is responsibility for their learning. This again will not necessarily develop without structured support at first. Giving pupils opportunity to plan their learning activities and to review their learning through a range of appropriate methods is the key to them seeing themselves as active agents in a cycle of learning. For this to happen, it will be necessary for us to:

- clarify the overall curriculum and its goals in pupil-friendly ways
- make plain the tasks and how the assessment will work
- arrange for resources to be accessible
- support pupils' planning and organization skills, together with monitoring and review.

N. Classroom rules and routines

Rules in classrooms are not operative just because the teacher says so. They have to be set up, agreed, used and periodically re-examined. This is not a once-and-for-all process. Routines also make a contribution: they may not be framed as a 'rule', but they are the way of making regular events happen: how resources are accessed, how homework is handed in, how the classroom is entered and so on. The purpose of any rule or routine needs to be clarified in the way it is framed and through review with the class. If the operation of these becomes erratic then the momentum of the classroom can be at risk. On such occasions, it can be useful to review the steps which are needed for effectiveness:

1. *Establishing* – needs a lot of communication/teaching at the early stage.
2. *Agreeing* – pupils are likely to agree if rules are few in number and their purpose is clear.
3. *Using* – all parties need to publicize and refer to the rules, and mediate them in so doing.
4. *Reviewing* – periodically the class examines whether the rules in use are fulfilling their purpose.

Most classroom rules can be grouped under these five headings (Hargreaves, Hester and Mellor, 1975):

- talk
- movement

- time
- teacher-pupil relationships
- pupil-pupil relationships.

Negotiation of classroom rules is something which cannot be avoided, indeed Rogers (1991) focuses on this as a major strategy in maintaining effective classrooms. If teachers act as though it was their role to impose a rule system, pupils will spend some of their time testing it out, especially self-respecting adolescents. If more is negotiated from the start, pupils will be more involved in applying it and are likely to learn more about themselves and behaviour in the process.

The level of detail at which rules are phrased can be a trap: if they become too detailed, it is possible to end up with too many and some of them will be easy targets. Once, when working abroad, we remember being presented with a six-page list of rules which newcomers to primary school were given!

O. Discussing the climate

'Climate' can seem like a broad, even nebulous, word, but it is necessary and appropriate for the more general level of considerations which we have now reached regarding difficult behaviour in classrooms. Ever since the studies of Lewin, Lippitt and White (1939) we have known that the teacher's style of running a group has a major effect on young people's behaviour. Classrooms which are run on *laissez-faire* lines are linked to more aggression between pupils – as are those run on authoritarian lines, but in the latter case the evidence may only become clear when the leader leaves the room. Developing a democratic climate is the productive approach.

Classroom climate can be led by the teacher, but you cannot be a leader without followers, so pupils will need to be engaged and supported in a variety of ways as mentioned in preceding sections. Fraser (1989) has reviewed many studies of the social climate of classrooms: his work highlights two recurring aspects: affiliation (pupils' sense of wanting to join in and be a part) and cohesiveness (pupils' sense of wanting to work with each other). These combine with the purposes of the classroom to create a productive climate for learning.

P. Building classroom community

Building classroom community helps to achieve many of the wider and important goals of school. When classes meet periodically to discuss issues of general concern, work collaboratively with the teacher to develop solutions to discipline problems and the teachers help students to think about the importance of community values, pupils develop more pro-social values, helping, conflict resolution skill and motivation to help others learn (Schaps and Solomon, 1990). Kohn (1996) has argued that classroom community-building is the necessary antidote to those methods which seem designed to produce compliance. As for community-building at the school level, and in parallel with the above consideration of classroom climate, the central themes which compose community recur: membership, purposefulness and coherence. The link to improved behaviour occurs because students who experience their classroom as a community attempt to abide by its norms and values (Solomon *et al.*, 1996).

Community in a classroom is built slowly but surely through:

- paying attention to how pupils affiliate to the class: do newcomers get included effectively? Do class members feel comfortable to describe the class positively?
- challenging pupils to become engaged in the class, and to support the activities related to it
- encouraging a wide variety of roles and contacts between all members of the class.

When teachers emphasize pro-social values, elicit student ideas, and encourage co-operation, there is higher student engagement and positive behaviour (Solomon *et al.*, 1997). Teachers' encouragement of co-operative activities appears to be particularly important.

Some of the additional methods which may contribute to this development include:

- class meetings, perhaps using a range of methodologies, to plan new tasks and arrange events for the class
- class reviews, which specifically address how the community feels and what would improve its working
- class problem-solving which addresses issues which arise, and through its workings creates more effective solutions at the same time as building self-discipline.

For the teacher responding to difficult behaviour, this means a shift from 'What will I do as a result of this incident?' to 'How are we all going to solve this problem?' and conveying that acts (not actors) are unacceptable when they break a community agreement or damage the community and its goals. Development of a classroom community also needs the pupils to learn skills of listening, anger control, seeing other's point of view and solving problems collaboratively. Teachers need to display these skills.

An underlying theme to these methods is that of regularly asking 'What sort of classroom do we want?' and following through with the responsibilities which we take on in order to achieve the things we want. The teacher can feel challenged at times by really taking on class ideas which she or he may not have chosen. The teacher will also have to challenge any community outcomes which are not genuine solutions, for example false compromises or subtle bargains.

The image of classrooms which we hope to convey

The themes and issues raised in the foregoing sections have not tried to advance a nostalgic, seductive picture of classrooms in which teachers had unquestioned authority and pupils were happily compliant. Rather, the overall position is one of trying to manage this complex situation in such a way that it promotes the qualities and skills which pupils will need to develop for their unknown and changing futures – learning skills and pro-social skills. The teacher who manages such a setting knows that they are not 'in control' of this complexity, but in a myriad of ways they are exercising control.

Keeping classrooms healthy: school practices

The previous sections, which make up the bulk of the chapter on improving classroom behaviour, are presented as though they are frameworks for an individual teacher. It is of course possible that such a scenario would be productive, after all teachers do a lot of their own problem-solving without anyone else knowing. However, you may have noticed that the sections occasionally suggested conversations with colleagues. We believe that on most occasions this can be more productive, since an external dialogue with a colleague can develop further than an internal dialogue with oneself. We now consider some of the wider ways through which colleagues in a school might be helped to interact with each other so as to support each other's learning and practice.

Teacher collaboration is an important part of building a professional learning community in school. Even in a context of pressure and constraint a school can and should, provide support to teacher motivation and effectiveness in this way. The image of teachers' working life which we should aim for is one where teachers' classroom practice has been de-privatized. No longer should we hear the idea that 'change stops at the classroom door'.

It is clear that a professional learning community is not built on the staff development practices of the recent past, which too often consisted of staff going to one-off off-site courses, and INSET days where little professional learning took place because the agenda came from elsewhere, the teachers were treated as functionaries rather than professionals and the lack of rigour often led to a dissatisfying process of recycling ignorance. Instead, the development of widespread professional learning in a school requires structural support and human and social resources. What might these be? We comment on some school practices which might be episodic (i.e. called on under certain conditions) and some which are more likely to be regular.

Meetings of teachers over a particular class

We have hardly ever met an example where a meeting of teachers discussing the learning and behaviour of a particular class was not productive. It is common in our experience for teachers who have recently experienced such meetings to say they should have more of them: if they did, the contribution to de-privatization of classroom practice would be significant. In the primary school it is likely that the class teacher remains a central figure in any such meeting, and the more peripheral perspectives of others attending could illuminate and enrich that view. In the secondary school the teachers of a particular group (even though the group may disperse somewhat in later years) can have a productive exchange, especially if it is well facilitated and has a structure to ensure information exchange. In the secondary school, regular meetings of this sort would be helped if the structure of teams focused more on pupil learning (Watkins, 1999).

Paired observation

Perhaps the most powerful form of professional learning is where pairs of colleagues choose to enter into a partnership with the intention of exploring developments in each others' classroom practice. Such partnerships have to be set up with care, and choice is an important aspect. In many schools, any hint of a central scheme allocating an observer, especially if it is tinged with hierarchical messages, will significantly increase the chances of defensiveness.

For paired work to develop, partners need to establish guidelines and agree on their responsibilities to one another and to others who may have an interest or involvement in the work. Time spent clarifying the purpose of the partnership is well spent at an early stage, so that trust can be built. Some practice and experimentation is welcome on the issues of how to choose a focus for an observation, if and how to collect and record information, etc. We have witnessed some pitfalls here, such as agreeing an oversafe focus in a collusive fashion, or the observer pressing their own interests or agenda as a focus, thereby risking the quality of learning relationship from the start.

The quality of observation is probably subservient to the quality of review which takes place following observation. Here the richness of professional conversation can be very significant – under the right conditions. These are likely to include that the observer will be explicit about the relativity of her or his observations, not casting them as more 'objective' than the teacher's, and that both will join in a dialogue which is triggered from the observations, and which elicits both parties' images and hopes for the classroom.

We are used to hearing that many teachers are resistant to observation of their classroom, and we understand such comments as reflecting past histories of isolation and current hostile perceptions in inspection. But these are not the only conditions under which observation might take place. Little (1988, p. 90) puts it well from her studies: 'Teachers welcome observation and profit from qualified observers, who will not waste the teacher's time, who will not insult the teacher's intelligence, and who will work as hard to understand classroom events as the teachers do to conduct them.' We find most UK teachers agree with this remark and can enter more actively into well-designed co-working as a result.

The following principles, devised from the work of Argyris (1993), have been well received:

- Negotiate your role explicitly, taking care over the evaluative dimension.
- Ask the teacher what they want you to report on and discuss.
- If you ask questions, give your rationale for asking.
- Do not make judgements without clarifying their basis, in detail.
- Beware handling the discussion as a control or influence interaction.

Change is not a problem in an atmosphere where it is recognized that change is continually part of a teacher's professionalism. But if one person takes it upon themselves to think that their job is to get their colleague to change, then the work suffers. Professionally supported teachers move their practice on in a variety of ways. In the current climate of target-mania in education, one conventional message is that action plans must be made for change to take place. We do not find this necessary in many cases, especially in schools where good levels of trust and professional practice are prevalent.

One of the key tests of this paired work, and of the learning climate of the school, is whether colleagues take or make opportunities to share the learning more widely, for example, between partnerships or with wider audiences. If few do, it may reflect on the school culture and, conversely, any pairs who do share more widely deserve real support for their contribution to change.

Mentoring

Mentoring seems to be promoted as a panacea, not always with sufficient attention to goals and processes (Watkins, 1997). Where mentoring is for teachers and has a focus on classroom practice, the mentoring schemes for beginner teachers and for the induction of newly qualified teachers often show the hallmarks of bad practice: agendas are decided elsewhere, mentors talk too much, criticism is confused with feedback, choice and power are not considered openly. The challenge is to find ways of building the learning agenda, building in choice, keeping the relationship under review and supporting action learning at all times (Watkins and Whalley, 1993).

Mentoring pairs who reach the stage of real dialogue (Dixon, 1998) often report a real excitement with their learning and practice. While we know of no direct evidence linking effective mentoring with lesser classroom difficulties, we would confidently expect that a school with quality mentoring on a widespread basis would be showing more signs of a learning community, and these are characterized by reduced difficulty.

Conclusion

At this point we reflect back over the chapter on improving classrooms, and consider a further way of keeping classrooms healthy. We wish to emphasize that although this chapter was constructed with the perspective of teachers in mind, and that most of the proposals indicate some action on the teacher's part, a theme runs through them all which is crucial to improving classroom life: improving the quality of communication between teachers and pupils. When difficulty arises in the classroom we may think that things are worse than they are, or that pupils are antagonistic to our goals, and so on. These are thoughts which usually indicate a limitation to communication between us and our pupils. Various studies show us that the picture may not be as we feel it is in those moments. For example, Munn, Johnstone and Holligan (1990) elicited the comments of 543 secondary pupils about the strategies used by their teachers which got the class to work well. The 4,300 comments were grouped into 21 categories, none of which dominated, but the most frequent was 'explains and helps'. A wide variety of strategies was seen as effective by the pupils, and through asking each pupil to select three teachers and their effective strategies, over 75 per cent of the staff in the four schools were identified as being best at getting the class to work well. Staff found this 'an immensely encouraging finding'.

Similarly when it comes to interventions which seek to improve behaviour, the process of eliciting pupil views has been identified in various sections of the chapter and can have long-lasting impact. Swinson (1990) adopted an approach which demonstrated this with a class in the second year of a Liverpool comprehensive, whom their teachers described as 'disruptive, disobedient, and therefore difficult to teach' (Swinson, 1990, p. 82). An early step was to gather their views on their classes, and to find that pupils rated 'being allowed to take a greater part in lessons by discussing rather than just writing/copying' (ibid., p. 84) as the most important item. This item was ranked equally highly by those pupils who had been mentioned as particularly disruptive, as those who were not. 'The teachers were generally surprised and encouraged at the very positive response of the class' (ibid., p. 86). A further step was for a meeting of staff to devise proactive strategies for improvement, agreeing that more emphasis should be given to encouraging feedback from the class. The class were supported in developing social and communication skills, and developed mutually supportive check-ups of equipment at the beginning of the day. Improvements in behaviour, attendance and schoolwork were noticeable, and Swinson concludes that a crucial element was the staff change to a more positive attitude as a result of the questionnaire feedback. In this example, better communication helped the improvement attempt get off the ground, and the improvement attempt itself focused on better communication, both between pupils and teachers and between pupils and pupils.

References

Admiraal, W. F., Wubbels, T. and Korthagen, F. A. J. (1996), Student teacher behaviour in response to daily hassles in the classroom, *Social Psychology of Education*, 1(1): 25–46.

Ames, C. (1992a), Achievement goals and the classroom motivational climate, in D. H. Schunk and J. L. Meece (eds.), *Student Perceptions in the Classroom*. Hillsdale, NJ: Lawrence Erlbaum.

Ames, C. (1992b), Classrooms: goals, structures, and student motivation, *Journal of Educational Psychology*, 84(3): 261–71.

Anderson, V. and Merrett, F. (1997), The use of correspondence 'training in improving the in-class behaviour of very troublesome secondary school children, *Educational Psychology*, 17(3): 313-28.

Argyris, C. (1993), *Knowledge for Action*. San Francisco: Jossey-Bass.

Arlin, M. (1979), Teacher transitions can disrupt time flow in classrooms, *American Educational Research Journal*, 16(1): 42–56.

Bach, G. and Wyden, P. (1968), *The Intimate Enemy: How to Fight Fair in Love and Marriage*. New York: William Morrow.

Bain, A., Houghton, S. and Williams, S. (1991), The effects of a school-wide behaviour management programme on teachers' use of encouragement in the classroom, *Educational Studies*, 17(3): 249-60.

Bales, R. F. (1970), *Personality and Interpersonal Behavior*. New York: Holt, Rinehart & Winston.

Ball, S. J. (1980), Initial encounters in the classroom and the process of establishment, in P. Woods (ed.), *Pupil Strategies: Explorations in the Sociology of the School*. London: Croom Helm.

Beynon, J. (1985), *Initial Encounters in the Secondary School*. London: Falmer Press.

Bossert, S. T. (1977), Tasks, group management, and teacher control behaviour: a study of classroom organisation and teacher style, *School Review*, 85(August): 552–65.

Brown, J. E. (1986), The use of paradoxical injunction with oppositional behaviour in the classroom, *Psychology in the Schools*, 23(1): 77–81.

Bullough, R. V. (1991), Exploring personal teaching metaphors in preservice teacher education, *Journal of Teacher Education*, 42(1): 43-51.

Bullough, R. V. and Stokes, D. K. (1994), Analyzing personal teaching metaphors in preservice teacher education as a means for encouraging professional development, *American Educational Research Journal*, 31(1):197-224.

Clandinin, J. D. (1985), Personal practical knowledge: a study of teachers' classroom images, *Curriculum Inquiry*, 15(4): 361-85.

Clarke, D. D., Parry-Jones, W. L., Gay, B. M. and Smith, C. M. B. (1981), Disruptive incidents in secondary school classrooms: a sequence analysis approach, *Oxford Review of Education*, 7(2): 111-7.

Connelly, M. F. and Clandinin, J. D. (1994), Telling teaching stories, *Teacher Education Quarterly*, 21(1): 145-58.

Cooper, P. and McIntyre, D. (1993), Commonality in teachers' and pupils' perceptions of effective classroom learning, *British Journal of Educational Psychology*, 63(3): 381–99.

Corrie, L. (1997), The interaction between teachers' knowledge and skills when managing a troublesome classroom behaviour, *Cambridge Journal of Education*, 27(1): 93-105.

Créton, H. A., Wubbels, T. and Hooymayers, H. P. (1989), Escalated disorderly situations in the classroom and the improvement of these situations, *Teaching and Teacher Education*, 5(3): 205–15.

Department for Education and Science (1989), *Discipline in Schools: Report of the Committee of Enquiry Chaired by Lord Elton*. London: HMSO.

Dickson, A. (1982), *A Woman In Your Own Right: Assertiveness and You*. London: Quartet Books.

Dixon, N. M. (1998), *Dialogue at Work: Making Talk Developmental for People and Organizations*. London: Lemos & Crane.

Doyle, W. (1980), *Classroom Management*. West Lafayette, IN: Kappa Delta Pi.

Doyle, W. (1986a), Academic work, in T. M. Tomlinson and H. J. Walberg (eds), *Academic Work and Educational Excellence: Raising Student Productivity*. Berkeley, CA: McCutchan.

Doyle, W. (1986b), Classroom organization and management, in M. C. Wittrock (ed.), *Handbook of Research on Teaching*, 3rd edn. New York: Macmillan.

Doyle, W. (1990), Classroom knowledge as a foundation for teaching, *Teachers College Record*, 91(3): 347–60.

Emmer, E. T., Evertson, C. M. and Anderson, L. M. (1980), Effective classroom management at the beginning of the school year, *Elementary School Journal*, 80(5): 219–31.

Fraser, B. J. (1989), Twenty years of classroom climate work: progress and prospect, *Journal of Curriculum Studies*, 21(4): 307–27.

Gannaway, H. (1984), Making sense of school, in M. Hammersley and P. Woods (eds), *Life in School: The Sociology of Pupil Culture*. Milton Keynes: Open University Press.

Gay, B. M. and Parry-Jones, W. L. (1980), The anatomy of disruption: a preliminary consideration of interaction sequences within disruptive incidents, *Oxford Review of Education*, 6(3): 213-20.

Goleman, D. (1996), *Emotional Intelligence: Why it Can Matter More than IQ*. London: Bloomsbury Paperbacks.

Gray, J. and Sime, N. (1989), Findings from the national survey of teachers in England and Wales, in Department for Education and Science (ed.), *Discipline in Schools: Report on the Committee of Enquiry Chaired by Lord Elton*. London: HMSO.

Hargreaves, D. H., Hester, S. and Mellor, F. (1975), *Deviance in Classrooms*. London: Routledge & Kegan Paul.

Houghton, S., Wheldall, K. and Merrett, F. (1988), Classroom behaviour problems which secondary school teachers say they find most troublesome, *British Educational Research Journal*, 14(3): 297-312.

Hughes, M. (1997), *Lessons are For Learning*. Stafford: Network Educational Press.

Johnson, B., Oswald, M. and Adey, K. (1993), Discipline in South Australian primary schools, *Educational Studies*, 19(3): 289-305.

Jones, K., Quah, M. L. and Charlton, T. (1996), Behaviour which primary and special school teachers in Singapore find most troublesome, *Research in Education*, (55): 62-73.

Jones, K., Wilkin, J. and Charlton, T. (1995), Classroom behaviours which first and middle school teachers in St. Helena find troublesome, *Educational Studies*, 21(2): 139-53.

Jordan, J. (1974), The organisation of perspectives in teacher-pupil relations: an interactionist approach, MEd thesis, University of Manchester.

Katz, N. H. and Lawyer, J. W. (1994), *Preventing and Managing Conflict in Schools*. Thousand Oaks, CA: Corwin Press.

Kohn, A. (1996), *Beyond Discipline: From Compliance to Community*. Alexandria, VA: Association for Supervision and Curriculum Development.

Kounin, J. S. (1977), *Discipline and Group Management in Classrooms*. (repr. edn). Huntington, NY: Krieger.

Lewin, K., Lippitt, R. and White, R. (1939), Patterns of aggressive behavior in experimentally created social climates, *Journal of Social Psychology*, 10 (May): 271–99.

Little, J. W. (1988), Assessing the prospects for teacher leadership, in A. Lieberman (ed.), Building a Professional Culture in Schools. New York: Teachers College Press.

Munn, P., Johnstone, M. and Holligan, C. (1990), Pupils' perceptions of 'effective disciplinarians', *British Educational Research Journal*, 16(2): 191–8.

Newmann, F. M., Marks, H. M. and Gamoran, A. (1995), Authentic pedagogy and student performance, *American Journal of Education*, 104(4): 280–312.

O'Hagan, F. J. and Edmunds, G. (1982), Pupils' attitudes towards teachers' strategies for controlling disruptive behaviour, *British Journal of Educational Psychology*, 52(3): 331-40.

Poyner, B. and Warne, C. (1988), *Preventing Violence to Staff*. London: HMSO/Health and Safety Executive.

Rogers, B. (1991), *'You Know the Fair Rule': Strategies for Making the Hard Job of Discipline in School Easier*. Harlow: Longman.

Rogers, B. (1992), Students who want the last word, *Support for Learning*, 7(4): 166–70.

Ryans, D. G. (1968), *Characteristics of Teachers: Their Description, Comparison and Approval: A Research Study*. Washington, DC: American Council on Education.

Schaps, E. and Solomon, D. (1990), Schools and classrooms as caring communities, *Educational Leadership*, 48(3): 38–42.

Solomon, D., Battistich, V., Kim, D.-I. and Watson, M. (1997), Teacher practices associated with students' sense of the classroom as a community, *Social Psychology of Education*, 1(3): 235–67.

Solomon, D., Watson, M., Battistich, V., Schaps, E. and Delucchi, K. (1996), Creating classrooms that students experience as communities, *American Journal of Community Psychology*, 24(6): 719–48.

Swinson, J. (1990), Improving behaviour: a whole-class approach using pupil perceptions and social skills training, *Educational Psychology in Practice*, 6(2): 82–9.

Sykes, G. and Matza, D. (1957), Techniques for neutralising deviant identity, *American Sociological Review*, 22(6): 667–70.

Watkins, C. (1997), Clarifying mentoring goals in their context, in J. Stephenson (ed.), *Mentoring – the New Panacea?* Dereham: Peter Francis.

Watkins, C. (1999), The case for restructuring the UK secondary school, *Pastoral Care in Education*, 17(4): 3–10.

Watkins, C. and Whalley, C. (1993), *Mentoring: Resources for School-Based Development*. Harlow: Longman.

Weinstein, C. S. (1979), The physical environment of the school: a review of the research, *Review of Educational Research*, 49(4): 577–610.

Weinstein, C. S. (1991), The classroom as a social context for learning, *Annual Review of Psychology*, 42: 493–525.

Wheldall, K. and Merrett, E (1988), Which classroom behaviours do primary school teachers say they find most troublesome?, *Educational Review*, 40(1): 13-27.

Chapter 16

Confrontation in the classroom

Colin J. Smith

Introduction

This chapter is a revised and updated version of ideas from Smith and
Laslett (1993) *Effective Classroom Management: A Teacher's Guide*. Its model of
relationships within the classroom is interpreted in terms of two conceptual
approaches: one based on applied behavioural analysis and the other on an
ecosystemic perspective.

A behavioural approach 'looks outside the child to the classroom
environment and learning experiences to find ways of changing behaviour ...
any problems are the teacher's responsibility not the child's fault' (Cooper,
Smith and Upton, 1994 p.75).

The ABC model of behavioural analysis applied in this chapter is summarised
by Ayers, Clarke and Murray (1995 p.20) as involving: *A*ntecedents which
precede a student's behaviour; *B*ehaviour itself, what the student is actually
doing, and *C*onsequences, what happens as a result and the reaction of others.

An ecosystemic approach also focuses on context: 'problem behaviour in the
classroom does not originate from within the individual who displays the
behaviour but is a product of social interaction' (Cooper, Smith and Upton,
1994 p.97).

This model draws on experience from systems theory and family therapy to
encourage teachers 'to engage in non-judgmental, problem-solving analysis
that avoids self-perpetuating cycles of negative interactions' (Ayers, Clarke and
Murray, 1995 p.50).

Both these approaches depend for effectiveness on teachers putting time and
effort into getting to know students and establishing warm, positive

relationships with them; involving students in continuous discussion and negotiation in taking collaborative ownership of classroom rules, and planning lesson activities and tasks which are positive and enjoyable.

A behavioural approach requires the teacher to specify precisely the behaviour that is to be observed, devising measures for counting and charting its frequency, setting goals for change and evaluating whether these outcomes are attained.

An ecosystemic approach involves the teacher seeking new plausible and possible interpretations of behaviour in order to 'reframe' them in a more positive light and change the interactional pattern from conflict to co-operation.

Classroom confrontation

When the variety of factors that affect the interactions between teachers and students in classrooms are considered, it is clear that it is not possible to suggest ways in which teachers can *always* manage to avoid unnecessary or unhelpful confrontations. The most that anyone who is not present in a classroom can do is to point to some guidelines, which can help teachers to avoid confrontations and suggest how they might be successfully managed if avoidance is impossible.

Some teachers seek confrontations without proper occasion and there is nothing commendable about that, but others, either through tension or inexperience, blunder into confrontations, which they do not intend and cannot manage and which are of no value to them, to the student concerned, or to those who witness it. The danger is that when the confrontation between a student and a teacher is started and when there is tension in a classroom, it only needs one of them to say the wrong thing or do the wrong thing for the situation to get out of control with consequences both regret. The following vignette illustrates how easily confrontations can arise and ignite.

Escalation and detonation in confrontations

There are inevitably some students whose behaviour makes a confrontation probable. When teachers know who such students are, they can adapt their approaches to avoid conflict, or reduce the chances of a conflict escalating into a confrontation. Sometimes, however, a teacher will bring about a confrontation with a student who is usually reasonably behaved but has reasons for surliness or unwillingness to co-operate on a particular occasion. The confrontation described below is an ugly and serious one, but not unfamiliar. The teacher concerned makes a reasonable request not knowing about previous events affecting the student's mood. The teacher's manner unfortunately aggravates the situation and events swiftly move towards a confrontation that gets out of control.

Martin was in the third year of a secondary school with the usual uncertainties of mood associated with adolescence, but on the whole pleasant and co-operative. However, on the morning of the confrontation, matters had not gone well for him, and the history lesson was the climax to a series of unfortunate events. These can be seen as antecedents or as factors in a wider ecosystem, which contribute to his oppositional behaviour. He had overslept and missed his paper round, which meant that he was going to have to face his employer's wrath. He was also late for school, and that meant detention later in the week. He had come to school without his PE kit, and so could not join in the PE lesson, which he usually enjoyed. He had had words with the PE teacher and had come off the worse in that encounter.

The history lesson was one in which the teacher talked to the class and then asked them to read passages from their history books. It had been rather lifeless and dreary until Martin leaned across to his neighbour and said loudly 'Who cares about the flipping Renaissance anyway?' In leaning across his desk he accidentally knocked his history book on to the floor.

The teacher, explaining the finer points of renaissance architecture, was aware that he had only a tenuous hold on the attention of the class, that the lesson had not gone well and that he should have found a more interesting way of presenting his material. These were the antecedents for his behaviour in the chain of actions and interactions which followed.

He was, in fact, just holding on till the bell rang, glad that this was due in ten minutes. When interrupted, he called out 'What did you say?' He had heard what was said well enough and his challenging tone was intended to convey annoyance expecting a noncommittal reply to avoid further trouble. Unfortunately already sore at the morning's events, this student rose to the challenge. He repeated his remark, loudly and clearly with challenge in *his* voice. It produced a silence that had not hitherto been a feature of the lesson.

Escalation

Whatever the teacher might have done about the first interruption, when he asked the student to repeat it, he made a mistake, which had serious consequences. Angry at the impertinence, though he had only himself to blame for it, the teacher walked towards the student, pointing and commanding, 'Pick up that book!' The teacher's look, movement and demeanour were intended to overawe the boy, but instead incited further defiance. Both teacher and student were now on the 'escalation–detonation' staircase, and continued challenges and responses drove them further up it. The student's surly rejoinder 'Pick it up yourself!' took another step up the staircase. The teacher now shouting, 'Pick it up *at once!*' went several steps higher. The silence of the class had given way to noisy interchanges, encouraging the student and discomfiting the teacher, who realised that the affair was slipping out of control. Flustered and angry, he was now standing over the boy, raising tension by his close presence.

For all his apparent coolness, the student was now beginning to panic. He had defied the teacher to the point of no return and felt he could not back down and be seen to have been worsted, as the whole class was watching with excited interest. At the same time he was uneasy, as he was not a practised disruptive and defiant student. The teacher also gave way to panic as he realised the corner into which he had been manoeuvred. He made a last unsuccessful attempt to overawe Martin, despite the evidence that this was unlikely to succeed and what he said took the last few steps up the staircase from which the confrontation detonated. He made a furious verbal assault in passionate terms which he would not normally contemplate, 'Pick it up! Pick it up! How dare you speak to me like that? You are a lout! You look like one and you behave like one. Pick up that book or I will …' No one knew what the end of the sentence might have been, what threat or ultimatum might have followed. When he called Martin a lout, this so stung the boy that he got to his feet in a reflex action to the verbal assault. What then happened was confused and illustrated exactly the way in which tension and panic leads to the misperception of intentions and actions.

Detonation

Martin stood up. The teacher reached out his hand. What he had intended to do, he explained afterwards, was to push him down into his seat, a risky thing to attempt in the circumstances. Seeing the hand coming towards him, the student raised his hand to push it aside. Thinking the boy was going to strike him, the teacher struck him first with his other hand, 'in self-defence'. This was returned with a more directed punch, its deliverer claimed, 'in self-defence', which knocked the teacher off balance and cut his lip. In the awful silence that followed, Martin ran out of the classroom. The whole confrontation had taken just under a minute. At the subsequent enquiry, the student was excluded. Both he and the teacher regretted what had happened, but neither would accept the other's version of what had transpired when both raised their hands.

Analysis

Although the history teacher's control of the class was not very good, it was not generally disastrous. The most obvious weakness was not so much his control but the dreary and tepid presentation. The diminishing interest in the lesson had a direct bearing on the interruption, which led to so much trouble. Crises do not usually erupt without some warning signals. The alert teacher picks up the need to inject some stimulation into lessons when students' attention wanders and does something to bring their attention back. The history teacher seemed unconcerned about the shuffling and whispering and other signs of boredom in the room until the electrifying interruption. The boy's comment began the series of events; the book falling to the floor, which played such a crucial part in the confrontation, was accidental. As it was simultaneous with the interruption, it strongly influenced the teacher's reaction.

De-escalation

The teacher found it difficult to ignore the interruption. It was not an outrageous comment but in the prevailing atmosphere of resigned boredom, some other student could have laughed loudly at it, or expressed agreement. But how different the outcome would have been if the teacher had expressed displeasure at the interruption in more reasonable terms. He could have said 'that will do, keep your comments to yourself. Just pick up the book like a good lad and give me your attention for a few minutes'. Or he could have made a more light-hearted comment, such as 'Well, Brunelleschi's cupola might not sound like your cup of tea, but wait until you see it one day. Now come on. It will soon be dinnertime', or even 'What's the matter? You have been sitting like a bear with a sore head all morning'.

This would have given Martin the opportunity to step down rather than up the escalation–detonation staircase by saying something about his frustrations. He may not have taken the opportunity, but if the request had been put in a way that did not slight him, and if posed with concern and not as a challenge, it is quite probable that he would have responded reasonably. The repetition of the comment increased the tension in the exchange, which was already beginning to show in the teacher's challenging tone.

The whole class was now an alert audience waiting for the next development. The two protagonists between them maintained the momentum of the confrontation, but the presence of the other students added to it, increasing the tension both felt, and making it difficult to step back down the escalation staircase. Having repeated his comment, it was clear that the student was not going to be overawed, and that he was ready to engage in a power struggle. The situation could probably still have been saved, even after the mistake of asking the student to repeat what had been said, if the teacher had stayed where he was and not increased his challenge by striding towards and closing on the student, his body language emphasising his challenge, and prompting a counter-challenge.

Once both began to panic, almost inevitably one or both of them would misperceive each other's intention and act precipitately. Neither could, at that stage, easily retreat from the confrontation, but unless one of them did something to slow down the swift ascent up the escalation staircase, it was certain that they would reach the top of it and detonation point. As the student showed it was not going to be him who would arrest the ascent, then the teacher should have done it. The situation was deplorable, but as it had reached the stage it had, all that was left to the teacher was to save his dignity. Retreating in such a situation is not pleasant but it has to be weighed against the alternative. In a physical encounter the outcome would at best be demeaning and against the teacher's professional code and at worst it could have had a disastrous consequence. With contact avoided, the teacher would at least have preserved some adult status by drawing back. This would not have precluded following matters up later away from an audience.

The confrontation began with an interruption and an accident. Within sixty seconds it ended in a disaster, which neither of the principals foresaw and neither of them wanted. The outcome was out of all proportion to the original offence. This confrontation shows how rapidly difficult situations in a classroom will deteriorate when an initial error in management is compounded by confused thinking, anger and panic, combining to propel the participants towards an unpredictable and unwanted outcome. It also illustrates how reflection on consequences or alternative explanations of oppositional behaviour can help a teacher de-escalate a situation before it reaches detonation point.

Students experiencing problems

In any circumstances when the stability of a class is at risk, it pays teachers to be careful in their interactions with students who cannot cope with unexpected change. When thinking about ways in which you might avoid unhelpful confrontations, it is useful to consider what it is that upsets the stability of a class of students, making the probability of confrontations greater.

Behavioural psychologists have helped teachers to understand that many incidents of disruptive or unacceptable behaviour tend to be specific to particular situations, to particular individuals and to particular environments

(Bull and Solity, 1987; Wheldall and Merrett, 1992). Features in an environment can either reinforce behaviour or extinguish it. This explanation has helped teachers to recognise that much unacceptable behaviour is not 'within child', and that teachers can organise classroom environments that will significantly reduce the probability of disruptive behaviour and increase the probability of successful learning and social progress.

Application of the principles of applied behaviour analysis and the use of behaviour modification techniques have undoubtedly helped teachers to find ways of establishing effective methods of classroom management. Excellent as these techniques are, it is important for teachers to recognise that many students whose disruptive behaviour is a persistent problem have had experiences of other people and of themselves that go a long way to account for their difficulties in the classroom. This is not to deny that the actual classroom environment may or may not increase their tendency to misbehave, but rather to emphasise that there are causative factors and patterns of interaction outside the control of teachers, which influence why these students become the centres of instability in the classroom.

Students 'with emotional and behavioural difficulties'

Certain students become notorious for their disruptive or attention-seeking behaviour. Whilst it is useful to look at why such children behave as they do, it is important to resist any temptation to use prescriptive and negative labels as an excuse for inaction on the part of the teacher in the face of an irredeemable 'lost cause'. The intention of reflecting on characteristics of problem behaviour is to offer insight into antecedents and reasons for apparently irrational behaviour and use this to plan appropriate responses, later discussed as teachers' strategies.

Some students bring with them from their pasts, previous school and personal experiences that bear upon contemporary attitudes and performance. Their need for counselling and support, for assessment of their problems at home, help for their parents and the involvement of personnel from outside the school, testify to the fact that their problems do not concern management of behaviour alone.

Among these students are those whose experiences of parent figures have led them to regard themselves as unworthy and undeserving. Because they were not wanted or loved, they have not received esteem from those from whom they might legitimately expect it. Consequently they do not esteem themselves, they have negative self-concepts, and this can be a serious bar to successful achievement. Experiences of alienation and of failure, not only in school-based learning tasks but elsewhere, produce a lack of security, which makes them resentful of criticism. They may not be much influenced by punishment because over-familiarity with it has made them indifferent to it. Indeed, it is just as likely to increase the probability of unwanted behaviour because the punishment, unpleasant though it is, at least provides the attention, which they seek.

Not only do they perceive themselves as unworthy and unsuccessful, these students also tend to perceive adults in authority as potentially uncaring and hostile. This perception has developed because experiences of hostile and uncaring adults in their past has led them to displace hostility they feel towards these adults on to teachers, especially when rules and school codes of conduct frustrate them. Lacking steadfast attention, adequate care and nurture, sometimes over-punished and emotionally disturbed, these students present you with difficult problems of management, which may be exacerbated by the application of normal disciplinary sanctions.

Rejected and deprived children are likely to be prompted by feelings of revenge because of the treatment they have received in the past from those who failed them and acted with hostility to them. Some of them feel ready to take it out on somebody without knowing just what it is that makes them feel bitter or angry. Here the process of displacement is operating. Teachers make very convenient targets for displaced and hostile feelings, which students dare not express towards their parents. Many children with emotional and behavioural difficulties have a limited repertoire of behavioural responses and tend to over-use displacement. This fixity of response limits their adaptability. They seem particularly inept at differentiating between people and circumstances so that they behave inappropriately, whereas students with more behavioural responses to call upon manage successfully.

Most students, however much they may protest, usually accept criticism or punishment as fair, and are able to make the connection between their offence and the punishment it brings about. But it is not wise to make this assumption about disruptive children who have problems of adjustment. Because they have not been able to trust others, and because their relationships have been impaired by injustice, hostility and rejection, they are likely to regard punishment as evidence of vindictiveness or spite. They are bankrupt in terms of the 'emotional and social capital, which homes and families supply' for more fortunate children (Laslett, 1998 p.38).

Difficulties in relationships

The students who cause the worst trouble in schools are often those with whom it is difficult to make meaningful relationships. Many students with emotional and behavioural difficulties find the making and sustaining of good relationships with others difficult, and some never succeed in doing this. They are either selfish or inconsiderate, or unapproachable and remote, or demanding and impetuous. They give way to temper and to anger which other students find unpleasant or frightening. They are wary of making relationships with adults because relationships with some of them have caused much pain and disappointment in the past when they were let down or rejected outright. When they have evidence that a teacher is friendly and caring, predictable and reliable, then many of these students do react positively and their behaviour improves but this does not always happen.

Another explanation for difficult behaviour is that some children have learned to behave in the ways they do from inappropriate models in their family. In the face of disappointment or frustration, they copy or imitate the ways in which parents, carers or siblings behave. The father who vents his frustrations at home relies on this to bring him the attention or solace he needs. Siblings who make demands and clamour for attention are given it and are indulged or gratified according to the frequency, intensity and duration of their demanding behaviour. They witness this inappropriate behaviour at home, see it bringing rewards and follow the example both at home and elsewhere.

When there has been persistent and damaging emotional deprivation, some students exhibit their most unattractive and demanding characteristics towards a teacher who demonstrates concern and patience. This seems to be paradoxical and self-defeating behaviour and it is wounding and perplexing. At the conscious level, it seems that the students are declaring that they have heard expressions of goodwill before, but as this goodwill is rapidly withdrawn when they make demands upon it, they will see how you will stand up to their demands. They then proceed to make these demands, sometimes taking care to direct them towards whatever vulnerabilities you have disclosed by your behaviour. It is when this happens that teachers are heard to remark that they have tried being kind and patient and it did not work. The teacher takes the student's reaction as evidence that the initial approach was mistaken and the students take it as evidence that they are unlikable and adults are hostile. The students have succeeded in dragging into their contemporary relationships just those features that destroyed previous ones. They have manipulated benevolent adults in behaving towards them as they did not intend to behave. If this process continues, their reactions harden into fixed patterns of behaviour, which are not quickly or easily changed.

Difficulties in learning

Many students with emotional and behavioural difficulties experience difficulties in, or barriers to, their learning. Much of the time when they should be listening to what teachers are telling them, or when they should be participating in learning activities, they are either disrupting lessons with some form of attention-seeking behaviour, or their attention is distracted by thinking of unsettling events that take place in their homes. Many of them have marked difficulties in motor control and in perception of printed words or other printed material, which interferes with their reading and writing. They may be clumsy and poorly co-ordinated in their movements or hyperactive.

Such students may pose a considerable threat to the stability of the class. If they are not actively engaged in learning tasks themselves, these students are unlikely to sit passively watching others succeed where they fail. Unless given a great deal of individual help, they are quite likely to interfere with others. Attention not received for successful performance may be sought through unacceptable behaviour. Often they find a role, which gains attention and provides apparent esteem through satisfying the expectations of their classmates for entertainment and distraction.

Students fulfilling class expectations

It is likely that there will be more students with emotional and behavioural difficulties in schools as the programmes of inclusive education of children with special needs in mainstream schools gains momentum from government initiatives (DfES, 2001) and legislation designed to reduce discrimination against students with disabilities (SENDA, 2001). Not all students with emotional and behavioural difficulties are difficult to manage, but many are disruptive and unstable. They find the excitement and the inevitable attention that goes with challenging a teacher temptation that they cannot resist. This applies equally to other students who may not be responding to the life-distorting experiences outlined above but who for a variety of reasons become trapped in a disruptive pattern of behaviour. It is important for teachers not to apply descriptions of behaviour as a label, which takes the focus away from antecedents and consequences, but the following examples illustrate how teachers may characterise the behaviour of some students.

The 'class wit'

In many classes there is one student who some teachers might call the 'class wit', not aggressive or unpleasant to deal with, resentful of authority or unco-operative, and not set on confronting the teacher, although a confrontation may arise from what is said and done. Motivation is more complicated and to do with relationships with the class and the dynamics of group behaviour rather than with the teacher. The antecedent of this behaviour is that, uncertain of the status that goes with approval given to successful students, and wanting recognition and attention, for this student status comes through drawing attention by ready wit and its intrepid display. On the whole, for this student, the consequence of status and popularity with the peer group is worth the cost of the punishments that follow from witty asides and comments.

This student appears to be licensed by the other students, whose approval may be withdrawn if limits are overstepped and the whole class is punished, perhaps for laughing too loudly or too frequently. Usually this student manages well enough within the rules, as they are understood; striking a balance between going just far enough to retain class approval and avoiding their disapproval contributes to the excitement. As other students encourage and sustain this behaviour, it is not easy to abandon it. When as a teacher, exasperated by continued interjections, you take this student to task, you might also be confronting the other members of the class, thus rewarding the behaviour. Applying an ABC model would suggest that it is better to ignore or tolerate the attempted humour and avoid being drawn into a negative reinforcement trap.

From an ecosystemic perspective, what is needed is not just criticism or punishment but assistance with relationships with the other students and help towards a new role. This is more easily given if you are aware of the dynamics in the class group, which sustain the role. In talking to the class, make them aware of what has been going on, their part in it, and explain that they can best help the student and themselves by enjoying the occasional and pertinent jibe but not encouraging repeated interruptions. In effect you are making the licensing process explicit and establishing ground rules that 'minimise a child's inappropriate ways of belonging through attention seeking and power-play and maximize appropriate ways to belong' (Rogers, 1991 p.29).

The 'rebel leader'

There is another aspect of group dynamics that may account for the disruptive behaviour of a student whose disruptive behaviour satisfies class feelings, and functions as a means of gaining rewarding consequences from enhanced status with the peer group. If a teacher gets on badly with a class and stirs up resentment and unco-operative attitudes, it is not uncommon for one bold individual to respond to the prevailing mood and to gather up the feelings in the class and act them out. Sharing the negativity that others may feel, but have not the temerity to express, gives this individual the impetus to act for the rest of the class. It is as if they take on a role, which could be perceived by some teachers as a 'rebel leader' who provides a focus for group dissent.

In these circumstances, criticism or punishment of the individual's misbehaviour is not the most effective way of stopping it. Indeed, it is more likely to reinforce it. One way in which a teacher can alter the behaviour of this disruptive student is to be found in changing the antecedent through altering his/her relationship with the class, by avoiding whatever behaviour stirs up resentment and prevents him/her from wanting to co-operate. From an ecosystemic perspective, this could mean 'reframing' the problem as one of group rather than individual relationships. While this explanation does not account for all the disruptive behaviour where one student continually takes a leading part, it is worthwhile to reflect on whether or not this student is doing something that satisfies the other members of the class. If so, then it is necessary to repair relationships with them and not only the relationship with the disruptive student.

The 'unpopular/victim' student

In many classes there is one unfortunate student who is unpopular with all the others, and who, whilst unlikely to confront the teacher, may be the source of exasperation and irritation which upsets the stability of the class. Frequently teased or bullied, this student's perception of these events is that of being an innocent victim. It is true that many bullies will attack those who are weaker than them, however their victims behave, but with the perpetually unpopular victim student there are aspects of behaviour that elicit hostile responses in others. Reactions to behaviour may arise from irritating ways, such as continual interference or the giving of unwanted and usually unwelcome advice, making undue demands upon the friendship of other students, being possessive of them and jealous of anyone else who may seek to join the relationship.

Unlikely as it may seem, this behaviour can be rewarding for a student through the consequences of excitement and attention. Aware of unpopularity but uncomprehending of the reasons for it, this student may be perceived by others as a chatterbox and a sneak, fussy and over-dependent, and so muddled in personal organisation that friendship is a burden. Whatever it is, other students will not tolerate from him or her what they tolerate in other children. It is this intolerance of exasperating behaviour that makes this student a threat to group stability, being likely to do or say something that is too much for the self-control of other students, and so becoming the centre of angry exchanges in the classroom. From a behavioural perspective the teacher can seek ways of ensuring more rewarding consequences for other students when they are able to ignore what irritates them. Applying an ecosystemic approach, a teacher may best help individuals who see themselves as 'victims' by pointing out that they cannot forever blame others for their misfortunes and that they should begin to think about their own behaviour. It is probable that the boy or girl will stoutly deny that any fault lies within themselves and they will need help in understanding how certain behaviours can bring trouble.

A good example of teacher intervention, which helped a student begin to understand how this victimisation worked, was given in a class where Stella, who was generally regarded as a nuisance by her classmates, complained that her sweets had been taken from her desk. The teacher asked who in the class knew that the sweets were there, and discovered that most of them did because Stella had broadcast the fact. Inevitably, less honourable classmates had taken them. The culprit admitted this and said it would not have been done if Stella had not kept on 'showing off about them and getting on people's nerves'. How she did this was discussed further, and other students described other exasperating behaviours. This discussion was painful for Stella and the teacher intervened from time to time to prevent it from becoming too unbearable. Fortunately she weathered the storm, and for the first time realised that her own behaviour was responsible for many difficulties. Once this was realised she was able, with appropriate help from the teacher, to avoid behaving in ways that elicited hostile responses from others.

The 'saboteur'

The student who enjoys the drama of a teacher in conflict with another student or other students may also threaten the stability of a class. Not as noticeable as the student with more obvious signs of adjustment difficulties, and not engaged in openly disruptive behaviour, he or she has developed strategies for egging others on towards a confrontation. Some teachers may think of this student as a 'saboteur' who undermines a teacher's intention to ignore minor unacceptable behaviour by drawing attention to it. A classroom crisis on the wane can flare up again through this student's uncanny knack of knowing just what to say or do to reignite it.

In managing a 'saboteur', it is better if the teacher avoids questioning at length about what has been done because this provides an enjoyable opportunity and rewarding consequence for making capital from the situation. If the teacher makes any error or inexactitude in accusations of or about the behaviour, the opportunity to deny the accusation will be seized. One exasperated teacher following the late arrival in his class of a girl, seen minutes earlier combing her hair before a mirror in the domestic science room, asked her why she had stopped 'to comb her hair in the mirror.' The girl replied that she had *not* been combing her hair in the mirror. This flat denial and untruth, repeated several times during the exchange, made the teacher increasingly angry. The girl at last announced that she had not been combing her hair *in* the mirror because that was impossible.

It is this kind of cool and exasperating exchange which demonstrates the dangers of involving such students in questioning, and it is better to avoid doing it whenever possible. It is better to describe precisely what they have done, making sure that there are no possibilities for ingenious wordplay and restating any antecedent rule that has been infringed and detailing any consequences that may follow. It is also reassuring to other students when a teacher does this and keeps the initiative. In this context, applying a systemic approach could involve 'reconstructing' the behaviour in terms of the student's concern for consistent application of rules and developing the possible improvements in the classroom ecosystem which can arise from a more flexible approach.

Teacher strategies

Understanding the behaviour of students who threaten the stability of a class goes a long way in helping you to avoid conflicts. Not making hasty responses when exasperated is helped by knowing more about students with emotional and behavioural difficulties; being aware of group pressures which sustained the class wit or rebel leader in role; not getting taken in by the complaints against other students from the victim child and taking the measure of the saboteur. Olsen (1997) writes about how students use 'gambits', which like those in chess are moves used to trick or gain advantage. Much misbehaviour, he argues, are gambits aimed at taking power by getting you off balance and distracted from the lesson. Temporary reductions in student misbehaviour can negatively reinforce teacher criticism. What start as quiet admonitions about too much noise become increasingly louder reprimands until control and dignity are lost, providing drama and distraction which positively reinforce the undesired student behaviour. It is important to avoid this aversive cycle or negative reinforcement trap.

The best response to this form of 'teacher baiting' is not to rise to the bait, thus denying the instigator satisfaction of seeing you are provoked. 'Arguing with students in front of their peers: wastes time, heats up the conflict, leads to irrational exchanges and often forces either side into a win/lose situation' (Rogers, 1991 p.63).

Guidelines for avoiding confrontations

On the whole it is wise for teachers to avoid confrontations with students when these can be avoided, but there are occasions when they cannot be, and there are circumstances when a confrontation is beneficial. You cannot always avoid a confrontation, for instance, if you are summoned by a colleague to help in some crisis. The angry student may turn on you and continue with you what began with your colleague. There are some circumstances when you may decide that you are not going to put up with a student's provocative or stupid behaviour any longer, or decide to demonstrate to a student who continually bullies or teases others that he or she has met their match. A confrontation could then be beneficial to the student concerned, to other students who witnessed it, and to your classroom management.

If convinced that confrontation will be beneficial, you have next to be sure that you can manage it. If, once it has started, the student continues to be defiant or provocative, and if the worst comes to the worst, you have to be sure that you can manage the situation should the student attempt a physical challenge. Once started, confrontations sometimes develop very quickly and unpredictably, so that it is foolish to initiate one and then find that it has gone out of control and escalated into a situation which cannot be managed successfully, becoming demeaning and undignified.

Useful ground rules for both avoiding and managing confrontations are to take care about language, consider whether to respond at all to minor irritations, reflect on non-verbal cues and signals you may be giving, refrain from physical intervention, and plan responses which lower rather than raise the temperature of the classroom climate.

Avoiding public denigration of a student

Although criticism of some students cannot be avoided, it is a mistake for a teacher loudly and publicly to denigrate some offender. This stirs up resentment and hostility if it is frequent, and even if the student dare not express this openly, it sours relationships, and is a poor example of adult behaviour. If a student is spoken to in a demeaning way there is loss of face with peers, and some way of regaining it will be sought when there is an opportunity to put you at a disadvantage. Students, especially older ones, resent being 'bawled out' as much as adults dislike it, and they see it as a form of bullying, which it is.

Smith and Laslett (1993 p.67) note what children perceive to be unacceptable behaviour in teachers. It is the teacher who speaks to them in contemptuous terms, and who is sarcastic, who frequently brings on confrontations. Students credit teachers with authority and expect them to exercise it to provide the right conditions for learning and acceptable behaviour in class. They accept that criticism or reprimands and punishment, when deserved, were legitimate. But if teachers treat them as if they had no status, if they are sarcastic, or punish unfairly, then such behaviour falls outside the unformulated but mutually understood social contract which operates in classrooms. Thus feeling no longer bound by the contract themselves, subsequent disruptive and antagonistic behaviour is legitimised. Their behaviour is then governed by the principles of 'reciprocity' and 'equilibration' (Marsh, Rosser and Harre, 1978). If the teacher is nasty, they are nasty; if insulting, they are insulting; treated as not entitled to respect, they show none. If they are unfairly put down or denigrated, an equilibrated reaction in a similar fashion restores status.

Rogers (1995 p.47) points out how easy it is for teachers to use negative language in moments of stress and therefore argues the importance of planning 'the language of correction' in advance. This also involves tone, timing and posture but essential principles include: calming yourself first, focusing on behaviour not the person, and balancing correction with encouragement and the re-establishment of working relationships (Rogers, 1995 p.104).

Ignoring unwanted behaviour

Another useful strategy is using planned or tactical ignoring of attention seeking or provocative behaviour. This is not the same as deliberately overlooking it because you cannot do anything else. It is about ensuring that you don't 'create more disruption by disciplining students than misbehaving students cause in the first place' (Olsen, 1997 p.35). It is about keeping the focus on the flow of the lesson by responding to other students who are behaving more appropriately and not rewarding the distraction. Often a non-verbal signal, a frown, a raised eyebrow or shake of the head can be linked to the tactical ignoring to make the offender aware that you are choosing not to react with admonition but would prefer them to desist. A teacher cannot rely upon the effectiveness of ignoring behaviour if there are no other strategies to deploy, and Rogers (1991 p.48) suggests the next level of action might be a quietly spoken simple direction, addressed to the individual, or a restatement or reminder of a rule.

Awareness of the effects of non-verbal communications

It is very easy for a teacher, especially if angry, to forget the effects that non-verbal communications and body language have on students. For some, they show that you are flustered and they take advantage of this; for others, a threatening demeanour communicates a challenge, which they take up. Many confrontations begin, or are maintained, not only by what you say, but by the way you walk, or stride towards a student, glare or point. In a confrontation the angry presence of the teacher in close proximity to a student can act as a powerful irritant, which prolongs and sharpens the crisis. Most people feel uncomfortable if another individual invades our 'private space'. These feelings are aggravated when an angry or unfriendly individual does this. In the same way, especially with older students, a teacher who is obviously annoyed and is not approaching a student with any friendly intention, risks making an aggressive response much more probable.

Proximity that is not threatening can help by offering an opportunity for offering help with a task rather than confrontation over behaviour. Assuming that distraction results from inability to cope rather than malevolent intent to disrupt enables you to reduce the potential for confrontation by focusing on the work in hand rather than the initial misbehaviour. You can also defuse the tension in a situation by humour or making any reprimand or redirection quiet and personal rather than public and dramatic.

Role-play can be an excellent way of demonstrating to teachers in training what messages they are conveying by their gestures, gait or demeanour, which are often a more accurate indication of their feelings than what they are saying. Another useful way for teachers to realise how facial expressions and bodily movements are likely to affect students is for them to simulate anger or exasperation and walk up to a full-length mirror. They could also profit from similar rehearsals while they extend their arms and hands and notice the difference in the effects of those movements, some of them noticeably expressing neutral or positive intentions and some expressing negative or hostile ones. A good deal of effective teaching is theatre, and teachers can learn a great deal from observation of experienced actors.

Avoiding physical interventions

A very common feature of a crisis in the classroom, which makes a confrontation more probable, is a teacher's attempting to grab some object a child has which is preventing him from paying attention or distracting others. In these circumstances, especially if the teacher is bigger and stronger than the student, it is tempting to make a grab at the personal stereo, or whatever it is that has not been put away or surrendered when asked to do so.

The teacher may be successful in doing this, but grabbing at the offending item or pushing the student aside to get hold of it moves the situation into a much more unpredictable dimension, and may well become the first step in a confrontation. The student may begin the tantalising manoeuvres of moving it out of the teacher's reach, perhaps by passing it on to others. There is no way of controlling this catch-as-catch-can manoeuvre, and each move in it increases the teacher's discomfort, increases the student's satisfaction, and adds to the tension. For the spectators in the class, it is hard to beat as a diverting spectacle.

For the teacher, it has few equals as an exasperating and undignified display of impotence.

Lowering the temperature

Individual strategies are not applied within a vacuum but within a classroom climate, which is defined by collective perceptions of what it feels like to be a student in your classroom. One research report on teacher effectiveness identifies nine dimensions or elements of classroom life, which have an impact on capacity and motivation to learn. Essentially, it concludes, students look towards the teacher for a sense of security and order, an opportunity to participate actively in the class and for it to be an interesting and exciting place (Hay McBer, 2000). Such conditions are most easily realised where teachers follow what have been characterised as the 'four rules' of classroom management:

> get them in, by starting lessons smoothly and promptly;
> get them out, by arranging an orderly conclusion to lessons;
> get on with it, by selecting suitable content with appropriate methods and materials;
> get on with them, by awareness of each student as an individual.
> (Smith and Laslett, 1993 pp.3–13)

Teachers are greatly helped by school behaviour policies, which establish procedures, rules and routines, which are rational and clearly understood, but also they need a personal discipline plan with a hierarchy of possible steps in mind (Rogers, 1991 p.48). In effect, you think in terms of an 'escalation–defusion' staircase as an alternative to the 'escalation–detonation' staircase mounted by teacher and student in the vignette that introduced this discussion. Teachers' responses will escalate and become increasingly intrusive but at each step there is an opportunity to step off the escalator. If the misbehaviour continues despite the diversionary tactics outlined above, then a further request for compliance can be accompanied by a choice indicating a sanction if the behaviour continues. Your plan should conclude with some arrangement for support from colleagues if necessary, for time-out and exit procedures if the student is determined to escalate the confrontation (Rogers, 1995 p.86) but there is a lot you could do to avoid this last resort.

Summary

Establishing a few essential rules and clarifying what is acceptable conduct will not prevent a calculated provocation but should deter the casual transgressor. Even when convinced that misbehaviour is deliberate, a teacher should be wary of overreaction. Anger uses too much adrenalin, and harsh punishment for minor misdemeanours leaves nothing in reserve for more serious infractions. In coping with potential confrontations, s/he should always look for a series of responses that are cool, calm and carefully calculated to reduce the chances of losing both temper and dignity.

References

Ayers, H., Clarke, D. and Murray, A. (1995) *Perspectives on Behaviour: A practical guide to effective interventions for teachers*, London: David Fulton Publishers

Bull, S.L. and Solity, J.E. (1987) *Classroom Management: Principles to practice*, London: Croom Helm

Cooper, P., Smith, C.J. and Upton, G. (1994) *Emotional and Behavioural Difficulties: Theory to practice*, London: Routledge

DfES (2001a) *SEN Code of Practice*, DfES Ref. 581/2001

DfES (2001b) *Inclusive Schooling: Children with SEN*, DfES Ref. 0774/2001

Laslett, R. (1998) 'Changing perceptions of maladjusted children, 1945–1981' in Laslett, R., Cooper, P., Maras, P., Rimmer, A. and Law, B. *Changing Perceptions: Emotional and behavioural difficulties since 1945*, Maidstone: Association of Workers for Children with Emotional and Behavioural Difficulties

Hay McBer Report (2000) *A Model of Teacher Effectiveness*, London: DfEE

Marsh, P., Rosser, E. and Harre, R. (1978) *The Rules of Disorder*, London: Routledge and Kegan Paul

Olsen, J. (1997) *Managing Classroom Gambits: Working with difficult classes in schools*, Canberra: University of Canberra

Rogers, W.A. (1991) *'You Know The Fair Rule': Strategies for making the hard job of discipline easier for the teacher* (British Edition), London: Pitman Publishing

Rogers, W.A. (1995) *Behaviour Management: A whole-school approach*, Gosford: Scholastic

SENDA (Special Educational Needs and Disability Act) 2001

Smith, C.J. and Laslett, R. (1993) *Effective Classroom Management: A teacher's guide* (2nd Edition), London: Routledge

Wheldall, K. and Merrett, F. (1992) 'Effective classroom behaviour management: positive teaching' in Wheldall, K. (ed.) *Discipline in Schools: Psychological perspectives on the Elton Report*, London: Routledge

PART 4
Individual student level

Chapter 17

A three-level approach to intervention for individual behaviour difficulties

H. Williams, Birmingham City Council

Introduction

These levels of intervention for individual behaviour problems should be seen as an extension of the normal provision made by the school through general curricular activity, work in PSE/PSME, extra-class activities and other aspects of the Behaviour Policy.

The paragraphs below describe a model of intervention which schools can use to respond effectively, efficiently and fairly to pupils exhibiting any of a wide range of possible behaviour problems.

Schools may wish to develop their own models of intervention reflecting their own individual circumstances. However, they should consult with the LEA when implementing their approach and should have regard to a number of principles that are central to all quality work with children exhibiting behavioural difficulties:

- Response to a child's behavioural difficulties should commence with an audit of the behavioural environment and remedial action where the evaluation determines that the environment is not optimal
- Individual programmes should be proportional to the problem and the least intrusive required to effect positive change
- Response to a child's behavioural difficulties should be appropriate, in that the action taken is likely to meet the aims of the intervention
- There should be careful recording of the nature of the problem, the action taken and the outcomes

- Children should be involved in their individual programmes to the greatest possible extent
- There should be close consultation and partnership with the child's parents where individual action is contemplated
- It should be recognised that all persons in professions working with children are likely to have, at some time in their career, difficulties in the conduct of their work related to the behaviour of children. In such situations it is appropriate that assistance be sought and that it should be given in a non-judgemental manner
- Systems for working with children exhibiting behavioural difficulties should be complementary to the Stages process for SEN allowing for all needs to be met in the most appropriate way.

In summary, the levels of intervention adopted by this Framework are:

Level 1 which follows an expression of concern and is characterised by an 'audit' approach to the behavioural environment, seeking areas for improvement and adopting a plan of action. At this level the child's class or subject teacher (or form teacher if the behaviour occurs outside lessons), with guidance from appropriate colleagues (including advice and assistance from outside agencies wherever possible and appropriate):

- checks the level of the behaviour causing concern (baselining)
- uses a checklist to audit the class and school environment
- ensures school's behaviour co-ordinator is informed
- makes a plan to effect change in the environment (Behavioural Environment Plan – BEP)
- implements the plan
- responds to individual problem behaviours by continuing to follow regular school disciplinary approaches
- monitors progress on the plan's objectives
- monitors the behaviour causing concern
- reviews progress.

Level 2 is characterised by a continued audit and plan to improve the behavioural environment alongside the use of an Individual Behaviour Plan (IBP). The responsibility for the IBP and BEP is held jointly at this level between the behaviour co-ordinator and the class or subject teacher expressing concern. Parents are informed and involved. The Behaviour Coordinator and class, subject or form teacher:

- ensures that the child's parents are informed
- informs head teacher
- re-checks the audit of the class and school environment

- marshals further relevant information (including from outside the school)
- re-establishes baseline
- modifies as necessary and continues operating a Behavioural Environment Plan
- establishes and operates an Individual Behaviour Plan
- monitors progress on the plans' objectives (including the behaviour causing concern)
- reviews progress.

Level 3 is characterised by an emphasis on the Individual Behaviour Plan with the involvement of outside agencies. The Behaviour Coordinator, taking the leading role and working closely with the child's teacher(s):

- keeps the head teacher informed
- draws on the advice of outside specialists, for example educational psychologists and advisory teachers
- ensures that the child's parents are consulted and involved as fully as is possible
- establishes and operates an Individual Behaviour Plan
- modifies as necessary and continues operating a Behavioural Environment Plan
- monitors progress on the plans' objectives
- reviews progress with outside specialists and parents.

Should the behaviour problem exhibited by the child not be resolved through work conducted at Level 3, outside specialists will be able to assist the school in determining whether other forms of provision might be appropriate.

Children may have learning difficulties more or less related to their behavioural difficulties. In such cases, the provisions and planning made at Levels 1 to 3 of this Framework should be carried out in conjunction with relevant intervention based on the Staged process of Code of Practice on the Identification and Assessment of Special Educational Needs. Children placed on any of the three Levels of this Framework might be at any Stage of the Code of Practice. Schools will already know of the importance of coordination between work on behaviour problems and Special Educational Need. Use of these levels for intervention with behaviour should make such coordination clearer.

All schools will recognise the importance of consulting and working in partnership with parents. They should be informed, at least in an informal way, when an expression of concern is lodged. Since Level 1 intervention will not include intervention that targets the individual child directly (outside of 'normal' disciplinary practices) there will be no need to detail precisely what response is being undertaken at this level. Good practice suggests, however, that all parents should be informed of any changes stemming from a plan following an audit of the behavioural environment that might affect their children. Intervention at Levels 2 and 3 should increasingly involve parents and suggest full information exchange.

(If for any reason a person suspects that any pupil is, or has been, the subject of abuse, the local authority's procedures for responding to such suspicions should take place with no delay and should precede any other action. Nothing within this guidance should be taken as suggesting any action contrary to child abuse procedures. However, sensitive level 1 work in such situations may not be precluded since it does not involve working individually with the child or children causing concern.)

Level 1

Level 1 involves the initial registration of a concern about a child's or children's behaviour, the gathering of basic information about the behavioural environment, planning and taking early action to improve the environment and monitoring and reviewing the progress of the plans.

Trigger

The trigger for Level 1 is an expression of concern that a child or children are exhibiting behaviour difficulties that are greater than those expected as a normal part of school life. Such expression will usually be made by a class or subject teacher when the behaviour is exhibited in lessons, but may also be made by others, for example; lunchtime supervisors or site staff, where the problems occur elsewhere.

Level 1 should be triggered if appropriate to the concern and where the behaviour occurs at times related to school activities. Detailed plans for dealing with behaviour problems occurring outside school times and premises should be made by the most appropriate agencies.

Roles and responsibilities

Where the expression of concern comes from a class or subject teacher and relates to a child's or children's behaviour in their class they will take on the lead responsibility at Level 1 (called the 'lead teacher' in the following text). Where the problem behaviour occurs outside class this lead responsibility could be assumed by the child's or children's form or class teacher or, in exceptional circumstances, the school's Behaviour Coordinator. **It is important**

to the chances of effectiveness of work at Level 1 that those dealing directly with the child or children whose behaviour causes concern feel that they have a significant degree of control over the process.

The lead person at Level 1 should have access to advice and support from colleagues in planning, conducting and evaluating the intervention. The Behaviour Coordinator will always be important here, but the lead person may also wish to use class or subject teacher colleagues as consultants or may wish to discuss plans with other members of the school's senior management team. Specialist support services to schools should organise to offer maximum possible access at Level 1 through advice and assistance with information gathering. **In some cases this initial advice will be sufficient to meet the concern – whenever this is the case there will be no need for further action**.

The Behaviour Coordinator will wish to keep a note of the Level 1 intervention and support and advise as appropriate.

Level 1 characteristics

The first activity at Level 1 is the 'baselining' of the problem behaviour. The purpose is to describe the concern with sufficient accuracy to be able to compare the position at the beginning of the intervention with that at the end. This means that a record is made of the occurrences of the behaviour stating, as appropriate:

- frequency
- place
- time
- social situation
- setting events
- description of problem behaviour
- duration of problem behaviour
- severity of behaviour (if appropriate)
- consequences to exhibiting child
- consequences to others.

An audit of the behavioural environment carried out at Level 1 is general in scope, and while it should relate to particular circumstances surrounding the behaviour(s) causing concern it should not focus in too closely. While there will be no Individual Behaviour Plan at this level some information concerning the child or children should be considered:

- possible sensory difficulty – particularly with hearing
- significant medical factors affecting the child
- significant life events which may affect the child.

When problems of this type are identified direct action is required; the Behaviour Coordinator and Special Needs Coordinator (or in the case of suspected abuse, the school's designated teacher) should be consulted. Seldom should such factors alter the basic approach taken to remedy behaviour difficulties as the principles underlying these procedures are pertinent in almost all cases. However, dissemination of relevant information to all concerned staff is often crucial to solutions being found.

The **behavioural audit** will seek to evaluate all the changeable factors having an effect on children's behaviour in the environment where the problem is occurring. The object is to compare these factors against the best they could reasonably be expected to be, the **'optimal behavioural environment'**. To carry out this audit, teachers will need a checklist of areas to assess which will cover aspects of:

- classroom physical environment, organisation and equipment
- classroom management
- classroom rules and routines
- environment, routines and rules outside class
- whole school policies and support for staff
- roles of parents and governors.

Since it is almost inconceivable that such a review will find perfection in all these areas, on the basis of the audit the teacher will isolate an area or areas for improvement. These should form the basis for a **Behavioural Environment Plan**; an action plan containing specific objectives for changing some aspect(s) of the behavioural environment. The plan should also include the methods proposed for effecting change, those who will be responsible, a date for completion of the changes and a date to review the effects. The full period of the plan should not normally be less than half a term, with at least 6 weeks of implementation, in order to allow sufficient time to show effects on behaviour.

Behavioural Environment Plans will inevitably vary in their scope and complexity. The purpose of record keeping is to ensure that all who need to know are clear what is being done, and that there is sufficient information recorded so that any information resulting from the plan can be used to guide future action. Commensurate with these aims, record keeping should be kept to the minimum necessary.

Direct responses to the child's or children's behaviour at Level 1 should be restricted to those in normal use under the school's behaviour and disciplinary policy. Only in the most exceptional circumstances should a Behaviour Coordinator accept a request to move to Level 2 in order to utilise an Individual Behaviour Plan without previous action at Level 1.

Implementation

Where the plan involves action that can be carried out by the lead person, the changes can be effected simply. All changes should be recorded and kept with the Behavioural Environment Plan. School staff may seek to work in partnership with colleagues who may have some interest in making similar changes, or who might agree to act as peer-advisers during the process. It is appropriate for Behavioural Environment Plans to extend to cover significant improvement projects within a school. However, it remains important that the lead person retains a high degree of ownership and control whilst such activity remains closely related to the original triggering concern.

There are many occasions where the behavioural audit will suggest changes that are not within the power of the lead teacher to effect. In such cases the drawing up of the Behavioural Environment Plan should be subject to negotiation with such others who will be involved in making the changes. It should be appreciated that changes envisaged by the aims of the plan are liable to have beneficial effects extending far beyond the limits of the original concern. Head teachers and governors should therefore ensure that the whole school is committed to supporting this process as far as is possible.

Evaluation and review

Evaluation of a Behavioural Environment Plan looks at three areas:

- progress made in implementing the changes
- changes in the general behaviour of children
- changes in the target behaviours causing concern

The first of these will be relatively easy to assess so long as the changes were clearly described in the plan. Evaluation of the expected 'general effects' will inevitably be somewhat subjective though perceptions of colleagues and the children may be of value in making judgements.

The behaviour causing concern should be monitored throughout the period of operation of the process and the data set against the information gained through baselining. In some cases the outcome will be obvious; the behaviour has increased or the behaviour has disappeared for example. In most cases there will be lesser effects.

Review should focus on:

- whether the changes described in the plan have been implemented
- whether the expected general effect of the changes has occurred

- whether there has been a consequent change in the behaviour causing concern
- future action.

  The outcomes of the Review may be:

- **the intervention continues at Level 1:** where the evidence from the evaluation suggests that the proposed changes in the environment have not been completed and that work on this should continue, or the behaviour has improved or not worsened and there should be a further amendment to the environment or continuation of the monitoring process, or the behaviour of a number of children has worsened possibly as a result of environmental change; a new or modified Behavioural Environment Plan should be set and the process repeated. In principle, Level 1 could be repeated any number of times, but there is an expectation that success at this level will mean that specific intervention will no longer be necessary. Schools may therefore wish to examine all factors more generally if there is a need, stemming from failure to effect plans or through negative outcomes from planned changes, for repeated plans at any one level.
- **intervention is no longer necessary:** where the Behavioural Environment Plan has been operated and has had the desired effect on behaviour. The records from this intervention should be shared with appropriate colleagues and the Behaviour Coordinator may wish to set up a library of information on successful interventions.
- **there is a move to Level 2:** where the Behavioural Environment Plan has been effected but the environmental changes have failed to be reflected in the target behaviour. This choice should only occur when the lead teacher and Behaviour Coordinator agree that there has been a move towards an optimal behavioural environment for the target behaviours but that general measures are insufficient to deal with the problems.

Level 2

At **Level 2** the Behaviour Coordinator takes the lead in 'baselining' the behaviour difficulty, designing and implementing a joint **Individual Behaviour Plan** and Behavioural Environment Plan, monitoring and reviewing, coordinating all staff involved and informing and involving the child's parents.

Trigger

The trigger for Level 2 intervention is a decision at a Level 1 review, or where, following an assessment of the behavioural environment which shows little need for change, the Behaviour Coordinator considers that an individual programme is necessary. The conduct and results of such an assessment should be recorded.

Roles and responsibilities

At Level 2 the responsibility is usually shared between the Behaviour Coordinator and the lead teacher. The Behaviour Coordinator will have the responsibility to ensure that the plans comply with the school's behaviour policy and are carried out efficiently, effectively and fairly. In addition, the Behaviour Coordinator will be responsible for any liaison with the Special Needs Coordinator, liaison with parents and keeping the head teacher informed.

The lead teacher will usually be responsible for carrying out the plan, working with the child directly and liaising with the Behaviour Coordinator.

There may be circumstances where the behaviour causing concern exists outside the classroom and where it is appropriate for the Behaviour Coordinator to act as the lead teacher. In such circumstances Behaviour Coordinators may well benefit from utilising another member of staff, perhaps the head teacher or deputy, as advisor to their conduct of the programmes.

Level 2 characteristics

Continuance of Behavioural Environment Plan

Move to Level 2 intervention is marked by the introduction of an Individual Behaviour Plan (or plans if more than one child is involved) but with a continuance of the audit process started at Level 1. If there has been no Level 1 intervention with a Behavioural Environment Plan, one should be established at the commencement of Level 2.

The process for establishing and running a Behavioural Environment Plan at Level 2 is similar to that at Level 1 though the responsibility is now shared between the lead teacher and the Behaviour Coordinator. Where there has been a previous plan, the decision at the start of Level 2 can be one of the following:

- to continue with the previous Behavioural Environment Plan to effect further improvements
- to modify the previous Behavioural Environment Plan in order to work towards a new outcome using tried methods
- to formulate and run a completely new plan.

Whichever course is chosen will depend on the previous experience and the judgement of those involved, particularly the Behaviour Coordinator.

It is important that the parents of the child or children for whom Individual Behaviour Plans are proposed are consulted and know of the Behavioural Environment Plan and how it connects with their children's programmes.

Whilst each child will have a separate Individual Behaviour Plan, the linked Behavioural Environment Plan may be common to more than one where there is a clear connection between the children's exhibited behaviour problems and the aims of the environmental plan. (For example, the Behavioural Environment Plan might be concentrating on the development of School-wide bullying policy and practice whilst particular acts of bullying are the subject of a number of children's individual plans.)

Formulation of Individual Behaviour Plan

The Behaviour Coordinator, consulting the lead teacher, any other relevant staff (including the SEN coordinator) and the child's parents should gather together all relevant information about the child which may affect:

- the decision to draw up an Individual Behaviour Plan
- the nature and conduct of the Individual Behaviour Plan
- whether SEN provision is required in parallel.

Such information may come from:

- the child
- parents
- support teachers
- educational psychologists
- medical practitioners
- social workers

and others as appropriate.

The Behaviour Coordinator should consider all available information before formulating the Individual Behaviour Plan in consultation with the lead teacher. However, the Behaviour Coordinator may decide that the information gained is not sufficient or that further advice is required before commencement. In such a case the Behaviour Coordinator should record

- what further advice or information is being sought
- what the arrangements will be pending receipt
- review arrangements.

Implementation

The Behaviour Coordinator working in consultation with the lead teacher will reestablish the baseline information relating to the current situation repeating the process described in Level 1 characteristics (p.273).

The Behaviour Coordinator will ensure that an Individual Behaviour Plan is drawn up which conforms to the principles laid out in the introduction to this chapter (pp.269–270). The plan should set out:

Level 2 – Individual Behaviour Plan

- nature of the behaviour difficulties exhibited by the child
- targets to be achieved in a given time and steps towards those targets
- action to meet targets:
  - the behavioural provision
  - staff involved including frequency of support
  - specific programmes/activities/materials/equipment
- help from and involvement of parents
- any direct involvement in the operation of the plan by the child, e.g. self-recording
- indication of concurrent SEN provision
- monitoring and assessment arrangements
- review arrangements and date.

Individual Behaviour Plans at Level 2 will be carried out normally in the place where the child's behaviour causes concern; the classroom or the playground, for example. Seldom should it be necessary at this level to incorporate any facility for withdrawal from regular activities and where this is included it must be for the least possible time. Rather, interventions at Level 2 will be characterised by a systematic approach to the child in his or her usual environment with an emphasis on positive responses to improvement in behaviour.

Schools should seek the involvement of children in their Individual Behaviour Plans to the greatest degree possible according to their age and understanding. It is easy to underestimate the degree to which this can be done, especially with younger or apparently 'disaffected' children. Involvement of the child can usefully start with the discussion of the difficulty and formulation of the plan.

Parents must be informed and involved as far as possible with the plan. In most cases it will be expected that they have agreed with the methods and targets involved. Certainly such agreement will significantly enhance the chances of success. Schools, understandably, might feel reluctant to see some parents as partners when, for example, there have been previous differences of opinion, or where the difficulty itself is seen as a function of home management problems. Nevertheless, the school should use its best endeavours at every occasion to secure maximum involvement of parents.

The content of the Individual Behaviour Plan will be similar to that of an Individual Education Plan. This means that an Individual Behaviour Plan and an Individual Education Plan can be used together as part of a unified plan covering behaviour and learning, and utilise common consultation and review.

Level 2 interventions will normally need to last for at least half a term with 6 clear weeks of implementation in order to allow sufficient time to show effects on behaviour.

Evaluation and review

Evaluation of the implementation of an Individual Behaviour Plan will consider to what extent the proposed actions have been carried out, the extent of help from home and the involvement of the child.

The behaviour causing concern should be monitored throughout the period of operation of the plans and the data set against the information gained through baselining.

Review should focus on:

- whether there has been a change in the behaviour causing concern about the child
- whether the changes described in the plans have been implemented
- whether the expected general effect of the environmental change has occurred
- any other information gained during the operation of the plans
- the views and feelings of the participants
- future action.

The outcomes of the review may be:

- **the intervention continues at Level 2:** where the evidence from the evaluation suggests that the proposed changes in the environment have not been completed and that work on this should continue, or the Individual Behaviour Plan has not been implemented fully or the behaviour has improved or not worsened and there should be a further amendment to the environment and implementation of an Individual Behaviour Plan, or the behaviour of a number of children has worsened possibly as a result of environmental change. In principle, Level 2 could be repeated any number of times, but there is an expectation that success at this level will mean that specific intervention will no longer be necessary or might revert to Level 1.

Schools may therefore wish to examine all factors more generally if there is a need, stemming from failure to effect plans or through negative outcomes from planned changes, for repeated plans at any one level.

- **the intervention reverts to Level 1 or is no longer necessary:** where the Behavioural Environment Plan and Individual Behaviour Plan has been operated and has had the desired effect on behaviour or there is sufficient improvement so that the Individual Behaviour Plan is no longer needed. The records from this intervention should be shared with appropriate colleagues and the Behaviour Coordinator may wish to set up a library of information on successful interventions.
- **there is a move to Level 3:** where the Behavioural Environment Plan and Individual Behaviour Plan have been operated in an appropriate way but have failed to be reflected in the target behaviour. This choice should only occur when the Behaviour Coordinator is satisfied that there has been an improvement or sustaining of the Behavioural Environment for the target behaviours but that the problems call for a more intensive individual plan with a greater emphasis on external advice.

Parents should be invited to Level 2 reviews. They should always be told the outcome. It is particularly important to talk with parents if the school is considering moving the child to Level 3. In addition, Schools should always consider the possibility of the child attending all or part of the Level 2 review.

Level 3

At **Level 3** the Behaviour Coordinator again takes the lead in 'baselining' the behaviour difficulty, designing and implementing an Individual Behaviour Plan and, if indicated, a further Behavioural Environment Plan. The Behaviour Coordinator also has responsibility for monitoring and reviewing, coordinating all staff involved and informing and involving the child's parents, liaising with outside agencies. The head teacher, or possibly in a large school the head teacher's representative, will be informed and will sanction the intervention. The head teacher may wish to inform the governing body.

Trigger

The trigger for Level 3 will normally be the decision to move to Level 3 at a Level 2 review.

Exceptionally, Level 3 might be triggered where the Behaviour Coordinator and the head teacher agree that a difficulty has suddenly arisen that is sufficiently great that it requires an immediate move to Level 3. The reasons for such a move should always be recorded. The intervention should always include an audit of the behavioural environment and usually a consequent Behavioural Environment Plan.

Parents must always be involved in the decision to move to Level 3 and their agreement sought.

Roles and responsibilities

As at Level 2 the Behaviour Coordinator will take the major role in coordination of the plans. At Level 3 responsibility will be shared with the head teacher, and, in situations where there are joint behaviour and education plans, the Special Needs Coordinator.

Normally, at Level 3 there will be consultation with education support services specialising in behavioural difficulties. The Behaviour Coordinator will also exchange information, where appropriate, with Social Services and Health Services.

It is likely that there will be a number of people who will have a role in putting plans into operation. At Level 3 there will be a high degree of monitoring and supervision conducted by the Behaviour Coordinator.

Depending upon the nature of the difficulties experienced by the child, where there is a joint IBP and IEP, either the Behaviour Coordinator or the Special Needs Coordinator should assume the lead responsibility for ensuring coordination and consistency of intervention. A Level 3 intervention for behaviour may operate in conjunction with intervention for special educational needs at any Stage described in the Code of Practice for the Assessment and Identification of Special Educational Needs.

The head teacher should have close involvement with any decision regarding the need for, and provision of, a Behavioural Environment Plan at Level 3. Where a Level 3 intervention occurs without a Behavioural Environment Plan the head teacher should be sure that there is no further need for one in the context of the particular child causing concern. Such a decision should be noted in the child's record.

Level 3 characteristics

Particularly when successful Behavioural Environment Plans have been operated at Levels 1 and 2 it may be decided not to extend their use to Level 3. However, if there is any doubt over this it is recommended that a further

Behavioural Environment Plan be adopted at this level in conjunction with the Individual Behaviour Plan.

The Individual Behaviour Plan may follow on from any adopted at Level 2, but will involve a greater degree of provision for operation and monitoring, and be more subject to advice from external specialists.

Where there is a joint IBP and IEP most of the liaison and consultation with parents and outside agencies will cover both plans. There will almost always be a close relationship between the actions in the plans and it will be efficient and effective for the plans themselves to be contained in one document and presented as a unified strategy.

At Level 3 there will be consultation with the child and the parents at all possible points in the formulation and conduct of the Individual Behaviour Plan. This is of the greatest importance given the degree of intervention implied by working at this level. In general, agreement of the parents (and often the child) should always be sought, particularly where operation of the plan may involve the child spending any time outside the normal classroom environment.

There may be a number of types of provision included in combination within the plan, for example:

- counselling
- therapies
- peer involvement
- self monitoring
- behavioural approaches:
  - use of systematic reinforcement (reward) for improved behaviour
  - stimulus-based training
  - 'token economies'
  - systematic non-reinforcement of unwanted behaviours
- use of sanctions.

At Level 3 there may be provision, as an essential and positive part of the plan, for the child to be removed from the normal environment in response to unwanted behaviour. Where this or any other sanction is planned, it is especially important for the Behaviour Coordinator to gain specialist advice. However, schools should avoid the understandable tendency to over-use 'internal exclusion'. The school should seek other ways of supporting any class teacher or other member of staff who may be put under a high degree of pressure by the child's behaviour.

It is especially important that there is a specific check to ensure that the level and quality of the curriculum being presented to the child is appropriate and that any modification following from such a check is carried out.

Implementation

The Behaviour Coordinator will re-establish the baseline information for the situation current at the beginning of Level 3.

The Behaviour Coordinator, following consultation with the head teacher, colleagues and outside specialists, will ensure that an Individual Behaviour Plan is drawn up. The plan should set out:

Level 3 – Individual Behaviour Plan

- nature of the behaviour difficulties exhibited by the child
- targets to be achieved in a given time and steps towards those targets
- action to meet targets – the behavioural provision
  - staff involved including frequency of support
  - specific programmes/activities/materials/equipment
  - involvement of external specialists
- help from and involvement of parents
- any direct involvement in the operation of the plan by the child, e.g. self-recording
- indication of any concurrent SEN provision (when not presented as a unified plan)
- monitoring and assessment arrangements
- review arrangements and date.

The Individual Behaviour Plans at Level 3 will have specific targets relating to the child's behaviour, progress towards which will be monitored on a regular basis (that is, at least weekly) by the Behaviour Coordinator. There should be facility for amending the plan before the review date should this monitoring suggest it, though it should be remembered that children's behaviour can often deteriorate for a short period before improving as a response to intervention. Progress towards targets and any changes made should be recorded contemporaneously.

The plan should ensure that all staff who need to know are informed of its content and know their role, if any, in its operation.

Where external specialists have been involved in the formulation of Individual Behaviour Plans they should be kept informed of any changes and offer further advice if indicated.

Evaluation and review

Evaluation of the implementation of an Individual Behaviour Plan will consider to what extent the proposed actions have been carried out, the extent of help from home and the involvement of the child.

The behaviour causing concern will have been monitored throughout the period of operation of the plans and such data should be set against the information gained through baselining.

Review should focus on:

- whether there has been a change in the behaviour causing concern about the child
- whether the changes described in the plans have been implemented
- whether any expected general effect of the environmental changes has occurred
- any other information gained during the operation of the plans
- the views and feelings of the participants
- future action.

The outcomes of the review may be:

- **the intervention continues at Level 3:** where the evidence from the evaluation suggests that the proposed changes in the environment have not been completed and that work on this should continue, or the Individual Behaviour Plan has not been implemented fully or the behaviour has improved or not worsened and there should be a further amendment to the environment and implementation of an Individual Behaviour Plan. In principle, Level 3 could be repeated any number of times, but there is an expectation that success at this level will mean that specific intervention will no longer be necessary or might revert to Levels 1 or 2. Schools may therefore wish to examine all factors more generally if there is a need, stemming from failure to effect plans or through negative outcomes from planned changes, for repeated plans at any one level.
- **the intervention reverts to Level 1 or 2 or is no longer necessary:** where the Individual Behaviour Plan and Behavioural Environment Plan has been operated and has had the desired effect on behaviour or there is sufficient improvement so that the Individual Behaviour Plan can be scaled down or is no longer needed. The records from this intervention should be shared with appropriate colleagues and the Behaviour Coordinator may wish to set up a library of information on successful interventions.
- **the intervention continues at the same level but the school seeks action beyond Level 3:** where the Behavioural Environment Plan and Individual Behaviour Plan have been operated in an appropriate way but have failed to be reflected in the target behaviour. This choice should only occur when the head teacher is satisfied that there is clear evidence that, even with the advice of external specialists, the school requires further provision to be made in order to meet the needs indicated by the behaviour difficulties.

Parents should be invited to Level 3 reviews. They should always be told the outcome. It is particularly important to talk with parents if the school is considering requesting action beyond Level 3. In addition, schools should always consider the possibility of the child attending all or part of the Level 3 review.

Action beyond Level 3

Unless the decision taken at Review was to reduce or discontinue intervention, when the school seeks action beyond Level 3 it should continue with present Level 3 interventions until other arrangements to meet the difficulty are made.

This framework does not extend to any single procedure for going beyond Level 3 (a 'Level 4') as there are a number of possible and distinctively different consequences to a decision at a Level 3 Review to ask for further action including:

- following an Individual Behaviour Plan at Level 3 and an Individual Education Plan, the head teacher considers referring the child to the LEA for statutory assessment
- The school consults the LEA regarding the development of a joint action plan where the school shares responsibility for meeting the child's needs with appropriate agencies.

The LEA should provide a detailed framework for the development of a system of joint action plans where schools may share the responsibility and provision for children with significant and complex and intransigent behavioural difficulties with the LEA, and, if indicated, with the social services department, health services, the housing department, and others such as voluntary agencies, probation services etc.

The place of exclusion, fixed term or permanent, is not covered by this Framework; it is a response made available to headteachers as a last resort to deal with situations where allowing the child to remain in school would be seriously detrimental to the education or welfare of the child, or to that of others at the school.

Therefore, this Framework does not attempt to offer advice to head teachers on the use of exclusion; that decision must be for them. LEA guidance should always be followed. However, it is believed that the utilisation of this Framework may well avoid, in a significant number of cases, the need for exclusion to be used. Where exclusion is found to be required, use of the Framework will furnish significant evidence of the effects of interventions to guide those taking future responsibility for the child.

Chapter 18

Behaviour in context: functional assessment of disruptive behaviour in classrooms

Dennis Moore

Introduction

Students who are non-compliant or display anti-social behaviours are an ongoing concern for school staff and parents throughout the world (Church, 1996; Fields, 1986; Whelan, 1998; Walker, et al., 1996). The literature is replete with diagnostic categories and terms describing these students including:

- children with emotional and behavioural difficulties (EBD) (Belknap & Mosca, 1999; Chazan, Laing, & Davies, 1994; Eber, Nelson, & Miles, 1997; Whelan, 1998; Ysseldyke, 1991),
- conduct disordered (CD) (Fox & Stinnett, 1996; Murray & Myers, 1998; Prinz, Blechman, & Dumas, 1994; Tainsh & Izard, 1994; Webster-Stratton, 1993),
- delinquent (Murray & Myers, 1998),
- emotionally handicapped (EH) (Indiana State Dept. of Education, 1988),
- oppositional defiant disorder (ODD) (Webster-Stratton, 1993),
- severely emotionally/behaviourally disordered (Ellis & Magee, 1999; Rutherford & Mathur, 1993; Swan, Brown, & Jacob, 1987),
- (severely) emotionally disturbed ((S)ED) (Brondolo, Baruch, Conway, & Marsh, 1994; Levine-Brown, 1993; Solnit, Adnopoz, Saxe, Gardner, & Fallon, 1997)

- socially maladjusted (Murray & Myers, 1998),
- troubled and troubling students (Whelan, 1998),

as well as other descriptors including:

- aggressive (Hudley & Graham, 1995; Pepler & Craig, 1995; Rosenberg, 1986),
- disruptive and distractable (Rosenberg, 1986),
- maladjusted (Murray & Myers, 1998; Rutherford & DiGangi, 1991; Wearmouth, 1999), and
- severely disruptive, (Younkin & Blasik, 1992).

In the United States alone over 17 different terms are in use to describe this population, reflecting the diverse conceptual frameworks which are brought to bear in the attempt to understand problem behaviour in classrooms as well as the sheer number of different agencies and professional groups that deal with this population (Shatz, 1994). For the purposes of this chapter the terms *conduct problems*, *disruptive behaviour* and *antisocial behaviour* will be used to encompass the field.

Effects of disruptive behaviour

On a daily basis many teachers deal with disruptions arising from student behaviours such as talking out of turn, not following instructions, and not interacting properly with peers (Corrie, 1997). Such disruptive classroom behaviour significantly impacts teachers' capacity to maintain a productive and orderly learning environment and has been repeatedly found to be a major factor contributing to teacher stress, discontent, and burn-out (Chazan, et al., 1994; Ellis & Magee, 1999; Hawe, Tuck, Manthei, Adair, & Moore, 2000; Merrett & Wheldall, 1993; Rutherford & DiGangi, 1991; Sterling-Turner, Robinson, & Wilczynski, 2001). Many teachers find the management of disruptive behaviour very aversive and stressful.

In extreme situations such behaviour can jeopardise not only the smooth functioning of classrooms, interfering with the process of teaching and learning, but also can threaten the safety of self and others. Further, recurrent inappropriate classroom behaviour has been shown to be predictive of present and future academic under-achievement for the students involved (Malecki & Elliott, 2002; Wentzel, 1993). Researchers have identified that persistent disruptive behaviour may interfere not only with the task of academic learning, but importantly also with the development of social skills, depriving students of social support from their peers. The absence of social skills has been correlated with student loneliness (Cassidy & Asher 1992). Children with negative and destructive interaction patterns often become catalysts for conflict with peers (Broadhead, 1998), which in turn may result in peer rejection and social isolation. There is clear evidence that conduct problems are associated with negative long-term outcomes for the students involved including lowered rates of successful school-completion, increased unemployment, and a higher risk of incarceration (Bear, 1999; Blechman, 1996; Chazan, et al., 1994; Little & Hudson, 1998; Tobin & Sugai, 1999) with associated costs to society.

Furthermore, recurrent disruptive and antisocial classroom behaviour has also been shown to be a problem for other students, compromising their participation in academic and social learning opportunities, diverting teacher attention from academic instruction, or simply through the general disruption caused (Kern, Childs, Dunlap, Clarke, & Falk, 1994; Kern, Delaney, Clarke, Dunlap, & Childs, 2001; Sterling-Turner et al., 2001). In extreme cases class peers can also be put at risk of personal harm or injury.

In-service courses in the effective management of disruptive classroom behaviour continue to be among the most frequently requested professional development programmes for teachers. Fortunately, there is now an extensive research literature contributing to our understanding of the aetiology of disruptive behaviour in the class, its prevalence, as well as the social and cultural factors with which it is correlated, and, importantly, with the effective management of such behaviour within the classroom and school.

One point of consensus among researchers is that schools are increasingly resorting to suspension and expulsion to deal with the problem of disruptive behaviour (Bain & Macpherson, 1990; Chazan et al., 1994; Farrell, 1995). Similarly, the published incidence figures show consistent and differential patterns in the frequency with which students are identified as having conduct problems as a function of gender, ethnicity, and socio-economic status, with over-representation of boys (Chazan et al., 1994; Harris, 1993; Macmillan, Gresham, Lopez, & Bocian, 1996; Thomas, Byrne, Offord, & Boyle, 1991) particular (country specific) ethnic minority groups (Macmillan et al., 1996; Hosp & Reschly, 2003) and of children from low socio-economic status households (Farrell, 1995; Grimshaw, 1995; Macmillan et al., 1996; Zima, Forness, Bussing, & Benjamin, 1998).

Based on these findings some have argued (see for example, Bear, 1999) that the use of suspension and expulsion from schools as a means of dealing with disruptive behaviour should be prevented as it is a systemic violation of the rights of these identifiable minority groups to an effective and meaningful education, one that provides learning opportunities of equal quality for all students.

Issues of identification

As is reflected in the different categorical labels listed above, an assumption underlying much of the research in this field has been that particular children have identifiable deficits or deficiencies and that the task of researchers and teachers is to develop procedures to reliably identify these children and to develop specific instructional procedures which address these deficiencies in a targeted way. However, as teachers know, the level of adaptive functioning of individual students varies markedly in different contexts (Whelan, 1998). Further, researchers have shown that schools of comparable socio-economic status and cultural composition differ markedly in their capacity to both prevent and manage behaviour problems (Banks, 1995; Chazan et al., 1994; Farrell, 1995), illustrating that behaviour problems do not occur in isolation but may be seen as the result of interactions between students and the learning contexts provided (Cantrell & Cantrell, 1985). A long-standing theoretical tradition which conceptualises person–environment interactions as the genesis of human behaviour (Bandura, 1977; Lewin, 1952; Skinner, 1953; Vygotsky, 1993) has contributed to our understanding of the critical role that environmental factors play in the development of children's behaviour and learning. Within this socio-ecological conceptualisation of the learning process, the locus of origin for disruptive or antisocial behaviour is not solely within specific individuals but rather within a complex array of individual and contextual factors. Our understanding of the problem and the development of procedures to address an instructional need requires analysis of both personal and environmental factors (Banks, 1995; Cantrell & Cantrell, 1985; Chazan et al., 1994; Kryzanowski, 1992; Peagam, 1995; Wheeler, 1999; Ysseldyke & Christenson, 1987).

Over the past 30 or 40 years researchers have been studying the processes of teaching and learning in schools and, in particular, working to understand the aetiology and effective management of conduct problems in classrooms. From this work we now have a much better understanding of both.[1] Recent meta-analyses and systematic reviews of this research have provided clear indications of what works and (sometimes) what does not work by way of interventions for disruptive classroom behaviour (see for example Farmer, Farmer, & Gut, 1999; Fisher, Schumaker, & Deshler,1995; Forness, Kavale, Blum,

---

[1] Factors known to be significant include the need to get the basics of classroom instruction right (good classroom management/routines, and an appropriate curriculum), the need for early intervention (Chazan et al., 1994), and to explicitly focus on the development of social skills (Marthur, Kavale, Quinn, Forness, & Rutherford, 1998; Quinn, Kavale, Marthur, Rutherford, & Forness, 1999). Furthermore the importance played by teacher beliefs/attitudes (Little & Hudson, 1998; Wilson et al., 2001) is well known as is a need to develop integrated, multi-tiered school-wide discipline/support systems to underpin the work of the classroom teacher (Walker et al., 1996). This material is beyond the scope of the present chapter.

& Lloyd, 1997; Goldstein, 1999; King-Sears, 1997; Little & Hudson, 1998; Wilson, Gottfredson, & Nahaka, 2001).

Addressing disruptive behaviour

Though much more work is needed before education could be described as an evidence-based profession, there is now strong empirical support for the effectiveness of particular instructional approaches. We know from the empirical research that cooperative learning approaches (including peer tutoring), and both behavioural (including antecedent interventions such as changes in seating arrangements and curriculum/instructional adaptation, reinforcement-based strategies such as differential reinforcement and token economies, direct instruction, incidental learning, and feedback), and cognitive behavioural strategies (strategy instruction, and mnemonic training) have powerful effects on behaviour and learning in the classroom. We know also that some strategies (for example, learning styles/modality training, withdrawal-based social skills training, perceptual training, non-behavioural counselling, and the Feingold diet) have produced minimal and possibly negative effects on learning and behaviour (Forness et al., 1997; Wilson et al., 2001). So strong is the convergence of findings across diverse systematic reviews and meta-analyses in support of the claims summarised above that these claims no longer appear either radical or contentious to the research community. However, as Vaughn and her colleagues recently noted in a review of intervention research with learning disabled students (Vaughn, Gersten, & Chard, 2000), this knowledge is too rarely implemented in classrooms. A puzzling mismatch can be observed between educational research findings and classroom practice in this regard. Expensive professional development programmes on kinaesthetic programming and modality training, for example, flourish, and counsellors, psychologists and other educational consultants continue to offer counselling for disruptive students and regular social skills training sessions for those who display inadequate self control. Similarly, teachers often report that particular well-researched and validated procedures for either reducing inappropriate behaviour or for shaping new, more adaptive responses prove ineffective in some situations and with some students. This is a vexing problem for teachers and researchers alike. In line with developments in the fields of health, social welfare and clinical psychology there is a resurgence of interest within education in 'evidence based practice' (Pring, 2004). Substantial research programmes designed to develop and empirically validate effective instructional procedures are under way in many parts of the world including Britain, the United States, Australia, and New Zealand.

Decision-making in interventions

When considering the application of particular instructional practices in classrooms, success involves recognising the importance of two issues: the fidelity with which the practice is implemented and, critically, the appropriateness of application of the procedure to a targeted problem. When confronted with a problem around which a number of empirically validated teaching procedures are known that will either increase or decrease the probability of occurrence of specific behaviours, on what basis should a teacher or a school-based multidisciplinary assistance team decide which of the procedures to apply?

A number of factors are known to influence teachers' decisions, including: the teacher's philosophy about behaviour change and the availability of necessary personal resources (Elliott, 1988; Miller, 1995), the severity of the problem (the more severe the problem the more acceptable are reductive or punitive procedures), the complexity of the intervention and the amount of time and effort it involves (Elliott, Witt, Galvin, & Peterson, 1984), personal characteristics of the student performing the behaviour (age, size and gender) (Pisecco, Huzinec, & Curtis, 2001; Power, Hess, & Bennet, 1995).

Interestingly, the most salient dimension of the behaviour in this decision-making process has been its *form* (topography, rate and or intensity) rather than its function (the function served by that behaviour). In selecting an intervention procedure, teachers and classroom management consultants alike typically have relied on their previous experience with a procedure that was thought to have been effective in dealing with behaviour of a similar form (for example, calling out or throwing objects) or which they have heard of or perhaps read about in the professional or more popular literature (Watson & Steege, 2003). Class-based interventions have all too frequently relied heavily on the application of arbitrary reinforcers and punishers to increase specific desired behaviour or suppress undesired behaviour, and thereby effectively overriding discovery of the conditions that brought about the undesired behaviour. If an intervention was found to be unsuccessful, another more intense intervention would be implemented and this process continued until a successful intervention was found. As a result of this process the learning histories behind the problem behaviour and the variables responsible for that behaviour were largely ignored in the development of an intervention strategy (Gable, 1996; Mace, Lalli, Lalli, & Shea, 1993; Sasso, Harrell, & Doeling, 1997).

In this context the educational community can learn, and has learned, some important lessons from researchers working in more clinical psycho-educational settings. Since the 1950s, researchers in the field of Applied Behaviour Analysis have been concerned with the analysis and treatment of socially important behaviour (for example, Ayllon & Michael, 1959; Baer, Wolf & Risley, 1968). Careful behavioural assessment was an integral part of this process, the purpose of this assessment being essentially to identify the environmental variables that significantly influenced the behaviour under examination. The results of the assessment were then utilised in the selection of an appropriate intervention. Early writers in clinical and psycho-educational settings stressed that considering only the topography or physical features of a behaviour (for example, head banging, biting), was not adequate for the selection of appropriate interventions as it could be shown that topographically similar behaviour could be maintained by different consequences (Bijou, Peterson, & Ault, 1968). Thus, the variables maintaining the behaviour were considered to be important, and identifying the *function* that behaviour served for different individuals was seen as central to the assessment and treatment of individual aberrant behaviour.

The place of functional analysis of behaviour

Initially research in the area illustrated the utility of analysing the function of the behaviour (for example, Ferster, 1961; Hasazi & Hasazi 1972; Hawkins, Peterson, & Schweid, 1966; Lovaas, Freitag, Gold, & Kassorla, 1965; Wahler, Winkel, Peterson & Morrison, 1965; Williams, 1959). However, throughout the late 1960s and 1970s, due largely to methodological difficulties in reliably identifying the function of aberrant behaviour, there was a shift in research focus, away from the analysis of the *function* of the behaviour, and towards analysing the *topography* of the behaviour (Carr, 1994). Through this period interventions were primarily selected on the basis of the procedures having previously been successful when utilised for reducing or eliminating a similar type of aberrant behaviour (Fowler & Schnacker, 1994). Thus, the critical interaction between the environmental antecedents and consequences maintaining the target behaviour was often neglected. Behavioural interventions through this period frequently involved the application of reinforcers and punishers that were able to prevail over the existing contingencies (Glynn, 1982; Wheldall, 1982). Problems with maintenance and generalisation of treatment effects emerged as this approach largely ignored the variables that regulate the target behaviour in the natural environment (Mace, 1994). Thus interventions selected on the basis of response topography and previous success, rather than an analysis of the function of the behaviour, proved less effective in reducing or eliminating aberrant behaviour.

Carr (1977), in a seminal review concerned with the treatment of self-injurious behaviour, concluded that one reason many of the interventions were largely unsuccessful was because little attention was given to the function and aetiology of the behaviour. He observed that similar behaviours may serve different functions for different individuals concluding that set interventions for particular behaviours will not always be appropriate. Carr suggested that self-injurious behaviour (SIB) could be viewed as communicating an individual's need, and advised that if professionals focussed on what individuals were trying to communicate through their behaviour, rather than on the form the behaviour took, interventions would be more effective.

Applying Carr's theory, Iwata, Dorsey, Slifer, Bauman and Richman (1982) developed the first comprehensive and standardised 'functional analysis'. Iwata and his colleagues sought to identify variables that were associated with, and may serve to maintain, self-injurious behaviour (SIB). Functional analysis is an experimental approach to behavioural assessment. Variables that are hypothesised to maintain the target behaviour are systematically manipulated under analogue conditions, while extraneous variables are held constant or eliminated. This allows the experimenter to examine one independent variable at a time in order to isolate the effect of each, (Conroy, Fox, Crain, Jenkins, & Belcher, 1996; Horner, 1994; Mace & Lalli, 1991; Mace et al., 1993; Schill, Kratochwill, & Gardner, 1996).

Iwata et al. (1982) examined four experimental conditions: social disapproval (testing whether positive reinforcement, contingent on the target behaviour, maintained SIB), academic demand (testing whether negative reinforcement, contingent on the target behaviour, maintained SIB), unstructured play (a control condition paralleling an enriched environment), and alone (testing whether self-produced reinforcement due to self-stimulation maintained SIB). Results indicated that the function of SIB varied across the nine participants in the study, supporting Carr's argument. For treatment to be effective, specific interventions were required, tailored to the individual needs of each participant. This study demonstrated that it is possible empirically to identify factors influencing levels of SIB before implementing treatments, therefore fostering more efficient development of interventions.

The development of this procedure has led to substantially improved behavioural interventions and is now widely used in clinical settings to identify the functional properties of problem behaviour (Carr, 1994; Kern et al., 1994; Mace, 1994; Repp & Karsh, 1994).

Effectiveness of functional analysis

Functional analysis which involves a detailed, often labour intensive experimental analysis of the ecology of the behaviour has proven very effective in the management of low incidence, severe or persistent difficulties that are highly resistant to intervention. As a recent illustration, Mildon, Moore, and

Dixon (2003) reported a study with a 4-year-old boy previously diagnosed with autism. He was referred for treatment because of a history of extremely aggressive (for example, hitting and head banging) and disruptive behaviour (for example, screaming and throwing objects). He had a limited non-functional vocal repertoire that consisted mainly of immediate and/or delayed echolalia, and was resistant to pre-academic instructional sessions. Prior to treatment, a functional analysis demonstrated that the disruptive behaviour of the participant was maintained by escape from demands. Throughout the analysis the participant's disruptive behaviour occurred almost exclusively during a demand condition, indicating that the behaviour was maintained by negative reinforcement in the form of escape from instructional demands. Data from this analysis were used to develop a tailored intervention in which non-contingent escape (Carr et al., 2000) and functional communication training (Durand, 1990; Durand & Carr, 1991) were employed to reduce disruptive behaviour, increase compliance to task demands, and the use of appropriate verbal responses. The data showed that with non-contingent escape and functional communication training in combination, rates of disruptive behaviour remained at near zero levels while compliance with task demands and appropriate verbal responses increased substantially.

From 1982 to the present a large and ever-expanding body of research has been published using functional analysis procedures. This work demonstrates conclusively that the identification of the function/s of problem behaviour is crucial in the design and implementation of successful behavioural interventions for low incidence, severe or persistent behaviour difficulties. A functional analysis is a powerful assessment tool because, through experimental manipulation, it provides a direct and reliable means of identifying functional relationships between particular behaviours and specific antecedent or consequent events. The technique involves precise, objective procedures that result in the development and selection of effective and efficient treatments (Broussard & Northup, 1995; Carr, 1994; Conroy et al., 1996; Kern et al., 1994; Mace, 1994; Sasso et al., 1992). Functional analysis procedures have been described as providing the most conclusive information of all assessment techniques (Northup et al., 1994).

Functional analysis in practice

A number of researchers have been exploring the application of functional analysis to the regular classroom setting (Dunlap et al., 1993; Ellis & Magee, 1999; Meyer, 1999; Repp, 1994; Umbreit, 1996). However, a full school-based functional analysis can take several months to complete (Broussard & Northup, 1995; Watson, Ray, Turner, & Logan, 1999), so that costs and other considerations, both ethical and practical, associated with standard functional analysis procedures have proven major stumbling blocks to its implementation with more high incidence disruptive behaviours in authentic regular education settings. School administrators and teachers, and government educational authorities may be reluctant to allow experimental assessments that (for example) purposely act to increase problem behaviours for short periods of time (Conroy et al., 1996; Ervin, DuPaul, Kern & Friman, 1998; Repp, 1994; Repp & Karsh, 1994). Functional analysis procedures have been criticised for being too complex and burdensome to complete in a natural environment such as a classroom (Northup et al., 1994; Sasso et al., 1992). It may be unrealistic to expect school personnel or regular caregivers to have the time, knowledge or resources to be able to conduct a functional analysis following Iwata et al.'s (1982) complex methodology (Sasso et al., 1992; Schill et al., 1996). It is also likely that conditions will exist in the natural environment that will make it impractical to carry out a complete functional analysis (for example, time restrictions, school timetables or schedules) (Desrochers, Hile & Williams-Moseley, 1997).

However, a range of non-experimental functional assessment procedures have been developed which are designed to identify functional relationships between events in the natural environment and the occurrence or non-occurrence of a target behaviour (Cone, 1997; Conroy et al., 1996; Dunlap et al., 1993; Foster-Johnson & Dunlap, 1993; Horner & Carr, 1997; Umbreit, 1995). Functional assessment aims to discover the antecedents, setting events and consequences that serve to occasion and/or maintain challenging behaviours. Functional analysis attempts to explain why a particular individual engages in such behaviour (Carr, Levin, McConnachie, Carlson, Kemp & Smith, 1994; Foster-Johnson & Dunlap, 1993; Horner, 1994; Storey, Lawry, Ashworth, Danko & Stain, 1994; Taylor, 1994). As noted previously, the underlying assumption of a functional assessment is that if interventions and behavioural support plans are based on the function that the target behaviour serves for a given individual, interventions will be more effective and efficient in controlling and reducing levels of challenging behaviours (Gable, 1996; Skiba, Waldron, Bahamonde & Michalek, 1998).

While functional analysis procedures have been used primarily for children with intellectual and developmental disabilities in restrictive settings, these procedures have been extended recently to the population of 'typically-developing' children exhibiting more high incidence inappropriate behaviour in less restrictive settings (Skiba et al., 1998; Watson & Steege, 2003). Although methodological problems concerning the reliability and validity of data obtained through these procedures (see Sasso, Conroy, Stichter, & Fox, 2001 for a current critique), the past 20 years have seen a marked increase in the direct and indirect assessment and analysis of problem behaviour-in-context to determine the function of disruptive behaviour in school settings and to develop more targeted interventions based on these assessments (Broussard &

Northup, 1995; Derby et al., 1992; Lewis & Sugai, 1996a, 1996b; Shapiro & Kratochwill, 2000; Umbreit, 1996). Indeed, since the reauthorisation of the Individuals with Disabilities Education Act in 1997 in the United States functional assessment has been mandatory for some disability categories.

Disruptive behaviour and curricular mismatch

Curricular expectations and instructional practices within the classroom are antecedent events that form a large and important part of any student's school day. A number of these curricular and instructional variables have been shown to be associated with the occurrence of undesirable behaviour (see Conroy & Stichter, 2003; Smith & Iwata, 1997; and Wilder & Carr, 1998 for reviews of the antecedent research literature). A clear functional relationship has been found between disruptive behaviour in the classroom and curricular mismatch. Researchers (Dunlap, Kern-Dunlap, Clarke, & Robbins, 1991; Kern et al., 1994; Lalli, Browder, Mace, & Brown, 1993; Roberts, Marshall, Nelson, & Albers, 2001; Umbreit, 1996) have demonstrated that significantly lower levels of off-task behaviour are observed in no or low-demand situations, with higher levels of off-task behaviour evident in situations with greater task demand. However, merely manipulating the difficulty level of academic content may not always be either appropriate or desirable. Presenting students with easier tasks may be effective in managing escape-maintained behaviour occasioned by task demands, but is unlikely always adequately to address students' educational requirements. As Winett and Winkler (1972) noted over 30 years ago, interventions that aim to remediate the behavioural problems of students may simply reduce the targeted disruptive behaviour and not improve their learning opportunity. While this may make instruction more accessible, undue simplification of academic content may continue to restrict the learning opportunity available. It is important that students are provided with ample opportunity to acquire new skills and expand their behavioural repertoire.

Students may display inappropriate classroom behaviour in order to escape from a task that is within their behavioural repertoire, but which is aversive for other reasons. Research has shown that student preference (Cole & Levinson, 2002; Cooper et al., 1992; Dunlap et al., 1994; Dyer, Dunlap, & Winterling, 1990; Kern et al., 2001), the reinforcement rate for a task (Smith & Iwata, 1997), the requirement that the task be completed in a distracting environment, and the presence of competing activities or competing reinforcement (Munk & Repp, 1994), task duration (Dunlap et al., 1991; Kern et al., 1994), and task sequencing (Horner, Day, Sprauge, O'Brien, & Heathfield, 1991) are all task dimensions that have the potential to impact negatively on student behaviour and academic performance.

Thus in class-based functional assessments, priority should be given to ensuring there is an appropriate match between the curriculum, and instructional materials and methods, and the existing level of students' academic skills with a view to developing effective interventions that target both behavioural and learning needs. Traditional norm-referenced tests are unsuitable for this purpose (Shapiro & Derr, 1987; Shapiro & Eckert, 1993, 1994). However, there have been interesting recent developments in curriculum-based assessment (CBA) procedures which directly link assessment to the curriculum and instruction (Blakenship, 1985; Rathvon, 1997; Shapiro, 1990, 1996; Shapiro & Derr, 1990). CBA consists of a direct evaluation of student performance on materials that are being taught in the classroom, thereby providing a measure of the goodness of fit of instructional expectations and students' performance capability. Roberts et al. (2001) suggested that CBA could usefully be incorporated into functional assessment procedures to assess student performance levels, and simultaneously to generate a hypothesis regarding the function of disruptive behaviour in the classroom.

Review

Moore, Anderson, and Kumar (2003) recently reported a study in which they examined the effects of an instructional adaptation (reduction of task duration) on inappropriate behaviour. The study implemented a functional behavioural assessment which indicated that a student's disruptive behaviour was escape-maintained as well as a curriculum-based assessment which showed appropriate curriculum/performance match. Results of the study indicated that a reduction in task duration was successful in decreasing the participant's level of escape-maintained off-task behaviour during independent work in mathematics, from around 40% to less than 10% of the time without having to alter the curriculum content of the lessons. The intervention did not entail additional, time-consuming forward planning for the teacher, nor did it require significant variation to the daily routine of the classroom. Most importantly it did not involve unnecessary simplification of the academic content or the level of difficulty of daily mathematics lessons for the participating student. Although assessment of the external validity of these findings requires systematic replication, the study demonstrates that curriculum-based assessment can provide a reliable and valid tool to assess the instructional context of problem behaviour and determine the current level of student performance. Incorporating the CBA process into the initial hypothesis development phase of the functional behavioural assessment in a regular classroom lesson added an important dimension to the information gathered. Continued work on the integration of curriculum-based assessment into functional assessment procedures in regular classroom settings is recommended.

References

Ayllon, T., & Michael, J. (1959). The psychiatric nurse as a behavioral engineer. *Journal of the Experimental Analysis of Behavior*, 2, 323–334.

Baer, D. M., Wolf, M. M., & Risley, T. R. (1968). Some current dimensions of applied behavior analysis. *Journal of Applied Behaviour Analysis*, 1, 91–97.

Bain, A., & Macpherson, A. (1990). An examination of the system-wide use of exclusion with disruptive students. *Australia & New Zealand Journal of Developmental Disabilities*, 16, 109–123.

Bandura, A. (1977). *Social Learning Theory.* London: Prentice Hall.

Banks, J. (1995). Integrating children with emotional and behavioural difficulties: The effect on Self-esteem. In P. Farrell (Ed.), *Children with emotional and behavioural difficulties: Strategies for assessment and intervention* (pp. 60–72). London: Falmer Press/Taylor & Francis.

Bear, G. G. (1999). *Interim Alternative Educational Settings: Related Research and Program Considerations* (Information Analysis). Alexandria, VA: National Association of State Directors of Special Education.

Belknap, N., & Mosca, F. J. (1999). *Preparing Teachers for Students with Emotional or Behavioral Disabilities in Professional Development Schools.* EDRS manuscript. ED429039.

Bijou, S. W., Peterson, R. F., & Ault, M. H. (1968). A method to integrate descriptive and experimental field studies at the level of data and empirical concepts. *Journal of Applied Behaviour Analysis*, 1, 175–191.

Blakenship, C. S. (1985). Using curriculum-based assessment data to make instructional decisions. *Exceptional children*, 52, 233–238.

Blechman, E. A. (1996). Coping, competence, and aggression prevention: II. Universal school-based prevention. *Applied & Preventive Psychology*, 5, 19–35.

Broadhead, P. (1998). *Can we let the children play?* Paper presented at the British Education Conference Annual Conference, Belfast, Northern Ireland.

Brondolo, E., Baruch, C., Conway, E., & Marsh, L. (1994). Aggression among inner-city minority youth: A biopsychosocial model for school-based evaluation and treatment. *Journal of Social Distress & the Homeless*, 3, 53–80.

Broussard, C. D., & Northup, J. (1995). An approach to functional assessment and analysis of disruptive behavior in regular education classrooms. *School Psychology Quarterly*, 10, 151–164.

Cantrell, M. L., & Cantrell, R. P. (1985). Assessment of the natural environment. *Education & Treatment of Children*, 8, 275–295.

Carr, J. E. (1977). The motivation of self-injurious behavior: A review of some hypotheses. *Psychological Bulletin*, 84, 800–816.

Carr, J. E. (1994). Emerging themes in the functional analysis of problem behavior. *Journal of Applied Behavior Analysis*, 27, 393–399.

Carr, J. E., Coriaty, S., Wilder, D. A., Gaunt, B. T., Dozier, C. L., Breitton, L. N., Avina, C., & Reed, C. L. (2000). A review of 'noncontingent' reinforcement as treatment for the aberrant behavior of individuals with developmental disabilities. *Research in Developmental Disabilities*, 21, 377–391.

Carr, J. E., Levin, L., McConnachie, G., Carlson, J.I., Kemp, D.C. & Smith, C.E. (1994). *Communication-based Intervention for Problem Behavior: A user's guide for producing positive change*. Baltimore: Brookes Publishing.

Cassidy, J., & Asher, S.R. (1992). Loneliness and peer relations in young children. *Child Development*, 63, 350–365.

Chazan, M., Laing, A. F., & Davies, D. (1994). *Emotional and Behavioural Difficulties in Middle Childhood: Identification, assessment and intervention in school*. London: Falmer Press/Taylor & Francis.

Church, J. (1996). *The prevalence of children with behaviour disorders in Canterbury primary schools* (Research Report 96–1). Canterbury: Education Department, University of Canterbury.

Cole, C. L., & Levinson, T. R. (2002). Effects of within-activity choices on the challenging behaviour of children with severe developmental disabilities. *Journal of Positive Behavior Interventions*, 4, 29–38.

Cone, J. D. (1997). Issues in functional analysis in behavioral assessment. *Behavior Research and Therapy*, 35, 259–275.

Conroy, M., Fox, J., Crain, L., Jenkins, A. & Belcher, K. (1996). Evaluating the social and ecological validity of analog assessment procedures for challenging behaviors in young children. *Education and Treatment of Children*, 19, 233–256.

Conroy, M. A., & Stichter, J. P. (2003). The application of antecedents in the functional assessment process: Existing research, issues, and recommendations. *The Journal of Special Education*, 37, 15–25.

Cooper, L. J., Wacker, D. P., Thursby, D. L. P., Harding, J., Millard, T., & Derby, M. (1992). Analysis of the effects of task preferences, task demands, and adult attention on child behavior in outpatient and classroom settings. *Journal of Applied Behavior Analysis*, 25, 823–840.

Corrie, L. (1997). The interaction between teacher knowledge and skills when managing troublesome classroom behaviour. *Cambridge Journal of Education*, 27, 93–105.

Derby, M., Wacker, D. P., Sasso, G. M., Steege, M., Northup, J., Cigrand, K., & Asmus, J. M. (1992). Brief functional assessment techniques to evaluate aberrant behavior in an outpatient setting: A summary of 79 cases. *Journal of Applied Behavior Analysis*, 25, 713–721.

Desrochers, M.N., Hile, M.G. & Williams-Moseley, T.L. (1997). Survey of functional assessment procedures used with individuals who display mental retardation and severe problem behaviors. *American Journal on Mental Retardation*, 101, 535–546.

Dunlap, G., dePerczel, M., Clarke, S., Wilson, D., Wright, S., White, R., & Gomez, A. (1994). Choice making to promote adaptive behavior for students with emotional and behavioral difficulties. *Journal of Applied Behavior Analysis*, 27, 505–518.

Dunlap, G., Kern, L., dePerczel, M., Clarke, S., Wilson, D., Childs, K.E., White, R. & Falk, G.D. (1993). Functional analysis of classroom variables for students with emotional and behavioral disorders. *Behavioral Disorders*, 18, 275–291.

Dunlap, G., Kern-Dunlap, L., Clarke, S., & Robbins, F. R. (1991). Functional assessment, curricular revision, and severe behavior problems. *Journal of Applied Behavior Analysis*, 24, 387–397.

Durand, V. M. (1990). *Severe behavior problems: A functional communication training approach.* New York: Guilford.

Durand, V. M., & Carr, E. G. (1991). Functional communication training to reduce challenging behavior: Maintenance and application in new settings. *Journal of Applied Behavior Analysis*, 24, 251–264.

Dyer, K., Dunlap, G., & Winterling, V. (1990). Effects of choice making on the serious problem behaviors of students with severe handicaps. *Journal of Applied Behavior Analysis*, 23, 515–524.

Eber, L., Nelson, C. M., & Miles, P. (1997). School-based wraparound for students with emotional and behavioural challenges. *Exceptional Children*, 63, 539–555.

Elliott, S. N. (1988). Acceptability of behavioral treatments: Review of variables that influence treatment selection. *Professional Psychology – Research and Practice*, 19, 68–80.

Elliott, S. N., Witt, J. C., Galvin, G. A., & Peterson, R. (1984). Acceptability of positive and reductive behavioral interventions: Factors that influence teachers' decisions. *Journal of School Psychology*, 22, 353–360.

Ellis, J., & Magee, S. K. (1999). Determination of environmental correlates of disruptive classroom behavior: Integration of functional analysis into public school assessment process. *Education & Treatment of Children*, 22, 291–316.

Ervin, R.A., DuPaul, G.J., Kern, L. & Friman, P.C. (1998). Classroom-based functional and adjunctive assessments: Proactive approaches to intervention selection for adolescents with Attention Deficit Hyperactivity Disorder. *Journal of Applied Behavior Analysis*, 31, 65–78.

Farmer, T. W., Farmer, E. M. Z., & Gut, D. M. (1999) Implications of social development research for school-based interventions for aggressive youth with EBD. *Journal of Emotional and Behavioral Disorders*, 7, 130–136.

Farrell, P. (Ed.). (1995). *Children with Emotional and Behavioural Difficulties: Strategies for assessment and intervention.* London: Falmer Press/Taylor & Francis.

Ferster, C. B. (1961). Positive reinforcement and behavioral deficits of young children. *Child Development*, 32, 437–456.

Fields, B. A. (1986). The nature and incidence of classroom behaviour problems and their remediation through preventive management. *Behaviour Change*, 3, 53–57.

Fisher, J.B., Schumaker, J.B., & Deshler, D.D. (1995). Searching for validated inclusive practices. *Focus on Exceptional Children*, 28, 1–20.

Forness, S.R., Kavale, K.A., Blum, I.M., & Lloyd, J. (1997). Mega-analysis of meta-analysis. What works in special education and related services. *Teaching Exceptional Children*, 29, 4–9.

Foster-Johnson, L. & Dunlap, G. (1993). Using functional assessment to develop effective, individualized interventions for challenging behaviors. *Teaching Exceptional Children*, 25, 44–50.

Fowler, R. C. & Schnacker, L. E. (1994). The changing character of behavioral assessment and treatment: An historical introduction and review of functional analysis research. *Diagnostique*, 19, 79–102.

Fox, J. D., & Stinnett, T. A. (1996). The effects of labeling bias on prognostic outlook for children as a function of diagnostic label and profession. *Psychology in the Schools*, 33, 143–152.

Gable, R.A. (1996). A critical analysis of functional assessment: Issues for researchers and practitioners. *Behavioral Disorders*, 22, 36–40.

Glynn, T. (1982). Antecedent control of behaviour in educational contexts. *Educational Psychology*, 2, 215–229.

Goldstein, A. P. (1999). Aggression reduction strategies: Effective and ineffective. *School Psychology Quarterly*, 14, 40–58.

Grimshaw, R. (1995). Placement and progress in residential special schools for children with emotional and behavioural difficulties. In P. Farrell (Ed.), *Children with Emotional and Behavioural Difficulties: Strategies for assessment and intervention.* (p 73–86). London: Falmer Press/Taylor & Francis.

Harris, P. (1993). The nature and extent of aggressive behaviour amongst people with learning difficulties (mental handicap) in a single health district. *Journal of Intellectual Disability Research*, 37, 221–242.

Hasazi, J. E. & Hasazi, S. E. (1972). Effects of teacher attention on digit-reversal behavior in an elementary school child. *Journal of Applied Behavior Analysis*, 5, 157–162.

Hawe, E., Tuck, B., Manthei, R., Adair, V., & Moore, D. W. (2000). Job satisfaction and stress in New Zealand primary teachers. *New Zealand Journal of Educational Studies*, 35, 193–205.

Hawkins, R. P., Peterson, R. F., & Schweid, E. (1966). Behavior therapy in the home: Amelioration of problem parent-child relations with the parent in a therapeutic role. *Journal of Experimental Child Psychology, 4,* 99–107.

Horner, R.H. (1994). Functional assessment: Contributions and future directions. *Journal of Applied Behavior Analysis, 27,* 401–404.

Horner, R.H. & Carr, J. E. (1997). Behavioral support for students with severe disabilities: Functional assessment and comprehensive intervention. *The Journal of Special Education, 31,* 84–104.

Horner, R. H., Day, M. H., Sprauge, J. R., O'Brien, M., & Heathfield, L. T. (1991). Interspersed requests: A nonaversive procedure for reducing aggression and self-injury during instruction. *Journal of Applied Behavior Analysis, 24,* 265–278.

Hosp, J. L., & Reschly, D. J. (2003). Referral rates for intervention or assessment: A meta-analysis of racial differences. *Journal of Special Education, 37,* 67–80.

Hudley, C., & Graham, S. (1995). School-based interventions for aggressive African-American boys. *Applied & Preventive Psychology, 4,* 185–195.

Indiana State Dept. of Education, (1988). *Module for Training Paraprofessionals Working in Classrooms for Students with Emotional Handicaps.*

Iwata, B.A., Dorsey, M.F., Slifer, K.J., Bauman, K.E. & Richman, G.S. (1982). Toward a functional analysis of self-injury. *Analysis and Intervention in Developmental Disabilities, 2,* 3–20.

Kern, L., Childs, K.E., Dunlap, G., Clarke, S. & Falk, G.D. (1994). Using assessment-based curricular intervention to improve the classroom behavior of a student with emotional and behavioral challenges. *Journal of Applied Behavior Analysis, 27,* 7–19.

Kern, L., Delaney, B., Clarke, S., Dunlap, G., & Childs, K. E. (2001). Improving the classroom behaviour of students with emotional and behavioural disorders using individualised curricular modifications. *Journal of Emotional and Behavioral Disorders, 9,* 239–247.

King-Sears, M.E. (1997). Best academic practices for inclusive classrooms. Focus on *Exceptional Children, 29,* 1–22.

Kryzanowski, E. (1992). *Youth with severe behaviour disorders: A literature review and survey results.* (89p). Edmonton: Learning Resources Distributing Centre.

Lalli, J. S., Browder, D. M., Mace, F. C., & Brown, D. K. (1993). Teacher use of descriptive analysis data to implement interventions to decrease students' problem behaviors. *Journal of Applied Behavior Analysis, 26,* 227–238.

Levine-Brown, L. S. (1993). *Pre-Crisis Intervention Strategies for Reducing Unacceptable Behaviors by Exceptional Students in a Public Elementary School.* Unpublished Ed.D. Practicum Report, Nova University.

Lewin, K. (Ed.). (1952). *Field Theory in Social Science.* London: Tavistock.

Lewis, T. J., & Sugai, G. (1996a). Descriptive and experimental analysis of teacher and peer attention and the use of assessment-based intervention to improve prosocial behaviour. *Journal of Behavioral Education, 6,* 7–24.

Lewis, T. J. & Sugai, G. (1996b). Functional assessment of problem behavior: A pilot investigation of the comparative and interactive effects of teacher and peer social attention on students in general education settings. *School Psychology Quarterly*, 11, 1–19.

Little, E., & Hudson, A. (1998). Conduct problems and treatment across home and school: A review of the literature. *Behaviour Change*, 15, 213–227.

Lovaas, O. I; Freitag, G., Gold, V. J., & Kassorla, I. C. (1965). Recording apparatus and procedure for observation of behaviors of children in free play settings. *Journal of Experimental Child Psychology*, 2, 108–120.

Mace, F.C. (1994). The significance and future of functional analysis methodologies. *Journal of Applied Behavior Analysis*, 27, 385–392.

Mace, F.C. & Lalli, J.S. (1991). Linking descriptive and experimental analyses in the treatment of bizarre speech. *Journal of Applied Behavior Analysis*, 24, 553–562.

Mace, F.C., Lalli, J.S., Lalli, E.P. & Shea, M.C. (1993). *Functional analysis and treatment of aberrant behavior.* In R. Van Houten & S. Axelrod (Eds.), Behavior Analysis and Treatment (pp. 75–95). New York: Plenum Press.

Macmillan, D. L., Gresham, F. M., Lopez, M. F., & Bocian, K. M. (1996). Comparison of students nominated for prereferral interventions by ethnicity and gender. *Journal of Special Education*, 30, 133–151.

Malecki, C. K., & Elliott, S. N. (2002). Children's social behaviors as predictors of academic achievement: A longitudinal analysis. *School Psychology Quarterly*, 17, 1–23.

Marthur, S. R., Kavale, K. A., Quinn, M. M., Forness, S. R., & Rutherford, R. B. Jr. (1998). Social skills interventions with students with emotional and behavioral problems: A quantitative synthesis of single-subject research. *Behavioral Disorders*, 23, 193–201.

Meyer, K. A., (1999). Functional analysis and the treatment of problem behaviour exhibited by elementary school children. *Journal of Applied Behavior Analysis*, 32, 229–232.

Merrett, F., & Wheldall, K. (1993). How do teachers learn to manage classroom behaviour? A study of teachers' opinions about their initial training with special reference to classroom behavior management. *Educational Studies*, 19, 91–106.

Mildon, R., Moore, D. W., & Dixon, R.S. (2003). Combining noncontingent escape and functional communication training as a treatment for negatively reinforced disruptive behaviour. *Journal of Positive Behavior Interventions, in press, anticipated publication: 6, (1)*

Miller, A. (1995). Teachers' attributions of causality, control and responsibility in respect of difficult pupil behaviour and its successful management. *Educational Psychology*, 15, 457–471.

Moore, D. W., Anderson, A., & Kumar, K. (2003). *Inclusive Instruction: Considering Behaviour Function and Instructional Match in Meeting a Student's Behaviour and Learning Needs.* Paper Presented at annual AACBT National Conference, Adelaide, September.

Munk, D. D., & Repp, A. C. (1994). The relationship between instructional variables and problem behavior: A review. *Exceptional Children*, 60, 390–401.

Murray, B. A., & Myers, M. A. (1998). Avoiding the special education trap for conduct disordered students. *NASSP Bulletin*, 82(594), 65–73.

Northup, J., Wacker, D. P., Berg, W. K., Kelly, L., Sasso, G. & DeRaad, A. (1994). The treatment of severe behavior problems in school settings using a technical assistance model. *Journal of Applied Behavior Analysis*, 27, 33–47.

Peagam, E., (1995). Emotional and behavioural difficulties: The primary school experience. In P. Farrell (Ed.). *Children with emotional and behavioural difficulties: Strategies for assessment and intervention.* (pp 32–44). London : Falmer Press/Taylor & Francis.

Pepler, D. J., & Craig, W. M. (1995). A peek behind the fence: Naturalistic observations of aggressive children with remote audiovisual recording. *Developmental Psychology*, 31, 548–553.

Pisecco, S., Huzinec, C., & Curtis, D. (2001). The effect of child characteristics on teachers' acceptability of classroom-based behavioural strategies and psychostimulant medication for the treatment of ADHD. *Journal of Clinical Child Psychology*, 30, 413–421.

Power, T. J., Hess, L. E., & Bennet, D. S. (1995). The acceptability of interventions for attention deficit hyperactivity disorder among elementary and middle school teachers. *Developmental and Behavioral Paediatrics*, 16, 238–243.

Pring, T. (2004). *Evidence Based Practice in Education.* Maidenhead: Open University Press.

Prinz, R. J., Blechman, E. A., & Dumas, J. E. (1994). An evaluation of peer coping-skills training for childhood aggression. *Journal of Clinical Child Psychology*, 23, 193–203.

Quinn, M. M., Kavale, K. A., Marthur, S. R., Rutherford, R. B. Jr., & Forness, S. R., (1999). A meta-analysis of social skill interventions for students with emotional or behavioral disorders. *Journal of Emotional and Behavioral Disorders*, 7, 54–64.

Rathvon, N. (1997). *Effective School Interventions.* New York: Guilford Press.

Repp, A. (1994). Comments on functional analysis procedures for school-based behavior problems. *Journal of Applied Behavior Analysis*, 27, 409–411.

Repp, A.C. & Karsh, K.G. (1994). Hypothesis-based interventions for tantrum behaviors of persons with developmental disabilities in school settings. *Journal of Applied Behavior Analysis*, 27, 21–31.

Roberts, L. M., Marshall, J., Nelson, R., & Albers, C. A. (2001). Curriculum-based assessment procedures embedded within functional behavioral assessments:

Identifying escape-motivated behaviors in a general education classroom. *School Psychology Review*, 30, 264–272.

Rosenberg, M. S. (1986). Maximizing the effectiveness of structured classroom management programs: Implementing rule-review procedures with disruptive and distractible students. *Behavioral Disorders*, 11, 239–248.

Rutherford, R. B., & DiGangi, S. A. E. (1991). Severe Behavior Disorders of Children and Youth. Monograph in *Behavioral Disorders*, 13, EDRS, ED331220

Rutherford, R. B., & Mathur, S. R. E. (1993). Severe Behavior Disorders of Children and Youth. Monograph in *Behavioral Disorders*, 16, EDRS, ED370301

Sasso, G. M, Conroy, M. A., Stichter, J. P., & Fox, J. J. (2001). Slowing down the bandwagon: The misapplication of functional assessment for students with emotional or behavioral disorders. *Behavioral Disorders*, 26, 282–296.

Sasso, G. M., Harrell, L.G., & Doelling, J. E. (1997). Functional assessment and treatment of problematic behavior. In P. Zionts, (Ed.). *Inclusion Strategies for Students with Learning and Behavior Problems: Perspectives, experiences, and best practices.* EDRS, ED406802 (pp. 197–227).

Sasso, G. M., Reimers, T. M., Cooper, L. J., Wacker, D., Berg, W., Steege, M., Kelly, L. & Allaire, A. (1992). Use of descriptive and experimental analyses to identify the functional properties of aberrant behavior in school settings. *Journal of Applied Behavior Analysis*, 25, 809–821.

Schill, M. T., Kratochwill, T. R., & Gardner, W. I. (1996). Conducting a functional analysis of behavior. In M. J. Breen & C. R. Fielder (Eds.), *Behavioral Approach to Assessment of Youth with Emotional/Behavioral Disorders.* Austin, Texas: Pro-Ed.

Shapiro, E. S. (1990). An integrated model for curriculum-based assessment. *School Psychology Review*, 19, 331–350.

Shapiro, E. S. (1996). *Academic Skills Problems: Direct assessment and intervention.* New York: Guilford Press.

Shapiro, E. S., & Derr, T. F. (1987). An examination of overlap between reading curricula and standardized achievement tests. *The Journal of Special Education*, 21, 59–67.

Shapiro, E. S., & Derr, T. F. (Eds.). (1990). *Curriculum-based Assessment, 2nd ed.* New York: Wiley.

Shapiro, E. S., & Eckert, T. L. (1993). Curriculum-based assessment among school psychologists: Knowledge, use, and attitudes. *The Journal of School Psychology*, 31, 375–384.

Shapiro, E. S., & Eckert, T. L. (1994). Acceptability of curriculum-based assessment by school psychologists. *Journal of School Psychology*, 32, 167–183.

Shapiro, E. S. & Kratochwill, T. R. (2000). *Behavioral Assessment in Schools, 2nd ed.* New York: Guilford Press.

Shatz, E. (1994). Programs for behaviourally disordered children and youth. *SSTA Research Centre Report #94–08.*

Skiba, R., Waldron, N., Bahamonde, C. & Michalek, D. (1998). A four-step model for functional behavior assessment. *Communique*, 26, 24–35.

Skinner, B. F. (1953). *Science and Human Behaviour.* New York: The Free Press.

Smith, R. G., & Iwata, B. A. (1997). Antecedent influences on behavioral disorders. *Journal of Applied Behavior Analysis*, 30, 343–375.

Solnit, A. J., Adnopoz, J., Saxe, L., Gardner, J., & Fallon, T. (1997). Evaluating systems of care for children: Utility of the clinical case conference. *American Journal of Orthopsychiatry*, 67, 554–567.

Sterling-Turner, H. E., Robinson, S. L., & Wilczynski, S. W. (2001). Functional assessment of distracting and disruptive behaviors in the school setting. *School Psychology Review*, 30, 211–220.

Storey, K., Lawry, J.R., Ashworth, R., Danko, C.D. & Strain, P.S. (1994). Functional analysis and intervention for disruptive behaviors of a kindergarten student. *Journal of Educational Research*, 87, 361–370.

Swan, W. W., Brown, C. L., & Jacob, R. T. (1987). Types of service delivery models used in the reintegration of severely emotionally disturbed/ behaviorally disordered students. *Behavioral Disorders*, 12, 99–103.

Tainsh, M. E., & Izard, J. E. (1994). *Widening Horizons: New Challenges, Directions and Achievements*. Selected Papers from the 6th National Conference on Behaviour Management and Behaviour Change of Children and Youth with Emotional and/or Behaviour Problems, Adelaide, South Australia.

Taylor, J.C. (1994). Functional assessment and functionally-derived treatment for child behavior problems. *Special Services in the Schools*, 9, 39–67.

Thomas, B. H., Byrne, C., Offord, D. R., & Boyle, M. H. (1991). Prevalence of behavioural symptoms and the relationship of child, parent, and family variables in 4- and 5-year-olds: Results from the Ontario Child Health Study. *Journal of Developmental & Behavioral Pediatrics*, 12, 177–184.

Tobin, T. J., & Sugai, G. M. (1999). Using sixth-grade school records to predict school violence, chronic discipline problems, and high school outcomes. *Journal of Emotional & Behavioral Disorders*, 7, 40–53.

Umbreit, J. (1995). Functional assessment and intervention in a regular classroom setting for the disruptive behavior of a student with Attention Deficit Hyperactivity Disorder. *Behavioral Disorders*, 20, 267–278.

Umbreit, J. (1996). Functional analysis of disruptive behavior in an inclusive classroom. *Journal of Early Intervention*, 20, 18–29.

Vaughn, S., Gersten, R., & Chard, D. J. (2000). The underlying message in LD intervention research: Findings from research syntheses. *Exceptional Children*, 67, 99–114.

Vygotsky, L. S. (1993). *The Collected Works of L. S. Vygotsky* (J. E. Knox & C. B. Stevens trans.) (Vol. 2). New York: Plenum Press.

Wahler, R. G., Winkel, G. H., Peterson, R. F., & Morrison, D. C. (1965). Mothers as behavior therapists for their own children. *Behaviour Research & Therapy.* 3, 113–124.

Walker, H. M., Horner, R. H., Sugai, G., Bullis, M., Sprague, J. R., Bricker, D., & Kaufman, M. J. (1996). Integrated approaches to preventing antisocial behavior patterns among school-age children and youth. *Journal of Emotional & Behavioral Disorders,* 4, 194–209.

Watson, T. S., Ray, K. P., Turner, H. S., & Logan, P. (1999). Teacher-implemented functional analysis and treatment: A method for linking assessment to intervention. *School Psychology Review,* 28, 292–302.

Watson, T. S., & Steege, M. W. (2003). *Conducting School-based Functional Behavioral Assessments: A Practitioner's Guide.* New York: The Guilford Press.

Wearmouth, J. (1999). Another one flew over: 'Maladjusted' Jack's perception of his label. *British Journal of Special Education,* 26, 15–22.

Webster-Stratton, C. (1993). Strategies for helping early school-aged children with oppositional defiant and conduct disorders: The importance of home-school partnerships. *School Psychology Review,* 22, 437–457.

Wentzel, K. R. (1993). Does being good make the grade? Social behavior and academic competence in middle school. *Journal of Educational Psychology,* 85, 357–64.

Whelan, R. J. E. (1998). *Emotional and Behavioral Disorders: A 25-year-focus.* Denver, Colorado: Love Publishing.

Wheldall, K. (1982). Behavioural pedagogy or behavioral overkill? *Educational Psychology,* 2, 181–184.

Wheeler, N. S. (1999). *Troubled Students and Schools.* Paper presented at the Summit of Education, Nashville, TN, June.

Wilder, D. A., & Carr, J. E. (1998). Recent advances in the modification of establishing operations to reduce aberrant behavior. *Behavioral Interventions,* 13, 43–59.

Williams, C. D. (1959). Case report: The elimination of tantrum behaviour by extinction procedures. *Journal of Abnormal and Social Psychology,* 59, 269.

Wilson, D. B., Gottfredson, D. C., & Nahaka, S. S. (2001). School-based prevention of problem behaviors: A meta-analysis. *Journal of Quantitative Criminology,* 17, 247–272.

Winett, R. A., & Winkler, R. C. (1972). Current behavior modification in the classroom: Be still, be quiet, be docile. *Journal of Applied Behavior Analysis,* 5, 499–504.

Younkin, W., & Blasik, K. (1992). *Behavior Change Program: A Successful Approach to Changing the Behavior of Disruptive Elementary Students; Program Evaluation.* EDRS, ED362313

Ysseldyke, J. E., & Christenson, S. L. (1987). Evaluating students' instructional environments. *Rase: Remedial & Special Education,* 8, 17–24.

Ysseldyke, J. E., Thurlow, M. L., Christenson, S. L., & Muyskens, P. (1991). Classroom and home learning differences between students labeled as educable mentally retarded and their peers. *Education and Training in Mental Retardation*, 26, 3–7.

Zima, B. T., Forness, S. R., Bussing, R., & Benjamin, B. (1998). Homeless children in emergency shelters – need for prereferral intervention and potential eligibility for special education. *Behavioral Disorders*, 23, 98–110.

Chapter 19

An introduction to multi-element planning for primary aged children

Mick Pitchford

Introduction

Over a number of years Derby City Educational Psychology Service (EPS) in England has developed and disseminated the use of Multi-Element Plans. Design and development of effective individual intervention programmes in schools to address children's behaviour that is problematic in some respect requires detailed assessment of the child and the learning environment. It also requires awareness of ethical considerations. This chapter outlines the practice of multi-element planning for primary aged children and provides a framework based on clear behavioural principles (Glynn, 1982; Wheldall, 1982) and the discipline of applied behaviour analysis (Kazdin, 1975; Grant and Evans, 1994) within which account can be taken of:

- potential causes of the problems experienced by the child
- factors that appear to maintain behaviour seen as problematic
- a range of strategies related to the learning environment, the development of skills that will be useful to the child, and intervention that will prevent the recurrence of the problematic behaviour or provide a way of safeguarding the child, peers and staff when the behaviour does recur.

The principles of Multi-Element Plans

Managing or changing the behaviour of individuals is fraught with ethical questions. The chief of these are:

- What gives us the right to manipulate or change someone's behaviour?
- How certain are we that the problem behaviour is not a perfectly reasonable response to unreasonable circumstances?
- If we do intervene, how ethically sound are our techniques and what is their record of effectiveness (Cooper, Heron and Heward, 1987; Grant and Evans, 1994)?

Therefore our actions and the technology we use have to be guided by the following principles (LaVigna and Donnellan, 1986):

- A commitment to improving the child's quality of life:
  If we can show that the problems the child is causing or encountering is detrimental to his/her quality of life and that our attempts to intervene are intended to improve it we are on much safer ground than if we are merely trying to stop the child doing something because they are troublesome to the school or family. This should be the litmus test we apply when considering the content of Individual Education Plans or Pastoral Support Plans that we write for students who experience difficulties in learning or whose behaviour is challenging, in order to focus, co-ordinate and monitor the efforts of family and professionals. Will the successful implementation of this plan lead to a happier more fulfilled life for this child?
- Do no harm:
  However effective or ineffective the recommendations we make turn out to be, at a minimum we should do no harm. This in turn leads to three imperatives.

  1 Firstly, in our analysis of the child and his/her problems we need to examine in detail the effect on them of his/her personal, physical and instructional environments. It may be that these environments, not the child, need changing (for example removal of abuse or bullying from the child's environment or improvements in instruction to remove frequent failure in the child's life).

  2 Secondly, we need a commitment to a careful assessment of the child in order to understand why they are doing what they are doing. In this way we show respect for the child and their predicament and have a much better chance of designing programmes that meet their needs rather than simply imposing programmes designed to meet institutional needs.

3 Finally, we should not build a plan that uses punishment. Although punishment can be 'effective' in the short term (if by that we mean 'stopping troublesome behaviour for a limited period of time') in the long term it may be ineffective, unnecessary, unethical, and has a number of negative side effects that make its use dangerous. As long ago as 1975 Kazdin noted that, even though punishment may eliminate the target behaviour, it might result in other consequences which are problematic in their own right or even worse than the original behaviour (Kazdin, 1975). These side effects include such dangers as punishment-elicited aggression (the child fights back), imitation (the child becomes more punitive towards others in his or her environment), inhibition of learning (the child is less likely to learn because of increased levels of stress and anxiety arising from the use of punishment), absconding (the child either physically or mentally removes her/himself from situations s/he associates with punishment).

• The right to effective support:
  If we have decided to intervene, have established that to do so would improve the child's quality of life and believe that we understand the child, the next requirement is to use a range of techniques whose effectiveness has been demonstrated clearly. Given the complexity of possible causes for the child's problems (for example, history of learning, history of reinforcement, impact of environments that do not match developmental needs) and the fact that it has probably developed and been maintained by a number of factors, it follows that we need to draw up an Individual Education Plan or Pastoral Support Plan that comprises a comprehensive multi-element plan (MEP) addressing all of these issues if we are to have a good chance of success. The MEP should have four main components:

  • **Ecological strategies**
  • **Positive programming**
  • **Preventive strategies**
  • **Reactive strategies.**

This four-part model is comprehensively described in LaVigna and Donnellan (1986). In the sections that follow each of these is considered in more detail.

Ecological strategies

Based on our assessment of the child we need to consider whether there are features of his or her environment that are contributing directly or indirectly to the behaviour problems we are encountering. In particular we need to examine whether there are mismatches between the child and his/her environment that require a change in the environment, not a change in the child. Change strategies should be considered under a number of subheadings: interpersonal environment, physical environment and instructional environment.

Interpersonal environment

At the most extreme an ecological strategy could involve the removal of a child from settings in which they were suffering physical, sexual or emotional abuse. In less extreme circumstances it might involved the use of a 'Circle Time' (Mosley, 1998) to increase the level of informal support he or she receives from peers.

Physical environment

An obvious example here would be changing the physical environment so that a child with sensory difficulties had better access to the curriculum. Other examples might include moving a child so they have easier informal contact with the teacher or a 'chill out' area where they can go unobtrusively to calm down or engage in less demanding work, subject to the teacher's agreement.

Instructional environment

The frequency of both positive feedback about a child's success or negative feedback about failure in class affects behaviour. If failure and negative feedback occur regularly, we might consider what can be done to differentiate the work so the child starts to experience frequent positive feedback about their success in class.

Positive programming

Positive programming involves teaching children skills that will have a positive impact on their lives. Our assumption is that learning is empowering, gives dignity to the individual, helps them get their needs met and helps them cope with an imperfect world. There are three areas of skill development that should be addressed: general, functionally equivalent and coping.

General skill development

There may be academic or life skills that the child has not mastered that are having a negative impact on his/her quality of life. For example, the major means of getting teacher approval and status in the classroom is through written work. If the child has problems in this area or with spelling then s/he is less likely to attract teacher approval and respect from peers than if s/he can produce written work to an acceptable standard. Similar considerations also apply in those parts of the curriculum that rely on a basic level of numeracy.

Functionally equivalent skills

No matter how strange, behaviour always has a purpose or a function (LaVigna and Donnellan, op. cit.). If we understand that purpose or function we are more likely to be able to channel it in a constructive way.

Behaviour often serves these functions:

- Stimulation or excitement
  The child is bored.He finds if he makes silly noises then his friends laugh. This is exciting and so is the teacher's reaction.
- Initiate social contact (attention seeking)
  The child finds that if she shouts out the teacher will usually give her attention.
- Escape or avoid situations
  The child has a history of failure in maths and discovers that if he throws things during maths he will be taken out of the lesson and so avoids doing maths.
- Obtain things or events
  The child has no friends and doesn't know how to share. He finds he can get sweets and toys off younger children if he uses violence or intimidation.
- Express emotion and reduce stress
  The child doesn't know how to defuse stress and simply feels better after a tantrum (many adults do too).

Below are some examples of problem behaviours, their functions together with the functionally equivalent skills that could be included in a multi-element plan to help the child achieve the same end.

Problem	Function	Functionally equivalent skill
Shouting out	Initiate social contact	Teach hand up and waiting quietly. Teach hand up and saying 'Excuse me Miss I've finished my work.'
Aggression (bullying)	Obtain things or events (e.g. children are made to share or give sweets unwillingly)	Teach play skills, turn-taking skills and negotiation skills.

Tantrums	Express emotion	Teach child to express emotions in writing or art or small world play.
Tantrums	Avoid situations (e.g. repeated failure in maths)	Teach key maths skills. Teach how to ask for help.
Makes silly noises	To gain excitement (children laugh)	Teach child • how to tell jokes • right and wrong time and place to tell jokes.

If the teacher teaches the child the functionally equivalent skill the child is less likely to resort to the problem behaviour because he or she can achieve the same end in a more acceptable way that will not result in trouble. Ethically this is far superior to simply suppressing behaviour through the use of punishment or sanctions.

Coping skills

Although we are committed to improving the environment of children so that they are less likely to resort to problem behaviour as a result of a mismatch between themselves and the environment, we have to recognise that they will have to cope with an imperfect world. Consequently we may need to teach the child a range of coping skills designed to help them manage and tolerate the frustrations and difficulties in their lives. For example, if a child is having tantrums as a result of teasing from peers it is important to do what we can to remove teasing from the environment. But we would also have to teach the child ways of coping with teasing on the grounds that we are unlikely to eliminate teasing entirely. Consequently we might teach the child how to use assertive statements in such situations. When including coping skills we have to be judicious. We might need to be certain the child should be expected to cope with this situation and that we have intervened to alter the environment as much as we can and that the coping skill is safe. For example, an assertive statement to a teasing peer in school might be safe in a way that an assertive statement to someone who is bigger and older out in the wider community might not be.

Other types of coping skills can include teaching children to cope with tasks in which they have a history of failure through the use of progressive relaxation and desensitisation.

Preventive strategies

There are two types of preventive strategy, the antecedent control strategy and the use of reward strategies (LaVigna and Donnellan, op. cit.).

Antecedent control strategies

The concept behind antecedent control strategies involves removing those events that act as a direct trigger to problem behaviours (Glynn, 1982). It is best illustrated by using examples as follows:

Antecedent and problem behaviour	Antecedent control strategy
When shouted at the child has tantrums	Don't shout at the child
If teacher refuses to open the door to let a child with severe learning difficulties leave the room, child bangs her head frequently and severely	Open the door for the child and provide supervision outside classroom
If the child makes more than five errors in his work and this is pointed out to him by teachers he refuses to do any further work	Give work where he is unlikely to make five errors
When the classroom gets noisy a child with Autism becomes distressed and difficult to manage and ultimately aggressive	Keep the classroom quiet or identify those lessons where noise is likely and make alternative arrangements, or agree a privately understood signal so the child can leave classroom and continue work somewhere quiet
When x happens the child exhibits problem behaviour y	Make sure x doesn't happen

Antecedent control can be highly effective but can only be a short-term expedient and so should always be used in conjunction with ecological and coping strategies. In all of the cases above we would want to change the environment to make sure that it was not putting unreasonable demands on the child. That said, however, if the child does not learn to cope with the rough as well as the smooth in life then his/her access to a whole range of activities and opportunities will be diminished along with their quality of life. We do not like going to the dentist, but for the sake of our teeth and quality of life (absence of pain) we have to learn to cope with it. Therefore we would also want to increase the child's ability to cope: in the instances above, with people who shout, with not being allowed out of the classroom, with failure and with noisy surroundings. Usually a combination of social skills (for example learning how to ask for help or a break) and desensitisation can accomplish this so that in the long run we can dispense with the antecedent control strategy.

Reward strategies

In the author's experience, the most commonly used strategy for tackling behaviour problems is the use of rewards. Reward strategies only work well when they are used in combination with the types of positive programming and ecological strategies described earlier. Rewards are artificial, the teacher will not always be there to reward the child, and since our aim is to teach the child to be independent, rewards can only be a short-term expedient. In particular, reward strategies are most effective when they run alongside the teaching of functionally equivalent skills.

From a behavioural perspective, basically there are three ways of rewarding children (LaVigna and Donnellan, op. cit.):

1 Rewarding children for being 'good'
2 Rewarding children for not being 'naughty'
3 Rewarding children for being 'naughty' less often than they were before.

1. Rewarding the child for being 'good' (Differential Reinforcement of an Alternative Response, Alt R)

To use this approach we need to know how often or how long the behaviour that we want to increase is happening on average. We need information from three different days. If our review of your records does not elicit the information, we need to get the teacher to collect the information using one of the charts illustrated in section two. We then have to make a judgement about what standard the child will have to meet to earn the reward. If the child only finishes work on average three times a day we might set the level at anything over that number. If the child only stays in his/her seat for five minutes on average in any one hour we might set the reward at anything over five minutes. The problem we will have in setting the level is of setting challenging but realistic standards. Unfortunately, unlike the other strategies we will discuss, there are no hard and fast guidelines to help us and this is partly why this technique can be tricky to use.

Another problem we may have with this approach is that it is difficult sometimes to monitor the behaviour. For example, a teacher would be hard-pressed to perform her duties and monitor the child staying in his seat to see whether or not s/he had met the standard set.

This approach is best used when teachers are trying to encourage new behaviour that the child can do but is not very good at or is not very enthusiastic about. Here are some examples:

Every time Inderjit finishes a piece of work she gets a star.

If John gets home on time after school his mother gives him his favourite pudding.

SUMMARY OF REWARD TECHNIQUES			
Technique	**Technical name**	**Advantages**	**Disadvantages**
Rewarding children for being 'good'	Differential Reinforcement of an **Al**ternative **R**esponse (Alt R)	Socially positive. Easily explained. Good for encouraging new positive behaviour.	Technically the most difficult to have success with. May have no effect on misbehaviour.
Rewarding children for not being 'naughty'	**D**ifferential **R**einforcement of the **O**mission of a Response (DRO)	Fairly easy to explain. Can result in rapid and dramatic reductions in behaviour problems if well designed. With some modifications the **most effective reward technique for severe and challenging behaviour.**	Can appear negative so should always be counterbalanced by positive programming that is teaching the child positive alternatives to problem behaviour. Need to have baseline information which tells you the **average time between episodes** of the problem behaviour.
Rewarding children for being 'naughty' less and less often	**D**ifferential **R**einforcement of **L**ower Rates of Responding (DRL)	The easiest to implement for frequent, irritating but not dangerous problems (e.g. shouting out). Can be used very effectively with groups or even classes of children. Very robust in classroom conditions. Easy to collect information before, during and after. Easy to give children visual feedback.	**Must not be used for dangerous or potentially dangerous behaviour.** Easy to implement but hard to explain. Teachers may be resistant to the idea of 'allowing' children to be badly behaved. Teachers need to be trained **not to be punitive** when points are removed.

When Kylie puts her hand up and waits quietly the teacher puts a marble in the jar for the whole class. Once the jar is full the whole class gets a reward.

Shaun is very shy, so every time he approaches the teacher and talks to her he gets a star on a card which he can take home to show his parents.

2. Rewarding the child for not being 'naughty' (Differential Reinforcement of the Omission of a Response, DRO)

To use this approach you need to know the average time interval between episodes. This is the system of choice for behaviour which is or could be dangerous (for example, fighting, self-injurious behaviour, reckless behaviour). Once we have done this it is easy to set the standard for reinforcement. We do it as follows.

- Calculate the average time between episodes of the problem behaviour.
- Halve the figure; that figure now becomes the basis for rewarding the child.

Below are some examples:

> For every hour that Wayne goes without teasing someone in class he gets a point. When he gets ten points he can take his points card and reading book to the headteacher who also listens to him read.

> If Amerjit goes a full session without destroying any of her work she gets ten minutes' choice time at the end of the session when she can choose from a menu of activities.

> If Karl goes for two hours without biting himself on the hand then he gets a point in a book. He trades the points in for extra pocket money at the rate of 5 pence per point when he gets home from school.

3. Rewarding children for being 'naughty' less and less often (Differential Reinforcement of Lower Rates of Responding, DRL)

To use this approach we need to know how often the behaviour problem happens on average. We then keep a tally of the problem behaviour using one of the charts from the previous issue and set the standard for reward at the present average. As the system begins to work, the average occurrence of problems will decrease, and as it decreases we can make the standard harder until we eventually fade out the reward entirely. It is particularly useful for frequent problem behaviours.

This technique, although it may meet with some resistance from teachers (because it 'allows' misbehaviour) is probably the most robust and successful in the classroom. However, it **MUST NOT BE USED FOR DANGEROUS OR POTENTIALLY DANGEROUS BEHAVIOUR**. If a problem behaviour is dangerous or potentially dangerous then the system described in the preceding section (DRO) should be used.

Below are some examples:

> Simon used to refuse to follow instructions straight away on average five times a session so that his teacher's time was often taken up cajoling him to do things. Simon is given five smiley faces at the beginning of each session. If he needs cajoling to do as he is told then one smiley

face is turned over by the teacher in a calm matter of fact way. Providing there is at least one smiley face at the end of the morning or afternoon Simon can choose from a menu of activities the one he would like to do at the end of the session. The following week Simon is only given four smiley faces at the beginning of the session, the week after that three smiley faces until eventually he has only one smiley face at the beginning of alternate sessions.

On a bad day class 5 break the rules 40 times a day, on a good day 10 times, on an average day 20 times. The class teacher tells the class they have 20 points at the beginning of the day and will lose a point every time someone breaks a rule. When this happens the class teacher calmly reminds the child or group what rule they should be following. At the end of the day if there is one point or more left then the class teacher picks the child she thinks has done well that day to come out to the front and spin The Wheel of Fortune which determines which class-wide reward they will receive. The following week the class has only 15 points at the beginning of the day, the week after 10, the week after that 5. From then on the system is only used every other day or when the teacher thinks the class is likely to be 'high'.

Hilary has a history of reacting very badly to mistakes and the teacher's attempts to correct her mistakes. As well as teaching her some very simple relaxation skills and asking her friends to show her how they cope with mistakes her teacher tells her to monitor her own performance. Every time she gets upset she removes a smiley face in her book. She has five smiley faces per day. If she has one smiley face at the end of the day she gets to read her favourite book to an ECO or a friend for five minutes. Occasionally the class teacher checks that Hilary is removing the smiley faces. As Hilary has more and more success meeting her targets, the number of smiley faces is reduced.

In some respects DRL is counter-intuitive so here are some further guidelines:

Guidelines for using DRL

There are a number of important guidelines that should be taken into account when using DRL.

- don't use reprimands. As has been illustrated from the examples above, the first rule for using this technique is not to tell the child off when we remove a point. It is unnecessary and adversely affects the system. A child who has ten points and is told off nine times and then is told s/he has been good, could be forgiven for being confused at best and resentful at worst. Instead give calm and matter-of-fact feedback.
- one point is as good as ten. Do not tie the level of reward to how many points are left. If a child has ten points left she should get the same level of reward as if s/he had only one point left, otherwise the child will resent seeing his/her level of reward being whittled away until it is at such a low level that it is not worthwhile to him/her – at which point his/her behaviour may rapidly worsen.
- use visual feedback: smiley faces, ladders, points, etc. Things that the children can see will help them monitor their own behaviour and will enhance the system.
- don't panic when they push their luck. The child may regularly lose all the points save one and so get his/her reward. This can be maddening for the

teacher but is a very good sign that the system is working. An appropriate response might be to reduce the number of points the child has at the beginning of the session.

Reactive strategies

Reactive strategies are included in the plan in order to safeguard the child, his or her peers and staff when things go wrong. We may have a thorough understanding of the child, and a highly effective multi-element plan, but we still need to plan for when things go wrong and problems occur. In particular we should know what safe non-punitive techniques will be used if the problem behaviour occurs and what support will be given to the child. Just as important is consideration of the practical and emotional help or support that should be given to the member of staff. When they do happen are behaviour problems so severe that there is a need for an emergency procedure that the teacher can use to summon help? If this is the case, is there a need for training in safe control and restraint such as Non-violent Crisis Intervention (NVCI) (Crisis Prevention Institute) or Safe Crisis Intervention and Prevention (Proact SCIP UK)?

Other questions that need to be asked to identify what strategies may need to be included in this section of the MEP are:

- How will staff be debriefed after major incidents in a way that addresses their emotional needs and promotes future improvements to the MEP?
- How will the relationship between the child and the teacher be rebuilt and how will the child's commitment to change be re-established?

Practical considerations in drawing up a Multi-Element Plan

In order to draw up a Multi-Element Plan it is necessary to take the following steps before drawing up the plan:

- Identify what the problems (special educational needs) are
- Determine which problem should have priority
- Collect data.

1. Identify what the problems (special educational needs) are

There are a number of questions to ask which will help with this:

- When was the last time the problem happened?

This will help to determine the frequency and seriousness of the problem.

- When, with whom, where does it happen?
- When, with whom, where doesn't it happen?
- How could you guarantee the problem would happen?

All these questions will help to see what triggers the problem and what preventive approaches it might be possible to use.

- If there is no clear idea of what is happening we should ask for a moment by moment description of what the child does, as though we were looking at it in slow motion. This will help clarify any misunderstandings about what colleagues mean when they use words such as tantrum, rudeness, aggressive, which can mean different things to different people.

The responses to these questions will clarify what Special Educational Needs should be written into the child's MEP and what consequences or rewards are maintaining the present behaviour problems.

2. Determine which problem should have priority

In deciding which problem should have priority we need to address a number of questions:

- Is there a problem which everything else stems from?

For example

> *Siraj kicks other pupils*
> *Siraj hits other pupils*
> *Siraj interferes with other pupils work*
> *Siraj gets out of his seat a lot to wander around the classroom*

The teacher realises that if Siraj were to stay in his place more he would not have opportunities to do all of the other things which are causing problems. Therefore the teacher and Special Educational Needs Co-ordinator (SENCO) decide to concentrate on ways of increasing the time Siraj stays in his chair.

- Is there a problem which effectively stops teaching occurring?

For example

> *Wayne goes under tables and shouts and swears at the teacher and other children so that no teaching or learning can take place*

- Is there a problem which is so dangerous it must have priority?

For example

> *Stephanie is a year one child who runs out of the building and on to the nearby road*

If the answer to any of these questions is yes then the problem should be considered as having a priority.

3. Collecting data

As well as identifying and prioritising problems we need to collect data in order to provide baseline information against which progress can be assessed. This is a step which is both vital and most often neglected. The commonest form of baseline information which teachers keep is some form of diary. Unfortunately this can be time consuming and inaccurate. Lack of entry for a particular day may or may not mean the child was well behaved, absent or the teacher was too busy to make an entry. How we collect baseline information will depend on the behaviour and how often it happens. Below are ideas for collecting this information.

- It is often not possible to keep a record of every time a particular problem happens, particularly if it is a high frequency problem such as shouting out or being out of seat or teasing other children. In these circumstances collect samples of baseline behaviour. Here is an example of how this might work:

  Harry's teacher and SENCO have decided that the most problematic behaviours are leaving his seat, shouting out, teasing peers and interfering with their work. These problems are happening so often it would not be feasible to keep a continuous record so the SENCO asks the teacher to keep a tally of these behaviours for 15 minutes three times during the coming week using the following chart. Here is a copy of the first chart they use:

Time: From 10.00 To 10.15 Date 11/12/97	Shouting out	Teasing	Interfering with work	Out of seat	Comments
	IIII	0	0	II	A better than average lesson

- For a more serious but less frequent behaviour such as running out of the classroom and serious tantrums we might keep a record of every instance of the behaviour during the day. Here is an example of how this might work:

  Sharon has serious tantrums lasting up to 15 minutes. She also sometimes runs out of the classroom. The SENCO and the classteacher decide to use the following chart every day.

Time of day	Tantrums	Runs out of class	Comments
Session 1	0	0	
Morning Break	0	not applicable	
Session 2	II	0	Trouble began when had difficulty with language
Lunch Break	0	not applicable	
Session 3	I	I	Trouble started when not allowed to choose activity she wanted
Totals	3	1	

- For other low frequency problems a chart which covers a whole week might be the best way of collecting information. Here is an example:

   There are frequent complaints about Elizabeth's bullying and name calling. The SENCO and class teacher decide to keep a record using this chart.

Day	Bullying reported	Comments
Monday	I	Jan complained of name calling
Tuesday	0	Absent
Wednesday	I	
Thursday	I	
Friday	I	
Total	4	

All of the data collected so far will help to set targets for the MEP; review whether the plan is succeeding and determine the criteria for rewards.

An example of a completed MEP

In this section we comment on an example of an MEP (see Figures 19.1 and 19.2) that was developed using the procedures described and successfully implemented in a mainstream classroom without additional resources other than advice and monitoring from the educational psychologist.

During the course of our assessment of the child (Fig. 19.1) the problem behaviours were defined (tantrums) using the questioning techniques discussed in section two, the final desired behaviours defined and alternative

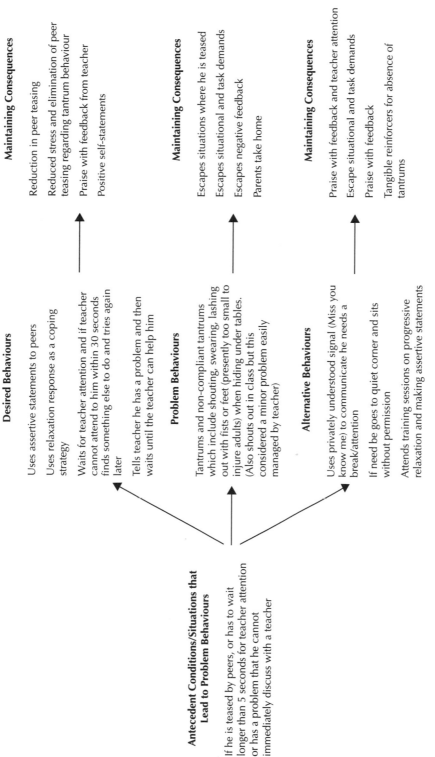

Summary of Key Information from Assessment

Background Information Speech problems have led to frustration at not being understood by adults and teased by peers. Parents have taught him to go behind settee when upset or angry in order to calm down. In school he tries to do this by hiding under tables but this has led to major problems.

Desired Behaviours

Uses assertive statements to peers

Uses relaxation response as a coping strategy

Waits for teacher attention and if teacher cannot attend to him within 30 seconds finds something else to do and tries again later

Tells teacher he has a problem and then waits until the teacher can help him

Maintaining Consequences

Reduction in peer teasing

Reduced stress and elimination of peer teasing regarding tantrum behaviour

Praise with feedback from teacher

Positive self-statements

Problem Behaviours

Tantrums and non-compliant tantrums which include shouting, swearing, lashing out with fists or feet (presently too small to injure adults) when hiding under tables. (Also shouts out in class but this considered a minor problem easily managed by teacher)

Maintaining Consequences

Escapes situations where he is teased

Escapes situational and task demands

Escapes negative feedback

Parents take home

Alternative Behaviours

Uses privately understood signal (Miss you know me) to communicate he needs a break/attention

If need be goes to quiet corner and sits without permission

Attends training sessions on progressive relaxation and making assertive statements

Maintaining Consequences

Praise with feedback and teacher attention

Escape situational and task demands

Praise with feedback

Tangible reinforcers for absence of tantrums

Antecedent Conditions/Situations that Lead to Problem Behaviours

If he is teased by peers, or has to wait longer than 5 seconds for teacher attention or has a problem that he cannot immediately discuss with a teacher

Figure 19.1

Summary of Multi-Element IEP

Possible Functions	Functions Identified by Assessment	
➢ Stimulation	Initiate social interaction	Shouting out
➢ Initiate social interaction	Escape or avoid	Non-compliance
➢ Escape or avoid events	Express emotion/reduce stress	Tantrum behaviour/hiding
➢ Obtain things or events		
➢ Express emotion/reduce stress		

Environmental Strategies

➢ Physical	Provision of a cooling off area
➢ Interpersonal	Personal and Social Education for class regarding teasing
➢ Instructional	Differentiated work on reading to improve phonics/pronunciation

Positive Programming

➢ Functionally Equivalent Skills	Using assertive statements using incident based role play
➢ Academic Skills	Instruction in phonic skills with additional advice from speech therapist
➢ Coping Skills	Relaxation response and learning to wait for five seconds for teacher attention

Preventive Strategies

➢ Antecedent Control Strategy	Not used
➢ For good behaviour (Alt R)	Contingent praise with feedback
➢ For no 'naughty' behaviour (DRO)	Notes home exchangeable for model making materials
➢ For 'naughty' behaviour less often (DRL)	Four smiley faces per day. One smiley face deducted in a non-punitive way for each refusal to comply with instructions. One smiley face remaining at the end of the day earned commendation in home school diary.

Reactive Strategies

➢ For the child	Non-punitive separation from the rest of the class/relaxation/feedback
➢ For the teacher	Reframing of problem (not as bad as it was, we now understand what's happening) time to discuss and express frustration to support staff/colleagues

Figure 19.2

behaviours that can be thought of as steps towards the final desired behaviours listed.

We might notice how all of the various elements in the plan (Fig. 19.2) combine to give the best chance of success. Notice also that although the plan is quite complex and sophisticated it is not time consuming for the teacher to implement. Finally, and most importantly, we might also notice how no punishments are recommended and how steps are taken to change the interpersonal environment of the young person concerned in order to improve his quality of life. The MEP was highly successful in eliminating dangerous tantrum behaviour and substituting a range of appropriate, positive skills. A full account of this case can be found in Eccles and Pitchford (1997).

References

Cooper, J. O., Heron, T. and Heward, W. E. (1987) *Applied Behavior Analysis*. Columbus: Merrill Publishing Co.

Crisis Prevention Institute, *Non-violent Crisis Intervention*, Crisis Prevention Institute Worldwide Ltd., IMEX Business Centre, Atlantic Street, Altrincham, Cheshire, WA14 5NQ.

Eccles, C. and Pitchford, M. (1997) 'Understanding and helping a boy with behaviour problems', *Educational Psychology in Practice*, 13 (2), 57–64.

Glynn, T. (1982) 'Antecedent control of behaviour in educational contexts', *Educational Psychology*, 2, 215–229.

Grant, L. and Evans, A. (1994) *Principles of Behavior Analysis*, New York: Harper Collins College Publishers.

Kazdin, A.E. (1975) *Behavior Modification in Applied Settings*, Homewood, Illinois: Dorsey Press.

LaVigna, G.W. and Donnellan, A.M. (1986) *Alternatives to Punishment: Solving behaviour problems with non-aversive strategies*, New York: Irvington Publishers.

Mosley, J. (1998) *The Whole School Quality Circle Time Model*, Trowbridge: All Round Success.

PROACT-SCIP-UK *Safe Crisis Intervention and Prevention*, The Loddon School, Wildmoor, Sherfield-on-Loddon, Hook, Hants, RG27 0JD.

Wheldall, K. (1982) 'Behavioural pedagogy or behavioural overkill?' *Educational Psychology*, 2, 181–4.

Chapter 20

What is the reality of 'inclusion' for children with emotional and behavioural difficulties in the primary classroom?

Sarah Shearman

Introduction

Current inclusion policy means that many children who in the past would have been in special schools are now in mainstream classrooms.

The question of how far inclusion should go has become more than just a practical question. It has become the focus of strong feelings which have tended towards moral stands. For example, Paul Cooper (1999) speaks of:

> Our sense of discomfort and fear regarding children in our society. It is almost as if, for the most part, we (at the societal level) do not know what to do with our children, especially when they are 'difficult'. Our first instinct is to want to ignore them and marginalize them; to send them away somewhere/anywhere.

In this chapter, I would like to look at some of the problems to do with children with emotional and behavioural difficulties (EBD) which are being thrown up by inclusion policy in my borough. I work in a primary outreach team, attached to a behaviour support service, whose work is designed to help primary schools to include children with EBD. Most of the children I see are on the verge of exclusion.

Our team works with individual children, classes and whole schools on improving behaviour policy and practices in order to reduce exclusions. At the same time as working in detail with individual children, their teachers and helpers, we also work in a broader way to help schools manage behaviour better, and so promote inclusion in the borough. Our input is usually requested by the headteacher or the special educational needs coordinator (SENCO).

In the last 2 years I have noticed that although inclusion policy has been beneficial for certain groups of children, and the more generous, inclusive ethos could be said to be beneficial for mainstream children in general, there have been extreme difficulties and stresses in trying to include children with EBD. I decided to explore how psychoanalytic thinking might illuminate what is happening for children with EBD, their teachers and helpers in the current climate.

How can we think about this topic?

I am finding that the inclusion of children with EBD, as it is beginning to be implemented in my borough, has led to enormous stresses and strains. I would like to use the psychoanalytic concepts of splitting, projective identification and denial to try and shed light on the current situation as exemplified in the cases of three primary children I have been concerned with recently. I would like to use these concepts to try and understand some of the unconscious processes at work.

After some general comments about inclusion policy, I will focus on three primary-age boys with EBD. I will introduce the children briefly and then use observations of them in school and of my work with them to explain how, in each case, inclusion has been working.

I will divide the observations and comments into three sections, to show first the impact of inclusion on the child, second the impact on the teachers and helpers, and third the impact on the visiting behaviour support teacher. I will also use some observation of whole-class situations to show how children with EBD can affect the class situation.

Methodology

In this article I use a qualitative approach. I have used observational material gathered from my work in order to look at the way children, teachers and learning support assistants (LSAs) behave in some primary schools in the borough where I work. It will be noticed that some of the observations quoted in this chapter are as objective as possible. These are the first observations made in the classroom, before I have been introduced to the child I am to work with. Others are participant observations, which show my involvement and something of my approach to the children I work with. In these participant observations, the impact of the child's behaviour on myself plays a large part in our interaction, and my understanding of this impact will be a factor in the outcome. It may also be noted that although my work methods are informed by psychoanalytic thinking, I also use behavioural methods. This combination of psychodynamic and behavioural approaches is, I believe, in common use nowadays in behaviour support work.

When I begin work with an individual child or a class, after talking to the staff involved and sometimes to the parents, I normally make an initial observation. The teacher introduces me just as someone who has come to see the class, so if I am observing an individual child, they are not aware of that fact on my first visit. This enables me to get a fairly objective view of how the child is operating in the situation I am observing. I usually spend about an hour in the classroom, paying careful attention to behaviour problems, their antecedents and their consequences. I then use my observations as a basis for devising a work plan.

About inclusion policy

Most literature about inclusion celebrates the inclusion of physically disabled children. However, children with EBD are also children with special educational needs. A feature of 'splitting', as described by Melanie Klein (1946), is that one situation tends to be idealized, another denigrated. If we think of this situation in terms of 'splitting', inclusion is at present idealized; special schools tend to be regarded as 'sinks' or 'bins' where 'very little meaningful education takes place'; and the difficulties of including children with EBD tend to be ignored or denied. The implication often seems to be that if a school is having problems including a behaviourally disturbed child, the fault lies with the school's behaviour policy, which is somehow not broad enough, not flexible enough, not welcoming enough. One could almost call this sort of idealization 'hallucinatory gratification', in which two interrelated processes take place: the omnipotent conjuring up of the ideal object and situation, and the equally omnipotent annihilation of the bad, persecutory object and the painful situation.

The setting

Implementation of inclusion policy takes place in a complex environment. Melanie Klein (1946) writes: 'Children unconsciously work to create a world which mirrors their own internal world.'

In many inner-city classrooms, a high proportion of children have social problems and/or dysfunctional families, or are suffering the traumas of recent loss of country or of war. Many of these children, to a greater or lesser degree, act out their need, their deprivation and their discomfort every day in the classroom.

Bion (1961) became aware in his work with groups that he was being made to feel the emotions which the individual or group was finding too painful to bear. The phenomenon of being able to engender feelings in another person is explained by Klein when she writes about projective identification. She explains that there exists, on an unconscious level, a phantasy that it is possible to split off part of one's personality and project it into another person. Often what are deposited are unbearable feelings such as helplessness, panic, guilt, despair or depression. Unsurprisingly, from this point of view, we find these are some of the feelings expressed by teachers and helpers who are working in inner-city classrooms, trying to include children with EBD.

Introduction to the children

In order to look in a detailed way at the reality of including children with EBD, I will be using observations taken from my work with three boys in primary classrooms.

Pablo is a 7-year-old boy whose family originally came to this country from Italy. He has moderate learning difficulties and obsessional behaviour. He finds it hard to relate to other children without getting very over-excited and violent. Pablo lives with his mother, who also has learning difficulties. She suffers from epilepsy and depression. The school where I saw Pablo had been directed by the local educational authority (LEA) to include him. They were doing so reluctantly. He had been more or less excluded from one primary school already.

Leroy is an 11-year-old Caribbean boy diagnosed as having attention deficit/hyperactivity disorder (ADHD), who was taking Ritalin for about 2 years. He is an intelligent boy who shows marked mood swings, lack of impulse control, hostility and aggression. He lives with his mother, who is a doctor's receptionist. She has found Leroy hard to manage since he was small, and his behaviour is beginning to affect his younger brother, who is now causing concern at his nursery. Leroy's father visits occasionally, but seems erratic in his treatment of the children, sometimes giving presents to one and not to the other.

Leroy has been 2 years at his present school. He was transferred there when his previous school was on the point of excluding him. The present school has been very committed to keeping him, but recently his behaviour has deteriorated markedly, possibly because he is refusing his Ritalin. The school is on the verge of giving up the struggle. At present he is part-time at the PRU, part-time at school.

Finally, Abdul is a 7-year-old boy who came to this country as a refugee. He has witnessed domestic violence. When he was 4, he spent about a year in a women's refuge with his mother and older brother. When he first came to his present school he had very little English. He was very withdrawn, only relating to other children by pushing them out of the way. Because he found it hard to put himself in other people's shoes, he found the classroom and playground situations very challenging. He is now learning well, with support from a full-time learning support assistant, but his behaviour is still problematic. He has just started therapy four times weekly at the local child and family consultation service (CFCS).

The impact of inclusion on the individual child

In each of the cases described in the previous section, the children were finding being in a mainstream classroom too difficult to manage.

Pablo

Pablo has a statement which allows him to have a full-time learning support assistant. Along with help with behaviour management, the school had asked me to show the LSA how to play with Pablo. I soon noticed that the school were finding Pablo too hard to manage and were wanting him out of the school. My job was to help the school with including him, so from the start our aims were different. This became apparent when I started to put plans forward.

Pablo certainly was having difficulties in the classroom, as the following shows.

Observation in class

Pablo starts to write his name at the top of the page. The child next to him says something disparaging. Pablo stands up. 'You don't even know!' he shouts, bashing his paper. 'Does anyone know what this picture is?' asks the teacher, 'It's a haystack.'

'Oh, for God's sake! It's a haystack!' says Pablo. 'Shall I write H? Underneath? Oh, I've done it wrong! I need a rubber!' Pablo is starting to get agitated. He marches round the table. 'He's going to hit me!' he calls out as he passes one boy. He starts to sing loudly, in a croaking, shouting voice. The other children have been taught to ignore him. They are amazingly tolerant.

Pablo sits down. He has found a rubber and puts it in his mouth. 'Don't put it in your mouth, you might swallow it,' the teacher tells him.

'Ow! I'm going to die!' he shouts, runs about and pretends to spit in the corner.

The LSA, Luke, arrives after his break. Pablo starts roaring and shaking his head. The teacher comes over. 'Pablo. What's the problem? Do you have to make so much noise? Give me the rubber – don't throw it at me, its rude.' Pablo throws a pencil, pushes his paper away, roars, lifts his chair as if to throw it, roars again. He starts to pile some chairs up behind the children's table. The chairs look as if they might fall down any second. The LSA takes him out of the room.

Comment

It seemed Pablo's reaction to his lack of success was to be overcome by feelings of rage, frustration and helplessness. I thought he was acting out these feelings in a dramatic way in order to provoke a response from the teacher. It appeared that Pablo needed a response, even a negative one, in order to convince him that he really existed.

In 'Therapeutic Consultations', Martha Harris (1987) writes about a very young child with a depressed mother:

> The mother's woodenness and depression intensify the child's anxiety and need to evoke some reassuring signs of life within her, to get into her and get something out of her. The violence and determination of his projection of himself into the mother bring concomitant fears of being caught and shut inside an object that contains and is coloured by his own hostile grabbing impulses.

I thought about how this configuration might have impacted on Pablo in his early years.

In this observation, it only takes a disparaging remark from another child to set off a whole chain of extreme reactions. Pablo's failures in the past have made him very sensitive to criticism. Although being with children who are succeeding gives him good models, it also can reinforce his deep sense of failure, a sense which is compounded by the school's inability to regard him in a positive light.

Leroy

The same sort of problems were noticeable in Leroy's case, although here the school were much more committed to including him, and he did not have specific learning difficulties. He is an intelligent boy, whose difficulties with accessing the curriculum come from his extreme restlessness and inability to concentrate.

I worked with Leroy and his teachers from September to February. He was finding it difficult to concentrate and was hurting children most days. The work I did with him was about becoming more aware of his habitual hostile reactions. The most successful period was when the whole school agreed to deal in the same way with his acts of aggression. This sort of consistent handling seemed to be helpful to the staff and to Leroy, but it required quite a concerted effort and it tailed off somewhat.

Observation in class

When I first visited Leroy in class, I noticed he was very restless and found it hard to concentrate. I watched him dabbing paint onto his picture and then, provocatively, start to dab it onto his neighbour's picture. He shifted from his own place to the teacher's seat and back again, sometimes putting his face right in front of another child's face and saying something to aggravate them. It was hard for me to take any notes or even look at him much, as he was super-sensitive to my observing him. His attention flicked constantly round the room, looking for reactions from other children. As he passed by children's chairs he would give an almost imperceptible kick or push, and they froze as he went past.

Comment

It seemed Leroy couldn't feel he existed unless he had an audience, and what is more, it needed to be an audience of his peers, applauding his opposition to authority. It looked to me as if Leroy's phantasy was to be the leader of a gang, but because he was constantly irritating, provoking and hurting other children, this phantasy was pathetically far from the reality of his situation. As in the case of Pablo, Leroy's sense of his previous failure, particularly his lack of ability to relate in a normal way to his peers, was being compounded by the lack of success in the continued attempts to include him in the mainstream classroom.

Abdul

Abdul was also having difficulty relating to other children.

Observation in class

Abdul came into the classroom. He looked a bit different from the other children, rather as if he had just come from somewhere far away. He is a thin little 7-year-old with enormous almond-shaped eyes and a beaky nose. He sat down with the others, but almost immediately rolled under the table. He started to push the chairs about by their legs.

I leaned down and put my hand firmly on his stomach. This seemed to surprise and calm him. He lay fairly still for a few moments. He sat up, and I held him loosely, with my arms round his chest. He swung in my arms a little. He didn't seem aware that the teacher was reading, although I tried to point this out to him. He found a rubber on the floor and started making marks on the chair with it. He decorated another chair with rubber marks and then got a bit fidgety.

I lifted him over to a chair and showed him a pen which writes in gold. He copied some letters. There were four other children at the table, some making bids for my attention, but Abdul ignored them all.

Comment

My instinct to put my hand on Abdul's stomach came from a feeling that he was fearful and holding himself together with difficulty. He seemed caught between pride and fear, not wanting to show he didn't understand anything that was going on. This was confirmed when I got to know him later by the fact that he found changing activities very difficult. Changing activity is often a problem for anxious children. They seem to be 'held together' by getting absorbed in one activity and experience the feeling of 'falling apart' when they have to change. Abdul was spending a lot of his time in the classroom playing with construction toys, ignoring what the other children were doing. He would also hide among the coats. In assemblies he would often roll about on the floor making barking noises.

One can observe very young children, beginning with their first relationship to their primary carer, work their way through their extreme fears and unconscious phantasies to a stage where they can begin to understand that the source of their gratification and the source of their frustration are one and the same person. This level of unconscious understanding brings with it the ability to spare the object (the mother) along with the wish to make reparation for the damage the infant imagines his hate has done. Abdul seemed at times to be still operating at the first level, where extreme fears and phantasies predominate.

In the normal development of the infant, feelings of disintegration are transitory. Their reintegration is effected by the primary carer, who mentally processes the infant's raw emotions and returns them to the infant in a digested form. This process is referred to by Bion (1961) as 'maternal reverie', a process in which the mother performs a containing function for the baby. When we consider that the three children I have mentioned are frequently falling in and out of disintegrated states, this containing function is constantly needed. If this sort of containment is not available at home, the question is whether it can realistically be provided at school.

In the cases of Pablo and Abdul, an LSA was employed full-time as part of the strategy to try and keep them in mainstream schooling. In the case of Leroy, this provision had not been put in place in time to help prevent his eventual exclusion.

The impact of inclusion on the learning support assistant

Special needs money is nowadays devolved to schools, who often, in the case of children with EBD, spend it on a learning support assistant who is with the child for a specified amount of time. It is often felt that when money has been provided, the problem is then settled, but this is often far from true. Children with EBD present complex behaviour including evasion, manipulation, projection, splitting between adults and sometimes violence, which makes them difficult to be with, even for very experienced teachers. It requires a very exceptional LSA to manage these sorts of behaviours. Much more than common sense is needed, and many LSAs feel a sense of outrage that their skills are effectively rubbished by children with EBD, a sense of outrage which they often do not feel at liberty to express. LSAs do not always receive special training for their job. They are often people from the local community, sometimes parents of children in the school, who have simply expressed an interest in the work. Sometimes LSAs have started work in the school as meals supervisors or playcentre volunteers. It is a lottery whether a child with EBD gets an LSA whose skills are appropriate for their task.

Pablo

Pablo's behaviour seemed to have been, at least partly, a product of his early years with a depressed mother. Unfortunately his LSA also seemed to be rather depressed, and had no notion that Pablo might be able to do some of his learning through play.

Observation in corridor

I went out to see what was happening outside. Pablo was throwing water out of the basin onto the floor and onto Luke (the LSA).

'Pablo, can you stop throwing water please. Could you stop it please,' says Luke in a level tone. Luke looks at me, expressing weariness and exasperation. Pablo is now running about, brandishing a pole. Luke is ignoring him and talking to the teacher from the nursery next door (the school is open plan).

'I wonder if you would like to make a sandpie and then go back to work,' suggests the nursery teacher. As soon as she suggests the sandpie, Pablo dries his hands, looks fascinated and goes over to the sandtray. 'I don't put sand on the floor,' Pablo says to me, anxiously. 'It'll be alright if you're careful,' I tell him, 'and if a bit goes on the floor, we'll sweep it up.'

'Look what I've found in the sand,' says Pablo to Luke, smiling and holding out a little animal. Luke comes over and goes through the motions of making a sandpie, but the sand is too dry, so it doesn't work. I show Pablo how he can pour it out of a teapot into a container. Luke looks as if he's a bit fed up with the sand play, but Pablo looks as if he could stay there forever.

Comment

It was an unfortunate fact that in some ways the depression of the LSA mirrored the depression of Pablo's mother. I thought this was bound to be stirring up a lot of uncontrollable feelings in Pablo.

Observation outside classroom

When I first sat down with Pablo, I showed him how to make a Plasticine snake and a little dish with pretend food in it. Pablo liked the simple game of making the snake pretend to eat. I felt all the time that Pablo might run off, so I arranged the table and chairs so he couldn't easily get out.

The next time we played, the LSA came to watch. I explained how children can learn through play and asked him about his own childhood. Adults playing with children in this way had not been part of his experience. I got a cardboard box and cut some windows and a door, got a handful of little toys and started pretending they were running out, hiding, calling out of the windows etc. Pablo was very excited by this and soon started to join in. The LSA looked on, sceptically.

Comment

The behaviour programme I made indicated that Pablo should complete about 10 minutes of classwork, and the teacher should then praise him and tell him he could go and play. The LSA should then play with him until the start of the next session. We made a little play place with toys. I asked the LSA to fill in a chart showing what they had done and how Pablo had liked it. The idea was that, as Pablo could not sustain a lengthy task, he would work in short, achievable sessions of about 10 minutes, so he could succeed and be praised, instead of dragging through a lengthy session, when he was likely to fail.

I also made a reward and sanction chart to help with Pablo's behaviour. He was to get a sticker on his chart for each session that he managed without preventing other children from learning. The stickers added up to a special time when he could do his favourite 'thing of the moment'. If he hurt another child or prevented children from learning by throwing things, shouting out etc., the LSA was to take him to a place near the pegs and sit him on a chair for 3 minutes, with a 3 minute sand-timer so he could watch the time.

When I returned the following week, after proposing these interventions, in each case the charts were still blank. The teacher and LSA were resistant to trying out my plans. They had not been fully involved in requesting my visits or in planning, so although we were meant to be working together, they were regarding my intervention as a threat. Because they couldn't manage Pablo, they were perhaps unconsciously hoping that I would also fail. This would prove no-one could manage him, and therefore they couldn't be blamed or blame themselves.

Abdul

An LSA was appointed to support Abdul, but he left after only a few weeks. After this false start, a young woman was chosen and she proved to have the energy, thoughtfulness and commitment necessary. Having someone at his side explaining and mediating the classroom experience was a great help and Abdul started to relate to some other children. Bowlby (1969), in his work on attachment, shows how a baby can start to explore the world from a secure base. We set up a table close to where the rest of the class were working. Abdul and his LSA would work or play at this table and she would 'join him in' as opportunities arose, at first just for a few minutes at a time. In the following observation I had taken the place of the LSA for an hour, to get the feel of how Abdul was getting on.

Observation in class

The children were being given different materials, microscopes and magnifying glasses. The lesson was on fabrics. I sat with Abdul at his little side-table. I thought this kind of open-ended activity might be difficult for him to manage.

I showed him the weave of my cardigan through the magnifying glass, and started to draw it for him, but he didn't show any interest. I realized the children were looking at the labels of their clothes to see what they were made of. I said 'What's your T-shirt made of?' and looked at the label. 'Polyester,' I told him. 'What was it?' I asked, but he looked blank. 'Polyester,' I repeated.

'What's your shirt made of?' I asked again. 'Polyester,' he answered, shyly, and looked pleased. I drew a picture of him and drew a label for his T-shirt. 'Can you write it?' I asked, writing it for him to copy. He shook his head and looked as if he might run off. I wrote it for him.

Later, we were doing some painting. Some water spilled on the table so I went to get a cloth. 'What's it made of?' he asked. He went on to ask 'What are we made of?' 'Bones, blood, skin, that sort of thing,' I told him. 'Bones' he said thoughtfully. 'What are teeth made of?' he asked.

Comment

Bion (1959) describes how a child may 'empty of meaning, and thus of feeling, a piece of insight he has just acquired'. Williams (1997) describes a boy using this sort of 'emptying of meaning' as the quickest remedy against any painful feelings, as he much preferred to be in a muddle to being in pain. I felt very encouraged by the evidence, shown in the above observation, of Abdul's capacity to think. It seemed that although he had been disturbed by his experiences in the past, his ability to make links was still intact. It also meant to me that Abdul's LSA had a good chance of working with him successfully.

Leroy

When I first met Leroy the application for him to get extra funding was not yet under way, so by the time it was completed he had fallen into the deteriorated state I mentioned earlier. We were in any case rather dubious about whether an LSA could be found who would be experienced and skilful enough to manage him. There was an applicant for the post, but unfortunately she encountered Leroy shortly after the interview. He abused her loudly in the street, and, understandably, she changed her mind. Nobody else had been found by the time Leroy had to be excluded from school.

The impact of inclusion on the teacher

Teachers can feel persecuted on all sides, by children who act out their pain and anxiety in the classroom, and by the political climate. The latter, by using league tables and a prescriptive curriculum, encourages competitiveness and exclusion, but at the same time dictates that a good teacher will be able to include all children, whatever their difficulties.

> I was often made to feel that challenging behaviour in my classroom was my fault and I should be able to handle it. (National Union of Teachers, 2000)

Teachers can also sometimes feel persecuted by 'specialists' who are called in to help, as I have described in the case of Pablo's class teacher.

Teachers under pressures of this sort can become demoralized. The following extract is from an observation in a Year 5 class with a long-term supply teacher.

Whole-class observation

I had started to pick out which children were having difficulties with the work, and consequently with their behaviour. There were some in such dire need of help that I felt I had to abandon my observer role, and I started helping two boys sitting near me. The work was too difficult for them; it involved carrying 10, which they didn't know how to do. I looked up from doing this and saw that R., the boy I had come to observe, had disappeared. I guessed he had 'gone to the toilet' because he couldn't do the work either.

An LSA came to see to a boy who was lying on the floor by the board, crying. She tried to cajole him into going with her, but he wouldn't, so she left him lying on the floor, his head in his arms. It was distressing to watch this interchange, and several children were obviously affected by it. Soon after, the deputy head came in and managed to remove the crying boy.

R. is back, but is under the table. He and another boy have got a pair of giant callipers and are measuring each other's heads and laughing. The teacher looks across at me and raises her eyes to heaven, a gesture which doesn't escape the children. R. is decorating his hair with gold marker pen. 'What are you putting gold pen on your hair for? Don't be so silly!' R. jumps up and down, making a 'silly' face.

'Get up off the floor! This is numeracy hour! Look me in the eyes when I'm talking to you! Don't hurt me by pushing your chair into me!'

About 17 children are managing to work quite well in spite of all this. However, the teacher's attention is entirely caught up by the malefactors. One boy is crawling under the desks, barking like a dog. R. looks relaxed, he is flicking little pellets of chewed-up paper around.

The teacher tells the boy with the callipers to sit down. The boy looks at her defiantly, laughing. 'But I'm having fun!' he replies. Teacher sits down and gets most children to sit on the carpet. It is time for her to read the story before break. R. is sitting at the back, laughing at the boy who is still clowning around with the callipers. The teacher now gets completely locked into telling these few children off. She puts the book down. 'Actually, I'm not bothering reading. I've had enough now.' Calliper boy flicks a rubber band at her. Three children are running in and out of the classroom. There is a fight in the classroom next door, and they want to see it.

Comment

Klein (1946) explains the origins of splitting in the earliest stage of infantile development:

> The first object is the mother's breast, which to the child becomes split into a 'good' (gratifying) and 'bad' (frustrating) breast. This splitting results in a severance of love and hate. The frustrating and persecuting object is kept widely apart from the idealised object. From the beginning, object-relations are moulded by an interaction between introjection and projection, between internal and external objects and situations.

One could say that in the previous observation, the children who are misbehaving are challenging the authority of the teacher in a hating way. We can see how this projected hatred pushes her to become more punitive and negative until she actually becomes, for the moment, a hateful figure, full of the split-off and projected feelings of the disturbed children. Watching children with EBD in classrooms, one can observe them sometimes regressing into states where persecutory anxiety is so high that they project their intolerable feelings into the object (the teacher) and turn her into a hated, persecutory figure, separate from the teacher they know and love. Although this process happens in unconscious phantasy, it propels the child to act it out in real life.

What is a mainstream teacher to make of the task of containing this amount of infantile rage and persecutory anxiety? In a specialized setting, with small groups of children and teachers with some notion of unconscious processes, one can imagine this sort of containment happening, but in a class of 26–30 children it becomes an impossibility. The teacher is constantly aware of the more disintegrated children's needs, but is unable to meet them; so she can fall, herself, into a state of persecutory anxiety and guilt.

Pablo

The reaction of Pablo's teacher seemed to be that of splitting off the feelings of anxiety provoked in her and the rest of the staff, by simply denying that there was any way in which her thinking could be enlarged to include Pablo. This became apparent when I started to put plans forward for the management of his behaviour. The class teacher and the LSA would listen politely and then firmly assert that the plans were unworkable. While sometimes the arrival of the behaviour support teacher may be greeted with relief, in this case my arrival provoked anxiety.

The only way to get a behaviour plan working seemed to be to involve the headteacher. After she had taken on the supervision of the plan, things improved quite rapidly. Pablo seemed to me to be feeling more secure now that some limits and boundaries had been defined, and he looked forward to our play sessions. I also noticed him being quieter and more aware in the classroom, but the teacher and the LSA felt that the improvement was not significant.

Leroy

Because Leroy was not able to manage for long in the classroom, he ended up spending a lot of time in the headteacher's office. The secretary and other staff were able to be very positive towards him, because they were not having to manage him in a classroom with other children, and he built up a strong relationship with the headteacher, James, who became a sort of surrogate father to him.

In the following observation, I am looking after Leroy in James's office, while James is out taking a class.

Observation in the office

When I reached the offices, I found the teacher had put Leroy in one office, and another boy who had been causing trouble in the other. Leroy started to try and get through the door to join the other boy. I held the door handle, and told him the teacher had said they weren't to be together. Leroy wrenched at the door handle, but I held on firmly. 'Why are you holding the door? I don't know you! I know your name, but I don't know you, you don't work here!' he told me. I laughed and said he should know me by now.

I showed Leroy what I had brought for him to do. I suggested he take his bag off, but he told me he always wears it as it has his Game Boy in it. He started to relax. I sat by the door. He started to rummage around the shelves, where James keeps some interesting things. He got out a Box Brownie camera. He came over to me and asked how it worked. I explained he couldn't use it as there wasn't any film in it. I showed him how it worked. It seemed by now he had remembered we were friends. 'It's James's camera,' he said. He then took out a huge sword in a scabbard. 'Be careful,' I said, 'I expect it's very sharp.'

'I felt the blade once,' Leroy told me. 'James took it out once, and I felt it.' He put the sword down and sat himself at James's desk, rattling the drawers importantly.

Comment

Leroy's class teacher was able to be fairly relaxed about the fact that she was barely able to include Leroy in her class, because she knew she had the total support of the headteacher, James, and that he was willing to look after Leroy whenever she had to exclude him from the classroom. In fact, Leroy spent more time with James than with anyone else except his mother during the few months before he was finally excluded from school.

When the time came for James to exclude him, it was a very painful moment. James had obviously had a very difficult time coming to the decision. We carefully arranged Leroy's goodbye to the school, and he was given the same parting gifts as would be given to a child leaving in a normal way. I was walking to the playground with Leroy some weeks later.

'Why did I have to leave school?' he asked me. I told him it was because he wasn't managing at school, that perhaps he could think of the present time as a little break, while people thought about where he should go next.

'I hate James,' he said 'He's a hard bastard.' Although Leroy had not shown any signs at the time that leaving school had been a severe blow to him, he expressed clearly here his anger at what he perceived as a rejection from the headteacher, who had spent so much time with him.

Abdul

When I first met Abdul, his teacher was managing the class and Abdul without any support. The only way he could do this was to ignore most of Abdul's behaviour, as to try and confront him would have meant dropping his attention to the rest of the class. He was obviously distressed at not being able to meet Abdul's needs, so when an LSA was appointed this gave great relief, and I was able to help her to set some boundaries around Abdul's behaviour. The next school year Abdul moved into a class where the teacher and his LSA were able to work very well together and his behaviour and socialization started to improve greatly.

Observation in class

Angela went to fetch Abdul from the playground. We paused on the stairs and looked down. 'There he is,' she said proudly. He was standing first in line and we saw him take the teacher's hand to go upstairs.

I went to the classroom and waited for them to come in. When the children came in, Abdul came up to me, smiling, with two pieces of red wool. 'They are snakes,' he told me, with a smiling, fierce look. 'They want to eat you.' He wriggled one of the snakes near my arm and I pretended to be scared.

Later, the teacher started to read 'Avocado Baby' to the class. Abdul suddenly realized he could understand it. He sat down at the back, and then moved forward so he could see well. Angela looked at me and at Abdul, sitting quietly on the carpet, absorbed in the story. 'Well, would you believe it?' she whispered to me.

Comment

It seemed to me that the degree to which containment could be offered to each of these three children depended on how much support was offered to the teachers and LSAs. In the first school, that of Pablo, the headteacher had already made up her mind that the school was not going to manage Pablo. Although the school was successfully including other children with learning difficulties, it seemed that Pablo, with his sometimes bizarre behaviour, was 'a bridge too far'.

Leroy's teacher was saved from excessive anxiety by the containment that the headteacher James was able to offer.

In the case of Abdul, I was able to support his LSA sufficiently for her to do a demanding job successfully.

The work of the behaviour support teacher

Most of the support offered by specialized behaviour support teachers in schools is in the form of short-term interventions. These can be either to support an individual child or a class, or to help a whole school revise their behaviour policy. The idea in the case of individual child support is that after getting to know the child and the whole situation, the support teacher gives advice which can be incorporated by the class teacher and school into their everyday practice.

The fact that this intervention is short term can make for difficulties. In psychoanalytic terms, one could say that when a good object is established, the ego is less liable to identify indiscriminately with a variety of objects, a process which is characteristic of a weak ego. There is a tendency in many EBD children, who have failed to internalize a sufficiently good object in their early infancy, or whose good object relations have been upset by trauma, to flit from one adult to another in an indiscriminate fashion. One could say that the present policy, to keep EBD children in mainstream classrooms, supported by a variety of professionals, some of whose work is designed to be short term, can actually reinforce this shallow, flitting tendency. The advantages of a 'secure base', shown by Bowlby (1969) in his work on attachment theory, appear at first to be supported by the inclusion policy, where children are kept in mainstream schools with their peers and siblings. However, in fact the individual, close and detailed work done with children with EBD in schools is often done by teachers whose intervention is only short term.

Klein (1946) writes:

> Among other factors, gratification by the external good object again and again helps to break through these schizoid states.

The 'again and again' of containing and managing children in disintegrated states, of repairing damages to the psyche, requires a high level of long-term commitment. This repairing work done again and again can gradually break a cycle of distortion and hostility. This long-term work should be done by child psychotherapists, but this facility is only at present reaching a very few of the children with EBD in our borough. In the case of Leroy, he and his mother were referred to the child and family consultation service, but after two or three sessions she felt it was not helping and stopped going. Pablo and his mother attend the CFCS weekly, and Abdul has recently started in therapy four times weekly.

Barton and Slee (1999) write of inclusive education as being about

> responding to diversity; it is about listening to unfamiliar voices, being open, empowering all members and about celebrating 'difference' in dignified ways. From this perspective, the goal is not to leave anyone out of school.

The rationale here is to accommodate differences, but hitherto the effort has been to help the child accommodate to the existing norms of school life. Some schools have undertaken radical restructuring to accommodate physically disabled children, but it is not yet clear how far schools are going to have to change in order to successfully include children with EBD.

Pablo

Given these constraints, the behaviour support teacher can still be quite a help in some cases. In the case of Pablo I was asked to support the LSA and look at behaviour strategies. I think, looking back at this case, that a good idea would have been to involve all the school staff from the beginning. This might have given more confidence to Pablo's teacher that the behaviour programme I suggested was workable. In fact, when the programme was finally implemented properly, things started to improve quite rapidly, but by this time the school had decided Pablo was to move to a special school for children with moderate learning difficulties.

I thought about Pablo's mental state with reference to the fact that his mother had been depressed when he was very young. In experiments described by Trevarthen (1974) mothers were asked to be deliberately unresponsive to their babies for a few seconds, to behave in the manner a depressed mother might behave. The infants reacted first of all by attempts to make the mother change her behaviour, and, when this failed, by self-comforting (turning away and thumb-sucking). When the mother resumed normal behaviour, the infant's negative mood and avoidance of eye contact continued for quite a few minutes. One could see the obsessive, repetitive aspects of Pablo's behaviour as a sort of self-comforting, which over time had become ritualized or stylized.

It seemed to me that Pablo's sense of self in relation to others was impaired or very underdeveloped. This could be partly due to some insufficiency in the capacity of his mother to respond in the way which allows an infant's raw feelings to be processed and returned to him in a digestible form, described by Winnicott (1956) as 'maternal containment'. It seemed that Pablo was at quite an infantile stage of emotional development, and it would certainly have needed a massive shift in thinking to provide the sort of environment which would meet his needs in a mainstream school.

There was evidently something about Pablo which deeply upset and disturbed people. What was it that made it so hard to plan for and think about this little boy? Perhaps Pablo's lack of empathy and obsessional behaviour were frightening to those who were not used to this sort of child. Somehow the fear of a mental state which perhaps cannot be cured or fixed could be very worrying.

Leroy

The work I did with Leroy was designed to make him more aware of his habitual hostile reactions. We also did some work about 'what do other people think, what do other people like'. Leroy found trying to put himself in another person's shoes difficult and distressing. The most successful intervention was when the whole school agreed to deal in the same way with his acts of aggression. This sort of consistent handling by all the staff seemed to be helpful to them and to Leroy, but it required a large concerted effort and it was difficult to keep the momentum going for long. Leroy desperately wanted to have friends and seemed to have no idea how to go about this. I gave him a picture of a magic box which could grant wishes. Leroy immediately drew a little figure coming out of it and labelled it 'a friend'.

Observation in the library

Leroy told me a story of his early childhood. He was staying in Jamaica with his grandparents. He was happy there. His grandparents had given him a puppy, but when they found he couldn't take the puppy back to England because of quarantine restrictions, they had it put down.

Comment

I expected to hear more of these stories but, as it turned out, in nearly 2 years this was the only account he gave me of his early life. I thought perhaps the story was about his extreme anxiety that because he was unacceptable, he would be 'put down'. This anxiety was reinforced by his mother, who wanted to send him to boarding school; by his father, who in effect had abandoned him; and by his school, from which he was often temporarily excluded for hurting children.

None of my interventions seemed to help to shift Leroy's uncompromisingly hostile position. When asked to write 'What do you like about school?' he wrote 'Nothing'. When asked 'What do you hate about school?' he wrote 'Teachers bossing you about. I'd give them one whack in the head.' He told me the first thing he remembered was 'hitting people with my rattle'. Later, in a more thoughtful mood, he said 'I'd like to stop hitting people' and 'I'd like to stop punching people', but it seemed he was unable to internalize any help directed towards achieving these goals.

Leroy reminded me of a boy described by Gianna Williams (1997): 'While provoking violent emotions in others, he himself appeared to be, most of the time, devoid of feelings.' She describes 'an alarming quality of numbness'.

In Leroy's case I thought this numb quality came from a specific lack of empathy. It seemed it was almost impossible for him to imagine what went on in other people's minds. I felt puzzled about whether this was an organic dysfunction which was part of his ADHD, or whether the numbness stemmed from his early experiences.

Abdul

When I first met Abdul the most important thing was to get him an LSA full-time to help him through his work and play times. When this was achieved, having someone at his elbow explaining and interpreting what was going on in the classroom was a great help, and Abdul began to relate to other children. It appeared that as soon as he was sufficiently contained by his LSA, he could venture to start making relationships with others. Just as a baby can begin to explore the world, while constantly returning to his carer, Abdul started to make tentative moves towards other children. His understanding and vocabulary also improved greatly. One of the things he continued to have difficulty with was changing activities. He would get absorbed in one activity, which served to give him the feeling of being 'held together'. When he had to change to another activity, he seemed to experience the feeling of 'falling apart'. His LSA became skilled at moving him from one activity to the next. Apart from a few setbacks, Abdul started to make steady progress in learning and socialization.

Conclusion

In looking at the reality of inclusion for three children in the primary classroom, from the point of view of the child, the teacher, the LSA and the behaviour support teacher, I have highlighted some of the problems thrown up by the inclusion of EBD children in the classroom.

> Inclusion involves restructuring the cultures, policies and practices in schools so that they respond to the diversity of students in their locality. (CSIE, 2000)

One of the main problems at present seems to be that although some schools are undertaking restructuring to include children with physical disabilities, it is still very unclear what restructuring is needed in order to include children with EBD.

A second difficulty I have highlighted in all three cases is that of containment. Without sufficient support and containment, the task of the teacher and the LSA to include EBD pupils becomes almost impossible. It seems to me that the CFCS could be extended to perform this important function in schools. Therapists are already working to support teachers in special units such as the PRU, and it would be very valuable if this work could be extended into mainstream schools.

At present, the work of therapists tends to be poorly understood by teachers and LSAs. It would be helpful if more work could be done to make links between the CFCS and schools, so the contribution of therapy and psychoanalytic thinking could be better understood. The case of Leroy, where his mother visited the CFCS a few times and then gave up, is very typical in my borough. Parents and teachers are often cynical about the value of therapeutic intervention and I believe this cynicism often comes from ignorance.

In each of the three cases I have described, my work as a behaviour support teacher was planned to last for one or two terms, but in fact after nearly 2 years I am still involved with these three children, although my support has now necessarily to be more limited. In the case of Pablo, my support is now limited to visiting him at home twice a week and keeping in touch with the relevant departments who will find a new school for him. In the case of Leroy, since his exclusion I will be working with him as part of a part-time PRU placement until alternative provision is found for him. In the case of Abdul, I am now visiting the school monthly to support teacher and LSA and to promote links between the CFCS, where he is in therapy, and the school.

It seems to me that to be successful, the sort of help offered by the behaviour support teacher needs to be longer term than was at first envisioned. In some cases this support may need to be continued for the whole of the child's time in primary school. As was seen in the case of Pablo, the behaviour teacher's work is more likely to succeed if the class teacher and LSA are involved initially with inviting and subsequently with planning the intervention.

I have described some of the difficulties encountered by teachers and LSAs. A positive result of the implementation of inclusion policy has been that more guidance is starting to be given to teachers about the management of behaviour, although this continues to be only a tiny part of initial teacher training. Guidance at present is given on in-service training days and in twilight sessions. There needs to be a greater focus on understanding of the underlying causes of EBD and the management of behaviour, now that EBD children are included in mainstream.

The success or failure of strategies to help children with EBD depend to a large extent on the work of the LSAs, whose training up to now has been inadequate or non-existent. Understanding of unconscious processes involved when working with disturbed pupils needs to be brought onto the training agenda. Although psychoanalytic thinking is informing, to some extent, those who devise policy, this thinking is not available to those working with children on a day-to-day basis.

A body of psychoanalytic literature exists about how institutions manage difficulty and change.

The institutional process involved in implementing inclusion policy is too large a subject to write about in this chapter, but I have been aware while collecting this material that the unconscious processes I have described are operating at the broader, institutional level as well as at the smaller, classroom and individual level. To manage the changes implied by inclusion policy successfully, these need to be understood.

Many would maintain that the needs of children with severe EBD cannot be met in mainstream classrooms; or, if they are, that the cost to teachers, LSAs and the other children in the class is too high. In our borough, as I write, plans are going ahead for learning support units and for a new EBD provision. It will be interesting to see how these plans can be developed so they do not turn out to be a step backwards from the ideal of inclusion for all children.

References

Barton, L. & Slee, R. (1999) 'Competition, Selection and Inclusive Education: Some Observations', *International Journal of Inclusive Education* 3 (1), 3–12.

Bion, W.R. (1959) 'Attacks on Linking', *International Journal of Psychoanalysis* 40.

Bion, W.R. (1961) *Experiences in Groups*. London: Tavistock.

Bowlby, J. (1969) *Attachment and Loss*. London: Hogarth.

Cooper, P. (1999) *Understanding and Supporting Children with Emotional and Behavioural Difficulties*. London: Jessica Kingsley.

CSIE (2000) *Index for Inclusion* (piloted from 1996). Bristol: Centre for Studies on Inclusive Education.

Harris, M. (1987) 'Therapeutic Consultations', in *The Collected Papers of Martha Harris and Esther Bick*. Clunie.

Klein, M. (1946) 'Notes on Some Schizoid Mechanisms', in *Envy and Gratitude and Other Works* (1946–63). London: Hogarth.

National Union of Teachers (2000) *Unacceptable Pupil Behaviour: Advice, Guidance, Protection*. Pamphlet. London: NUT.

Trevarthen, C. (1974) 'Conversations with a Two-Month-Old', in *Child Alive*. Temple Smith.

Williams, G. (1997) 'Double Deprivation', in *Internal Landscapes and Foreign Bodies*. London: Tavistock Clinic, Duckworth.

Winnicott, D. (1956) 'Primary Maternal Preoccupation', in *Through Paediatrics to Psychoanalysis*. London: Hogarth.

Chapter 21

What is to be done about bullying?

K. Rigby

Introduction

People are often divided about what (if anything) should be done. Among schoolteachers, some view bullying between schoolchildren as occurring with sickening regularity; others hardly notice it or think it is unimportant.

But the drift is unmistakably towards increasing concern about bullying. The media has become energetic in drawing attention to the problem of bullying. It can readily be sensationalised; it sells newspapers, is a boon to talk-back radio and attractive to television documentary producers. The effect is to get us to focus almost exclusively on the violent end of the bullying continuum and virtually ignore the day-to-day verbal and relational forms of bullying to which far more people are subjected, sometimes with equally or more devastating consequences for health and well-being.

Because of this preoccupation with the more overt and violent aspects of bullying, not surprisingly authorities sometimes view bullying as a crime for which legal responses are the most relevant. This is unfortunate, because only a quite small and limited amount of bullying is of direct interest to the law – principally bullying which results in grievous bodily harm.

Nevertheless, some authorities see the emphasis placed upon methods of behavioural control, such as we see in many schools (and prisons), as misguided and even counter-productive. What matters, it is sometimes argued, is promoting positive ways in which people treat each other.

These two perspectives on what to do about bullying are central to the current debate. It is a debate about both ends and means. One sees the desirable end as achieving constructive, respectful behaviour between people;

the other as the elimination of hostile, aggressive behaviour between people. Disputes often arise about the effectiveness of means, with one side urging that positive improvements in behaviour between people can be brought about through instruction, persuasion and modelling of respectful behaviour; the other that we can best proceed by identifying and punishing behaviour we wish to stop. These are of course diametrically opposed positions, and in practice we see some compromises, depending upon situations (e.g. school versus workplace) and the form of bullying behaviour encountered (e.g. teasing versus serious assault). Nevertheless, the perspectives I have described do in no small measure determine what people think should be done and what people in authority in schools and in other contexts actually do.

Education about bullying

It is generally agreed that those who make decisions about what is to be done about bullying should be 'educated' about bullying, and that there should be a 'policy' about bullying.

There has emerged a demand for detailed knowledge of what is actually going on between people in an organisation that can be termed 'bullying'. We find that this demand is being addressed in a number of ways. Members of a workforce sometimes get together to pool their perceptions and judgements of how people in their organisation are treating each other. Alternatively, members may be invited to inform about any bullying they have observed in their workplace or have experienced themselves. To this end, a 'bully box' may be provided into which complaints may be put. A 'hot line' may be opened to report incidents. Another way of obtaining information of this kind may be through the use of anonymous questionnaires. The information received in any or all of these ways may be used as a basis for discussion and planning what to do next. The great advantage of this approach to educating a workplace or school community is that it can be based upon a realistic appraisal of the situation to be addressed, rather than upon statistics and generalisations derived from samples of respondents whose experiences and responses could be quite different from one's own.

Policy

It remains true that conceptions of the nature of bullying may remain comparatively unaffected by the results from questionnaires or other forms of data collection or by sharing impressions. For example, where bullying is conceived as 'deviant behaviour' that must be 'stamped out' a policy may emerge that relies entirely on rules and sanctions and zero tolerance for rule infractions. Under these circumstances, there is typically a resolve to treat minor and major violations of rules in much the same way. On the other hand, where bullying is seen less as a matter of 'deviance' and more as a matter of unsatisfactory ways of relating to others that can be rectified by psychological and social means, some, if not all, instances of bullying may be treated as 'non-crimes' and sanctions will be seen as not always necessary. Hence, even when there is a common perception of what is happening between individuals in a social environment where an anti-bullying policy is needed, views on what kind of policy is appropriate may well diverge.

Differences may also have to do with whose responsibility it is to counter bullying. At one extreme, there may be authorities who set the rules, identify the bullies and impose the penalties. At the other extreme, members of the whole community may be expected to play a part in developing a plan to stop bullying and also in implementing that plan. A broadly based policy of this kind adopted by some schools (see Rigby 2001) is shown in the box below.

Elements in an Anti-bullying Policy for Schools

(i)   A strong statement of the school's stand against bullying.

(ii)   A succinct *definition* of bullying.

(iii)   A declaration of the *rights* of individuals in the school community – students, teachers, other workers and parents – to be free of bullying and (if bullied) to be provided with help and support.

(iv)   A statement of the *responsibilities* of members of the school community: to abstain personally from bullying others in any way; to actively discourage bullying when it occurs; and to give support to those who are victimised.

(v)   A general description of what the school will do to deal with incidents of bullying. (For example: the severity and seriousness of the bullying will be assessed and appropriate action taken. This may include the use of counselling practices, the imposition of sanctions, interviews with parents, and, in extreme cases, suspension from school.)

(vi)   An undertaking to *evaluate* the policy in the near and specified future.

Parenting the non-victim

Numerous writers have argued that children can be protected from being bullied by the efforts of wise parents (Berne 1996; E. Field 1999; Zarzour 1999).

We can distinguish several themes in the advice currently being offered. Prominent among these are: (i) the need to develop in children high self-esteem; (ii) training in social competence; and (iii) learning to act in a pro-social way.

High self-esteem is seen by many as the core quality that can prevent a child from being bullied. Sue Berne (1996) writes: 'Self-esteem is the single most important factor in determining whether your child will grow up to be happy and successful' (p. 107). She quotes approvingly the words of Stephanie Marston, an American psychologist: 'Self-esteem is the real magic wand that can form your child's future.' Berne defines self-esteem simply as 'how you feel about yourself'. She adds: 'High self-esteem means you can say: "I'm OK just as I am – always" ' (p. 108).

If we recall the research evidence on the connection between being bullied and self-esteem, we find that, indeed, victims of school bullying do tend to have below average self-esteem. However, existing research does not support the view that high global self-esteem or high esteem in general can 'bully-proof' a child, but rather it is that aspect of self-esteem relating to social competence that may do the trick. And further, such self-perceived social competence is probably a reflection of actual social competence which, as a result of repeated encounters with others, a child knows he or she possesses and can be applied in situations that might otherwise lead to being bullied by a peer.

Seligman (1995) in his book *The Optimistic Child* takes rather violent exception to the claims that have been made on behalf of self-esteem. And also the means by which parents are being urged to nurture this precious commodity. He argues that there are almost no findings anywhere showing that self-esteem causes anything. Rather, he argues, one's level of self-esteem is a by-product or consequence of success or failure. This does not mean that parents should not praise their children or that praise will not on some occasions actually raise self-esteem, especially when it comes as a confirmation that he or she has advanced towards a higher level of competence. The praise, he suggests, should be directed towards encouraging children's efforts towards laudable achievements – which could include asserting themselves in such a way as to deter others from bullying them – and not simply reinforcing everything a child does in the vain hope of developing an impregnable feel-good state.

Feeling good without anything to show for it, as Seligman would say, puts one in a highly vulnerable position. In behavioural terms, one has been reinforced for doing everything and anything. As long as one is with infinitely laudatory parents the feeling is good, but when the continuous positive reinforcement abruptly ends, as it may do when peers see nothing so wonderful in the little things you do, the consequences can be devastating. Serious depression may then follow, and act as a signal for peers to bully you and deepen a sad condition from which it is difficult to recover.

When books give advice on the development and reinforcement of skills that are relevant to countering bullying and harassment they are on firmer ground. In *Bully-Proof Your Child* Berne (1996) identifies a number of skills that parents can teach their children to help them become more socially competent. These include being able to approach people sensitively and to gain acceptance, communicate clearly, make friends, act cooperatively and to negotiate and resolve interpersonal difficulties. Where parents are able to both encourage the development of such skills and, most important, to model them through their interactions with others, children appear more likely to be able to interact positively – and more safely – with peers at school. But, as Berne correctly points out, children need other children with them continually if they are to learn to become socially competent with peers and not merely good at role-playing with mother. The steadily growing research showing a reliable association between non-involvement in bully/victim problems and the quality of home life, as indicated by positive family functioning and good child–parent relationships, provides some basis for the belief that parents can affect the ways in which children interact with others at school, although – yet again – we cannot discount the possible influence of heredity.

It must also be admitted that indicators of social competence that are relevant to family situations, especially those involving adults, may have diminished relevance when a child is being harassed in the school playground. Children rarely shake hands and introduce themselves politely when they meet, nor do they generally inquire about each other's health and begin conversations obliquely by making observations about the weather. There are clearly limitations to what social manners can be transferred from one situation to another. However, parents can, if they will, listen to their children when they want to talk about what happened at school, and react sympathetically to accounts of what went wrong. We know that having someone to turn to when one is bullied can greatly reduce the distress one feels (see Rigby 2000). Further, parents can do a number of practical things that can help to prevent a child from being picked on by other children. They can see to it that, as far as possible, the child looks right, wears the right (peer approved) clothes, has the right haircut. This may seem a trivial point almost, but the rules of conformity can be used cruelly and begin a cycle of violence that could with foresight have been avoided.

Actions to stop the bullying

Various solutions – or ameliorations – have been suggested to stop bullying from taking place. Different perspectives are taken according to whether the focus is on the victim, the bully, the bully and victim together, or the wider circle of people that could include peers and/or parents.

Focus on the victim

An essential element in defining bullying is the existence of a power imbalance between a potential target and a would-be perpetrator or perpetrators. Logically, remove the power imbalance and there is no more bullying. However, it is unrealistic to expect power imbalances of one kind or another to disappear, ever. The best we can hope for is the reduction of power differences, such that bullying becomes harder to sustain because the target has become tougher or more resilient. How can this be done? A good deal of attention has been given to what a potential victim (usually a child) can do when he or she is actually in a situation in which there is a threat of being bullied.

E. Field (1999) proposes that the victim looks the bully in the eye; puts on a friendly-looking face; stands straight – no jiggling; speaks clearly and calmly; and is prepared, not scared (p.163). Zarzour (1999) in general agrees but adds: 'Give him (sic) a stony-faced stare – look straight through the bully' (p.98).

An excellent website from New Zealand (http://www.nobully.org.nz/) draws on the wisdom of the Maoris: *Kia haha* meaning 'stand tall'. By all means, stand tall. The problem is how to do that in the actual situation when one is frightened or upset. Some offer further advice, beginning usually with: first practise before a mirror or (if possible) role-play with friends or members of your family. Then, when it happens – take a deep breath. Field advises 'fake it' until it becomes automatic. Given that most victims are rather timid, shy and introverted, one can see that isn't going to be easy.

Ignore it. This is sometimes suggested as the first thing you should do if somebody tries to bully you. Not everybody agrees. Miller (1999) writes: 'While kids are making fun of you, one of the worst things you can do is to pretend to ignore them in the hope that they will lose interest and stop. They won't. They know you can hear them, and if you act like you can't, they'll take that as a challenge and keep at you' (p.15). She adds: 'Even though you do not look at them or speak to them, your non-verbal reactions – clenching your teeth, staring straight ahead, frowning, etc – gives them enough proof that they are upsetting you. This is all the encouragement they need to continue' (p.19).

Zarzour (1999), who believes that acting assertively can be a first step, concedes that assertiveness may not always work, and that one might then go on to talk to the bully 'in a friendly manner'. If this fails, she says, one may calmly walk away – remembering 'to hide your fear'. This way of reacting to bullies does not appeal to many people. Parents typically would like to see a more positive or even aggressive response from their children. Children who see a child walking away following uncalled-for insults, hiding (or more probably *trying* to hide) their fear, are liable to deride the victim as a coward.

Many writers suggest that he or she should hit back verbally but not physically. The reason for differentiating between the two modes of reacting is sometimes unclear. The assumption is made that physical aggression is somehow worse than verbal aggression and, regardless of the situation, more culpable. Yet it is misleading to assume that physical aggression is always more reprehensible than verbal aggression. If we are concerned about the 'hurtfulness' of the two kinds of aggressive acts, then we need evidence that physical aggression is more hurtful than verbal aggression. In fact, in a recent study with 14-year-old Australian schoolchildren (Rigby and Bagshaw 2001), students rated 'name-calling' as more hurtful to them than a slap across the face. I think the real objections to physical counter-aggression when bullied at school are two-fold: first, the victim is likely to get the worst of it, in particular if he or she is outnumbered or confronted by a stronger person; and second, that physical aggression is seen as particularly objectionable by schools. Conspicuous violence, especially if it escalates, is always a major concern for schools.

In discussing how victims should or should not respond to bullying, we should make it clear in whose interest the advice is being given. Pepler, a Canadian psychologist who has specialised in addressing problems of bullying in schools, is quoted by Zarzour as having this to say about victims hitting back: 'I can't argue that it's not effective in some situations. It may well be ...' In short, it is recognised that in some situations it may be in the best interest of the individual child to hit back. Pepler continues: 'It is not a positive way to solve a problem' (p.96). But we need to ask again, from whose point of view is it not positive, the individual's or the school's? To the child who has got the bully on his or her back the outcome is very positive, if they successfully hit back. To the school, understandably concerned about its reputation, the totality of violent incidents are what concerns it most.

Rarely do we think about 'hitting back' from the point of view of the victimised child. Recently I came across an analysis of what victims should do from a young man who had just left school and posted his comments on the internet. He makes the very obvious point, curiously neglected, that it would be foolish not to distinguish between an extremely dangerous, even life-threatening situation, as when one's assailant is brandishing a knife or a group is intent on beating you up – in which case it is wise to 'play ball' or run like hell – and a situation in which a milder kind of bully is 'trying it on'. He goes on to point out that a countering blow struck in anger may on some occasions be the wiser option, even though one might subsequently pay for it by losing a fight or even a tooth; preferable maybe to being chased round the school for years to come by a rabble of insensitive kids who see you as a pushover who will not fight back.

Being assertive is widely seen as the answer, but how? It is often recommended that the victim states how he or she feels, as in: 'I don't like what you said then', followed by steady eye-contact. Or 'I don't think that's funny', when one has been deliberately insulted. Or more simply: 'I would like you to stop doing that.' If the bully is sufficiently empathic to care about the victim's feelings or opinions, the bullying may end. But many a time the bully or bullies will simply be receiving welcome, explicit confirmation that the barb has gone home as intended.

Some writers have spent considerable time and applied considerable ingenuity in devising the sort of 'come-backs' that can put the bully on the back foot and even back off for good. These tailor-made retorts vary in degree of offensiveness.

E. Field (1999) provides numerous examples of verbal tricks and questions that a victim may use. Some involve asking questions designed to put the pressure back on the bully.

> Bully: Hey homo…
> Reply: Could you explain that to me, I'm only a lay person
>
> Bully: Hey, fathead…
> Reply: Did you call me fat or obese. What is the difference?
>
> Bully: You're such a bitch
> Reply: Shall I go back to my kennel now or later?

Such a display of verbal dexterity is intended to convince the bully that he or she will surely lose in a battle of wits, in which case there is no verbal imbalance of power in the bully's favour (in this regard power has been equalised or maybe tilted the other way). Perhaps the bully would be advised to try a different medium of aggression. One is reminded of the mythical encounter that supposedly took place between two men on a narrow pavement in 18th-century London. The swaggering bully blocks an oncoming pedestrian saying: 'I never give way to a villain.' 'Oh,' says the other, stepping neatly aside, 'I always do.' Collapse of the real villain.

It is possible that some children who might otherwise be victimised could learn such tricks, but as I think the examples show, what they are asked to say must all too often appear unnatural and suggest a precocity that could afford further grounds for tormenting the child. A further problem is that such tricks are not easily learned or 'pulled off' by children who are naturally introverted and not verbally quick, which unfortunately is often the case among children whose peers ridicule them. Field recognises this problem and concludes: 'They (victims) should only say something when they can do it naturally and automatically' (p.185).

In her advice to parents, Field advises: 'Your child should always appear polite and respectful.' Never 'rude and aggressive'. Not all advisers agree.

Miller (1999) sees bully and victim engaged in a desperate struggle where desperate measures may be taken. 'Brace yourself for a power struggle,' she writes, 'and be ready to stand your ground. Don't give up when ridicule seems to get worse' (p.16). Here are her examples of insults and comebacks:

> Insult: You're so ugly
> Comeback: Then I must be like you
>
> Insult: You look like a witch
> Comeback: That's really funny coming from a hag
>
> Insult: You're such a skinny freak
> Comeback: Thanks fatso
>
> Insult: You're so stupid
> Comeback: So few brain cells. Don't waste them on speech.

With the possible exception of the last one, these have the virtue of lacking any sort of subtlety.

At a loftier level, Fuller (2000) has suggested that children learn to deflect or 'deconstruct' insults from bullies, thereby reducing their hurtfulness. Here are his examples: if you are called a slut, point out that a slut really means 'a woman of untidy domestic habits'. A clever response, he suggests, would then be: 'How do you know I haven't done the dishes?' If you are called a faggot recognise that a faggot is an English meatball. Hence the smart answer to being called a faggot could be: 'What makes you think I'm an English meatball?' One wonders on how many schoolyard bullies this display of erudition would be rather lost. Fuller adds that among his favourite responses to the jibes of bullies are 'snotgobbler' and 'weasel breath', said with gusto and determination – and (I should think) at least a 50-metre start.

Telling

'Make ours a telling school' is a catchcry of many schools that have adopted an anti-bullying policy. Although most children at some stage in their lives have told others that they have been bullied at school – and sometimes received effective help – many children prefer to keep it to themselves, either from a sense of pride or a sense of fear. There is for some children – and some adults too (for example in the armed forces) – a stigma attached to 'informing on your mates' or showing that 'you can't take it'.

From the perspective of organisations, 'telling' seems desirable. It is a means by which the authorities can find out what is going on. If it is out in the open, they reason, they can deal with it.

Hence, a great deal of pressure may be put on children to tell.

From the viewpoint of the individual child the picture may be different. Approximately 10 per cent of children in schools report that 'telling' led to matters getting worse – and with increasing age no improvement is evident. One can understand why many children, especially older children, are reluctant to ask others for help when they are being bullied. Telling everybody may be a recipe for disaster. Some will be glad to hear the news – and join in with the bullying. Limiting the 'telling' to people who can be trusted is an important proviso. As we have seen, school counsellors normally have a much better record of being helpful than others. But it is important for school authorities to recognize that from the perspective of individual children it is not clear whether it is in their interest to take the risk of informing. Hence, if school authorities are going to encourage informing on bullies as a matter of school policy, they need to assure children that the risk is non-existent or, at worst, minimal. They need to ensure that children who tell are well protected.

Taking action on behalf of the victim

What action and when? Authorities – whether teachers, parents, counsellors or managers – are often undecided as to what kind of action they should take and under what circumstances the action is justified. Most are agreed that it is best for victims to solve the problem themselves – if this is possible. The lift to self-esteem in overcoming a bullying problem oneself is remarkable. Hence, it is generally advisable to spend time exploring what can be done by the victim, without involving the authorities. In any case, often the victim does not want the authority to take direct action on his or her behalf, and, as we have seen, he or she may have grounds for suspecting that the situation could be made worse. Persuading a hesitant victim otherwise or over-riding the victim's wishes should obviously be done only in extreme circumstances, for instance when the victim's life or health is seriously threatened. It is known that in many cases the victim simply wants to be heard and receive moral support – and that such support can reduce the stress that is being experienced and lessen negative health effects (Rigby 2000). But there certainly are cases in which it would be desirable and sensible to provide more positive help. Where a child or older person has become traumatised by a severe bullying experience, professional help may be needed, and knowing how a relevant referral can be made is important. Where intervention on behalf of the victim is seen as necessary, a guiding principle must be to reduce the likelihood of that person being further victimised as a result of informing. This means providing adequate protection – which is sometimes not easy to do. It may be that on occasions effective action can be taken on the basis of information that cannot be traced back to what the victim may have said. The Method of Shared

Concern, as developed by Anatol Pikas (1989) (see below), suggests ways in which this may be achieved.

Focus on the bully

What can be done by parents to prevent a child from growing up a bully? Zarzour (1999) declares – and some others agree: 'Bullies are not born: they're created' (p.57). The jury in fact is still out (the jurymen and jurywomen of different persuasions – behavioural geneticists and developmental psychologists – are still arguing fiercely about the verdict). But in the meantime it would be foolish not to try to produce the conditions that we know are statistically associated with the home backgrounds of non-aggressive children. And we know the sort of families in which bullies do not usually thrive. They are non-authoritarian (also non-permissive); they are caring, accepting; they are places where children are happy rather than resentful. But more specifically, what if the child behaves aggressively, as children invariably do from time to time? Here viewpoints diverge. For example, Zarzour argues that when children act aggressively, regardless of circumstances, parents should tell them that they are upset about it, and ask them whether they could not have handled their feelings better. However, parents are generally *not* upset when their children stand up for their rights; as when they persist and push away another child who would take things from them. Most parents would see such counter-aggression as a legitimate use of force, not to be confused with bullying.

A further issue upon which there are alternative views is whether children should be exposed to violent media presentations. It is sometimes argued that the media is one thing and real life another, and that the former does not affect the latter. We may see violence as mere entertainment. Sometimes the argument is that viewing violence can have a cathartic effect and enable us to discharge aggressive feelings vicariously through fantasy. The research on this issue is now quite extensive. The verdict is not unanimous, but the drift is certainly towards believing that viewing high levels of media violence is likely to induce violent behaviour in children, especially among those predisposed to act aggressively and to bully others.

Action with the bully

What should one do to, with, or for the bully? The prepositions 'to', 'with' and 'for' are significant. For some people the question is simply what should we do 'to' the bully – what does he or she deserve to have happen and what might act as a deterrent to others? 'Making the punishment fit the crime' is a well respected principle in jurisprudence, widely supported. But is bullying a crime? Does it call for a response that is applicable to offences we call criminal? In some writings about bullying the word 'crime' is used loosely, to express the writer's feelings of repugnance. I think we should be clear that where bullying has been involved, legal action has been applied in relation to the nature of the assault and the damage it caused, rather than because it constituted 'bullying' as such. From a legal standpoint, it appears that bullying per se is not a crime, but actions that accompany bullying may be criminal, and incur legally justified punishment.

Most of what we call bullying does not invoke the law, not is it likely to do so. Yet quasi-legal structures are being mooted and in some cases introduced to cater for the relatively extreme forms of bullying, for instance, in the form of tribunals in industry which may examine cases of sexual and racial bullying and even personal bullying. In schools, procedures are sometimes introduced leading to decisions about the kinds of sanctions that should be applied, and these may include suspensions. Some writers have advocated the setting up of bully courts in which students may play a leading role in 'trying' suspected bullies and recommending to the principal of a school that one or more of their peers be punished for 'bullying' (see Elliott 1991). The notion of retributive justice as applicable to bullying, especially extreme forms, is also not without its supporters.

The buzz word until recently has been 'consequences'. This sounds better than 'punishment', in part perhaps because the latter has, for some, a sense of being arbitrary and vengeful, though of course it need not have. The appeal of 'consequences' also lies in its apparent independence of volition on the part of authorities who do hurtful things to rule-breakers. If rules can be formulated that are entirely reasonable then whoever breaks them brings the consequences on themselves. The rules relating to behaviour are seen as having an unquestionable validity. They are 'natural laws' akin to the law of gravity. Defy that and you are almost literally riding for a fall. The snag lies in the difficulty of formulating entirely reasonable rules for everything. Rules are always there to be questioned and defended or changed. Nevertheless, there is some evidence that in those US schools where students are more knowledgeable of the school rules for behavioural infractions and also know the consequences for infractions of those rules, the level of school disorder is significantly lower (Mayer and Leone 1999).

Responses to bullying sometimes invoke the concept of zero tolerance. Tolerate nothing. The theory of James Q. Wilson, the academic who introduced the notion, was that allowing small crimes to pass unpunished will encourage contempt for the law in larger matters. For instance, a school in which children tease and call each other names will also be one in which children physically assault each other. In practice, if we stamp on teasing we will simultaneously be reducing physical violence. The plausibility of this theory appeared to be supported by the introduction of zero-tolerance policing in New York and a corresponding observed reduction in crime in that city. Unfortunately for the theory, its introduction coincided with a period during which there was a dramatic reduction in the numbers of young men in New York between the ages of 15 and 24 years, the demographic category most associated with crime statistics (see 'Defeating the bad guys', *The Economist* 1998).

What disturbs people about the zero-tolerance policy is that in its execution, if not in its conception and intention, it appears to be undiscriminating. Cases of minor infringement have been treated as major crimes meriting suspension. In their examination of legal issues in the prevention of school violence, Yell and Rozalsky (2000) describe zero tolerance as relating to 'policies in which any violation of a specified type (e.g. violence, drug use) results in severe consequences (e.g. expulsion, arrest)' (p. 190). This suggests that the theory of zero tolerance applies to really serious anti-social activities. But this goes against the line of thinking that says don't let people get away with small things or they will go on to do the big things. No wonder people are confused. What is missing is a reasonable view on adjusting the reaction of school authorities to correspond to the seriousness of the student's misbehaviour.

We need a reasonable typology of seriousness as applied to bullying. Delwyn Tattum, the Welsh authority on bullying, has advised teachers to gather all the relevant evidence, then 'exercise the wisdom of Solomon'. Certainly an answer cannot be given in a nutshell. Unfortunately, that is what teachers and authorities in general want, and the notion of an irrefutable correspondence between offence, rule and consequence is what is yearned for. Some authorities have sought to provide guidelines to help teachers to gauge the seriousness of offences and the severity of the options open to them (Rigby 2001).

But when the focus is on the bully, the question is not just or simply what shall be done to him or her, because that would be just and that would deter others. There is also the question of what can be done with and for such a person. Tattum, for instance, has argued that it is not enough simply to apply an appropriate sanction to the school bully. We have to think about the miscreant's future. Should the label 'bully' remain like an albatross around his or her neck in perpetuity? Clearly not, if one wants to motivate that person to make a fresh start and, in time, wipe the slate clean.

Some would argue that (whether the individual wants it or not) bullies must be 'helped'. The means by which a bully can be helped to abandon bullying and act more pro-socially may, of course, vary from person to person. For example, some bullies do have well developed social skills; others may bully because they lack such accomplishments and can in fact be helped by appropriate social training. There are bullies who simply lack self-control and these people may benefit from anger-management training, whilst others are very deliberate and calculating and cannot be helped in this way. Some can be helped by being provided with better opportunities for cooperating with others or even leading others in pro-social activities. It would be foolish, however, to assume that all can be helped in the same way, or that every alternative is equally practicable. One may, for instance, seek to reform a bully in the workplace by promoting him to a position of greater authority (where he is less frustrated) only to find that this gives him greater scope for bullying and that his promotion is, in any case, deeply resented by other workers.

Finally we should recognise that there is one enormously important advantage in working 'with' bullies or 'for' bullies as opposed to against them. If one is successful in changing the basic motivation of people who bully (and no-one should underrate this difficulty) the task of monitoring what goes on in the school or workplace is made much easier. In fact, as far as the less overt forms of bullying are concerned, as in indirect aggression, rumour spreading, etc. – forms that are often highly destructive of individuals – they are practically impossible to stamp out by punitive action and sustained surveillance.

Focus on the bully or bullies and the victim

They say it takes two to tango – and at least two, often more, to produce a bully/victim situation. Hence some authorities have argued that it is no good dealing with each in isolation. The bully and the victim must be brought together and their conflict resolved in a satisfactory way. Accordingly, emphasis has been placed in some schools on conflict resolution. This has sometimes involved the training of selected students in ways in which they can intervene to stop bullying from continuing. There can be no doubt that some students are apt trainees and can develop useful conflict resolution skills and apply them in situations where aggressors and victims are prepared to talk about their differences. Indeed, some students are more willing to work with a fellow student-counsellor than with a teacher whom they think would be less able to understand the situation. However, as it has been frequently observed, mediation ideally requires a situation in which there is an equality in power between the people in dispute and a readiness in both of them to find a mutually acceptable solution. By definition bullying occurs when there is an imbalance of power, sometimes a very large imbalance of power. Moreover the bully often does not want his or her dominance over the other to end. There is little therefore for the bully to gain from mediation; much, it seems, to lose. What can be done directly through the use of it to resolve conflict in bully/victim cases must therefore be limited. (I should add that it may nevertheless help greatly in creating an ethos in a school or place of employment which is conducive to constructive relations between people; an ethos in which bullying is unlikely to thrive.)

Authority is generally seen as needed to redress the imbalance of power between bully and victim. In schools this means teachers; in the workplace, management – or a suitable tribunal or even a court of law. Typically, the bully or bullies are to be denounced; the victim (or victims) roundly supported. In schools I often hear of such a thing. The gang of bullies are 'invited' to the principal's office and dressed down in no uncertain terms in the presence of the child whom they have been tormenting. They are then each invited to go up and apologise sincerely to the poor child who is wishing the ground would swallow him up. Afterwards, he – or it could be she – has a fair idea of what will happen. The subsequent bullying could be more subtle but no less intense and no less hurtful.

Anatol Pikas (1989) has proposed a way in which authorities – that is credible authorities – can work with both bullies and victims. His method of dealing with bullies and victims is known as the Method of Shared Concern. It has been applied in numerous schools in Europe and in Australia, often with considerable success. It seems likely that the approach can be adapted for use in the workplace. The method is applicable especially in cases in which there is evidence of group bullying. It is assumed that bullies are generally insensitive to the harm, or the extent of the harm, they are doing to the victim. This insensitivity is due to their involvement in a group which seems to give legitimacy to their bullying activities and prevents them from feeling personally responsible for the outcomes. What they appear to gain mostly through bullying is a sense of being part of a group which is 'having fun'. Yet as individuals, bullies commonly feel uncomfortable about what is being done. Further, a hostile blaming attitude on the part of an authority figure is likely to increase the desire to continue bullying and unite the group of bullies more strongly.

Pikas recommends that one should work with members of a known bullying group individually, and always begin by sharing with them one's own sincere concern for the victim before asking them what they know about what has been happening to the victim. The method is in a sense confrontational – it does not involve making any accusations but it does strongly invite and expect a responsible response. Typically promises are elicited from each person in the group separately on how they will improve the situation for the victim. (A possible script for an encounter is given in Ken Rigby's website: http://www.education.unisa. edu.au/bullying/) What transpires is then carefully monitored.

Pikas believes strongly that victims should not be interviewed first, because then the bullies will suspect that they have informed on them and the victims will become more endangered. Victims, he points out, are not always 'innocent', and it is important to understand what they may be doing to provoke the bullying. One may need to work directly on changing the victim's provocative way of behaving. Once the victim becomes involved in the proceedings, the counsellor may sometimes need to engage in 'shuttle diplomacy', between the victim and members of the bullying group in a mediational role. Although the aim is to re-individualise bullies, the idea is *not* to 'break up' groups (students have a right to enjoy being in a group) but eventually to change their attitudes and behaviour towards the victim and other potential victims.

Finally, in employing this method, it is important to see the whole group of 'bullies' together, to congratulate them on what they have been able to achieve, and to work through any residual problems with the victim present. An important benefit from this approach is that it can lead to a 'change of heart' on the part of bullies and remove the need for constant surveillance. He points out that the use of punishment is often ineffective. It may breed resentment, increase group solidarity, jeopardise the victim further, and challenge bullies to practise ways of bullying that are hard to detect. There is research evidence that the method is effective in at least two cases in three and contributes significantly to reduction in peer victimisation (see Petersen and Rigby 1999; Smith and Sharp 1994).

Include the peers

A wider perspective on dealing with bully/victim problems includes not only bullies and victims but also peers. We can identify two contrasting ways in which this may be done, based upon quite different philosophies and premises. Both ways have been applied only in schools.

One way is to include peers in reaching a judgement about the culpability of the bully or bullies and the penalty or sanction that is to be applied. This approach was suggested by Michelle Elliott (1991) who advocated the setting up of so-called bully courts. The process (as described in Rigby 1997) can begin when, and only when, a student makes a formal complaint against another student. For this an official form is provided on which the details are written. The bully or bullies are invited to attend the next meeting of the bully court. The complainant is also to be present, together with any witnesses of the event(s). There is no audience. Each person attending the proceedings is asked to give evidence and is then questioned by the panel of students and staff. The panel then discusses each case in private and makes its judgement. Penalties or sanctions may be prescribed and steps taken to see that they are administered, unless there is a successful appeal to the principal who may apply a veto.

Finally, as in a system of law, a record is kept of all proceedings and verdicts and these become precedents for other cases.

Another, radically different way has been suggested by Maines and Robinson (1992) and is known as the No Blame Approach. The authors have provided a detailed description of the method; a critique is to be found in Rigby (1997). Again the use of the method has been limited to schools. They have proposed that a teacher or counsellor who learns about a child being bullied should discover as accurately as possible from the victim both how he or she has been feeling about the treatment and who the perpetrators are. With the victim's permission (and with assurances that it is safe to do so) the bullies are approached and a meeting convened which includes some peers of the bullies as well as the bullies themselves. At this meeting the convener describes in graphic detail the predicament of the victim and the distress that has been felt by him or her. As a group, they are asked to put things right, and left to do so. As with the Method of Shared Concern, the outcome is carefully monitored.

Despite involving the same persons – bullies, victim and peers – in an attempted resolution of the problem, the underlying rationales could hardly be more different. The bully courts assume there is probably somebody to blame, somebody to be tried and probably convicted. The No Blame Approach assumes that the allocation of blame is unnecessary and even counter-productive. The important thing is to change the situation for the victim. The role of the peers in bully courts is to apply principles of justice, as in the public courts. The role of the peers in the No Blame Approach is to help to exert positive social influence on the bullies so that they will be encouraged to do the right thing by the victim. The philosophy behind the bully courts is that bullies need to be punished and any would-be bullies deterred by the knowledge that they can be brought to justice. The philosophy behind the No Blame Courts is that punishment is unnecessary and moreover, bullies and would-be bullies will behave well if their consciences can be touched and if they are influenced – but not coerced – by others who know what is the right thing to do.

There is one more distinctive feature of the No Blame Approach setting it apart. The exponents believe that it is absurd to believe that the victim is in any sense to blame. He or she, they assert, are actually doing their best. They would stop the bully if they could. It is outrageous to suggest in any way that the victim is to blame, for example, in not having the necessary social skills or in being somehow provocative. Curiously, I have found that some people feel that the victim *is* being blamed if the bully is not punished, so deeply ingrained is the notion that one cannot reasonably deal with bullying cases without punishing someone.

Include the friends and families

Perhaps the broadest perspective employed is one in which the net is spread so wide as to include virtually everyone who has a personal interest in the way bullies and victims are going to be dealt with. This most inclusive approach has been advocated by those who run community or school conferences for the resolution of particularly extreme kinds of bullying, as in cases involving serious assaults which do not have to go to court. At such a conference the victim of bullying is encouraged to describe what had happened and the distress that resulted. Friends and relatives of both parties – bully and victim – listen to what is said. The victim has the satisfaction of knowing that what has happened has indeed been heard. The bully is expected to provide compensation for the hurt that was done, and typically feels shame. When this is done with the support of family and friends this can be 'reintegrative shame' rather than an enduring stigma (see Braithwaite 1989).

This approach is controversial and clearly requires a careful selection of cases that are suitable for conferences and the employment of a trained facilitator to manage proceedings. One difficulty is that if teachers are used as facilitators, the fact that they may be well known to the persons involved in the conflict, and are, in any case, seen as representing the school, may call into question their objectivity and reduce their effectiveness. Yet there have certainly been successful resolutions of bully/victim issues using this approach, and more important, true reconciliations between bullies and victims. The view of bullying as a community problem requiring a community response rather than one that involves a counsellor, detached from the broader social context and 'fixing up' individuals, has considerable appeal.

References

Berne, S. (1996) *Bully-Proof Your Child*. Port Melbourne: Lothian.

Braithwaite, J. (1989) *Crime, Shame and Reintegration*. Cambridge: Cambridge University Press.

'Defeating the Bad Guys' (1998) *The Economist 340*, 35–38.

Elliott, M. (1991) *Bullying: A Practical Guide to Coping in Schools*. London: Longman.

Field, E. M. (1999) *Bully Busting*. Lane Cove, NSW: Finch Publishing Pty.

Fuller, A. (2000) *Raising Resilient Young People, a Parents' Guide*. Sydney: Australian Scout Publication.

Maines, B. and Robinson, G. (1992) *Michael's Story: The 'No Blame' Approach*. Bristol: Lame Duck Publishing.

Mayer, M. J. and Leone, P. E. (1999) 'A structural analysis of school violence and disruption: implications for creating safer schools.' *Education and Treatment of Children 22*, 333–356.

Miller, D. (1999) 'Time to tell 'em off! A pocket guide to overcoming ridicule.' Unpublished manuscript.

Petersen, L. and Rigby, K. (1999) 'Countering bullying at an Australian secondary school.' *Journal of Adolescence 22*, 4, 481–492.

Pikas, A. (1989) 'The Common Concern Method for the treatment of mobbing.' In E. Roland and E. Munthe (eds) *Bullying: An International Perspective*. London: David Fulton in association with the Professional Development Foundation.

Rigby, K. (1997) *Bullying in Schools – And What to do About It*. British Edition. London: Jessica Kingsley Publishers.

Rigby, K. (2000) 'Effects of peer victimisation in schools and perceived social support on adolescent well-being.' *Journal of Adolescence 23*, 1, 57–68.

Rigby, K. (2001) *Stop the Bullying: A Handbook for Schools*. Melbourne: Australian Council for Educational Research.

Rigby, K. and Bagshaw D. (2001) 'The prevalence and hurtfulness of acts of aggression from peers experienced by Australian male and female adolescents at school.' *Children Australia*.

Seligman, M.E.P. (1995) *The Optimistic Child*. London: Houghton Mifflin.

Smith, P. K. and Sharp, S. (eds) (1994) *School Bullying: Insights and Perspectives*. London: Routledge.

Yell, M. L. and Rozalsky, M. E. (2000) 'Searching for safe schools: Legal issues in the prevention of school violence.' *Journal of Emotional and Behavioural Disorders 8*, 187–197.

Zarzour, K. (1999) *The Schoolyard Bully*. Toronto: HarperCollins.

Chapter 22

Might is right? A discussion of the ethics and practicalities of control and restraint in education

John Cornwall

Introduction

This chapter sets out to challenge some of the assumptions underlying current guidance and strategies for physical restraint in schools. Teachers and managers are worried about the consequences of violence and extreme behaviour in schools. All of us lack confidence in dealing with these problems because they have not yet been set on a firm ethical and psychological footing. The threat of the medico-legal system and the demands of social accountability that surround teachers and schools is such that too many assumptions have been made about what is on offer. Short term training 'packages' have been accepted without sufficient questioning of their provenance and schools are currently reaping the whirlwind in terms of staff subjected to litigation and disciplinary procedures not to mention damaged young lives that deserve a more rigorous professional response. This chapter deliberately throws up questions, challenges some key assumptions and hopes to encourage further practical research and improve the quality of debate and training.

The skills required to develop and maintain good workable relationships with troubled and troublesome young people are complex and require much practice. Children and young people who exhibit extremes of challenging behaviour are often involved in restraint situations and are amongst the most troubled and emotionally vulnerable. They may also have significant or severe learning disabilities or be suffering from post-traumatic stress (Randall, 1998). In addition to this, the wider impact of brief (and even isolated) incidents of challenging behaviour, violence and subsequent restraint on the lives of both staff and children or young people is out of all proportion to the number of pupils involved (Harris, 1995). Yet there is little attempt to engage in discourse and research on important ethical and educational issues or the psychological impact of physically controlling and restraining young people (Peagam, 1993; Cooper, 1999). Circular 10/98 does not deal with the training required for individuals to 'live up to' school policies nor does it acknowledge the complexity of the situations encountered. For example, the tensions encountered between individual emotional requirements of young people and the demands of the national curriculum and OfSTED. The response in research and literature seems to be equally indifferent in the UK. An illuminative but statistically imprecise search of ERIC (Educational Resources Information Center) revealed in excess of 800 citations worldwide, but mostly from the USA, using the parameters of 'violence', 'aggression', 'physical restraint' and 'education' in various combinations. An equivalent search of the British Education Index revealed little more than one percent of this number (8) with a similar percentage on ERIC (12) representing UK work. This indicates an inattention to the ethics and the human consequences of current practice. It also reflects a lack of focus on:

- the many potential layers of non-confrontational advanced communication skills;
- an understanding of the psychology and psychological consequences; and,
- alternative (to physical restraint) strategies that should be available to schools and teachers.

It could be argued that the recognition by service managers and policy makers of the impact of violence on pupils, teachers and in schools is too little and too focused on short-term reaction rather than prevention or longer-term psychological and educational responses.

Assumption [1] – that violence is the result of individual derangement and that a 'control and restraint' ethic is appropriate or understood

Conflict is a transaction between people and there is an assumed consensus about what constitutes violent or aggressive behaviour in schools. This is misleading. Such challenging behaviour and the influences that promote it are complex. When these complex social and psychological factors are taken into account, particularly with younger children, it is more useful to regard such behaviour as 'growth not pathology' (Bennathan, 1997). For example, the discussion and debate about the influence of media and computer games still continues (e.g. Charlton & Gunter, 1999; Charlton, Gunter & Coles, 1998) unabated and unresolved. There has been some discussion about stress as a cause of challenging behaviour with implications for the way we respond to it (Cornwall, 1998; Varma, 1973; Wolff, 1969) and only a small amount about the educational impact of the mental health of children and young people (Varma, 1973). Similar confusions still exist about what warrants physical intervention and whether (self-) protection is the same as control and is this, in turn, the same as restraint? In other words the lack of informed and publicised or open debate means that individual schools and teachers are forced into making quick and crucial decisions without sufficient shared knowledge and strategy or well-developed skills. The Education Act 1997 (Section 1) refers to specific purposes by teachers and learning support staff which includes the following justification for physical restraint, in preventing pupils or students from...

- committing a criminal offence
- injuring themselves or others
- causing damage to property
- engaging in any behaviour prejudicial to maintaining good order and discipline.

Whilst this might seem reasonable enough, there are a range of ethical problems attached to using restraint to maintain order and discipline. It is here that the confusions exist between general human right to self protection (and the protection of others) and restraint as coercion; over the use of restraint as 'discipline', when teachers are trying to maintain positive relationships and encourage self-discipline, and self-restraint; and finally, over the need to choose an ethically based system for staff to use within the commercial base from which training is promoted these days. To add a practical note, Circular 10/98 adds that 'property' includes the pupil's own property. One has to question whether physically restraining a pupil from damaging his or her own property is appropriate as a general rule. For example, breaking your own pencil in class could be interpreted as a 'restrainable' action, depending on the timing of the event. There is still much confusion about the conditions that should trigger off physical intervention and the application of the terminology associated with violence and control. Hewett & Arnett (1996) asked pertinent questions about the key judgements that staff have to make in difficult and sometimes traumatic circumstances:

- Are there grounds for believing immediate action is necessary to prevent injury?

- Are there grounds for believing that someone might be 'significantly' injured?
- Are there grounds for believing that there will be serious damage to property if physical restraint is not used?
- Are there more steps that can be taken in advance to avoid the necessity for physical restraint?

There are also issues involved in what is expected of teachers. Is there a range of activity stemming from a 'control' ethic to an 'educational' ethic (exemplified in McGuiness, 1994)? Should teachers really be working in the 'control' part of this spectrum – along with control by drugs, strict behaviour modification techniques, sarcasm, verbal aggression and legal sanctions? Is this compatible with their position as a teacher and mentor? If challenging and physically aggressive behaviour is seen as a form of communication – then what is communicated to pupils when they are physically restrained by a group of adults? Might is right?

The control ethic stems from a medico-individualistic perspective where the remedy lies in control and treatment of an aberration or problem within the individual. Where does the social and educational perspective come in? For example, sufficient opportunity for personal and social development for certain young people, including such areas as anger management, inter-personal or assertive skills and stress management. A longer term perspective might include the use of early years and primary strategies (e.g. Kochanska, Tjebkes and Forman, 1998; Bennathan, 1997; Jewett, 1992). There is still something of an authoritarian or hard-baked reaction to extreme and challenging behaviour in young people characterised over the years by an emphasis on 'behavioural' (and disciplinary) rather than 'emotional' (Bowers, 1996) and self-restraint. In all areas of education provision, there are still issues of power and control that remain unexplored and still confusion between disciplinary and therapeutic responses in schools (Smith & Cooper, 1996). These are probably linked to a lack of 'ethics' in this area, particularly with respect to the rights of young people and issues of choice and autonomy. Do children have a right to absent themselves from the classroom if it is failing them? Are other means of expression open to them?

Assumption [2] – that 'control and restraint' training is sufficient and appropriate as a major response by schools and LEAs to violent or aggressive behaviour by certain individuals

A young person's emotional growth depends as much on 'how things are done' as 'what is done' and attitudes and relationships are key to this process (Greenhalgh, 1994; Bowers, 1996) as well as to effective teaching and learning.

In probation services there has been some effort expended to understand the nature of violence in the context of helping clients and, for example, the role of gender and gender stereotyping (Buckley, 1999) and in Scotland, interventions in the playground (e.g. Briggs, McKay & Miller, 1995) have shed light on the effect of the school environment. In schools it is predominantly a male problem but little discussion or research of the implications of this has taken place in the educational context. Recent NfER research (Kinder et al, 1999) points clearly to the importance of a humane approach to young people with 'techniques and attitudes that enable teachers and other staff to recognise and relate successfully to troubled youngsters'. This could be argued to be the opposite of a hard line coercive education system whose end result 'in extremis' is physical control and physical superiority. The concepts of emotional and social growth and learning 'self-restraint' could be at odds with the foundation of Circular 10/98 that implies we are saving young people from themselves (i.e. when they are out of control).

There are also considerable dangers and long-term consequences for adults and children when physical control goes wrong. For example, the lack of trust in services, the indignity and increasing disaffection of young people and the consequences for the careers of teachers and carers. Incidents of disciplinary procedures and whole school investigations point to…

a)   a lack of skills and understanding of the range of techniques and mediating strategies that could be used before resorting to physical intervention techniques;
b)   a lack of recognition of the psychological factors working within all parties involved in violent or potentially violent situations and of the psychological consequences for all parties; and,
c)   inappropriate and uninformed management ethics, compounded by lack of training and poor attitudes – particularly with people who are learning disabled.

A lack of the proper study of violence, control and restraint practices in schools could lead us towards a culture where physical control is practised as a means of achieving compliance, not as the ultimate last resort. The ultimate horror is where control and restraint actually satisfies the need for power and sadistic satisfaction of the staff involved (see McIntyre, 1999).

There appears to be an increasing number of troubled and troublesome youngsters who resort to extremes of aggressive and violent behaviour. There has been a lack of cohesion and a history of sparse research and writing in this country as yet (also noted by Cooper, Smith and Upton in 1994) that gives a clear picture of these trends and their causes. Historically, inaction in addressing the needs of this group (Peagam, 1993) has led to a lack of proper psychological and ethical rationale in dealing with troubled young people who resort to violence and aggression (McDonnell, Dearden & Richens, 1991). Certainly exclusions from school (many due to confrontations) increased in the 90s from 2,910 in 1990/91 to 13,581 by 1996/97 (Castle & Parsons, 1997). Many of these exclusions can be traced back to confrontations with individual teachers and their lack of skill and understanding in handling these situations or the lack of time and positive school strategies to minimise risks (Peagam, 1993).

Despite lack of recognition of the social, cultural and affective psychological factors at play (Bowers, 1996; Cooper, 1999) and the importance of an ethical response, there has been a growth in the marketing of 'packaged' control and restraint or physical intervention programmes nationally. Head Teachers and Managers are currently choosing training programmes for their staff without...

- any objective or shared evaluative criteria as to their efficacy and ethical base or any significant background comparative research;
- regard to the importance of·previous training in conflict management technique, de-escalation, advanced communication or anger management skills; and,
- incorporating a necessary review of teamwork, institutional ethos, practices and policy that might contribute to violent and aggressive incidents.

Assumption [3] – that it is the role of the teacher, to restrain, control and enforce an essentially coercive system

What do teachers say? There is very little national research that clearly states teachers' feelings and thoughts about the apparent necessity to adopt physical intervention techniques. So far, significant resources have been allocated to a 'fire brigade' (McGuiness, 1994) model of intervention where there is violence, aggression or extremely challenging behaviour. In this country we have concentrated on behaviour management whereas elsewhere there has been recognition given to emotional and diverse capabilities as well as social projects (Goleman, 1996; Gardner, 1993; Goldstein, 1987; Gibbs, Potter, Goldstein & Brendtro, 1996). In America, a number of specific approaches for teachers have developed (e.g. Gibbs et al., 1996; Pappas, 1997; Graves et al., 1997) and work has been done in the early years development of cooperation and self-restraint (e.g. Kochanska et al., 1998; Jewett, 1992). In Washington State, USA, the 'Second Step' Elementary School programme combines an ethical and humane approach to youth violence that includes empathy, impulse control and anger management training and has been properly evaluated (Grossman, 1997). This behavioural research has indicated that early intervention programmes like these are effective in reducing youth violence as students get older. It is an 'educational' – not a 'controlling' approach.

A pilot study (Cornwall, 2000) of teachers' concerns and successes in working with challenging behaviour has been undertaken over the past five years. It has involved the analysis of over 400 teacher (and learning support assistant) statements and disclosures. The following concerns have been expressed by a significant number of adults who work with troubled and challenging children…

- they may not be able to exert sufficient self-control themselves in extremely challenging situations;
- they do not have sufficient time and opportunity (apart from brief training) to practise physical intervention skills and they are not confident in their safe use;
- they don't feel armed with sufficiently broad or well-founded skills to handle often very difficult situations in a non-confrontational way;
- they are concerned that it will become an expectation and will also affect their relationships with pupils.

It is fairly clear that they feel unskilled and clearly point up the need for broader and deeper training that will enable them to deal with challenging behaviour and aggressive responses. They are also very concerned about maintaining positive relationships with their pupils and implicit in this is the fear that using physical coercion (or control) will fracture that relationship. Let us be clear that training in 'control and restraint' is not the same as training in self-preservation or getting away from threat and attack. Or that, above a certain age, 'control and restraint' is an appropriate response to actions that, in adult life, are illegal. Suggestions in the CSIE document 'Money for Inclusion' (2000) regarding Section 19 funding for social inclusion (pupil support) concern many of the preventative measures, including multi-agency work. Surely, physical aggression is an area for collaborative and preventative work with both mental health services and the police and probation service, depending on the circumstances?

Violent behaviour could also be interpreted as uncensored and antisocial reaction to schools that have formerly been concerned with the wider outcomes of education but are now concentrating exclusively on exam performance (Raven, 1997). The effect of this is to deny pupils who possess any of the wide variety of hugely important talents that do not show up on traditional examinations, and more recent standardised tests, the opportunity to develop or to get recognition for these talents.

> What we are witnessing is a world-wide reinforcement of a move towards widespread acceptance (of the kind most desired by fascists) of the right of others to dictate what one will do and what one will learn, of the right of

others to issue demeaning and degrading orders and expect compliance, and of the right of authority to test one, assess one's "integrity" according to their standards, and allocate one's life chances on the basis of criteria they have established.

(Raven, 1997)

Teachers are aware of the incompatibility of being seen as the 'Government enforcer' and at the same time as the young person's motivator for personal growth and development. Physical restraint practices give out a very strong 'enforcement' message to young people. Should we accept that it is the teachers' role to coerce and control young people to remain in the classroom against their will? There is little research evidence that would indicate exactly what physical restraint is being used for in this country, whether it is effective and what the consequences are, so these questions need to be raised. Surely education should be moving away from the 'controlling classical' and into a 'nurturing and humanistic' (Parsons, 1999) approach to children's education?

Using physical control whilst at the same time motivating and socialising troubled children does not seem compatible. It is but one of many conflicting demands upon teachers. At a recent European Conference on 'Initiatives to Combat School Bullying', one workshop on the concept of Institutional Violence recorded some interesting comments…

> …it was pointed out that institutions were faced with the challenge of creating environments where people with difficulties do not feel excluded. As it stands, institutions tend to promote conformity (and mediocrity!) and these attempts to put everyone into the same mould provoke violence, which the institutions are not equipped to deal with. The response of the institutions (e.g. schools) is too often to exclude the individuals who are creating the disturbance. The way institutions deal with dissent then ultimately leads to discrimination … teachers do not have the training needed to deal with the attitude problems of students. Teachers traditionally perceive themselves as being there "to teach the curriculum". It was suggested that teachers be equipped (with training) to deal with violence (and emotions) to counter this institutional neglect of a sizeable sub-group of pupils – violence that was built into the system.

The school climate is related to the degree to which pupils and students have some influence within it. It is desirable to try to involve all parites (in the school) to tackle the problems of violence in schools – follow a 'bottom up' approach, rather than imposing solutions from the top. Training in and using specific control and restraint techniques may be seen as a necessity in some circumstances but it is not any kind of solution to the problem. The example set by teachers is also important: there is no point in teaching caring values if the teachers themselves are violent, which can be the case. Creating an 'accepting' environment where people are encouraged to show their emotions, frustrations and aggressions without the institution breaking apart is a challenge for those who believe that discipline, rather than self-discipline, is the key. Enabling teachers and support staff to deal with the 'deviations from the norm' is more desirable than 'bottling up' needs and ultimately being rejected by the institution. The aim should be to incorporate young people who are troubled and troublesome and to empower schools and units to deal affectively, not just effectively, with them.

Conclusion

In America, there seems to be current debate and research into restraint, self-restraint and the wide range of methods that can be used to cope with aggressive students. An example is the concept of 'verbal judo' for defusing tense situations with students (Blendinger, 1995). Staff working with troubled and troublesome youngsters do need to be armed with skills, knowledge and understanding. There is much concern in the USA and Canada about challenging behaviour or violence in schools and colleges evidenced by State and Federal responses (APA, 2000–182 documents; Sprott & Doob, 1998; NSSC, 1998). In this country some texts have explored psychological consequences (for both victim and perpetuator) of violent and aggressive behaviour (e.g. Breakwell, 1997) but only very few have put this into the educational context (e.g. Peagam, 1993; Hewett and Arnett, 1996; Russell, 1997). Some of this has been translated into practical training or support for pupils, teachers or other education staff in the UK but mainly there is a focus on physical control. Circular 10/98 and subsequent papers emphasise policy and physical intervention and, as such, outline 'rules of engagement'. The 'packaged' training programmes have emanated from an immediate practical need. They have grown out of a demand from schools and staff to have pre-planned physical interventions that pass over a real understanding of the complex factors that contribute to violent incidents. A whole area of skill and understanding has been missed out in the training that currently exists. This area is characterised by advanced communication skills for teachers, conflict management and reduction techniques, specific programmes for dealing with antisocial behaviour (e.g. Gibbs et al., 1996), analysis of the efficacy of pre-school programmes, conflict resolution through literature, peer mediation programmes, anger management programmes and many more examples. There are undoubtedly programmes emerging in this country but there is a lack of community when it comes to sharing practice and developing an appropriately evaluative base. Perhaps it has something to do with the competitive, commercial basis on which the training is provided and the lack of involvement of the psychology and educational research community?

The emphasis should be much more on prevention of violent and aggressive behaviour and on questioning the conditions that produce it. We should not be operating the 'fire service' (McGuiness, 1994) approach that is evident at the moment. Much of the current British literature and research deals with challenging behaviour, bullying and discipline issues. It does not extend generally to understanding physically aggressive or violent behaviour, to skilled educational responses to pupils who are violent or to the many social and ethical issues that aggressive or violent behaviour raises. There is a gap in the literature and research. Research in the USA seems to bridge the gap between 'behaviour management' and a much broader psychological and educational perspective. This has led to a broader range of strategies available to teachers in coping with violent and aggressive behaviour. Perhaps this has been born out of necessity in what is regarded generally as a more violent society and because they have always taken the subject more seriously. Circular 10/98 was a reactive and postural response from the Government and it has been accompanied by some equally limited local authority responses. It is not a question of enabling teachers to do the job, no matter what it entails. It may be time to question or to change the job itself and many teachers are now questioning some of the things they are required to do. We have spent too long sweeping these issues under the carpet.

References

APA (American Psychological Association) (2000) Search phrase – 'violence in schools' on their web site – *http://www.apa.org*

Bennathan, M (1997) Effective intervention in primary schools: What nurture groups achieve. *Emotional and Behavioural Difficulties*. Vol. 2. No. 3. Winter.

Blendinger, J (1995) *Controlling Aggressive Students*. Fastback Series No. 387. Phi Delta Kappa, 408, N. Union, PO Box 789, Bloomington, In 47402–0789.

Bowers, T (1996) Putting back the 'E' in EBD. *Emotional and Behavioural Difficulties*. Vol. 1. No. 1. Spring.

Breakwell, G (1997) *Coping with Aggressive Behaviour*. Leicester: BPS Books (Personal & Professional Development Series).

Briggs, S., Mckay, T & Miller, S (1995) The Edinbarnet playground project: changing aggressive behaviour through structured intervention. *Educational Psychology in Practice*. Vol. 11. No. 2. July.

Buckley, K (1999) *Managing Violence; Managing Masculinity*. In Kemshall, H. & Pritchard, J. (eds) *Good Practice in Working with Violence*. London: Jessica Kingsley.

Castle, F & Parsons, C (1997) Disruptive behaviour and exclusions from schools: redefining and responding to the problem. *Emotional and Behavioural Difficulties.* Vol. 2. No. 3. Winter.

Charlton, T & Gunter, B (1999) TV violence effects: Exceptionally vulnerable viewers? *Emotional and Behavioural Difficulties.* Vol. 2. No. 3. Winter.

Charlton, T., Gunter, B & Coles, D (1998) Broadcast television as a cause of aggression? *Emotional and Behavioural Difficulties.* Vol. 4. No. 1. Spring.

Cooper, P (1999) Changing perceptions of EBD: maladjustment, EBD and beyond. *Emotional and Behavioural Difficulties.* Vol. 4. No. 1. Spring.

Cooper, P., Smith, C & Upton, G (1994) *Emotional and Behavioural Difficulties: Theory to Practice.* Page 96. London: Routledge.

Cornwall, J (1998) *Stress and Challenging Behaviour.* In David, P. (Ed.) *Young Children Learning.* London: Paul Chapman.

Cornwall, J (2000) Unpublished pilot research for Doctorate. For further details email – J.V. Cornwall@cant.ac.uk – mark your email 'Violent behaviour'.

CSIE (2000) *Money for Inclusion. 2nd Edition.* Bristol: Centre for Studies on Inclusive Education.

Gardner, H (1993) *Multiple Intelligences: The Theory In Practice.* New York: BasicBooks.

Gibbs, J., Potter, G., Goldstein, A & Brendtro, L (1996) From harassment to helping with antisocial youth: The EQUIP Program. *Reclaiming Children and Youth: Journal of Emotional & Behavioural Problems.* Vol. 5. pp. 40–46. Spring.

Goldstein, A (1987) *Aggressive Behaviour: Assessment and Intervention.* Oxford: Pergamon Press.

Goleman, D (1996) *Emotional Intelligence: Why it can matter more than IQ.* London: Bloomsbury.

Graves, M., Nordling, G., Roberts, D & Taylor, C (1997) *Conflict Resolution through Literature.* Illinois: ERIC Digest of field based action research.

Greenhalgh, P (1994) *Emotional Growth and Learning.* Pages 27 & 83. London: Routledge.

Grossman, D. (1997) The effectiveness of a violence prevention curriculum among children in elementary school. *Journal of the American Medical Association.* Vol. 277, No. 20, 1605–1611.

Harris, J (1995) Responding to pupils with severe learning disabilities, who present challenging behaviour. *British Journal of Special Education.* Volume 22. No 3. (September).

Hewett, D & Arnett, A (1996) Guidance on the use of physical force by staff in educational establishments. *Emotional and Behavioural Difficulties,* Vol. 23. No. 3. September.

Kinder, K., Wilkin, A., Moor, H., Derrington, C & Hogarth, S (1999) *Raising Behaviour. 3 – A School View.* Slough: NfER.

McDonnell, A., Dearden, B & Richens, A (1991) Staff training in the management of violence and aggression. *Mental Handicap*. Vol. 19. pp. 73–151. June.

McGuiness, J (1994) *Teachers, Pupils and Behaviour: A managerial approach*. London: Cassell.

McIntyre, T (1999) *McIntyre Undercover: Privatised Home Care*. BBC1. 16th November.

NSSC (National Schools Safety Centre) (1998) Web site: http://www.nssc1.org/

Pappas, R (1997) *Using Children's Stories with Conflict Themes To Help Four-Year-Olds Deal with Aggressive Behaviours in the Classroom*. New York: ERIC Digest.

Parsons, C (1999) *Education, Exclusion and Citizenship*. London: Routledge.

Peagam, E (1993) Who cares about control? *British Journal of Special Education*. Vol. 20. No. 3. September.

Randall, P (1998) *Aggression at school, post-traumatic stress disorder and peer relations*. In Slee, P. & Rigby, K. (Eds) *Children's Peer Relations*. London: Routledge.

Raven, J (1997) 'Education, Educational Research, Ethics and the BPS'. The British Psychological Society. *Education Section Review*. Vol. 21, No. 2.

Russell, P (1997) Don't forget us! Messages from the Mental Health Foundation Committee's Report on Services for Children with Learning Disabilities and Severe Challenging Behaviour. *British Journal of Special Education*. Vol. 24. No. 2. June.

Sprott, J & Doob, A (1998) *Who Are The Most Violent Ten And Eleven Year Olds? An Introduction To Future Delinquency*? ARB (Applied Research Branch), Human Resources Development Canada.

Varma, V. P (Ed) (1973) *Stresses in Children*. London: University of London Press.

Wolff, S (1969) *Children Under Stress*. Harmondsworth: Penguin.

Index